Acknowledgments My deepest gratitude to all who provided footage for this book. A huge thank you to executive producer and star of *Monk*, Tony Shalhoub, co-star Stanley Kamel, co-producer Scott Collins, and editor Scott Boyd; to the team members of SeaWorld Inc. and Busch Entertainment Corp. for their generous use of *The Making of Believe*; Kristy Manning and Michael Albright from the BBC Motion Gallery for the BBC short-form program, *Living Colour: Yellow*; and to John Dames, of coreaudiovisual, for his branded content material.

Special thanks to my editorial team: Serena Herr, Bob Lindstrom, Mary Plummer, Brendan Boykin, and Nancy Peterson; to my Apple support team: Patty Montesion, Steve Bayes, and Brian Meaney.

For equipment and technical support, Roger Mabon at G-Technology, Inc., for the G-RAID drive; Manny Gaudier, Alejandro Navarro, and Steve Ruiz at Sony for the HVR M15U deck; Victoria Battison and Joshua Helling at Blackmagic Design USA for the DeckLink HD Extreme card; and Andrew Robbins of Megatrax.

Finally, to my business partner Shirley Craig, our Weynand Training team (www.weynand.com) and to Susan Merzbach, my grateful thanks.

Apple Pro Training Series
Final Cut Pro 6
Diana Weynand

Apple
Certified

Apple Pro Training Series: Final Cut Pro 6
Diana Weynand
Copyright © 2007 by Diana Weynand and Shirley Craig

Published by Peachpit Press. For information on Peachpit Press books, contact:

Peachpit Press
1249 Eighth Street
Berkeley, CA 94710
(510) 524-2178
Fax: (510) 524-2221
http://www.peachpit.com
To report errors, please send a note to errata@peachpit.com
Peachpit Press is a division of Pearson Education

Editor: Bob Lindstrom
Apple Series Editor: Serena Herr
Project Director: Shirley Craig
Production Coordinator: Laurie Stewart, Happenstance Type-O-Rama
Technical Editor: Mary Plummer
Technical Reviewer: Brendan Boykin
Copy Editors: Darren Meiss, Karen Seriguchi
Proofreader: Karen Seriguchi
Compositor: Kate Kaminski, Happenstance Type-O-Rama
Indexer: Jack Lewis
Cover Illustration: Kent Oberheu
Cover Production: Maureen Forys, Happenstance Type-O-Rama
Media Reviewers: Eric Geoffroy, Jay Payne

ISBN 0-321-50265-5
9 8 7 6 5 4 3 2 1
Printed and bound in the United States of America

Contents at a Glance

Table of Contents

Completing the Cut

Adding Effects and Finishing

Getting Started

Welcome to the official Apple Pro Training Series course for Final Cut Pro 6, Apple's dynamic nonlinear editing package. This book is a comprehensive guide to editing with Final Cut Pro. It uses exciting, real-world footage from NBC/Universal, Seaworld, and the BBC—in both NTSC and PAL formats—to demonstrate both the features of the application and the practical techniques you'll use daily in your editing projects.

Whether you're a seasoned veteran or just getting started in the editing field, Final Cut Pro 6 is flexible enough to meet all your editing needs. So let's get started!

The Methodology

This is, first and foremost, a hands-on course. Every exercise is designed to enable professional-quality editing in Final Cut Pro as quickly as possible. Each lesson builds on previous lessons to guide you through the program's functions and capabilities. If you are new to Final Cut Pro, start at the beginning and progress through each lesson in order. If you are familiar with an earlier version of Final Cut Pro, you can go directly to a specific section and focus on that topic, because every lesson is self-contained.

Course Structure

The book is designed to guide you through the editing process as it teaches Final Cut Pro. You will begin by learning basic editing techniques and then refine your project by trimming and adjusting edit points and clip location. While exploring all of Final Cut Pro's editing tools, you'll learn to customize your interface, work with different types of edits, and even edit multi-camera footage. After working on several projects, you'll complete them by mixing the audio and adding transitions and titles. Finally, you'll add effects to your project, prepare it for broadcast, and export it as a file or output it to tape.

The lessons are grouped into the following categories:

▶ Creating a Rough Cut   Lessons 1–3

▶ Refining the Rough Cut   Lessons 4–6

▶ Supporting the Process   Lessons 7–8

▶ Completing the Cut   Lessons 9–11

▶ Adding Effects and Finishing the Cut   Lessons 12–14

In addition to the exercises, most lessons include "project tasks" that give you an opportunity to practice what you've learned before moving on to new material. Throughout the book, review sections will guide you in evaluating your project before moving to the next editing stage.

Using the DVD Book Files

The *Apple Pro Training Series: Final Cut Pro 6* DVD (included with the book) contains the project files you will use for each lesson, as well as media files that contain the video and audio content you will need for each exercise. After you transfer the files to your hard drive, each lesson will instruct you in the use of the project and media files.

A comprehensive glossary of Final Cut Pro terms is also included in PDF form on the DVD.

Installing the Final Cut Pro 6 Lesson Files

On the DVD, you'll find a folder titled FCP6 Book Files, which contains two subfolders: Lessons and Media. These folders contain the lessons and media files for this course. Make sure you keep these two folders together in the FCP6 Book Files folder on your hard drive. If you do so, Final Cut Pro should be able to maintain the original links between the lessons and media files.

1   Insert the *Apple Pro Training Series: Final Cut Pro 6* DVD into your DVD drive.

2   Drag the FCP6 Book Files folder from the DVD to your hard drive to copy it. The DVD contains about 7.8 GB of data.

Each lesson will explain which files to open for that lesson's exercises.

Reconnecting Media

When copying files from the DVD to your hard drive, you may unintentionally break a link between a project file and its media files. If this happens, a dialog appears asking you to relink the project files. Relinking the project files is a simple process that's covered in more depth in the "Reconnecting Media" section in Lesson 7. But should the dialog appear when you are opening a lesson, follow these steps:

1   If an Offline Files dialog appears, click the Reconnect button.

A Reconnect Files dialog opens. Under the Files To Connect portion of the dialog, the offline file is listed along with its possible location.

2 In the Reconnect Files dialog, click Search.

Final Cut Pro will search for the missing file. If you already know where the file is located, you can click the Locate button and find the file manually.

3 After the correct file is found, click Choose in the Reconnect dialog.

4 When the file is displayed in the Files Located section of the Reconnect Files dialog, click Connect.

When the link between the project file and the media file is reestablished, Final Cut Pro will be able to access the media within the project.

Changing System Preferences

A few editing functions within Final Cut Pro use function keys also used by other programs, such as Exposé and the Dashboard. If you want to use the FCP editing shortcuts, you will need to reassign the functions keys in these other programs.

1 From your desktop, open System Preferences.

2 In the Personal section, click Dashboard & Exposé.

3 Reassign the keyboard shortcuts for F9, F10, F11, and F12 to other keys.

Reassigning the shortcuts will allow Final Cut Pro to use these shortcut keys exclusively.

At any time when using Final Cut Pro, you can return to System Preferences and change these key assignments.

About the Footage

Four sets of footage are used throughout this book. Together they represent different types of projects and media formats. The exercises instruct you to edit the footage in a particular way, but you can use any part of this footage to practice editing methods. Techniques you've learned using one set of footage in a lesson can be practiced with a different set of footage to create a new project. Due to copyright restrictions, however, you cannot use this footage for any purpose outside this book.

The footage includes the following:

SeaWorld Inc. and Busch Entertainment's "The Making of 'Believe'"—This documentary material was shot by SeaWorld Inc.'s San Antonio and Orlando media divisions while the theme park's training staff joined with Broadway directors, choreographers, and designers to create and rehearse the Shamu show "Believe." The rehearsal and performance footage was shot on HDV at the San Antonio, Texas, SeaWorld facility, and the underwater material was shot on Betacam SP at the SeaWorld facility in Orlando, Florida.

Monk—This footage is from the popular television series *Monk*, starring Tony Shalhoub. The scene is from an episode titled "Mr. Monk and the Actor," which aired during season five. It was written by Hy Conrad and Joe Toplyn, directed by Randy Zisk, and edited by Scott Boyd. Executive producers for the series are Andy Breckman, David Hoberman, Tony Shalhoub, and Randy Zisk. Co-executive producers are Fern Field and Tom Scharpling. The supervising producer is David Breckman, and the producer is Anthony Santa Croce. The program is produced by NBC Universal Television Studios in association with Mandeville Films and Touchstone Television.

The *Monk* series is shot on Super 16mm film and transferred to D5 HD tape. It is captured using the DVCPRO HD codec at 23.98 fps (frames per second). For this book, the DVCPRO HD files were recompressed using the new Apple ProRes 422 codec.

"Living Colour: Yellow"—This set of media is from the British Broadcasting Corporation (BBC) and was created as *interstitials,* short sequences that play between programs. In this instance, rather than shooting new material, the BBC assembled clips from all of its long-form programming for use in a series of five-minute interstitials titled *Living Colour*. The interstitial used in this book is about the color yellow. It is an excellent example of how a filmmaker can use individual, disparate clips to tell a complete story.

The original footage for "Living Colour: Yellow" was culled from many different programs shot on a variety of formats. It was mastered on PAL DigiBeta and captured for use in this book using the DVCPRO PAL codec. Many of the shots within this program are searchable online via BBC Motion Gallery (www.bbcmotiongallery.com).

"Commercial"—This media file was shot as a branded-content piece provided by the motion design company coreaudiovisual. Branded content is typically more entertainment than commercial, but it is often underwritten by a company whose brand or product is present in the piece. For this piece, the directorial vision was to create all of the elements of a great drama without shooting an entire film. These elements refer to a narrative without explaining it, leaving interpretation and detail to the viewer's imagination. It was shot in HD at 23.98 fps, and captured using the DVCPRO HD codec. It was recompressed for the book using the Apple ProRes 422 codec.

System Requirements

Before using *Apple Pro Training Series: Final Cut Pro 6,* you should have a working knowledge of your Macintosh and the Mac OS X operating system. Make sure that you know how to use the mouse and standard menus and commands; and also how to open, save, and close files. If you need to review these techniques, see the printed or online documentation included with your system. For the basic system requirements for Final Cut Pro 6, refer to the Final Cut Pro 6 documentation.

About the Apple Pro Training Series

Apple Pro Training Series: Final Cut Pro 6 is part of the official training series for Apple Pro applications developed by experts in the field. The lessons are designed to let you learn at your own pace. If you're new to Final Cut Pro, you'll learn the fundamental concepts and features you'll need to master the program. If you've been using Final Cut Pro for a while, you'll find that this book covers most of the new features found in Final Cut Pro 6.

Although each lesson provides step-by-step instructions for creating specific projects, there's room for exploration and experimentation. However, try to follow the book from start to finish, or at least complete the first three lessons before jumping around. Each lesson concludes with a review section summarizing what you've covered.

Apple Pro Certification Program

The Apple Pro Training and Certification Programs are designed to keep you at the forefront of Apple's digital media technology while giving you a competitive edge in today's ever-changing job market. Whether you're an editor, graphic designer, sound designer, special effects artist, or teacher, these training tools are meant to help you expand your skills.

Upon completing the course material in this book, you can become an Apple Certified Pro by taking the certification exam at an Apple Authorized Training Center. Certification is offered in Final Cut Pro, Motion, Color, Soundtrack Pro, DVD Studio Pro, Shake, and Logic Pro. Certification as an Apple Pro gives you official recognition of your knowledge of Apple's professional applications while allowing you to market yourself to employers and clients as a skilled, pro-level user of Apple products.

To find an Authorized Training Center near you, go to www.apple.com/software/pro/training.

For those who prefer to learn in an instructor-led setting, Apple also offers training courses at Apple Authorized Training Centers worldwide. These courses, which use the Apple Pro Training Series books as their curriculum, are taught by Apple Certified Trainers and balance concepts and lectures with hands-on labs and exercises. Apple Authorized Training Centers for Pro products have been carefully selected and have met Apple's highest standards in all areas, including facilities, instructors, course delivery, and infrastructure. The goal of the program is to offer Apple customers, from beginners to the most seasoned professionals, the highest-quality training experience.

Resources

Apple Pro Training Series: Final Cut Pro 6 is not intended as a comprehensive reference manual, nor does it replace the documentation that comes with the application. For comprehensive information about program features, refer to these resources:

▶ The Reference Guide. Accessed through the Final Cut Pro Help menu, the Reference Guide contains a complete description of all features.

▶ Apple's Web site: www.apple.com.

Creating a Rough Cut

1

Screening and Marking in the Final Cut Pro Interface

Final Cut Pro is a dynamic, flexible, and efficient editing system that allows you to organize, view, and edit your footage. While there are numerous ways to edit a project in Final Cut Pro, certain aspects of the editing process remain consistent.

The first stage in editing is to take stock of what you've shot, and figure out what works and what doesn't. The next stage is to choose and combine selected portions of your footage to shape your story into a *rough cut*. Next, you adjust and refine the cut, and finally you add music and sound or visual effects to dress it up. Simply put, editing is the most powerful stage of the production process because it's when the separate parts become a meaningful whole.

This section focuses on the first step, the rough cut. In the next three lessons, you will be editing footage from a short documentary about the making of SeaWorld's newest killer whale production, "Believe." In this lesson, you will work with the Final Cut Pro interface, learn about the workflow of a project, organize project elements, play source footage and edited footage, and mark clips in preparation for editing. You will also learn about Final Cut Pro menus and shortcuts, as well as features available using a two-button mouse.

Launching Final Cut Pro

Before you get started, install the Final Cut Pro application and copy the lessons and media from the book's DVD onto your hard drive. Instructions for doing this are in the Getting Started section of this book. After those two tasks are complete, you can move forward with this lesson.

You can open, or *launch*, Final Cut Pro in one of three ways:

▶ In the Applications folder on the hard drive, double-click the Final Cut Pro application icon.

▶ In the Dock, click the Final Cut Pro icon once.

▶ Double-click any Final Cut Pro project file.

Placing the Final Cut Pro icon in the Dock will make it easier to launch the program in future lessons.

1 If the Final Cut Pro icon does not already appear in your Dock, find the icon in your hard drive Applications folder, drag it into the Dock, and release the mouse.

2 In the Dock, click the Final Cut Pro icon once to launch the program.

If this is the first time you've launched Final Cut Pro, a Choose Setup window appears, where you choose the type of footage you are editing.

The default is DV-NTSC. For now, you can click OK to bypass this dialog because the settings you need are contained within these lessons. You will work with this window and these options in a later lesson.If an External A/V window appears with a warning that it can't locate the external video device, click Continue. You do not need an external video device for these lessons.

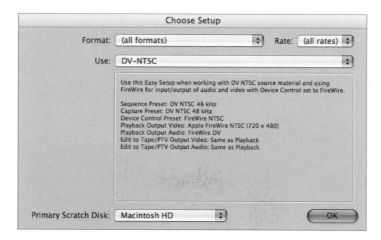

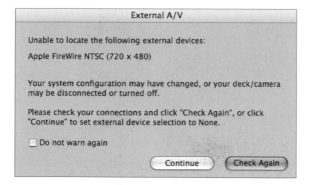

The program interface opens with a default project titled Untitled Project 1 in the Browser window. The Browser is located in the upper-left corner of the interface. If you have already worked on other projects, they may appear here as well.

Final Cut Pro Interface

Four primary windows make up the Final Cut Pro interface: the Browser, Viewer, Canvas, and Timeline. The most basic functions of these windows can be broken down into two areas: The Browser and Viewer windows are where you organize and view your *unedited* material, and the Canvas and Timeline are where you view your *edited* material.

There are two secondary windows: The Tool palette contains an assortment of editing tools, and the audio meters allow you to monitor audio levels.

Browser   Viewer   Canvas

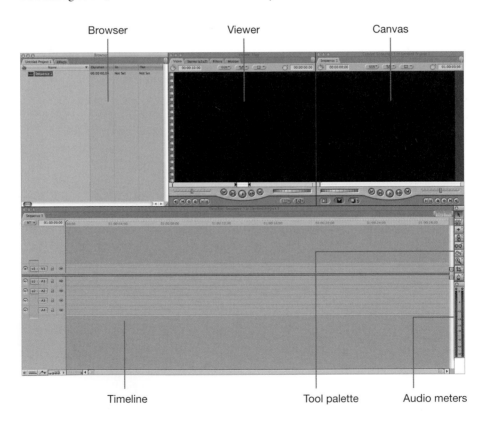

Timeline   Tool palette   Audio meters

Each window fulfills a unique purpose in the editing process:

Browser

The Browser is where you organize all of the project elements you use when editing. You can view the different elements as a list or as icons.

Viewer

The Viewer is where you view your source material and choose edit points. But you can also edit audio, modify transitions and effects, and build titles here.

Timeline

The Timeline is a graphical representation of all the editing decisions you make. This is your workbench area, where you edit your material, trim it, move it, stack it, and adjust it. Here you can see all your edits at a glance.

Canvas

The Canvas and Timeline windows are different sides of the same coin. Both display your edited project, but whereas the Timeline shows your editing choices graphically, the Canvas displays those edits visually like a movie.

Tool Palette

The Tool palette is a collection of Final Cut Pro editing tools. Each tool has a shortcut key, so you can access each one directly from the keyboard.

Audio Meters

The audio meters window displays two audio meters that reflect the volume level of whatever audio is playing. It could be a source clip in the Viewer you screen before editing or the final edited piece you view in the Canvas.

Project tab   Browser   Shuttle control   Viewer

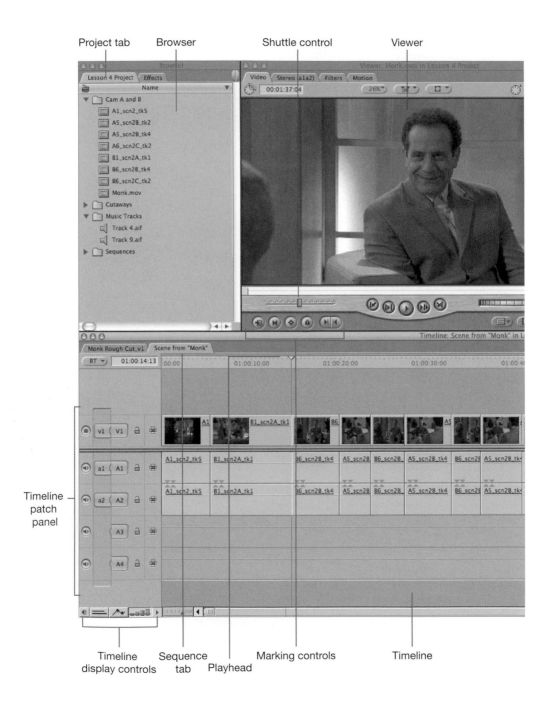

Timeline
patch
panel

Timeline   Sequence   Marking controls   Timeline
display controls   tab   Playhead

Viewer
Scrubber bar   Jog control

Timecode
Duration field

Sequence tab

Canvas

Current
Timecode field

Timeline
ruler area

Generator
pop-up menu

Edit
buttons

Transport
controls

Audio meters

Tool palette

Window Properties

The Final Cut Pro interface windows share similar properties with other OS X windows. They can be opened, closed, minimized, and repositioned using the OS X Close, Minimize, and Zoom buttons in the upper-left corner of the window. Each window displays its name in the title bar area.

1 Click the Browser to make it the active window.

Active Browser window when selected

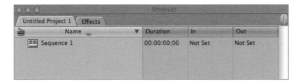

Inactive Browser window when another window is selected

An active window has a lighter title bar, and you can easily read the window name. An inactive window has a dark gray, or *dimmed*, title bar that blends in with the name. Only one window can be active at a time. Making a window active in the interface is an important part of the editing process because some editing functions will be available only if a specific window is active.

2 Click the Viewer window to make it active, and then click the Close button
in the upper-left corner.

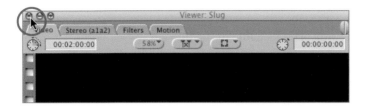

In most OS X windows, the Close button is red. In Final Cut Pro, this set
of buttons—Close, Minimize, and Zoom—takes on the gray of the interface. But these buttons still perform the same functions that they do in
other OS X windows.

3 To restore the Viewer window, choose Window > Viewer, or press
Command-1.

You can open and close each interface window by choosing the window
name in the Window menu or using a keyboard shortcut.

NOTE ▶ Because of the small size of the Tool palette and audio meters,
they each have just one button, which closes the window.

4 Drag the Browser window title bar to move this window away from its
current position. Drag it again and allow it to snap back into its original
position.

All Final Cut Pro interface windows snap into place, even though they are
separate windows.

Menus, Shortcuts, and the Mouse

Some editors enjoy using keyboard shortcuts for editing functions, and others prefer choosing menu selections or clicking buttons or objects within the Final Cut Pro interface. In addition, Final Cut Pro has a position-sensitive mouse pointer. When you move it over certain parts of the interface, the pointer will automatically change to allow you to perform a specific function in that location.

1   Move the pointer over the boundary line between the Browser and Viewer. When the pointer changes to the vertical Resize pointer, drag right to dynamically increase the size of the Browser window and view more columns.

As you drag the Browser boundary line, the Viewer and Canvas windows automatically resize to accommodate the larger Browser. The Resize pointer may appear in several places throughout the Final Cut Pro interface. Whenever you see the pointer icon automatically change, you click or drag the mouse at that location.

2   In the Tool palette, move the pointer over the icon that looks like a magnifying glass.

A tooltip appears with the tool name and keyboard shortcut. Tooltips also appear when you hold the mouse pointer over buttons and other areas in the interface. If you wanted to use the keyboard shortcut to select this tool, you would press the letter *Z* on the keyboard.

NOTE ▶ You can turn tooltips off and on in the General tab of the User Preferences window (Option-Q).

3   Move the pointer over the first tool in the Tool palette.

The Selection tool is the default tool you use most frequently. Its shortcut is the letter *A*.

TIP▶ You will use different tools throughout the editing process, but it's a good habit to return to your Selection tool after you've used another tool.

4 Choose File in the menu bar of the interface.

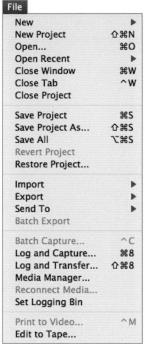

The Final Cut Pro menu bar organizes editing functions by category, such as View, Modify, Effects, and so on. Within each menu, specific functions are grouped together if they share a similar purpose or topic. In the File menu, the New and Open functions are grouped together, as are the Save functions, Import, and so on. As in all Apple menus, black menu options can be selected, but dimmed options cannot.

NOTE ▶ When directed in the book exercises to choose an item from a menu, such as Open from the File menu, it will appear as "Choose File > Open."

5 From the menu bar, choose Window > Arrange.

A submenu appears.

6 Drag the pointer over Standard in the submenu, but *don't release the mouse.*

Keyboard shortcuts appear in menus and submenus to the right of the listed function. Similar functions often share the same shortcut letter.

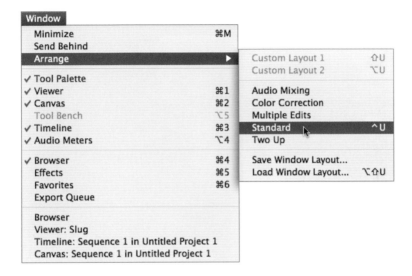

The shortcuts in this submenu all use the letter U with one or more modifier keys. There are four modifier keys: Shift, Control, Option, and Command (the Apple key).

7 Click Standard, or release the menu and press Control-U, to choose the default Standard window layout. This returns all windows to their default layout.

8 Hold down the Control key and click in the gray area of the Name column in the Browser window.

A shortcut menu appears with a list of options for that specific area. Control-clicking in different areas of the Final Cut Pro interface will produce different shortcut menus from which you can choose or change your editing options.

TIP You can also access this shortcut menu by clicking in the same area with the right button of a two-button mouse.

Following a Workflow

Before you work with project elements, let's take a minute to review the nonlinear editing process and some of the terminology you'll need to know. Final Cut Pro follows the normal conventions of the nonlinear editing process. That process usually begins with *capturing* material from the original source tape, thereby converting it into digital media files. The media files are actually QuickTime movies that play like any other QuickTime movie on your computer. One file is created for each portion of source footage you choose to capture. Each media file may be a different length, as measured in minutes, seconds, and frames.

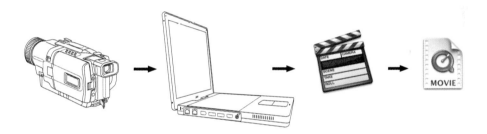

The Final Cut Pro editing process is nondestructive, which means that you never make changes to the actual media files. Instead, you work with *clips* that represent these media files. For example, you can change the audio level or add an effect to a clip inside Final Cut Pro, which causes the media file to be played back with those changes. But the actual media file itself is still unchanged.

You mark edit points on clips and combine clips with other edited clips to form a *sequence*. When you edit the sequence of shots together, you are not actually making changes to your original media. You are only specifying what portions and in what order you want Final Cut Pro to show you the original media. You can change your mind over and over again about the placement or length of a shot without affecting the original captured media files.

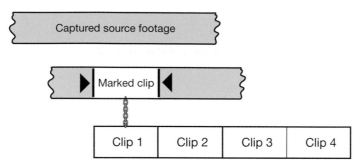

Edited sequence of clips

You can also save the initial captured media files to a separate hard drive connected through FireWire, or to a CD or DVD. The material in the accompanying DVD in this book has already been captured for the purposes of preparing these lessons. You will learn to capture your own source footage and export it in different ways in later lessons.

Working with Projects

Every time you begin editing a new body of material, you create a new *project file* to contain that material. Each project may have several kinds of elements, such as QuickTime clips, music, sound effects, narration, and graphics, which you will combine to form an edited version of the material. Project elements are displayed in the Browser window under a project tab.

Opening and Closing Projects

When you launch Final Cut Pro, it opens the last project you worked on or a new untitled project. In the Browser, there is a tab with the project name on it.

To work with the project file created for this lesson, you will open it from the files you transferred from the DVD in this book.

1   Choose File > Open.

2   In the Choose a File window, click the column view option.

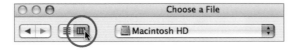

3   In the sidebar, or first column, of the Choose a File window, click the Macintosh HD icon; in the next column, click the FCP6 Book Files folder; and in the third column, click the Lessons folder.

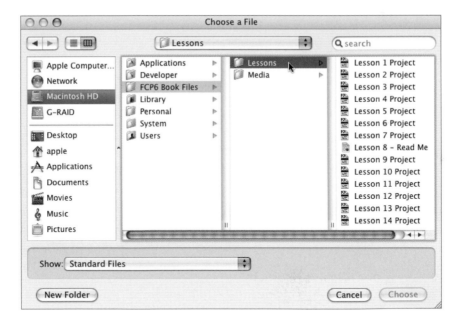

NOTE ▸ If you copied the FCP6 Book Files folder to a FireWire drive, select that drive in the first column.

4   Select the **Lesson 1 Project** file, and click Choose.

In the Browser window, Lesson 1 Project appears as a separate tab next to the Effects tab. (If you already worked on another project before starting these lessons, that project's tab may appear here as well.)

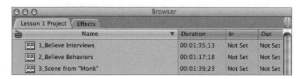

5   In the Browser window, click the Effects tab.

This is where you select effects such as video and audio transitions and filters. Effects are covered in later lessons.

NOTE ▶ The use of tabs throughout Final Cut Pro helps maximize space in the interface while keeping windows organized.

6   If any projects other than **Lesson 1 Project** are open, click the project's tab to make it the active project.

7   To close that project, choose File > Close Project.

With the **Lesson 1 Project** open in the Browser, you are ready to begin. However, if you want to preserve the original project, and make your changes in a duplicate project, continue with the next step.

8   To duplicate this project, choose File > Save Project As. In the Save window, rename the project *My Lesson 1* or just use the default, *Lesson 1 Project copy.* Create a new destination folder on your desktop called *My FCP Projects,* and click Save.

TIP ▶ Saved projects default to include the Final Cut Pro file extension .fcp. If you don't want this extension to appear on your project files, select the "Hide extension" checkbox in the Save window.

The project tab in the Browser reflects the new project name. Working in a backup version of this project allows you to make and save changes without disturbing the original project, which you can use for future reference.

NOTE ▶ Throughout this book, the original project lesson file names are used.

Identifying Project Elements

Lesson 1 Project has four different types of project elements. Each is represented by a unique icon, which can appear larger or smaller depending on what view you select. You'll learn about views in the next exercise, but in the following examples you can see two views for each icon. The first image represents the view you see in the current project, which is a list view. The second image represents an icon or picture view.

Clip

Each clip in your project represents some portion of your original captured source footage. It links back to a digital media file on your hard drive. This type of clip icon can represent video only or video and audio combined. When viewed as a list, such as the current display in the Browser, the clip icon resembles a piece of film.

Audio Clip

An audio clip represents sound clips or files such as music, sound effects, narration, and so on. Like the video clips, these audio clips link back to the original audio files stored on your hard drive. Audio clips contain no video. The icon is an audio speaker.

Sequence

A sequence is a group of audio and video clips that have been edited together. A sequence might also contain effects and transitions you may have applied to the edited clips. When you view a sequence in the Canvas or work with it in the Timeline, Final Cut Pro links back to the media clips on the hard drive and plays just the selected portions of the clips you have identified and marked. The sequence icon, which looks like two pieces of overlapping film, represents combined audio and video elements.

Bin

A *bin* is a folder used to organize clips and sequences in the project. The term bin comes from the days of film editing when pieces of cut film hung on hooks over large canvas containers called bins. These pieces of film, or film clips, would hang there until the film editor selected them to use in a sequence.

Viewing Project Elements

As you begin to view your project elements, you can choose from one of two primary views: as image icons or as an alphabetized list. When you view elements as image icons, using one of the View as Icons options, you see a thumbnail image of each video clip. The thumbnail is a visual reminder of the clip's content and is especially helpful when screening material for the first time. With the View as List option, the clips are alphabetized in a list and you have access to more clips in a smaller space, which makes it an excellent option when organizing a lot of elements in a larger project.

1   To see what view is currently selected, hold down the Control key and click in the empty gray space of the Name column in the Browser window. (Or, if you use a two-button mouse, right-click in the same area.)

This shortcut menu contains three View as Icons options, each with a different-sized icon or image, and a View as List option. The checkmark next to View as List indicates that it is the current view.

2 Choose View as Medium Icons from the shortcut menu.

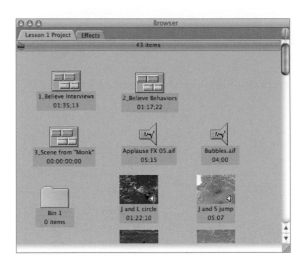

Each video clip is now represented by a medium-sized thumbnail image of the first frame of that clip. The name and duration of the clip appear under the thumbnail image. In this view, you may have to drag the blue vertical scroller in the Browser to see all of the elements.

TIP In this view, you can manually move the clips around in the bin to create your own clip layout. If you want a more ordered layout, you can choose Arrange > by Name from the same shortcut menu.

3 Click the Browser Zoom button to see all the clips in this view. Then press Control-U to return to the default Standard layout.

Like other Mac OS X window Zoom buttons, this one expands the Browser to display as many elements as possible.

4   Control-click again in the Browser gray area under the Name column and this time choose Text Size > Medium from the shortcut menu.

This option enlarges the type identifying the project elements in the Browser and Timeline.

5   Control-click again and choose View as List and whatever text size you prefer.

In this view, elements are sorted and listed alphabetically by name, making it easier to find a specific clip by name and organize a larger group of project elements.

NOTE ▸ The lessons in this book were often prepared with the View as List option so you can quickly find a clip by name. You may choose whichever view you prefer for your own editing.

Organizing Project Elements

The key to organizing a Final Cut Pro project is to sort clips and elements into bins, just as you would organize computer documents by placing them in folders. You can also place bins within bins, just as you would place a folder of files within another folder. Organizing your material into bins streamlines your editing process, making it easier to find and access project elements.

Creating and Naming Bins

The first step in organizing this project is to create new bins to sort the project elements. Typically with Final Cut Pro, you can accomplish the same task in several ways. For example, you can create a new bin in one of three ways:

▸   From the File menu, choose File > New > Bin.

▸   Use the keyboard shortcut, Command-B.

▸   In the Browser, Control-click in the gray area under the Name column and choose New Bin from the shortcut menu.

You will create three bins using these different methods.

1   Click in the Browser window to make it active.

2   Choose File > New > Bin.

A new bin appears in the Browser with the default name Bin 2.

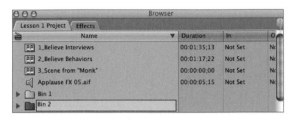

NOTE ▶ A default sequential number always appears in the name of new bins, sequences, and projects. Since this project already has a Bin 1, the new bin is named Bin 2.

3   If the bin name is already highlighted, type *Clips*.

4   Press Return or the Tab key to accept the name. If you need to correct it, click the text of the name itself, not the bin icon, to highlight the name again.

When you press Return, the newly named bin is placed in its appropriate alphabetical order.

TIP ▶ If you want to change a bin name, but the bin is not highlighted, click once to select the bin, and once again on the name to highlight the text. Pressing the Enter key is another way of highlighting just the name of a selected item.

5   To create another bin, press the keyboard shortcut Command-B.

6   Name this bin *Audio*, and press Return to accept the name.

7   To create the third bin, Control-click the gray area under the Name column and choose New Bin from the shortcut menu. You can also right-click using a two-button mouse.

8   Name this bin *Sequences*.

9   To remove the bin labeled Bin 1 from the project, click once to select it and press Delete.

Dragging Clips into Bins

You've created three bins to organize the different elements in this project. Now you will select the elements and drag them into their appropriate bins. You can drag a single clip or a group of clips at one time. The different ways to select items in the Browser follow standard Mac selecting options:

▶   Single-click to select one item.

▶   Command-click to add or remove another item to the current selection.

▶   To select a contiguous list of items, click the first item and Shift-click the last item.

▶   Drag a "marquee" around a group of items.

▶   Press Command-A to choose all items in the window.

The method you choose to select clips in the Browser depends entirely on where the clips are located: if they are side-by-side in a contiguous group, or spread out between other clips. Let's first make the Browser taller.

1   Move your pointer over the boundary line between the Browser and Timeline windows. When the pointer changes to a Resize pointer, drag down as far as possible.

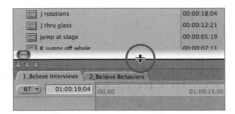

Now the Browser is taller, giving you more room to organize your clips.

2   Drag the **Applause FX 05.aif** audio clip (speaker icon) to the Audio bin. When the Audio bin becomes highlighted, release the mouse.

> **TIP** Whenever you drag and drop an item in Final Cut Pro, make sure the tip of the Selection tool pointer touches the specific destination, in this case the bin icon or name.

3   To place the remaining audio clips in this bin at the same time, click the **Bubbles.aif** clip, then hold down the Command key and click first the **narration_1** clip, then the **Track 12_believe finale.aif** clip, and finally the **Track 12_believe short.aif** clip to include them in the selection. Drag the selected audio clips into the Audio bin.

You can select any number of noncontiguous clips by holding down the Command key and clicking a clip to select or deselect it.

4   To select the three sequences, click the first sequence, *1_Believe Interviews,* and Shift-click the third sequence, *3_Scene from "Monk."*

Using Shift when you select the last item will highlight all items between the first and last.

5   Drag the selected sequences to the Sequences bin. When the Sequences bin becomes highlighted, release the mouse.

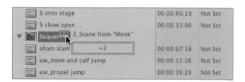

As you drag these sequences together, the name of only the sequence you clicked shows, as well as the number of other items you're dragging.

6   To select the upper group of remaining clips, click the **J and L circle** clip and Shift-click the **S show open** clip above the Sequences bin. Drag this group into the Clips bin.

7   To select the remaining group of contiguous clips, click to the left of the **sham slam** clip, and drag diagonally down and to the right, until the pointer touches the last clip in this group. Then, drag these clips into the Clips bin.

NOTE ▶ Dragging diagonally to select clips is often referred to as *marqueeing,* as in "drag a marquee around these clips."

All the project elements are now tucked away in their bins.

8   To return to the Standard default window layout, choose Window >
    Arrange > Standard, or press Control-U.

9   To save these organizational changes, press Command-S.

    TIP ▶ How you organize your own project is a personal choice. When
    others will be working on the same project, make sure the organizational
    structure is clearly defined.

Viewing Bin Contents

Now the arrangement of clips looks neat and organized. However, as you begin
to screen your clips for editing, you'll need to access the clips inside the bins
quickly and easily. There are several ways to do this. Some options work better
if you're using a two-display editing setup, while others are better for laptops
or one-display setups. Let's look at different ways to display the contents of a
bin so you can get to this material easily.

1   Click the disclosure triangle next to the Audio bin to display its
    contents. Click it again to hide the contents of that bin.

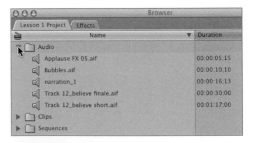

Clicking the disclosure triangle displays or hides the complete contents
of the bin. Depending on the number of items in a bin, you may have to
scroll down to see them all.

2   Double-click the Clips bin.

This opens the bin as a separate window, which you can move anywhere
in the interface.

If your editing setup includes two displays, a common practice is to move the entire Browser window to the left display, and open the bins you are working with as separate windows.

3 Drag the window by its title bar and position it away from the Browser.

In the Browser, the Clips bin icon changes to an open folder, indicating that the bin is open as a separate window or tab.

4 In the Clips bin window, click the Close button in the upper-left corner to close this bin window, or press Command-W.

In the Browser, the Clips bin icon changes back to a closed folder.

5 To view the contents of the Clips bin a different way, hold down the Option key and double-click the Clips bin.

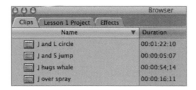

This opens the bin as a separate tab next to the Lesson 1 Project tab.

TIP▸ If you are working with just one display, opening a bin as a separate tab is a helpful way to view and access clips without placing an additional window in the interface.

6 To change the view of the Clips bin, Control-click in the gray area under the Name column and choose View as Medium Icons. Then click the Lesson 1 Project tab.

Each bin can be set to a different view option.

7 Control-click the Clips tab, or right-click it with a two-button mouse. Choose Close Tab from the shortcut menu.

This returns the Clips bin to its closed bin configuration in the Lesson 1 Project tab area. You can also display and hide bin contents by using the arrow keys on the keyboard.

8 To navigate to a specific clip using shortcuts, follow these steps:

▶ Select the Clips bin, then press the Right Arrow key to display the bin contents.

▶ Press the Left Arrow key to hide the bin contents.

▶ Press the Up or Down Arrow keys to select a different bin in the same level. Select the Clips bin again.

▶ Press the Right Arrow key once to open the bin and once again to move the highlight inside the bin to the first clip.

▶ Press the Down Arrow key several times until you highlight the **J thru glass** clip.

▶ To close the Clips bin, press the Left Arrow key twice.

9 Now display the contents of the Clips bin by clicking the disclosure triangle next to it. If you increased the text size and can't read all the clip names, move the cursor over the right edge of the Name column. When you see the Resize pointer appear, drag right to increase the Name column width.

NOTE ▶ When viewing bin contents as a list, you have access to over 60 columns of information in the Browser window. This may include information Final Cut Pro knows about an item (number of audio tracks, frame size, frame rate, and so on) or descriptive information you enter for further clarification, such as scene and take numbers. You will work more with these columns in later lessons.

Playing Clips in the Viewer

The Viewer window is where you play and mark your source clips in preparation for editing. It's also where you perform other tasks, such as adding and adjusting effects.

The Viewer has multiple tabs across the top. The default is the first tab, Video, where you can see, hear, and mark your clips. When you first open Final Cut Pro, the Video tab displays a black *slug*, or placeholder. The Audio tab is where you'll work more closely with the audio of a clip. If no Audio is present in the clip, no audio tab will appear. The Filters and Motion tabs will be used when you start to create effects in later lessons. In this exercise, you will learn different ways to open and play clips in the Viewer.

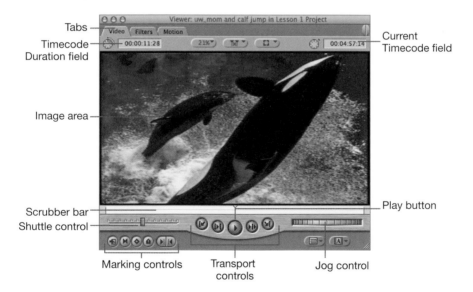

To view or "screen" a clip in the Viewer, you have to open it from the Browser window. There are several ways you can open a clip into the Viewer. For this exercise, you will work with three different ways:

▶ Double-click the clip in the Browser window.

▶ Drag the clip from the Browser to the Viewer window and release it.

▶ Select the clip in the Browser and press Return.

▶ **About the Footage**

▶ The footage you'll screen in this exercise is part of a documentary shot at SeaWorld in San Antonio as the creative teams developed an all-new killer whale show, "Believe." Over the course of two years, the Busch Entertainment Company brought together killer whales and killer whale trainers, a Broadway producer, a Las Vegas director, a Los Angeles composer, set designers, and technicians who created a unique production for their premier show. "Believe" opened to the public in spring 2006, in all three U.S. SeaWorld locations. The footage was shot as HDV 1080i60.

▶ As is the case with documentaries, reality television, and other projects where you don't have control over the surroundings, some of the audio is usable, and some is not. The trainers and whales rehearsed to a 20-minute music track that was used for the performance, and that music was recorded as part of the clips. For the book exercise, you will sometimes use just the video portion of the whale behavior clips, perhaps over a music track, narration, or dialogue clips.

1   In the Clips bin, double-click the **S onto stage** clip to open it in the Viewer.

In the Viewer title bar, the clip name and project appear. You can customize the Viewer window to see a larger image by simply dragging boundary lines between the windows.

2 To make the Viewer window larger, move your pointer over the boundary line between the Browser and Viewer. When the Resize pointer appears, drag left as far as you can. Drag the Viewer and Canvas boundary line to the right. Drag the Timeline boundary line down until the image in the Viewer fills that window.

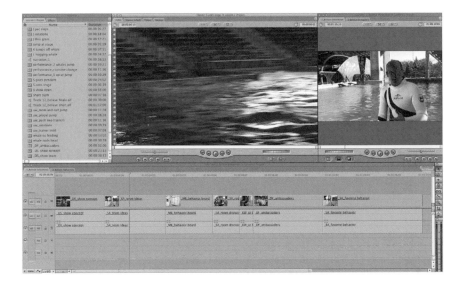

When you focus on one aspect of the editing process, such as screening your footage, it's helpful to arrange your interface for that purpose.

TIP You can dynamically resize more than one window at a time by dragging a boundary corner diagonally.

3 To save this window layout for future screening sessions, hold down Option and choose Window > Arrange > Set Custom Layout 1, then release the Option key.

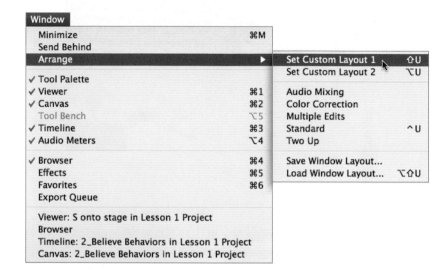

This custom window layout is now available for you to recall at another time.

4 To play the **S onto stage** clip, click the Viewer Play button in the transport controls area.

The next image shows Steve Aibel, assistant curator of animal training at SeaWorld, San Antonio, Texas. He is rehearsing the new killer whale show, "Believe." Other whale trainers you will see in the source clips include Julie Sigman, Katie Wright, Leslie Popiel, and Bridgette Pirtle. The initials of their first names were used to identify the clips they are in.

5 When the clip stops playing, press the Play button again and this time watch the bar beneath the image area.

This is called the *scrubber bar*. The length of the scrubber bar represents the duration of the clip. The actual time duration of the clip appears in the Timecode Duration field in the upper left of the Viewer window.

6 In the Clips bin in the Browser, find the **K jumps off whale** clip. To open this clip, drag it into the Viewer window and release it. Look at the Timecode Duration field to determine the length of this clip.

7 Press the spacebar to play this clip. When you see Katie jump off the whale, press the spacebar to stop playing. Press it again to play. Notice the thin vertical line topped with a yellow triangle in the scrubber bar as the clip plays.

This is called the *playhead*. The location of the playhead corresponds to a specific frame in the clip.

In the upper-right corner of the Viewer window is the Current Timecode field. The number that appears is the *timecode* of the frame where the playhead is currently located. Timecode is a video labeling system that records a unique eight-digit number—representing hours, minutes, seconds, and frames—onto each frame of a clip or sequence. As the clip plays and the playhead moves, the timecode number in this field changes to reflect the new timecode location.

8   Single-click the **_SA_favorite behavior** clip in the Browser to select it, and then press Return to open it in the Viewer. Whenever you open another clip in the Viewer, it replaces the previous clip in the Viewer display.

NOTE ▶ The Enter key is not used interchangeably with Return to open a clip. If you select a clip, bin, or sequence and press Enter, the name will become highlighted, allowing you to rename it.

9   As you play this clip, keep an eye on the Current Timecode field. Stop the clip just after you see the timecode number, 01:03:10:00, after Steve says, "…zoom to the bottom of the pool…."

TIP If necessary, take a moment to make sure your audio monitors or computer sound levels are set to a good level for screening and editing.

10 Click the Stereo (a1a2) tab in the Viewer. Play the clip from this location and watch the visual display of the sound signal as the playhead moves through the clip.

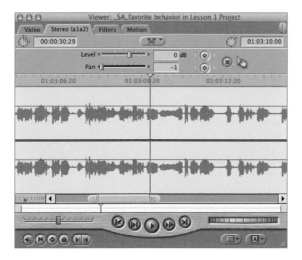

When you open a clip that has audio attached, either a Stereo or Mono audio tab appears in the Viewer, depending on how the clip was captured. If you have two channels of audio, they may be shown together as a stereo pair, as in the current clip, or as two separate Mono tabs. In any one of these tabs, audio is displayed in the form of waves and peaks that represent the sound signal. This display is referred to as a *waveform*.

TIP When you name clips during the capture process, choose a naming convention that will help you identify what that clip is. For example, all the interview clips in this project, such as **_SA_favorite behavior**, were labeled with an underscore and then the two initials of the interviewee. An underscore at the beginning of a clip name places it at the bottom of the list alphabetically, which helps separate the interview clips from the rehearsal and performance clips.

11 To access the **S onto stage** clip again, click the Recent Clips pop-up menu control in the lower-right corner of the Viewer window. From the pop-up menu, choose the **S onto stage** clip.

The Recent Clips pop-up menu displays the most recently opened clips, with the most recent clip at the top of the list. The menu displays a default of the 10 most recent clips, but you can change that in the User Preferences window (Option-Q) to save up to 20 clips.

TIP There are two additional ways to open a clip in the Viewer. You can select a clip and choose View > Clip, or you can Control-click the clip in the Browser and choose Open in Viewer from the shortcut menu.

Navigating Clips

As you begin to edit, playing or screening clips will always be one of your first steps. But after you've played through a clip, you will soon want greater navigational control. For example, you may want to go back a few seconds to review an action, play faster through an area that is less important, move quickly to the head or tail of a clip, or go backward or forward to find a specific frame, and so on. In the Viewer window, there are transport buttons, as well as keyboard shortcuts, to give you this control. There are also visual clues to indicate when you are on the first or last frame of a clip.

In this exercise, you will open one clip that has several actions in it. By using buttons and shortcuts, you will move to and screen different actions within this clip.

1   From the Clips bin in the Browser, open the **J and L circle** clip. Press the End key to see the last frame of this clip. Then press the Home key to move the playhead back to the first frame.

TIP ▶ If you are using a laptop, press the fn (function) key and the Left Arrow for Home, and the fn key and Right Arrow for End.

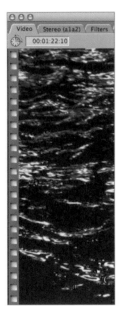

First frame of clip

Last frame of clip

In the Viewer, a filmstrip appears on the left side of the image area when the playhead is on the first frame, or *head*, of the clip. It appears on the right when the playhead is on the last frame, or *tail*, of the clip.

NOTE ▶ If the filmstrip overlays do not appear in your Viewer image area, choose View > Show Overlays. You can toggle overlays off or on during the editing process.

2 Press End to move the playhead to the tail of the clip. Press the Left Arrow key several times and watch the trainer's right hand move up and down on the whale's pectoral flipper.

The Left and Right Arrow keys are a great way to navigate frame by frame to the beginning or end of a specific action. You can also hold the Left or Right Arrow key down to move forward at a slow-motion speed.

3 Now press Shift–Left Arrow four times to move the playhead backward 4 seconds. Play from this position to the end of the clip.

Using the Shift key with either the Left or Right Arrow keys moves the playhead backward or forward, respectively, in 1-second increments. This is a helpful way to move the playhead quickly backward or forward a specific amount of time, in this case, to play the last section of the clip.

4 To move back to the head of this clip a different way, press the Up Arrow key to move the playhead to the beginning of the clip.

The Up and Down Arrow keys move the playhead backward or forward to the head or tail of the clip.

5   In the Viewer scrubber bar, drag the playhead forward through the first section where the two trainers move in a circle. Then drag the playhead backward to about 00:14:03:20 and play this section.

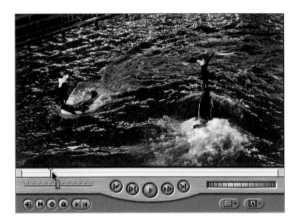

Dragging through a clip this way is called *scrubbing*. You are viewing the clip, but not at normal play speed. You can also drag the playhead to move quickly to the head or tail of a clip, or click in any part of the scrubber bar to bring the playhead to that location. As you scrub, you hear the digital audio of the clip.

TIP ▶ To toggle off or on the clip audio as you scrub, choose View > Audio Scrubbing, or press Shift-S.

6   Scrub the playhead forward to where the whale is pushing the trainer out of the water, around 00:14:32:00. Drag the jog control to the right, until you see the trainer's hands open up. Then drag the shuttle control to view the rest of this section. Stop at about 00:14:40:00.

The shuttle and jog controls act like traditional VCR controls, scrubbing or scrolling through frames of your clip. When you use the jog control, you hear the digital audio scrubbing sound. When you use the shuttle control, you hear an analog audio sound that can be useful when looking for a specific sound cue.

TIP ▶ A great use for the scroll button on a two-button mouse is to scrub frame by frame through an image as though you were using a jog control. Place the pointer over the image area in the Viewer and scroll up to scrub backward, and scroll down to scrub forward. The scroll ball on the Apple Mighty Mouse can move left and right as well.

7   The J-K-L keys provide additional ways to navigate a clip. Press L to play forward. Watch for when the whale lifts the trainer out of the water, and goes back under. Then press K to stop. Press the J key to play backward through this section.

These three keys—J, K, and L—provide a convenient way to screen a clip for specific actions. By using combinations of these keys, you can play a clip slow or fast, forward or backward, and view it frame by frame.

8   Move the playhead to the head of the clip. With your three fingers over the J, K, and L keys, try the following key combinations to reacquaint yourself with the whale's behaviors:

▶ Press L two or three times to play the clip faster. When you press L repeatedly, the clip speed is ramped up faster and faster.

▶ Press K to stop, then press J several times to play backward at faster speeds.

▶ Press and hold K and L together to play forward in slow motion.

▶ Press and hold K and J together to play backward in slow motion.

▶ Hold K and tap L to move forward one frame at a time.

▶ Hold K and tap J to move backward one frame at a time.

TIP ▶ You can also play backward by holding down the Shift key and then pressing the Viewer Play button or the spacebar.

9 To move the playhead to the head of the clip using a Viewer transport button, click the Go to Previous Edit button.

The Go to Next Edit button will move the playhead to the tail of the clip. The Up and Down Arrows are the shortcut keys for these functions.

10 To move to the exact location in this clip where the trainer opens her hands, click in the Current Timecode field and type *00:14:33:24*, then press Return.

The playhead moves to that specific timecode location. Often, in larger productions, an editor will receive a list of timecode numbers from a director, writer, or assistant that represents specific edit points or important locations in a clip. Editors often begin their editing process by screening these "selected" takes.

11 Move the playhead to the following timecode locations to review memorable frames from this clip:

00:15:16:27   Trainer lying on whale's chest

00:14:04:08   Two trainers in circle

00:14:45:13   Whale lifts trainer out of water

TIP When entering a timecode number, you don't need to click first in the Current Timecode field. Just make sure the Viewer window is active, then start typing the timecode number. Final Cut Pro knows that you are typing a timecode number and automatically places it in that field. Also, you never need to type preceding zeros or the colons or semicolons that separate numbers. However, the text of this book uses colons to make the timecode numbers easier to read.

Project Tasks

Take a moment to screen the following clips. Use the different navigation techniques to find specific trainer actions, killer whale shots, or interview segments that are interesting and that might be good to use in a sequence when you begin to edit:

▶ **uw_propel jump**

▶ **J thru glass**

▶ **_SA_team ideas**

▶ **jump at stage**

▶ **whale nods head**

▶ **sham slam**

▶ **performance_S spray jump**

▶ **_SA_room discussion**

To review, the different ways to navigate through a clip are:

▶ Use the navigation buttons and controls in the Viewer.

▶ Use the keyboard shortcuts, such as Up, Down, Left, and Right Arrows.

▶ Use the J-K-L keys to move forward or backward at different speeds.

▶ Enter a timecode number in the Current Timecode field and press Return to go to a specific location.

Playing and Navigating a Sequence

Now that you've screened some of the raw footage from the SeaWorld "Believe" project, let's take a look at how you can use that footage to create an edited sequence in the Timeline. Whereas the Browser is a container for *all* your project elements and full-length clips, the Timeline is a container for just those portions of clips that contain specific actions. These edited clips make up the sequence.

You can play and navigate a sequence in either the Canvas or Timeline window. In fact, all of the play and navigation commands you used in the Viewer can be applied in the Canvas and Timeline, sometimes with slightly different results. Sequence names appear on tabs at the top of both the Timeline and Canvas windows. There are two sequence tabs open in the Canvas and Timeline windows. Each tab represents a different sequence.

The Canvas has a playhead and a scrubber bar similar to the Viewer's. In the Timeline, blue video and green audio clips sit on horizontal tracks. These tracks are a linear representation of time proceeding from left to right. In the middle of the current sequence is the playhead, which functions just as the Viewer playhead does.

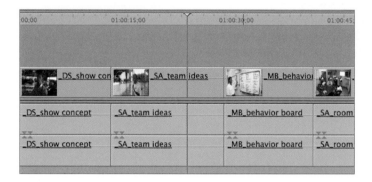

1 To focus on the sequence image in the Canvas, resize the windows by dragging the boundary line between the Viewer and Canvas as far left as possible. Then hold down Option and choose Window > Arrange > Set Custom Layout 2 to save this layout for future use.

2 In the Canvas, click the *2_Believe Behaviors* sequence tab to make sure it is the active sequence. Drag the playhead in the scrubber bar to the far left, or press the Home key. What's the duration of this sequence?

While the Viewer scrubber bar represents the length of one clip, the Canvas scrubber bar represents the length of the entire sequence. This length appears in the Timecode Duration field, positioned in the upper-left corner, just as in the Viewer.

3   To play this sequence, click the Canvas Play button, or press the spacebar. You can also use the L key as you did in the Viewer.

NOTE ▶ This sequence contains clips of trainers rehearsing with the killer whales accompanied by a single music track of the show's theme song, "Believe."

As you play the sequence, you see the playhead in the Timeline ruler area move in tandem with the Canvas playhead. They are each playing the same sequence; the Canvas is displaying the image while the Timeline displays a graphical representation of the individual edits. Notice that the Timeline ruler area displays the continuous timecode of the sequence, not of the individual clips. Entering a specific timecode number in the Canvas or Timeline moves you to a specific place in the sequence.

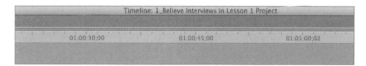

4   To see a mother whale and her calf jump together, click in the Canvas Current Timecode field and type *1:00:52:29*. Press Return.

The playhead moves to the specific timecode number you entered.

5 To see an edited portion of the **J and L circle** clip you just screened, click in the Timeline Current Timecode field and type *1:00:08:03*, and press Return. Play the edited version of that clip from the playhead location.

TIP ▶ Just as in the Viewer, you don't have to click in the Current Time-code field before typing the timecode number. With the Canvas or Time-line window active, just start typing the number and it automatically appears in this field.

Again, the playhead moves to that individual frame. You can also scrub through the Timeline to find interesting actions, just as you did in the Viewer and Canvas. You do this by dragging the playhead in the ruler area of the Timeline or the Canvas scrubber bar.

6 Drag the yellow triangle of the playhead slowly across the Timeline ruler area to the **whale nods head** clip. Drag through this clip to see the whale nod its head "no" and then "yes."

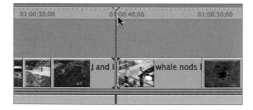

As you drag the playhead across other clips in the Timeline, the playhead snaps like a magnet at the edit point between each clip. When you drag within a clip, you don't feel the playhead snap.

NOTE ▶ The snapping function can be toggled off or on in the Timeline button bar. Make sure it is on, or green, for this exercise.

7   To move to edit points earlier in the sequence, press the Up Arrow key several times. To move forward to later edit points, press the Down Arrow key several times.

In the Canvas and Timeline, the Up and Down Arrow keys move the playhead to the first frame of the previous or next clip. The L-shaped symbol in the lower-left corner of the Canvas is a visual clue indicating the playhead is positioned on the first frame of the edited clip.

TIP ▶ Another way to move backward and forward to a clip is to use the Go to Previous Edit and Go to Next Edit buttons in the Canvas. You can also use the ; (semicolon) and ' (apostrophe) keys, which are conveniently located next to the J, K, and L keys.

8   Move the playhead to the first frame of the **whale nods head** clip. Now press the Left Arrow key to move one frame backward.

In the Canvas, the reverse L in the lower-right corner of the image area indicates that you are on the last frame of that clip. As in the Viewer, the Left and Right Arrow keys move the playhead one frame at a time.

9   The J, K, and L keys work in the Canvas and Timeline just as they did in the Viewer. They can play the sequence forward or backward, step through frame by frame, and play it in slow motion. Use the J, K, and L keys to move quickly through the sequence, stopping at interesting whale behaviors and playing them in slow motion or backward.

10   To jump to the end of the sequence, press the End key.

A blue vertical bar appears on the right side of the Canvas window, indicating that you are at the end of the sequence. There are no edits past this point.

11 To see this sequence play full-screen on your computer monitor, position the playhead at the head of the sequence and choose View > Video Playback > Digital Cinema Desktop Preview - Main. Then press Command-F12. When you see the image full-screen, use the spacebar or the J-K-L keys to play and navigate the sequence. To come out of the full-screen preview, press the Escape key.

Project Tasks

To practice playing and navigating a different sequence, or viewing a sequence in the Digital Cinema Desktop Preview mode, click the *1_Believe Interviews* sequence tab and play that sequence. You will edit this footage in the next lesson.

You can also open the *3_Scene from "Monk"* sequence in the Browser and play it full-screen. You will work with this footage in Lesson 4.

> **TIP** To open a sequence, double-click it in the Browser, or select it and press Return. It will open as a new tab in the Timeline and Canvas windows.

Marking Clips

Now that you've seen how clips can be edited together into a sequence, you can start to mark specific actions in your source clips.

First you will determine what portion of a clip to use, then mark the starting and ending points of the desired action or sound in the Viewer. For example, is the best starting point when the trainer picks the fish from the bucket? Or when the trainer throws the fish into the whale's mouth? Should you include everything the trainer says in the interview? Or just one sentence?

You can use the different navigation methods from the previous exercises to move to the precise starting point and then set an *In* point, which lets Final Cut Pro know where to begin using the clip content. Next, you play the clip from the In point to see where you might want to stop using the footage, and here you set an *Out* point.

There are two ways you can set edit points in the Viewer:

▶ Use the Mark In and Mark Out buttons in the Viewer window.

▶ Use the keyboard shortcuts: I for In and O for Out.

Mark In button ⏄ ⏄ Mark Out button

When you set In and Out points in a clip, they remain with that clip until you decide to change their location or remove them altogether. You can change, remove, and reposition edit points. Sometimes, when working with sound effects or static video shots, you may choose to enter a duration to define the length of an edit, rather than look for a specific action to mark.

In the next lesson, you will edit these marked clips into a sequence. But for now, prepare the clips by just marking the portion you want to use.

TIP ▶ To return to the larger Viewer window layout you saved, choose Window > Arrange > Custom Layout 1, or press the shortcut, Shift-U.

1   From the Clips bin in the Browser, open the **_DS_show team** clip into the Viewer. (This is David Smith, VP of entertainment for Busch Entertainment Corporation.) Play the clip and stop after David says, "…all around the country." Note the duration of this clip is 38:15.

TIP ▶ Throughout this exercise, take an extra moment to create *clean* edit points. For example, use the Left and Right Arrow keys, or J-K-L keys to position the playhead where David's eyes are open, and where his mouth is closed before he speaks again.

Currently, the Timecode Duration field in the Viewer is reflecting the full length of the clip. When you mark this clip, this duration will change to reflect the marked portion only.

2   To set an In point at this location, click the Mark In button (beneath the shuttle control and Viewer transport keys).

A new In point appears in the scrubber bar where the playhead is located. Notice the In point overlay in the upper-left corner of the image area, and the shorter duration that appears in the Timecode Duration field. This duration reflects the time from the new In point to the end of the clip.

3   Play the clip from this point and stop after David says, "…what the overall content of the show would be." In the Viewer, click the Mark Out button to set an Out point at this location.

A new Out point appears in the scrubber bar where the playhead is located and in the upper-right corner of the image area. The Timecode Duration field reflects the length of the marked portion of the clip, and the scrubber bar becomes gray outside the marked area.

4   Click the Play In to Out button to see just the marked portion of your clip.

This is the portion of the clip that will be edited into the sequence.

TIP ▶ Even though you haven't begun editing, the edit points you are setting can be saved as part of your project. To save the marks you create, choose File > Save Project, or press Command-S.

5   Now open the **_SA_room discussion** clip from the Clips bin and play it. Position the playhead at the end of Steve's comment, "…biggest one is immersion." This time, press I to mark an In point. Move the playhead to after Steve says, "…three or four, three or four, three or four." Then press O to mark an Out point.

Using keyboard shortcuts produces the same results as the mark buttons: They create In and Out marks in the scrubber bar and clip image.

6   To review the first frame of the marked portion of this clip, press Shift-I to move the playhead to that location. To review the Out point, press Shift-O.

All the keyboard shortcuts that relate to the In point use the letter *I* with or without a modifier key. All the shortcuts that relate to the Out point use the letter *O*.

TIP ▶ To remove an In point, press Option-I. To remove an Out point, press Option-O. To remove both marks at the same time, press Option-X.

7   From the Clips bin, open the **jump at stage** clip. Play this clip several times until you're familiar with and can anticipate where the trainer raises her hands and then lowers them. Mark an In and Out point at those locations. If you need to redo your marks, replay the clip and mark again.

Marking again after you already have an In or Out point simply replaces the old edit point with the new. Marking in real time as the clip is playing is called *marking on the fly*.

8   From the Audio clips bin, open the **Applause FX 05.aif** clip and play this clip. To mark the entire length of the sound effect, click the Mark Clip button, or use the keyboard shortcut, X.

Marking an audio-only clip follows the same process as marking a video clip, even though no Video tab appears in the Viewer. You can navigate through the clip by dragging the playhead in the scrubber bar. The Viewer's audio tab, like the Timeline's, has a ruler area and a second playhead. You can drag the playhead to scrub the clip in the ruler area or the Viewer scrubber bar.

NOTE ▶ Audio clips created using Apple's Audio Interchange File Format have an .aif file extension. Depending on how the clip was named, this extension may not always be visible.

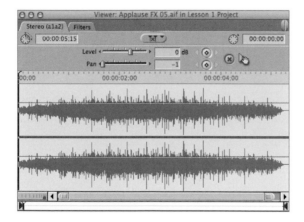

9   From the Clips bin, open the **_MB_behavior board** clip and play it. We may want just a portion of the camera zoom from this shot. A timecode reference for the In point is 00:31:11:20. Enter that number in the Current Timecode field and press Return. Then set an In point at this location. Set an Out point at 00:31:15:17.

TIP ▶ If you change your mind about an edit point, Command-Z or Edit > Undo removes the mark or returns you to a previous mark. The default number of undos is 10, but you can change that number in the General tab of the User Preferences window (Option-Q).

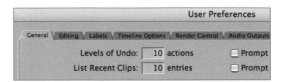

10 Open the **whale nods head** clip and play it from the beginning. After the whale nods "yes," mark an Out point.

   With just an Out point, the duration is calculated from the beginning of the clip. When you edit this clip, the material from the beginning of the clip to the Out point will be used in the edit. You can also mark an In point but not mark an Out point.

11 Open the **sham slam** clip and mark an In point at 00:17:59:10. Click the Play In to Out button.

   With no Out point, the clip plays to the end. When you edit this clip, the material from the In point to the end of the clip will be used in the edit.

12 Open the **Bubbles.aif** clip and play it. Since this sound effect is continuous, you can set a duration for how much of it you want to use. Mark an In point where the sound begins, then click the Timecode Duration field in the upper-left portion of the Viewer, and type *4:00*. Press Return to enter this duration.

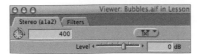

An Out point is automatically created in the scrubber bar 4 seconds from the In point, or in this case, from the head of the clip. It doesn't matter where the playhead is located when you enter a duration for a clip.

TIP You can also type this number without a colon (*400*), or with a period following the 4, such as *4.*, to represent two zeros, in this case zero frames. Substituting a period for double zeros is used throughout Final Cut Pro.

13 Open the **_DS_show concept** clip and mark an In point before David Smith says, "The idea of 'Believe.'…" Mark an Out point toward the end of the clip after David says, "…the whole concept of this particular show." To adjust the Out point to an earlier cue, move your pointer over the Out point in the scrubber bar and drag left toward the middle of the clip. Then drag right until after you hear David say, "…it all came from the animal itself."

Dragging an edit point left or right resets it to that location. It also changes the duration of the marked portion of the clip. When you release an edit point at its new location, the image in the Viewer reverts to the frame at the playhead location, which may not be the new In or Out point.

TIP Choose Mark > Go To to see the shortcuts for going to edit points. You can also choose other mark options here, or use this menu to remind yourself of the keyboard shortcuts.

Project Tasks

In the next lesson, you will edit marked clips to create new sequences. Take a moment to mark the portions of the following clips you will use in those sequences. You can play the sequences in the Timeline as a reference. For the whale behaviors, the times listed are those that were used for the *2_Believe Behaviors* sequence. These durations will create clips that fit the length of the current music track. You can also just mark whatever actions you'd like to use in your own sequence. (A complete set of marked clips will be available in the **Lesson 2 Project** file.)

Interviews (from *1_Believe Interviews* sequence):

- **_DF_ambassadors**   "We as trainers … with this species of animal."
- **_KW_at board**   "Kayla's got the … OK, great."
- **_SA_team ideas**   "From the trainers' … see in the 'Believe' show."
- **_SA_favorite behavior**   "There's a behavior … reason why we do this."
- **_MM_with trainers**   From head of clip to after Mark raises his arm.
- **S gives pendant**   Mark the beginning and end of camera zoom.
- **performance_S spray jump**   Mark In point 1 second before whale exits water; give this clip a 7-second duration.

Whale behaviors from *2_Believe Behaviors* sequence and their times:

- **J and L circle** (Trainer sitting on whale's nose, goes up and down = 3:00)
- **uw_push two trainers** (3:00)
- **J and S jump** (4:15)
- **K jumps off whale** (2:15)
- **J and L circle** (Circle together = 7:10)
- **uw_mom and calf jump** (7:15)
- **performance_S spray jump** (8:15)
- **S show open** (5:10)

Saving, Hiding, and Quitting Final Cut Pro

Make sure you save frequently throughout the editing process, whether you've made any edits or not. You may have made only minor organizational changes or marked a few clips. Saving your project ensures these decisions are included the next time you open that project. You can also hide the interface if you want to work on your desktop or in another program. You save, hide, and quit Final Cut Pro just as you would any Apple application: from the menu or by using a keyboard shortcut.

1 Press Command-S to save changes in the current project.

2 To hide the interface, choose Final Cut Pro > Hide Final Cut Pro, or press Command-H.

   The interface disappears, and you see your desktop or any other programs you may have open in the background.

3 Restore the Final Cut Pro interface by going to the Dock and clicking the program icon.

   The small black arrow or triangle next to the Final Cut Pro icon in the Dock is a reminder that the application is still open, even if it's not showing.

   NOTE ▶ If you made all of the suggested changes in the exercise steps and Project Tasks sections, you can leave this project open and use it for the next lesson. If not, close this project and open the **Lesson 2 Project**.

4 To close this project, choose File > Close Project.

   When you close a project or quit Final Cut Pro, a prompt to save appears if you have made any changes since the last time you saved the project. If this window appears, click Yes to ensure that you are saving the most recent changes.

   If you want to keep working on this project the next time you open Final Cut Pro, you don't have to close the project prior to quitting the program. If you quit with that project open, it will open along with the program the next time you launch Final Cut Pro.

5 If you are finished working, quit the program altogether by choosing Final Cut Pro > Quit Final Cut Pro, or by pressing Command-Q. If you are not finished working, leave the program open, and continue with the next lesson.

Lesson Review

1. Name three ways to launch Final Cut Pro.
2. To open and close projects, you select the appropriate item from which menu?
3. What are the four modifier keys that are often used in conjunction with keyboard shortcuts to initiate functions or commands?
4. How do you access a shortcut menu?
5. Name three ways to create a bin.
6. What are three ways to open a clip into the Viewer?
7. Besides using the Play button, what keys on your keyboard can you press to play a clip or sequence forward?
8. What keys move the playhead forward or backward in one-frame increments in the Viewer, Canvas, and Timeline?
9. How do you mark an In or Out point on a clip?
10. What is the visual indicator in the Viewer that lets you know you are on the first or last frame of the entire clip?
11. What is the visual indicator in the Canvas window that lets you know the playhead is on the first or last frame of an edited clip in the Timeline?
12. When viewing the audio portion of a clip, what do you see instead of a video image?
13. What are the shortcuts to save, hide, and quit Final Cut Pro?

Answers

1. Double-click the application in the Applications folder, click once on the icon in the Dock, or double-click a Final Cut Pro project file.
2. The File menu.
3. Shift, Control, Option, and Command.
4. Control-click, or right-click with a two-button mouse.
5. Choose File > New Bin, press Command-B, or Control-click in the gray area of the Browser.

6. Double-click the clip in the Browser, drag it to the Viewer, or select it and press Return.

7. The Spacebar and the L key.

8. The Left and Right Arrow keys.

9. Use the Mark In and Mark Out buttons in the Viewer, or the keyboard shortcuts, I and O.

10. A filmstrip appears on the left side of the image in the Viewer indicating the first available frame of media, and on the right side indicating the last.

11. An *L* in the lower left means you're on the first frame of the edited clip, and a reverse *L* in the lower right means you're on the last frame.

12. A waveform display.

13. Press Command-S to save current changes, press Command-H to hide the application, and press Command-Q to quit.

Keyboard Shortcuts

Organizing Project Elements

Command-B	Creates a new bin
Control-click (or right-click)	Opens shortcut menus throughout Final Cut Pro

Moving the Playhead and Playing a Clip or Sequence

Home	Takes playhead to head of the sequence
End	Takes playhead to end of the sequence
Down Arrow	Moves playhead forward in the Viewer to end of clip or next edit point, and in Timeline to the first frame of the next edit
Up Arrow	Moves playhead backward in the Viewer to head of clip or previous edit point, and in Timeline to previous first frame

Keyboard Shortcuts

Moving the Playhead and Playing a Clip or Sequence (continued)

Left Arrow	Moves playhead one frame to the left
Right Arrow	Moves playhead one frame to the right
L	Plays clip or sequence forward in Viewer, Timeline, or Canvas
K	Stops playing clip or sequence in Viewer, Timeline, or Canvas
J	Plays clip or sequence backward in Viewer, Timeline, or Canvas
K + L	Plays forward in slow motion
K + J	Plays backward in slow motion
K + tap L	Moves playhead one frame to the right
K + tap J	Moves playhead one frame to the left
Shift-spacebar	Plays a clip or sequence backward

Setting, Viewing, and Removing Marks

I	Sets an In point
O	Sets an Out point
X	Sets In and Out points at the head and tail of the clip
Shift-I	Moves the playhead to the In point
Shift-O	Moves the playhead to the Out point
Option-I	Removes the In point
Option-O	Removes the Out point
Option-X	Removes both In and Out points

Keyboard Shortcuts

Controlling the Application and Interface

Control-U	Selects the Standard window layout
Shift-U	Recalls Custom Layout 1
Option-U	Recalls Custom Layout 2
A	Selects the default Selection tool
Command-S	Saves changes in the project
Command-H	Hides the Final Cut Pro interface
Command-Q	Quits Final Cut Pro

2

Lesson Files	Lesson 2 Project
Media	SeaWorld > Believe, Narration, Music, and Sound Effects folders
Time	This lesson takes approximately 90 minutes to complete.
Goals	Manage project elements
	Make overwrite and insert edits
	Manage Timeline tracks
	Import clips
	Edit audio clips
	Move clips in the Timeline
	Use drag-and-drop editing
	Change volume of sequence clips

Editing Clips to the Timeline

In the previous lesson, you screened and marked clips from the SeaWorld "Believe" documentary in the Viewer window. Now you will edit the marked selections to the Timeline to build a rough cut of the footage.

In the simplest terms, building a rough cut consists of marking clips and placing them into the sequence in a specific order. But rather than focus on a specific action within a clip, you begin to focus on how clips fit together. Keep in mind that a rough-cut sequence will require trimming, adjusting, and finessing, but all of that comes in the next stage of the editing process.

There are two ways to edit a marked clip into a sequence. The first is somewhat automatic: You simply click a button to make an edit. The second approach is more hands-on. After determining its proper location, you use the mouse to manually place the clip into the Timeline. This approach is referred to as *drag-and-drop editing*.

While there are many types of edits you can make in Final Cut Pro, the two types of edits you will work with in this lesson are *overwrites* and *inserts*. As you begin building a sequence, you will also learn to work with audio clips, create new versions of sequences, and open and change clips in the Timeline.

Managing Project Elements

In Lesson 1, you dragged clips into bins to organize your project. On larger projects, such as documentaries and reality shows, there is often so much footage that additional organization is needed. For example, having one bin with 100 clips may not be as helpful as having 10 bins with 10 clips, each organized around a specific topic.

To further organize the elements in this project, you will create bins within bins and create two new sequences.

1   If Final Cut Pro is not open, launch it by clicking its icon in the Dock.

If a project was open when you last quit Final Cut Pro, such as the **Lesson 1 Project**, it will open automatically when you launch the application. Also, the windows will be arranged according to the last layout you used, such as the large Viewer layout you saved as Custom Layout 1.

NOTE ▶ If you marked all of the clips in the Lesson 1 project tasks, you can continue working within the **Lesson 1 Project**. If not, you can open the **Lesson 2 Project**, which contains marked clips ready for editing.

2   Choose File > Open, and navigate to the Lessons folder, as you did in Lesson 1. Select the **Lesson 2 Project** file, and click Choose.

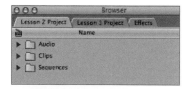

In the Browser, the project elements are organized into three bins, the way you organized the elements in the previous lesson. Also, the window layout remains unchanged when you open a new project.

3   If you have another project open, such as **Lesson 1 Project**, Control-click its tab in the Browser and choose Close Tab from the shortcut menu. Save the project when prompted.

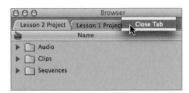

4   Click the disclosure triangle next to the Clips bin to view its contents.

There are three sets of clips from the SeaWorld "Believe" project inside this bin. One set is interview footage, another is the whale behaviors from the "Believe" show rehearsals and performances, and a third set is underwater footage. If each set of footage is put into a separate bin, it will be easier to locate specific clips when working on a particular section of the documentary. Let's organize this footage into separate bins *within* the Clips bin.

5   To create a bin inside another bin, Control-click the Clips bin in the Browser (or right-click when using a two-button mouse). From the shortcut menu, select New Bin. Repeat this two times to create a total of three new bins *inside* the Clips bin.

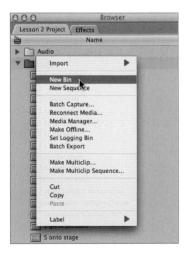

When you Control-click a specific bin to create a new bin, you are directing Final Cut Pro to place the new bin inside the bin you selected.

6   Rename the new bins *Interviews*, *Behaviors*, and *Underwater*. You can select the bin and click the name to highlight it, or select the bin and press Enter.

7   As you did in Lesson 1, drag the clips into their appropriate bins. Underwater clip names begin with *uw*, interview clip names begin with an underscore, such as *_SA*, and the remaining clips are behaviors from rehearsals and performances.

When clips are in their appropriate bins, it's easier to find a specific clip.

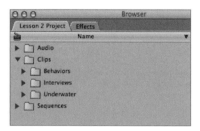

8   From the Clips > Interviews bin, open the **_SA_team ideas** clip. Click the Play In to Out button to see the marked portion of this clip.

The clip's marked duration determines how much of the clip is used. All of the clips in this project have been marked in preparation for this lesson.

You will be editing two sequences in this project, so you will need to create two new empty sequences for that purpose.

9 To create a new sequence, choose File > New > Sequence, or press the shortcut, Command-N.

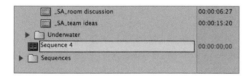

When you create a new sequence, a sequence icon appears with *Sequence 2, 3*, or other sequential number in the Name area depending on how many sequences have already been created in the project. Three sequences have already been created in this project, so this sequence name defaults to *Sequence 4*.

10 Rename this sequence *Behaviors_v1*, for version 1, and then drag this sequence inside the Sequences bin.

TIP ▶ Adding version numbers to a sequence name is a common and helpful practice. In later exercises, when you make changes to this sequence, you will duplicate it, change the version number, and make changes to the new version.

11 To create a sequence inside the Sequences bin, Control-click the bin and choose New Sequence from the shortcut menu. Name this new sequence *Interviews_v1*.

You will edit your first rough cut in this sequence.

Editing a Rough Cut

As you begin editing clips into a sequence, there are questions you need to ask about the edit. For example, do you want to edit both audio and video from the same clip? Or will you take the video from one clip and audio from another? If you are editing audio, you may need to adjust the audio level of the clip before editing it. You might also ask where in time you want to place a clip in the sequence. Before the whale jumps or after the underwater shot?

When deciding where to place a clip, you may also consider which Timeline track is the best to use. Often, a rough cut will utilize just one video track, though other video elements may be added later. However, you generally utilize several audio tracks in a rough cut. You may edit in the natural sound of a video action, a narration track, music, or sound effects. Even though this is a rough cut, it's important to follow a plan for where you want to place these audio tracks and to be consistent throughout the editing process.

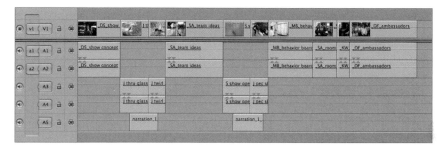

Organized use of audio tracks in the Timeline

MORE INFO ▶ You will learn more about mixing audio tracks in Lesson 10.

Some editors like to begin with a *prebuild* sequence, laying in all of the selected takes in rough order. Once the clips are in the Timeline, you can view them side by side and start to get a better sense of the story. Also, Final Cut Pro offers many functions that make it easy to change clips in the Timeline. In this lesson, you will edit into the sequence all the interview footage you will need, and then make changes to the arrangement or placement of the clips in the sequence.

Making Overwrite Edits

You can make different types of edits in Final Cut Pro, and each type places a clip in a sequence a little differently. An overwrite edit places a clip over whatever is on a Timeline track. The Timeline may be empty at that point, or another clip may be present. An insert edit positions a clip between other clips currently on a track. For this exercise, the audio and video will be edited to the V1, A1, and A2 tracks.

One clip overwriting another in a sequence

There are different ways to make overwrite edits. Later in this lesson you will drag an edit into the Timeline manually. For this exercise, you will use these more automatic methods:

▶   Click the Overwrite button.

▶   Press the keyboard shortcut, F10.

▶   Choose the Overwrite option from the Canvas Edit Overlay.

TIP ▶ Because you will be using the Viewer and Canvas windows equally in this exercise, you may want to press Control-U to revert to the Standard window layout. Or you can resize your interface according to your own preferences.

1   In the Browser, double-click the *Interviews_v1* sequence to open it in the
       Timeline.

When you open a new sequence in the Timeline, the playhead is always
positioned at the beginning of the sequence. When editing, you can use
the playhead as a *target* that identifies the exact placement of the edit
in the sequence. At the current target location, your first edit will appear
at the head of this sequence.

2   In the Viewer, click the Stereo tab to see the stereo waveform of the
       _SA_team ideas clip.

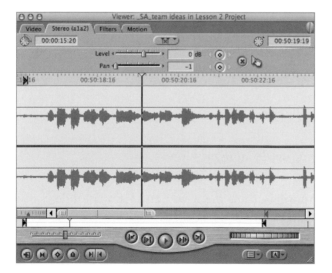

This clip has two tracks of audio. When you edit this clip, the video and both tracks of audio between the In and Out points will be edited.

3   To edit the **_SA_team ideas** clip at the playhead or target location in the Timeline, click the red Overwrite button in the Canvas window.

Before the clip is edited into the Timeline, you will most likely see a Warning box appear, letting you know that the settings of the sequence you've created don't match those of the clip you are editing.

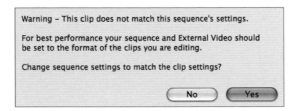

4   Click Yes to have Final Cut Pro automatically change the sequence settings for the *Interviews_v1* sequence to match the SeaWorld footage. Then play the edited clip in the Timeline.

MORE INFO ▶ You will learn more about changing sequence settings in Lesson 7.

The marked clip is automatically placed in the Timeline at the playhead location. The playhead jumps to the end of the clip, or more specifically, the first frame of the space following the clip, awaiting the next edit. Notice the blue end-of-sequence overlay in the Canvas, indicating that you are at the end of the sequence. Because the audio has stereo tracks, the clip occupies two audio tracks in the Timeline, A1 and A2. These are the default target audio tracks.

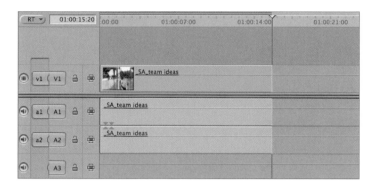

5 From the Interviews bin, open the **_MB_behavior board** clip. In the Viewer, click the Play In to Out button to see the portion you will edit.

All the clips you use in this exercise will be taken from the Interviews bin.

6 To edit this clip into the sequence at the end of the previous clip, make sure the playhead is targeting that location, and click the red Overwrite button.

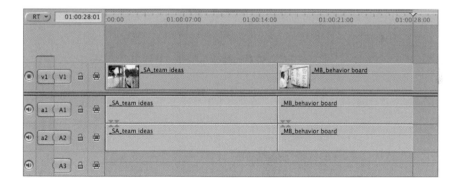

In the Timeline, the clip is edited at the playhead location, and the playhead is automatically moved to the end of the clip, awaiting the next edit.

NOTE ▶ To use the keyboard shortcut in step 7, make sure you have reassigned the OS X functions in the System Preferences. If you need help setting Preferences, go to the "Getting Started" chapter.

7 Open the **_SA_room discussion** clip and press Shift-\ (backslash) to play it from the In to the Out point. Now move your pointer over the red Overwrite button until you see the Overwrite shortcut, F10, appear in the tooltip. Press the F10 key to edit this clip into the sequence.

> **TIP** To find a shortcut for any button or function in the interface, simply move your pointer over that area. You can turn tooltips off or on in the General tab of User Preferences (Option-Q).

8 Open the **_KW_at board** clip and press Shift-\ to see the marked portion of the clip. To edit this clip a different way, click and hold your pointer in the image area of this clip.

In the Viewer, a clip thumbnail attaches to the pointer.

9 Drag the thumbnail image into the Canvas window, but *don't release the mouse.*

The Edit Overlay appears in the Canvas window with a palette of seven sections. These sections represent seven different types of edits. Overwrite is the default edit option. To indicate this, the red Overwrite section has a brighter border around it, and the red Overwrite button is brighter.

Notice that the icon in the Overwrite section, like the Overwrite button, has a downward-facing triangle or arrow. This is a visual clue that you will be covering, or overwriting, anything in its place in the Timeline.

10 Drag the **_KW_at board** thumbnail image onto the Overwrite section in the Edit Overlay, and release the mouse. Play this group of clips from the beginning of the sequence.

> **NOTE ▶** If the Overwrite section is highlighted in the overlay, you can drop the clip anywhere in the Canvas image area to make an overwrite edit.

Remember, this is a rough cut, and you will want to make many changes to it over the course of the editing process. One change you can make is to overwrite a portion of a clip you edited when you make the next edit. For example, the last clip in this sequence seems a little long. Let's shorten the end as you make the next edit.

11 Play the **_KW_at board** clip and stop after you hear Katie say, "…OK, great."

TIP ▶ To hear the audio as you drag the playhead through the clip, choose the View menu and make sure Audio Scrubbing is checked.

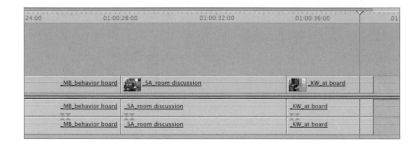

When you make the next edit, the new clip will overwrite the remaining portion of this clip.

12 Open the **_DF_ambassadors** clip and view the marked portion. Drag the clip into the Canvas and drop it over the Overwrite option in the Edit Overlay.

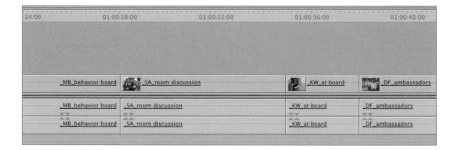

Now the **_KW_at board** clip is shorter in the Timeline than it was before. You can also overwrite an entire clip or group of clips as you make an overwrite edit.

Some editors consistently use this method of editing clips with extended lengths in the Timeline as a way to increase their flexibility in choosing where to place the next clip.

13 Press Command-S to save the changes you've made to your project.

Managing Timeline Tracks

After editing several clips to your rough cut, the earlier clips in the sequence will begin to move offscreen. Some Timeline management is required to shift the focus to a particular clip or area in the sequence, or to see all the clips in the Timeline window at the same time. Magnifying the tracks is one way to manage how you view your sequence. You can magnify or zoom into your clips two ways: horizontally, so the clips appear wider, or vertically, so the clips appear taller. Magnifying tracks does not in any way change the length of the clips in the sequence, only their appearance in the Timeline.

1   To zoom into the **_KW_at board** clip to read its name, move the playhead to that clip and press Option-+ (plus). Press it again to zoom in further.

In the ruler area, notice that the timecode numbers have expanded to reflect the zoom change.

Two Timeline controls allow you to zoom into a Timeline area or to slide the sequence left or right: the zoom control and zoom slider, both located on the very bottom of the Timeline beneath the audio tracks.

Zoom control   Zoom slider

2   To see the clips at the beginning of the sequence in this zoomed-in view, drag the zoom slider to the left.

TIP ▶ If you are using a mouse with a scroll ball, you can scroll through the sequence clips by dragging the scroll button left or right.

The zoom slider changes the portion of the sequence that's visible in the Timeline.

3   To zoom out to see all the clips in your rough cut, drag the zoom control to the right to decrease the size of the clips in the sequence. You can also use the shortcut for zooming out, Option-– (minus).

The zoom control adjusts the horizontal scale of the tracks. Using the keyboard shortcut or zoom control always zooms the sequence in or out around the playhead location.

4   Move the playhead to the beginning of the second clip, **_MB_behavior board**, and press Option-+ two times to zoom into that clip. Now drag the zoom slider to the right to position the fifth clip, **_DF_ambassadors**, in the center of the Timeline. To jump back to the playhead location at the second clip, click the tiny purple line in the zoom slider area.

This purple line represents the playhead in the sequence. Clicking it is a convenient way of bouncing back to the current playhead location.

5   To see the entire sequence in the Timeline window, press Shift-Z.

6   In the bottom of the Timeline, move the pointer over the the Track Height control (to the left of the zoom control). Click different columns to change the height of the tracks.

In addition to magnifying tracks horizontally, you can also stretch tracks vertically, making them taller in the Timeline. The taller the track, the larger the clip icon will be. When the track height is at its smallest, the clip icons will not be displayed.

7   Press Shift-T repeatedly to toggle through the height options. Choose the second- or third-tallest height to see a clear thumbnail image.

8   Click the Zoom In tool (magnifying glass) in the Tool palette, or press the shortcut key, Z. In the Viewer, find the whale's dorsal fin in the **_DF_ambassadors** clip and click it a few times to zoom into that area.

Sometimes you need to zoom into the video of a clip to see or understand something in the background, or add or create effects. And sometimes, perhaps when trying to press Command-Z or Shift-Z, you simply hit the Z key by itself and enlarge the image accidentally. If you see blue scrollers appear below or to the side of a clip in the Viewer or Canvas, you can resize the image as you did the sequence in the Timeline.

9   In the Viewer, press Shift-Z to see the entire image fit in the window. Then press A to return to the default Selection tool.

The blue scrollers no longer appear in the window.

TIP ▶ You can use the Zoom In tool in the Timeline to zoom into a clip area, or drag a marquee with the Zoom tool to zoom into a clip area.

Making Insert Edits

Regardless of what type of project you're editing—dramatic film, documentary, commercials, music video, or local soccer game—the beauty of the nonlinear editing process is that you don't have to make all of your editorial decisions in a linear fashion as you did in the previous exercise. In a dramatic project, if you don't have all the footage captured for Scene 1, you can start editing Scene 2 and insert Scene 1 at a later time. In the "Believe" documentary, you can edit together interview clips and later insert clips of whale behaviors.

When you insert a clip into a sequence, all clips *in all tracks* following the new clip are moved forward the length of the clip. Inserting a clip lengthens the sequence by the length of the clip.

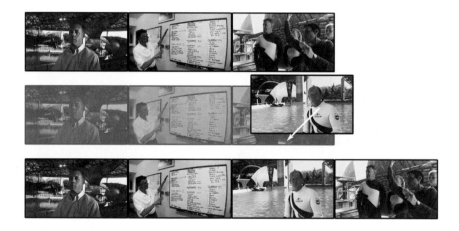

As with overwrite editing, you can use the location of the playhead to determine where a clip will be inserted. To make an insert edit, you use methods similar to those for overwrite editing:

▶ Click the yellow Insert button.

▶ Press the Insert keyboard shortcut, F9.

▶ Choose the Insert option from the Canvas Edit Overlay.

1 From the Interview clips bin, open the **_DS_show concept** clip, and play
the marked portion.

This introduction of the "Believe" concept really belongs at the head of the
sequence, before the trainers discuss their process.

2 In the Timeline, move the playhead to the beginning of the sequence,
where you will insert the new edit.

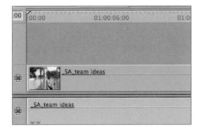

3 Click the yellow Insert button in the Canvas.

In the Timeline, the clip is inserted *before* the first clip in the sequence.
All the other clips are moved down to allow room for the new clip. Notice
the playhead is positioned on the first frame of the second clip. This
is the correct position to continue inserting clips at this location.

4 From the Behaviors bin, open the **J thru glass** clip, and play it from the
In to the Out point.

Let's discuss where you want the audio of this clip to be placed in the sequence.
You will edit the audio and video of this clip as marked at the current playhead

location after the first clip. However, in order to keep similar audio on the same tracks, you will edit the audio from this clip onto Timeline tracks A3 and A4.

On the far left is the Timeline patch panel, where you control certain aspects of each individual track. All the tracks in the Timeline have a different number, such as V1 for the video track, and A1, A2, A3, and A4 for the audio tracks. These are referred to as *destination tracks* and the controls with the track numbers are *destination controls*.

To the left of the destination controls are the source controls, labeled v1, a1, and a2. The source controls that appear in the Timeline represent the video and audio tracks of the source clip in the Viewer. Looking at the source controls, you know that the current clip in the Viewer has a video track and two audio tracks.

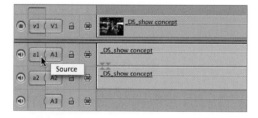

Although the order of the destination tracks is fixed, you can move and connect source controls, or *patch* them, to any destination track. To edit the **J thru glass** audio tracks onto the A3 and A4 tracks, you have to connect the a1 and a2 source controls to those tracks.

5   In the Timeline, drag the a1 source control down to the A3 destination track. Then drag the a2 source control down to the A4 destination track. Make sure that each source control is connected to the destination control, and that there is no break in between them.

6   To insert the **J thru glass** clip onto these tracks at this location, click the yellow Insert button in the Canvas.

The clip is inserted at the playhead location, and the remaining clips in the sequence are moved down the length of the new clip. The new clip's audio tracks appear on A3 and A4, separating them from the interview clips on A1 and A2. The playhead is at the edit point, ready for the next clip.

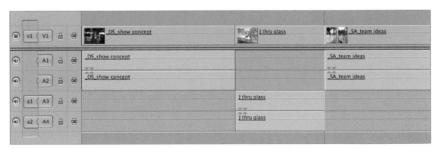

7   To insert a whale clip at this location, open the **J hugs whale** clip and press Shift-\ (backslash) to play from the In to the Out. To edit this clip at the Timeline playhead location, press the keyboard shortcut, F9.

With the source controls still patched to the A3 and A4 tracks, this clip's audio is placed on those tracks. Again, all the clips in the sequence are moved down the length of the new clip to allow room for it.

8   Let's insert a whale clip after the **_SA_team ideas** clip. Drag the playhead and snap it to the edit point between the **_SA_team ideas** clip and the **_MB_behavior board** clip.

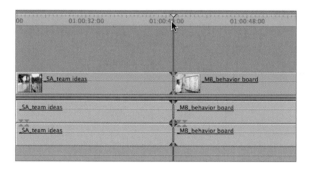

When the playhead snaps to an edit point in the Timeline, the playhead looks thicker, and brown snapping arrows appear around the clip's edit points. The snapping function is very helpful when inserting clips so you can be sure you are inserting a clip exactly at the edit point where the two clips meet.

9   From the Behaviors bin, open the **S show open** clip and play the marked portion. Click and drag the Viewer image into the Canvas Edit Overlay, but *don't release the mouse.*

Like the Insert button, the Insert section is yellow, and its icon is an arrow pointing to the right, indicating that all the following clips in the sequence will be moved forward to allow room for the new clip you are editing.

10 Drag the clip to the yellow Insert section, and when the section becomes highlighted, release the mouse.

11 From the Behaviors bin, open the **J pec slaps** clip and play the marked portion. Make sure the playhead is positioned after the **S show open** clip and insert this clip at that location.

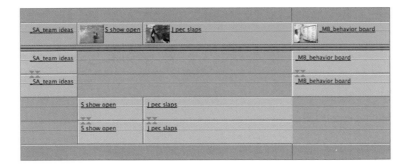

12 If necessary, press Shift-Z to see the entire sequence. Press Home to go to the head of the sequence and play it. Then press Command-S to save your changes.

Again, you are prebuilding a section of this documentary by placing all the clips in the sequence you want to use in a logical order. In the following exercises, you will continue adding clips and adjusting their placement.

Adding Audio Clips

As you build your rough cut, you may find that adding some additional audio clips, such as narration, music, or sound effects, improves your sequence. But you may not always have those clips in your project when you start editing. Perhaps the narration hasn't been recorded yet, or the composer is just starting to write a music track. You can import whatever source material you need along the way or as it becomes available. In this exercise, you will import some narration tracks, take a closer look at them in the Viewer, adjust the volume, and edit them into the current sequence.

1   Close all open bins in the Browser. Then choose File > Import > Files, or press Command-I.

A Choose a File window opens where you can browse to your file location.

2   In the Choose a File window, navigate to the narration files at the following path: Macintosh HD > FCP6 Book Files > Media > SeaWorld > Narration.

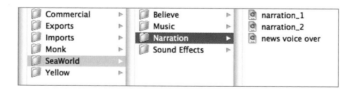

If you placed the book files from this book's DVD in a different location, such as a FireWire drive or on your desktop, navigate to that location.

3   In the Narration clips column, click the **narration_1** clip. To add the
narration_2 clip to the selection, Command-click that clip and click
Choose.

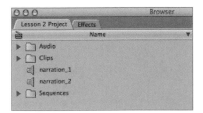

Imported clips come into the project and are available for editing. As with
other clips, these clips are links to the narration media files in the Media
folder.

4   Double-click the **narration_1** clip to open it in the Viewer. Click between
the two Mono tabs.

This narration was recorded using a single microphone input into channel 1
on a DV camera. Although both tracks were captured during the capture
process, only one track (Mono a1) has sound on it. In the Timeline patch
panel, there are two source controls because there are still two tracks of
audio. You will want to edit just the good one.

5   Click the Mono (a1) tab and play the clip. Mark an In point just before
the narrator begins speaking. Mark an Out point after the narrator says,
"…trainers have with the whales."

To navigate the waveform display in the Viewer, you use similar controls
as you did in the Timeline. Drag the zoom control to zoom in or out, and
drag the zoom slider to move forward or backward in the waveform.

6   Move the playhead to the In point and zoom in by dragging the zoom
control to the left.

These controls zoom and magnify the waveform display in the Viewer just as they magnified the sequence in the Timeline. When you zoom into a clip or a sequence as far as possible, the representation of time is expanded. The black bar next to the playhead indicates the width of a single frame.

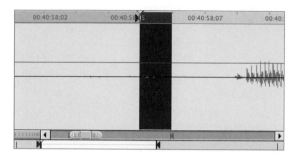

7   Press Shift-Z to display the entire audio track and see both edit points. Then play this clip again and look at the audio meters in your interface.

TIP ▶ Depending on your computer, the audio meters may appear beneath the Tool palette or to the side. If you don't see the audio meters in your interface, choose Window > Audio Meters, or press Option-4 to open them.

The audio meters display two channels of audio with tiny numbers between them that represent dB, or *decibels*. That is the unit of measurement for audio. A good rule of thumb is to have the narration average around –12 dB on the audio meters. However, depending on the level of the original media file, this may mean raising or lowering the audio level on the clip in the Viewer.

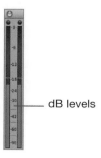

dB levels

Whether audio appears in the left or right audio meter, or both, depends on the number of tracks and how the audio is positioned, or *panned*, within the clip. Typically, stereo audio is distributed between both channels. With this clip, you see volume appear in both the audio meters because the sound from track 1 is panned toward the middle between both channels. Because there is only one good track of audio in this clip, let's direct it to one channel.

8   To pan the Mono (a1) audio track to the left, drag the Pan slider to the left, or enter *−1* in the Pan field. Now play the clip again.

The volume level for this clip appears only in channel 1.

Above the waveform display is the Level slider and entry field. When you import a new clip, the volume reference is always 0, indicating zero change to the imported audio level. You raise or lower the clip volume according to how you want to use it in the sequence. You will want to hear some audio clips as primary audio and others as background.

9   The goal is to keep the narration level at about −12 dB on the audio meters. Try each of the following options and preview the results until you reach that goal:

▶   Drag the Level slider to the left to lower the volume down to −3 dB.

▶   Enter *6* in the Level field and press Return.

▶   Move the pointer over the pink audio level overlay in the waveform area. When it changes to a Resize pointer, drag down to 2 dB.

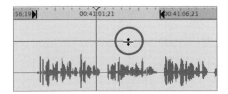

When you drag the Level slider, or enter a volume level, you see the pink volume line move in the waveform display. Likewise, when you drag the pink volume line, the Level slider moves and a new dB number appears in the Level field.

NOTE ▸ Remember, the dB number you see in the Level field represents a change of volume up or down relative to the original sound level of this clip, not to a specific dB on the audio meters.

Now for placement of the audio in the sequence. There are four tracks in the current sequence. A1 and A2 contain sync sound from the interview clips, and A3 and A4 contain sync sound from the whale clips. To keep the narration clips organized in the sequence, you need to create a new track.

10 In the Timeline, Control-click next to the A4 destination control and from the shortcut menu, choose Add Track.

A new track, A5, is added to the sequence.

11 To patch the source audio a different way, Control-click the A5 destination control and choose a1 from the shortcut menu. Then click the a2 control to disconnect it from its destination control.

TIP ▸ You can either Control-click a destination control and choose a source track, or Control-click a source control and choose a destination track.

When a source control is disconnected, that source track will not be part of the edit.

12 In the Timeline, position, or *snap*, the playhead at the head of the **J thru glass** clip.

Because there is no interview dialogue at this location, the narration can be the primary audio over the whale clip sound.

To edit an audio clip, you can use the Overwrite button or the keyboard shortcut. Or you can use a special icon to drag it into the Canvas Edit Overlay.

13 In the far right of the Viewer Mono (a1) tab, move your pointer over the icon of a hand on top of a speaker. The pointer changes to a hand icon.

This is the drag hand icon. An audio clip has no image to drag, so drag the hand icon to edit this clip.

14 Drag the drag hand icon from the **narration_1** clip in the Viewer into the Canvas and release the clip on the Overwrite edit option.

Now the clip is placed at the playhead location on the targeted track without changing the placement of the edits that follow it.

15 Play this section of the sequence.

Although the narration may be a good idea, the whale clip's audio level overpowers it. Ultimately, you will need to lower all the whale clips' volume to a background, or *mix*, level. For now, you can turn off the sound of the A3 and A4 audio tracks to focus on the narration.

16 In the Timeline patch panel, click the green Audible control for the A3 track. Then click the A4 Audible control and play the narration.

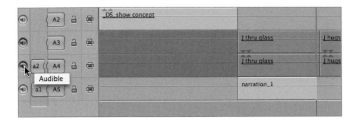

Each track has a green Track Visibility (video) or Audible (audio) control in the Timeline patch panel. When clicked, that track turns dark and will not be seen or heard as you play the sequence.

Project Tasks

There is another area in this sequence that could benefit from a narration track. Perform the following steps to add the track:

1   In the Timeline, move the playhead to the **S show open** clip.

2   In the **narration_1** clip in the Viewer, mark In and Out points around the section of the clip where the narrator says, "More than anything…as well as to every performance."

3   Click the Overwrite button to edit this clip.

   In the Timeline, each narration clip has the same name, indicating it was edited from the same source, or *master*, clip.

4   To keep the clips organized in the Browser, create a Narration bin and drag the two narration clips you imported into that bin.

Moving Clips in the Timeline

After you've edited a clip to the Timeline, you may want to move it earlier or later in the sequence. For example, to better match the narration to the whale activity, you can move the narration clips earlier or later. You can select and move one clip's position in the sequence or select and move a group of clips on one or more tracks.

Other times, you may want to select a clip during the editing process in order to delete it, add an effect, view its properties, or make other changes to the clip. Selecting a clip in the Timeline follows the general Apple selection principles: clicking a clip just once selects it, and clicking away from the clip deselects it.

1   In the Timeline, select the first **narration_1** clip by clicking once in the middle of the clip.

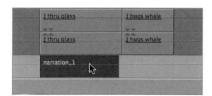

When you click the body or middle of a clip, the clip turns brown to indicate that it is the selected clip.

2   Press Option-+ (plus) to zoom into this area.

When a clip is selected in the Timeline, any zooming occurs around the selected clip, *not* the playhead location.

3   To deselect this clip, click in the empty Timeline area above or below the tracks. Don't click a track or you will select it.

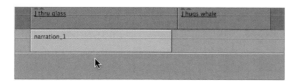

TIP Deselecting clips when you're not moving or changing them is always a good idea so you won't accidentally change them.

4   Click the same clip again and move the mouse pointer through the clip *without clicking or dragging it.*

The pointer changes to a move tool. Like the Resize pointer that appears when you can change the volume level, this tool indicates that you can move a clip. However, it's not a tool you select from the Tool palette.

5   Click and drag the **narration_1** clip to the right, so it's underneath both the whale clips above it, but *don't release the clip*.

Several things happen. A small duration box appears that displays a + sign and a number. This is how far in time you have moved the clip forward from its most recent position. Also, the pointer changes to a downward arrow.

6   Release the clip. This time drag the clip to the right until its Out point snaps to the Out point of the **J hugs whale** clip. Play this section of the sequence.

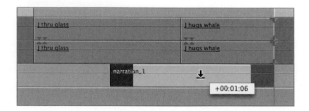

Just as the playhead snaps to edit points in the sequence, clip In and Out points can snap to each other as well. When a clip snaps to another clip's In or Out point, brown snapping arrows appear, just as they do when you snap the playhead to the same location.

TIP ▶ If the clips are not snapping to each other in the Timeline, make sure the snapping function is turned on in the Timeline button bar.

7   Drag the clip left until it's between the two whale clips above it. Play this section of the sequence.

This narration works better now that it covers the span of both whale clips.

You can also adjust clip placement by an amount of time.

8   Drag the zoom slider to the right so you can see the second **narration_1** clip, under the **S show open** clip. Select this clip and type *500*, for 5 seconds and zero frames.

NOTE ▶ It may seem strange to just start typing a number without typing it somewhere specific, but with the clip selected, Final Cut Pro anticipates what you want to do.

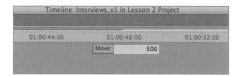

In the center of the Timeline, a Move box appears with the number you typed. As when entering durations, you can also type *5.* (5 period) to represent 5 seconds.

9   Press Return to enter this move amount and play the narration clip again.

The selected clip is moved forward 5 seconds. After you get the general placement of the clip, you can *nudge* the selected clip a little left or right to finesse its location.

10 With the clip still selected, press the > (right angle bracket) key to move the selected clip forward one frame in the sequence. Press Shift-> to move it forward 5 frames. Use these keys to move the clip forward, or the < (left angle bracket) and Shift-< keys to move it backward, until the narrator says "magic" where Julie pats the whale's tongue.

> **TIP** ▶ The amount of adjustment when you use the Shift key in this situation can be changed in User Preferences > Editing > Multi-Frame Trim Size (Option-Q).

11 To deselect the clip using the keyboard shortcut, press Shift-Command-A. Press Shift-Z to make the entire sequence fit in the Timeline window.

> **NOTE** ▶ As in other Apple applications, you can select the entire contents of a sequence by pressing Command-A.

Creating a New Rough-Cut Version

The editing process is all about making changes. You've just completed adding narration to the sequence. But you may not be sure if you like the narration and whale clips between the interview clips. Before you start making any major changes, it's a good idea to duplicate the current version of the sequence and make changes to the new version. This way, if you don't like the new changes, you can go back to the previous version and start again.

Sequence versions often use the original name with a version number and/or topic added to the name, such as *SeaWorld_v2_Inserts*, or *SeaWorld_v6_SFX*, to indicate what was new in this sequence. Duplicating a sequence makes an exact copy of the edit information. It does not duplicate the source media.

1 In the Browser, Control-click the *Interviews_v1* sequence icon and choose Duplicate from the shortcut menu.

A duplicate sequence is created and placed under the original sequence in the Sequences bin in the Browser. The word *Copy* is added to the sequence name.

2   To rename this sequence, click in the name area, and type *Interviews_v2_ no narr*. Press Return to accept it. Press Return again to open that sequence in the Timeline.

> **TIP** ▶ If you're not making a major change to your sequence but just want to back up the current version, you can add a date in the sequence name.

3   In the Timeline, click alternately the *Interviews_v1* and *Interviews_v2_no narr* sequence tabs.

At this point, the two sequences should be identical. The A3 and A4 tracks are dark in each sequence and even the playheads are in the same location.

4   To close the *Interviews_v1* sequence, Control-click its tab in the Timeline or Canvas and choose Close Tab from the shortcut menu.

You will continue working in the *Interviews_v2_no narr* sequence. In this sequence, you will remove or delete some narration clips and a few of the whale clips.

5   Click the first **narration_1** clip in the Timeline to select it. To delete this clip, press the Delete key. Delete the second narration clip the same way.

You can delete each of the narration clips individually, or you can select them both and delete them at the same time. Remember, deleting a clip removes it from the sequence but does not delete the media file or the original master clip in the Browser.

6 Press Command-Z two times to return both narration clips to the sequence. With the first narration clip selected, Command-click the second narration clip to add it to the selection. Then press Delete.

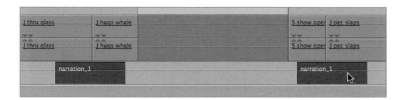

TIP ▶ Another way to delete a selected clip is to choose Sequence > Lift.

Both clips are deleted, or *lifted*, from the sequence at the same time. (You could have used other Apple selection techniques to select these clips, such as marqueeing them, or selecting one and Shift-clicking the other.)

7 Because there are no longer any narration tracks to compete with in this sequence, click the A3 and A4 Audible controls to turn sound back on for those tracks.

8 To remove the **J hugs whale** clip, click the clip on the V1 track to select it.

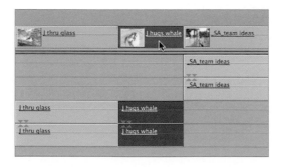

When a clip contains more than one track, such as video and two audio tracks, selecting one track also selects or highlights the others.

NOTE ▶ If clicking the V1 track of this clip did not select all tracks, make sure the Linked Selection function is active (green) in the Timeline button bar. You will work more with linked selection in later lessons.

9   To remove all the tracks of this clip from the sequence, press Delete, or choose Sequence > Lift.

Deleting this clip leaves a gap in the sequence because it was between two other clips. But the gap itself can be deleted.

10 Click the gap between the **J thru glass** clip and the **_SA_team ideas** clip. Press Delete.

With this action, the remaining clips in the sequence are pulled up, or *rippled*, by the length of the gap.

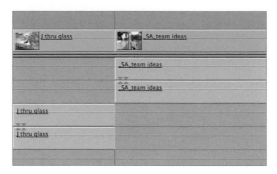

11   Let's remove the two whale clips, **S show open** and **J pec slap**, from this version of the interview rough cut. To select these clips, drag a marquee around them. To do this, position your pointer above the first clip, then drag down and to the right until both clips are highlighted.

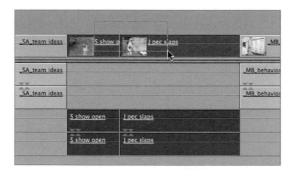

You can use the marquee approach to select one clip on one track, or many clips on several tracks. You can also use a different delete function, called ripple delete, to delete the clips. Ripple delete removes both clips, as well as the gap they would create, at the same time. In removing the gap, the remaining clips are pulled up by the length of the clips you delete.

12   To delete these two clips, press Shift-Delete, or choose Sequence > Ripple Delete.

TIP ▶ If you are using an extended keyboard, the Forward Delete key will remove the clip and gap at the same time.

Both clips are deleted, and the remaining clips are pulled up in their place.

Sometimes you want to reposition a clip to a different location. In the next step, you will move a clip with both audio and video through other clips to the end of the sequence.

13 Select the **J thru glass** clip and press Option-– (minus) to zoom out, creating gray space at the end of the clips in the sequence. Now drag this clip to the right through the clips in the V1 track and watch the Canvas as you drag, but *don't release the clip*.

In the Canvas window, two edit frames appear. This is referred to as a *two-up display*. The left frame displays the last frame of the clip before the clip you're dragging. The right frame displays the clip frame that follows the clip you're dragging. The overlay identifies the clip name and source timecode number.

As you drag a clip through other clips in the sequence, you can choose to drop it over another clip to overwrite that clip's material. Or you can drag *through* clips to position the clip elsewhere, such as at the end of the sequence.

> **TIP** ▶ If you accidentally release a clip over another one, it will overwrite the clip beneath it. To undo this action, press Command-Z.

14 Continue dragging the **J thru glass** clip to the right and snap its In point to the Out point of the **_DF_ambassadors** clip, the last clip in the sequence.

15 Delete the gap where this clip was originally located earlier in the sequence and press Command-S to save your work.

> **TIP** ▶ When you are working with a long sequence and can't easily see if you've left any gaps between your edits, move the playhead to the beginning of the sequence and press Shift-G. This moves the playhead forward to the next gap. Press Control-G to delete that gap, and press Shift-G again to move forward to the next gap. You can press Option-G to move backward to a gap.

Using Drag-and-Drop Editing

In the previous exercises, you've used the playhead to target an edit location and then pressed an edit button or dragged a clip to the Canvas Edit Overlay. But we are visual creatures. As you worked with clips in the Timeline, you may have identified a great spot for a new clip simply by eye-balling the target location. No need to go get the playhead, drag it back to where you're focused, and then click a button in a different window to edit it. With drag-and-drop editing, you simply rely on your own eyes to target the new location and manually drag a clip directly to where you want it to be.

As you drag and drop a clip, you can rely on snapping to position the clip immediately adjacent to another or to make a clean insert edit. Also, when you drag a clip to the Timeline, the position of your pointer in a track will determine the type of edit you make—overwrite or insert.

1   At the end of the clips in the sequence, move the tip of your pointer up and down over the thin gray raised line of the V1 track.

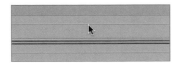

This line appears as a reference in each Timeline track. Nothing happens now without a clip, but this is the line you will focus on when you drag a clip to the Timeline. Even when there are clips on a track, you can see this raised line appear at the same level.

TIP ▶ Properly positioning your pointer is the key to drag-and-drop editing.

2   Find the Snapping button in the upper-right Timeline button bar. Click it several times, toggling it on and off. Leave snapping toggled on; the icon is green.

Snapping on   Snapping off

When snapping is on, or active, the icon design is green and looks concave. When the function is toggled off, the design is gray and appears flatter.

MORE INFO ▶ Every window has its own button bar that you can customize with a unique set of buttons representing functions, tools, or commands. You will learn how to customize button bars in Lesson 7.

3   Drag the playhead through the sequence and allow it to snap to the edit points. Then press N to toggle snapping off, and drag again without snapping. Toggle snapping back on for this exercise.

4   From the Clips > Interviews bin in the Browser, open the **_SA_favorite behavior** clip and play the marked portion. To target this clip's audio to

the A1 and A2 tracks, Control-click in the Timeline patch panel and choose Reset Panel from the shortcut menu.

Even though drag-and-drop editing is a more manual approach to making an edit, you still need to target which tracks will be edited and where.

5   Click in the Viewer image area, and drag the _SA_favorite behavior clip thumbnail to the end of the empty V1 track in the Timeline, clear of any other clips, but *don't release the mouse.*

Remember, this approach doesn't require that you position the playhead before making an edit.

TIP ▶ When dragging a clip from the Viewer, you can always return the clip to the Viewer to pause and rethink your edit before releasing a clip in the Timeline. You can also press Command-Z to undo that action and drag again.

6   With clip thumbnail in hand, focus on the tip of your pointer, and drag it up and down over the thin gray line in the V1 track just as you did before.

When the tip of the pointer is positioned below the thin gray line, an overwrite edit is indicated with a downward arrow and a solid dark box representing clip length.

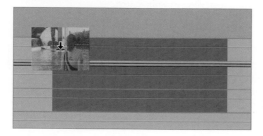

When the tip of the pointer is positioned above the thin gray line, an insert edit is indicated with a forward arrow and a hollow box representing clip length. In both situations, the thumbnail image remains the same.

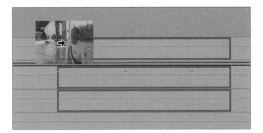

7   Still holding the clip, position the tip of the pointer *below* the thin gray line so the overwrite downward arrow appears, and release the clip clear of the last clip in the sequence.

Because the pointer tip was below the thin gray line when you released the clip, the clip was edited as an overwrite edit positioned just where you dropped it. Even though the playhead was not used in making this edit, it has repositioned itself after the new clip.

8   To snap the **_SA_favorite behavior** clip to the last clip in the sequence, drag it left until you see the brown snapping arrows between the two clips. Make sure you focus on snapping the shaded clip box on the track and not the clip thumbnail image.

The head of the shaded clip box beneath the thumbnail image snaps to the tail of the last clip in the sequence.

You can also add a clip to the sequence and position it in the same move.

9 From the Behaviors bin, open the **performance_S spray jump** clip, and play the marked portion. To edit just the video portion of this clip, click the a1 and a2 source controls to disconnect them.

10 Drag this clip into the Timeline but don't release it until you have followed these steps:

▶ Snap the clip to the end of the **_SA_favorite behavior** clip.

▶ Position the tip of the pointer below the thin gray line in the V1 track.

▶ Make sure you see the overwrite edit visual clues—the downward pointing arrow and the solid clip.

▶ Now release the clip as an overwrite edit.

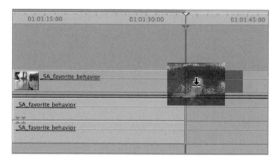

TIP ▶ When dragging a clip to the Timeline, always hold on to the clip with your pointer until you have positioned the clip exactly where you want it to go in the sequence and have chosen which type of edit you want to make—overwrite or insert.

You can drop a clip on top of another clip in the sequence, which will overwrite that clip or a portion of it. You can also insert a clip between two other clips.

11 From the Interviews clips bin, open the **_DS_show team** clip and play from the In to the Out.

To continue the explanation about the "Believe" show, let's insert this clip after the first clip in the sequence on the V1, A1, and A2 tracks. If you can't see the edit point between the first two clips, you can use the zoom control, the zoom slider, or zoom shortcuts to view that edit point.

12 Reconnect or reset the a1 and a2 source controls to the A1 and A2 destination tracks. Make sure snapping is on.

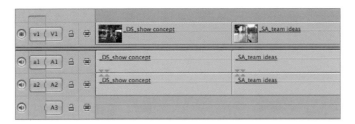

The zoom slider and zoom shortcuts will zoom in or out around the playhead location. So in this situation, you used the playhead not to place a clip, but to focus the zooming action on that area.

13 Drag the **_DS_show team** clip from the Viewer into the Timeline and snap it to the edit point between the first two clips, but *don't release the mouse.* Position the pointer above the thin gray line, which is indicated by a slight indent in the clip at that location. When you see the forward arrow and the hollow clip box, release the clip.

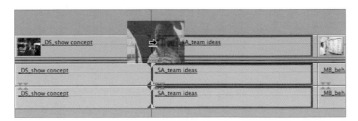

The clip is inserted, and the remaining clips are pushed down the length of the clip.

NOTE ▶ You can also insert a clip into the middle of another clip. For example, you might decide to break up the action of a long clip by inserting a different image for a few seconds. The long clip will be split into two parts, and after the new insert, the remaining portion of the original clip will continue to play.

14 From the Audio bin, open the **Applause FX 05.aif** clip and play it. To blend this clip's sound into the background, lower the volume to about –20 dB by dragging the audio level overlay or the Levels slider or by entering the value in the Levels field.

Let's say you want to edit additional sound effects into your sequence at a later time. To keep them organized, you may want to add an extra audio track or two, depending on whether the clips are mono or stereo. By dragging and dropping an audio clip below the lowest existing track (and a video clip above the highest existing track), Final Cut Pro will automatically create the new tracks for you.

15 To edit the **Applause FX 05.aif** clip, find the **performance_S spray jump** clip at the end of the sequence. In the Viewer, drag the drag hand icon into the Timeline beneath the A5 track, but *don't release the clip*. Snap the head of this clip to the head of the **performance_S spray jump** clip, and then release it in the gray nontrack area.

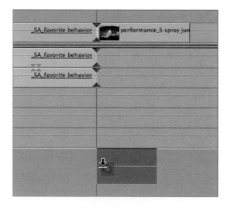

Two new audio tracks are automatically created for you to accommodate the stereo clip you just edited. Although this audio clip doesn't cover the entire whale jump clip above it, it serves as a target for when you come back to this sequence to add sound effects on this track.

TIP Don't forget to save frequently (Command-S) throughout your editing session.

Changing the Volume of the Edited Clips

After you edit a clip to the Timeline, it becomes part of the sequence and is referred to as a *sequence clip*. There are times you will need to change certain aspects of a sequence clip after it's already been edited. For example, in the *Interviews_v1* sequence, you had to click the Audible control for tracks A3 and A4 so the whale clips' audio wouldn't compete with the interview or narration clips. But it would be nice to hear them all together. You just have to decide which one is the priority and lower the other clips' volume.

1   From the Browser, double-click the *Interviews_v1* sequence to open it in the Timeline. Click the A3 and A4 Audible controls so you can hear those tracks.

     Because you created a new version of this sequence and made changes to that version, your original *Interviews_v1* sequence still has all the narration and whale clips you edited earlier.

2   Play the first few clips in this sequence. To adjust the volume of the **J thru glass** clip, double-click the clip in the Timeline.

     When you double-click a sequence clip in the Timeline, that clip opens up in the Viewer so you can play or adjust it by itself. There are two indications that this is not the original source clip from the Browser, but is the clip from the sequence. Look at the title bar of the Viewer.

     When you open a source clip from the Browser, the name of the clip appears in the Viewer along with the project name. Here the clip name appears along with the name of the sequence it is in.

     Now look at the scrubber bar. The two rows of dots, or sprocket holes, that appear throughout the scrubber bar is another indication that this is a sequence clip. It is not the original source clip from the Browser.

Whatever marks or settings you originally made to the clip prior to editing are exactly the same. In this case, the sound level is 0 dB, because you did not change it prior to editing.

3   In the Stereo tab, lower the volume of this clip to −15 dB. Click the Timeline to make it the active window, and play the area where the **J thru glass** and **narration_1** sequence clips overlap to see if you like the mix of sound.

   If the clip's audio tracks are a stereo pair, dragging one volume line automatically drags the other to the same level.

4   If the clip is too loud, lower the volume even further.

   As long as you don't open another clip, the sequence clip in the Viewer can still be actively changed.

   TIP▶ If you are using a mouse with a scroll knob, you can position your pointer over the Level slider and drag the scroll wheel up or down to change the volume. You can even do this as the clip is playing.

5   In the Timeline, double-click the **J hugs whale** clip. Lower this volume to −15 dB. Play this clip in the Timeline to see if you like the new level.

   You can also change the audio level of a sequence clip directly in the Timeline.

6   In the lower-left corner of the Timeline, click the Clip Overlays control.

A pink audio level overlay appears over the raised line of each audio clip, representing the volume of that clip. This is the same volume line you have adjusted in the Viewer waveform area.

NOTE ▸ With clip overlays toggled on, black overlay lines appear on the video clips. These represent the percentage of video opacity. You will work with these in a later lesson.

7 For greater control, let's make the tracks taller. In the lower-left corner of the Timeline, click the tallest column in the Track Height control, or press Shift-T to cycle through to the tallest option.

8 In the Timeline, find the **S show open** clip and move the pointer over the pink audio level overlay on the A3 track. When the pointer turns into a Resize pointer, drag down to –15 dB. Adjust the volume as necessary to create a good mix with the narration.

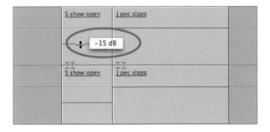

As you drag down the audio level overlay, both the volume lines of this clip's audio tracks are adjusted to the same level, because the audio is a stereo pair.

9 Adjust the level of the **J pec slaps** clip to a similar mix level and play these clips. Then press Command-S to save your project.

Project Tasks

Now that you have an arsenal of tools to edit a sequence, practice making overwrite and insert edits using both the automatic and manual drag-and-drop methods. Follow these steps:

1   Open the *Behaviors_v1* sequence into the Timeline.

2   Edit the **Track 12_believe finale.aif** music track onto the A1 and A2 tracks.

3   Mark different whale behaviors and edit them onto the V1 track.

   If you insert a clip, it will split the music track at the insert point. To protect the music track from being affected, you have to lock it.

4   Click the Lock Track controls for the A1 and A2 tracks to protect the music track as you make insert edits.

   Diagonal lines appear over these tracks, indicating that they are locked and cannot be changed.

   TIP ▶ If you prefer to practice editing dramatic footage, you can create a new sequence and import the Monk Clips folder from the FCP6 Book Files > Media folder.

Saving and Quitting

Always save frequently throughout your editing session, whether you've made any edits or not.

1   Press Command-S to save the current project.

2   Choose File > Close Project if you want to close this project.

If you want to keep working on this project the next time you open Final Cut Pro, you don't have to close the project prior to quitting the program. If you quit with a project open, it will open along with the program the next time you launch Final Cut Pro.

3   Press Command-Q to quit Final Cut Pro, or continue to the next lesson.

Lesson Review

1.   How do you create a bin inside another bin?

2.   What are the four methods you can use to create an overwrite or insert edit?

3.   What icon in the Viewer audio tab do you use to drag an audio clip into the Edit Overlay or into the Timeline?

4.   What are the keyboard shortcuts to zoom into or out of an area of the Timeline?

5.   How do you change the track heights in the Timeline?

6.   How do you target a track in the Timeline?

7.   Under what menu do you find the Import command?

8.   What controls in the Timeline patch panel toggle off or on the video and sound of individual tracks?

9.   To select a clip in the Timeline, you click it once. Name two ways to deselect it.

10.   How do you change a clip's location in the Timeline?

11.   What are two ways to turn snapping off or on?

12.   When dragging clips directly to the Timeline, your pointer changes as you position the clip depending on the type of edit you're making. When you're making an overwrite edit, what type of arrow does your pointer change into? What is it for an insert edit?

13.   When you open a clip in the Viewer, what do you see in the Timeline patch panel?

Answers

1. Control-click (or right-click) a bin and choose New Bin from the shortcut menu.

2. Click an edit button; use a keyboard shortcut; drag a clip from the Viewer into the Canvas Edit Overlay; or drag the clip directly into the Timeline and release it onto a track.

3. The drag hand icon.

4. Press Option-+ (plus) to zoom in, and press Option-– (minus) to zoom out.

5. In the Timeline display controls, click a track height in the Track Height control, or toggle to find an option by pressing Shift-T.

6. Drag a source control to the target destination track.

7. The File menu.

8. The Track Visibility and Audible controls.

9. Click in the empty gray space above the track, or press Shift-Command-A.

10. Drag the clip, or select it and enter a move amount.

11. Press N, or click the Snapping button in the Timeline.

12. The downward arrow is for an overwrite edit; the forward arrow is for an insert edit.

13. The representative source tracks from the clip appear as source controls in the Timeline patch panel.

Keyboard Shortcuts

Command-A	Selects all clips in the sequence
Shift-Command-A	Deselects all clips in the sequence
N	Toggles snapping off and on
Shift-Z	Shows the entire sequence in the Timeline
Z	Selects the Zoom In tool
Command-O	Opens a project
Control-click	Brings up a shortcut menu
Command-S	Saves the current status of a project
F10	Makes an overwrite edit
F9	Makes an insert edit

3

Lesson Files	Lesson 3 Project
Media	SeaWorld > Believe, Narration, Music, and Sound Effects folders
Time	This lesson takes approximately 90 minutes to complete.
Goals	Set edit points in the Timeline
	Add cutaways
	Edit narration and music tracks
	Import folders into the project
	Backtime clips
	Import and edit sound effects to video clips
	Link separate clips together
	Copy and paste clips
	Work with markers

Lesson 3
Finishing the Rough Cut

With your clips edited into sequences, you're now ready to put the finishing touches on your rough cut. To finish a rough cut, you often edit new clips into a sequence that refer to, relate to, or synchronize with clips that are already there.

This is an important editing technique and one you will use frequently. In order not to disturb other clips already in the sequence, you mark In and Out points around just the portion of the Timeline you want to change or edit.

One specific example of marking in the Timeline is when you cut to a music track. Just about every music video cuts to the beat of the music. So first you edit the music into the Timeline, mark where the beats occur, and then edit your video to those beats.

Another example involves cutting to narration. You will often want to illustrate what the narrator is referring to by cutting to an appropriate image. Again, you must mark the narrator's line in the sequence so you know exactly where to place the new visual and how much of it to use.

And then there's editing an interview or documentary. First, you juxtapose different shots of the same person talking, and then you cover the awkwardness of successive talking-head shots by adding video *cutaways.*

Marking in the Timeline follows the same procedures as marking in the Viewer, so you're already in the driver's seat in terms of knowing how it's done. But you will learn additional Timeline management and functionality in this lesson, such as copying and pasting clips or sections of your sequence, creating new edit points, and adding markers, all of which will help you finish your rough cut.

Preparing the Project

For this lesson, open the **Lesson 3 Project**, which contains the marked footage and sequences you need for this lesson. Then, you will duplicate a sequence to create a new version for this project.

1   With Final Cut Pro open, choose File > Open, or press Command-O.

2   Choose the **Lesson 3 Project** file from the FCP6 Book Files > Lessons folder on your hard drive.

3   Close any other projects that may be open from a previous session by Control-clicking the project name tab in the Browser and choosing Close Tab from the shortcut menu.

   NOTE ▶ Final Cut Pro allows you to work with multiple projects open at one time. Closing a project here is just a matter of simplifying what you're looking at in the interface as you move through the lesson.

4   In the Browser, display the contents of the Sequences bin. To edit a new version, Control-click the *Interviews_v2_no narr* sequence and choose Duplicate from the shortcut menu.

5   Name the new sequence *Interviews_v3_cutaways.* Press Return once to accept the name, and once again to open the sequence in the Timeline.

Image from the *Interviews_v3_cutaways* sequence

6 In the Timeline, close the *Interviews_v2_no_narr* sequence.

Adding Cutaways

To tell a story in the most concise way, you often have to edit together pieces of
one or more *talking head* clips—individuals speaking to the camera—and put
them in a logical order. Sometimes you have to edit different pieces from the
same clip. For example, in the previous lesson, you edited two clips of David
Smith, first talking about the "Believe" concept and then about the "Believe"
team. Both clips have *sync sound* of David talking on-camera. While he tells a
good story, it doesn't necessarily look good to cut from one on-camera clip of
David to another, especially since he was wearing two different shirts in the clips.

Cutting from a person in one clip to the *same* person in the next clip is referred
to as a *jump cut*. Jump cuts can be jarring to the viewer. The solution is to cover
them up by editing a new shot of something else over the actual edit point.

These replacement shots are referred to as *cutaways*. Cutaways can be selected from another area in the same clip or from completely different material. The cutaway source is often referred to as *B-roll* because it's not the primary footage, and there's no one talking directly to the camera.

The first step in covering a jump cut is to place In and Out marks in the Timeline where you want the cutaway to cover the "guilty" edit point. Then you choose the source you want to use for the cutaway and set an In point. Using three marks to make an edit is often referred to as three-point editing (see sidebar below). The combination of any three marks will answer the three important questions in making an edit: Where is the *location* in the sequence, what is the clip *duration*, and what is the source *content*?

> ▶ **Three-Point Editing**
>
> *Three-point editing* is the term used to describe editing a clip to the Timeline with any combination of three edit points that determine the duration, location, and content of a clip. When you made edits to the Timeline in the previous lesson, you identified the edit duration and content by setting In and Out points in the Viewer, and you identified the location of the edit by moving the playhead to a specific point in the Timeline. Those three points—Source In, Source Out, and playhead position—determined the duration, location, and content of this edit. That is one example of three-point editing. But you can also use Timeline In and Out points to determine the duration and location of a new edit.

1   In the Timeline, play the first two clips of the *Interviews_v3_cutaways* sequence. Press Option-+ (plus) to zoom into those two clips to enlarge your view of the edit point.

This is the *guilty* edit point, the jump cut that needs covering. To make this edit point smoother, you can position a cutaway directly over the edit point, at the end of the first clip or at the beginning of the second clip. Let's place a cutaway at the beginning of the second clip.

You follow the same general procedures for marking in the Timeline as you did when marking in the Viewer. You position the playhead where you want to set an edit point and use the shortcut keys, I and O, to set an In or Out point. You can also use the Mark In and Mark Out buttons in the Canvas window to set marks in the Timeline.

2 Snap the playhead to the beginning of the **_DS_show team** clip. You will see the first frame overlay in the lower left of the Canvas. Press I to set an In point at this location.

An In point appears in the ruler area of the Timeline, in the Canvas scrubber bar, and in the Canvas image area. In the Timeline, all the clips that follow the In point become lighter, or *highlighted*, to indicate they are part of the currently selected area.

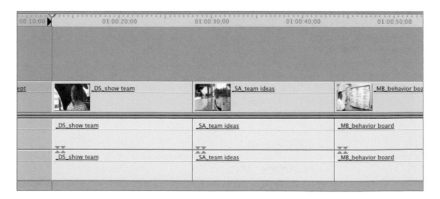

3 Position the playhead at the point when David finishes saying "…overall content of the show would be." In the Canvas, click the Mark Out button to set an Out point at this location. Then look at the Canvas Timecode Duration field.

The Canvas Timecode Duration field shows the duration of the marked portion, not that of the entire sequence.

In the Timeline, only the material that falls within the marked portion appears highlighted. Since there are many things you could do with this marked portion of the sequence—delete it, copy it, replace it, and so on— this color shade difference helps you to see at a glance which portion of the sequence and what specific clips might be affected depending on your action. In the next step, you won't change the existing clips, just add a new one.

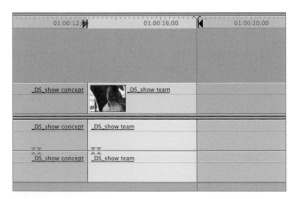

4 From the Clips > Interviews bin, open the **_MM_with trainers** clip. Since you don't want the audio to compete with the interview clip, lower the volume to about *–18 dB* in the Level field, and mark an In point at the head of the clip.

The two marks in the Timeline identify the clip location and duration. All you need is an In point to identify where to begin using the source content. The In point of the source clip will be lined up with the In point in the Timeline, just as it did when you edited to the playhead in the previous lesson. The source content will continue until the Timeline Out point.

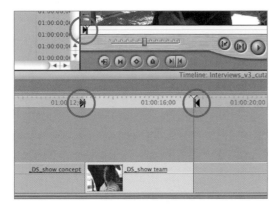

NOTE ▶ If you have In and Out points in both the Viewer source clip and the Timeline, and they represent different durations, the Timeline edit points will always take priority, and the Out point in the Viewer will be ignored.

Before you edit a cutaway at this location, think about track placement. As you did in the previous lesson, you can target, or patch, the source audio for the natural sound, or *nat sound*, from the secondary clips to the A3 and A4 tracks. For the video, you can organize all the B-roll footage, or cutaways, onto the V2 track. This will make the cutaways in the sequence easy to locate. But first you have to add a new video track.

5   In the Timeline patch panel, Control-click above the V1 track. Choose Add Track from the shortcut menu.

6   Patch the v1 source control to the V2 destination control. Then patch the
    a1 and a2 source controls to the A3 and A4 destination controls.

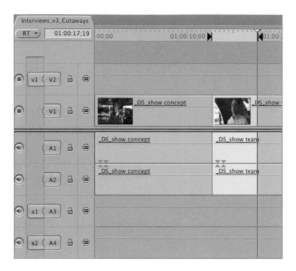

7   To edit this clip as an overwrite edit, click the Overwrite button.

    NOTE ▶ For this exercise, you must use the automatic methods of
    making overwrite edits—via the edit button, keyboard shortcut (F10),
    and Canvas Edit Overlay—because Final Cut Pro ignores Timeline edit
    points when you drag a clip into the sequence.

    The new clip's audio tracks are placed beneath the interview clips, and the
    video track is placed on the V2 track. The Timeline edit points have been
    removed, and the playhead is aligned to the first frame after this clip, where
    you will edit the next cutaway.

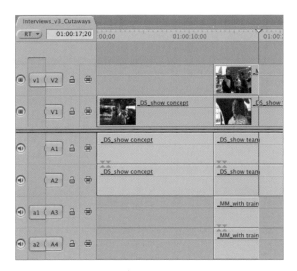

8   Play the area around the new clip, and focus on the Canvas window to see how the edit looks.

The adjacent placement of the two David Smith clips is not distracting because you cut *away* to a different shot between them. (There is still the problem of the two different shirts, which you will fix in the next step.)

9   Now play the clip area and focus on the layout of clips in the Timeline with an eye on what's happening in the Canvas.

When you stack clips on top of each other in a sequence, you get different results for audio and video. All of the audio clips combine into one mix of sound. Stacking video clips is different, however, in that whoever is on top wins.

In this sequence, you see the V1 video in the Canvas until the play-head reaches the V2 clip; then the V2 clip takes priority. When the playhead reaches the end of the cutaway on V2, you see the video on the V1 track again.

> **TIP** ▶ Placing cutaways onto separate tracks gives you the freedom to drag or reposition the clip after you've made the edit.

10 Experiment with the placement of the **_MM_with trainers** clip by dragging it left over the center of the edit point. Play this clip, then reposition it to its original location at the head of the **_DS_show team** clip.

Remember, you can position a cutaway anywhere over an edit point, as long as it covers the jump cut between the two talking-head clips.

11 In the Timeline, move the playhead to the first visible frame of the **_DS_show team** clip after the first cutaway and mark an In point for the next cutaway. Move the playhead to the last frame of this clip and mark an Out point.

> **TIP** ▶ An easy way to find the Out point of a clip is to press the Up or Down Arrow keys to move the playhead to the following clip's In point, then press the Left Arrow key to move back one frame.

12 Press Shift-I and then Shift-O to go to the In and Out points you set.

These shortcuts work just as they did in the Viewer. When you mark edit points in the Timeline, you don't need to reposition the playhead, because Timeline marks take priority over the playhead location.

13 In the Clips > Behaviors bin, open the **S gives pendant** clip. Mark an In point at the beginning of the zoom-out, around 00:22:05:24. Be sure to lower the volume of the clip to allow David's clip in the Timeline to be heard. Try *–20 dB*.

Again, since you have already defined the duration and location for this clip in the Timeline, you only need to indicate where you will begin using the source content.

14 Edit this clip as an overwrite edit, using one of the automatic methods of editing. Play the new clip.

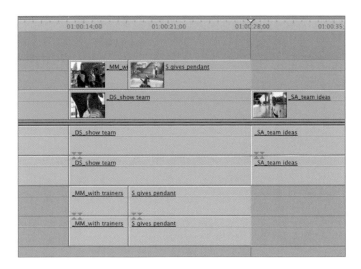

TIP In the Timeline, you can also set In and Out points on the fly as the sequence is playing, just as you did in the Viewer.

Project Tasks

In the current sequence, Steve Aibel talks about talking to his team of trainers; then we *see* him actually talk to them in the clips that follow. You can edit those clips on top of the **_SA_team ideas** clip, so you show and tell the story at the same time. Using the marking steps outlined in the previous exercise, mark and edit the following two clips as cutaways over Steve's dialogue. Make sure to lower volumes as needed.

> **TIP** ▶ If a clip opens with previous marks, press Option-X to remove both the In and Out points at the same time.

▶ **_SA_room discussion** to cover:

"We took those ideas back to the parks, talked about it with the in-house staff."

▶ **_KW_at board** to cover:

"Then we put those sequences, and those ideas…"

> **NOTE** ▶ Later in this lesson, you will delete the duplicate clips in the sequence, as well as other sections you no longer want.

Editing to Narration

Narration tracks are used in many film and video genres, including documentaries, news-based shows, reality television, and even dramas. In Lesson 2, you fit two short narration clips beneath the existing whale clips and positioned them to your liking. For many projects, the script or narration track comes first. Then you let it guide you in the selection of appropriate source material, based on what the narrator is saying.

In the next two exercises, you will edit a narration track in the Timeline, then mark portions of it to determine the duration and location for each new video clip.

Preparing the Narration Track

After editing the narration clip, there are a few things you can do to adjust the audio track in the Timeline to make it easier to edit. For example, in the Timeline audio tracks you can turn on audio waveforms, which appear similar to those in the Viewer. You can also save a Timeline track layout, as you did a window layout, and recall it for use at a later time.

1   From the Audio bin in the Browser, open the **narration_2** clip and click the Mono (a1) tab in the Viewer to see the audio waveform. Using the waveform as a guide, mark an In where the narrator begins to talk and an Out where she stops talking at the end of the clip. Then play from the In to the Out.

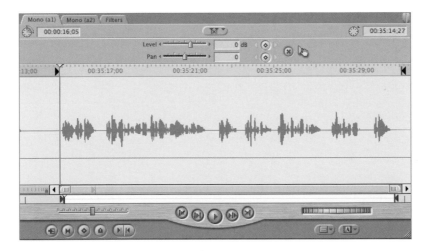

When you look at the audio waveform of this clip, it's easy to see where the narrator starts and stops talking. You could even mark an In and an Out based on the waveform display.

Since you will have just one narration clip in this sequence, you can place it on the A1 track along with the interview clips. If you were working in a sequence with a lot of narration clips, you might want to dedicate a separate track or tracks just for those clips.

2   To edit just the Mono (a1) track of this source clip, where the narration is actually recorded, patch the a1 source control to the A1 destination control in the Timeline. Then click the a2 source control to disconnect it.

3   Drag the playhead to the end of the sequence, or press the End key, and edit the narration clip as an overwrite edit at this location.

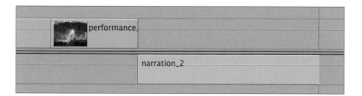

This is another example of a three-point edit. The two edit points in the Viewer identified content and duration, and the Timeline playhead determined location. As long as you haven't set an In or Out mark in the Timeline, you can use the playhead to target the edit location.

Since the audio waveforms were such a helpful reference in the Viewer, let's turn them on in the Timeline audio tracks.

4   In the lower-left corner of the Timeline, click the Track Layout control.

This pop-up menu provides several options to change the display of your clips in the Timeline tracks. You can also choose a different track height from the options on the bottom of the menu.

5   From the shortcut menu, choose Show Audio Waveforms.

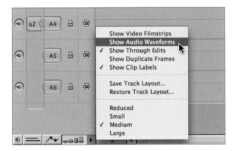

TIP ▶ The keyboard shortcut to toggle off and on audio waveforms is Option-Command-W. The shortcut to toggle off and on the pink audio level overlays is Option-W.

The same waveform display that you see in the Viewer appears on the audio tracks in the Timeline; it's just not as large. There are two ways you can make the waveform, and the narration clip, larger: make the track height taller, and zoom into the clip to expand it.

6   Position the playhead over the narration clip and press Option-+ (plus) a few times until this clip is wide across the Timeline window.

7 In the Timeline patch panel, position the pointer over the A1 lower boundary line. When you see the Resize pointer appear, drag down to make just the A1 track taller.

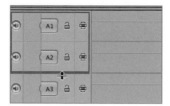

Pointer over A1 boundary line · Pointer dragging A1 boundary line down

Now you can clearly see where the narration stops and starts in this clip.

Each individual track in the Timeline can be adjusted for specific editing needs. You can save this track layout as you did the window layouts. But with the Timeline track layouts, you name the layout and recall it by name.

8 In the Timeline, click the Track Layout control again and choose Save Track Layout from the pop-up menu. In the Save window, name this track layout *A1 tall* and click Save.

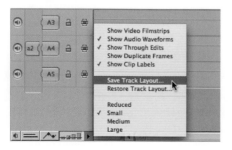

Final Cut Pro automatically saves this layout in a folder named Track Layouts located in the following path: Macintosh HD > Users > [User Name] > Library > Preferences > Final Cut Pro User Data > Track Layouts. When you save other named layouts, such as window or keyboard layouts, they are saved to their own folder within the Final Cut Pro User Data folder.

MORE INFO ▶ In Lesson 7, you will learn how to load these layouts and transfer them to other computer stations.

9   To recall this track layout at a later time, click the Track Layout control and you will see the saved track in the middle of the menu.

Dividing and Marking the Narration Track

To edit video clips to this narration track, you could quite easily play the narration clip and mark an In and Out at the appropriate times. But there are other Final Cut Pro tools and shortcuts you can use as well. To continue editing to this narration clip, you will use a special tool to divide the clip after each sentence, making that part of the narration its own clip. Then you will use a different marking function to automatically set In and Out points around that segment of narration.

NOTE ▶ Make sure snapping is on for this exercise.

1   In the **narration_2** clip in the Timeline, mark an In at the first frame of this clip and an Out after the narrator says, "…between man and killer whale."

Since the video you will edit in this location will be primary video, let's edit it to the V1 track. So as not to compete with the narration, you can edit just the video portion of the source clips for this section.

2   From the Clips > Behaviors bin, open the **J pec slaps** clip. Mark an In point where Julie starts to jump up and down, at around 00:06:45:15 (after the camera has panned past the other trainer).

3   Patch the v1 source control to the V1 track and disconnect the a1 source control. Edit just the video portion of this clip as an overwrite edit to the V1 track.

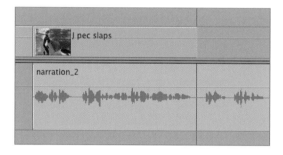

4   In the Tool palette, click the Razor Blade tool, or press the shortcut, B.

5   Move the Razor Blade tool into the A1 track, and snap it to the playhead location at the end of the **J pec slaps** clip. Click to create a new edit point in the audio track at this location.

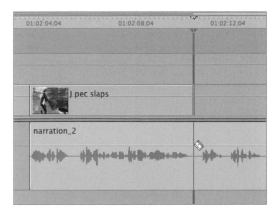

Through edit indicators (red arrows) appear at the edit point, which tell you that, although there are two separate clips now, the source material continues *through* this edit point as it did in the original clip.

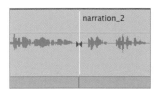

6 To create a new edit point at the end of the next sentence, play the clip and stop after the narrator says, "…two different species." Drag the Razor Blade through the A1 track, snap it to the playhead at this location, and click.

Notice that every time you divide the clip, the name **narration_2** appears on the new clip.

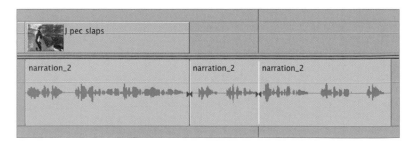

With the clip divided around this sentence, you can delete this portion of the clip, copy it, move it, and also mark it.

7   Move the playhead over this segment of the **narration_2** clip, between the through edit indicators. In the Canvas window, click the Mark Clip button, or press X.

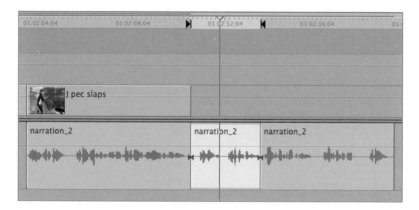

When you press X at the playhead location, In and Out points are placed at the first and last frames of the clip that the playhead is over in the Timeline. If you had not divided this clip, the entire length of the narration clip would have been marked.

NOTE ▶ Even though the Razor Blade tool is selected, when you move the pointer into the Timeline ruler area, the Selection tool reappears so that you can perform other functions such as play or mark the clip.

8   From the Behaviors bin, open the **J hugs whale** clip and press Option-X to remove any marks. Then mark an In point 4 seconds in from the head of the clip, at 00:00:04:00. Edit this clip as an overwrite edit onto the V1 track and play the clip.

9   In the Timeline, using the Razor Blade tool, add one more edit point after the narrator says, "…trying to bridge the gap between them." Move the

playhead over this segment and press X to mark this clip. Press A to return to the default Selection tool.

TIP ▶ You can also create new edit points at the playhead location by choosing Sequence > Add Edit. Using this function's shortcut, Control-V, you can create edit points on the fly as a clip is playing.

To edit the next video clip, you will determine the source content by where the clip ends instead of where it begins. To do this, you will set just an Out point on the source clip in the Viewer. Without an In point, the source Out point will align to the Timeline Out point. The source In point will be determined by *backtiming* the clip, or filling in the distance back to the Timeline In point. This is referred to as backtiming because Final Cut Pro starts from the end of the clip and measures the duration backward to determine where the clip begins.

10 Open the **L hugging whale** clip and find the point where Leslie is onstage with her arms around the whale. Mark an Out point just after she kisses the whale. Edit this clip and play it in the sequence.

Now the clip leads up to and stops just after Leslie kisses the whale, where you marked the Out point.

11 Use the Mark Clip function to mark the last segment of narration.

12 Open the **S show open** clip and press Option-X to remove any marks. To backtime this clip, mark an Out where Steve has his fist in the air, just after coming up out of the water. Edit this clip as an overwrite edit. Play this section of the Timeline to view your progress.

> **TIP** ▶ When backtiming clips, make sure there is no In point in the Viewer. Otherwise, the clip's In point will line up with the Timeline In point instead of lining up Out point to Out point. If you need to remove just the In point in the Viewer, press Option-I.

Editing to Music

Marking a music track is a little different from marking a narration track. With narration, you refer to a script or wait for the end of a sentence or other verbal cue to set your marks. With music, you respond to the rhythm of the beats and can usually anticipate when the next beat or musical phrase will occur. Final Cut Pro offers another way to mark a clip, and that is to add markers at specific points in a clip or sequence. Unlike setting a single In or Out point, you can create multiple markers in one clip or in an area of the Timeline.

Markers have a million great uses. You can think of them as sticky notes that remind you where you want to set an edit point, where the beats of music occur, where Scene 3 begins, or simply where in the Timeline you stopped editing for the day. They can even be converted to edit points if you want to edit at that location, which is how you will use them in this exercise. First, you will import a folder of music tracks.

1 In the Browser, Control-click in the empty gray area under the Name column, and from the shortcut menu, choose Import > Folder. In the Choose a Folder window, navigate to the FCP6 Book Files > Media > SeaWorld > Music folder.

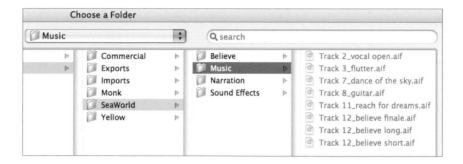

When you initiate the Import Folder command, as opposed to the Import File command, none of the clips in any of the folders are selectable. Only a single folder can be selected.

2   In the Choose a Folder window, click Choose to import the entire contents of the Music folder into the project.

The Music folder appears in the Browser.

TIP ▶ You can also use the drag-and-drop approach to import clips or folders into a Final Cut Pro project. To do this, arrange your interface windows so you can see the Browser and a Finder window on your desktop. Navigate to the location of the desired clip or folder in the Finder window. Drag the file or folder into the Browser and release it.

3   Display the Music bin contents and open **Track 12_believe finale.aif**. Play it in the Viewer and adjust the volume so it averages around –12 dB in the audio meters. You may have to lower the music volume about –8 to –10 dB. You will use this clip in its entirety.

This is the finale to the "Believe" soundtrack you've heard in a different sequence. You will cut underwater shots of whales and trainers to this music. Typically, you want all the music on its own tracks. With interviews and narration on A1 and A2, and natural sound from whale clips on A3 and A4, you can place this music on the A5 and A6 tracks.

4   In the Timeline, use the zoom slider, or a scroll ball on a two-button mouse, to scroll the sequence clips to the left so you see the end of the narration clips and empty Timeline space for your new edits. Press Shift-T to toggle through track heights until you are on the second-lowest height.

When you use one of the preset track heights, all audio and video tracks conform to that height. With shorter track heights, you will be able to see the music tracks more easily on A5 and A6.

5   With the playhead at the end of the last narration clip, patch the a1 and a2 source controls to the A5 and A6 destination controls, and edit this music track as an overwrite edit.

> **NOTE ▶** You will listen to the music to hear where you want to edit the video, so you won't need the audio waveforms turned on as a reference in the Timeline audio tracks. Press Option-Command-W to toggle off the audio waveforms.

6 Position the playhead at the head of the music clip and press M.

In the Timeline ruler area, a green marker appears. In the Canvas, a marker appears in the scrubber bar, and a marker name appears as an overlay in the image area. When editing music, setting markers on beats or phrases of music can be helpful and will allow you to utilize other Final Cut Pro functions.

7 With the playhead on the marker, press M again to open the Edit Marker window. In the name field, type *clip 1*, to indicate where the first clip will be edited over the music track. Take a look at the Edit Marker window before you click OK to close it.

The Edit Marker window has options to set a marker at a specific timecode location, to create a duration for a marker, and to delete a marker. You can also add other types of markers here, such as scoring markers for use with Apple's Soundtrack Pro application, and you can add compression and chapter markers if your Final Cut Pro sequence will be used in a DVD Studio Pro project. You will work with markers throughout these lessons.

NOTE ▶ You don't have to name markers, but if you're working with several in the Timeline, naming them is a smart way to find the one you need.

8   To add a marker at the next strong musical downbeat, play the **Track 12_believe finale.aif** clip and stop when the singer sings, "(Be)–LIEVE" again. It's about 8 seconds from the first marker. Press M once to set a new marker. Then press M again and name this marker *clip 2*. Click OK.

In the Canvas scrubber bar, when the playhead is directly over a marker, it appears yellow.

TIP ▶ To delete a marker, move the playhead to the marker, and press Command-` (grave key). If you want to reposition a marker you've already created, move the playhead forward to a new location and press Shift-`. Choose Mark > Markers to find other marker shortcuts.

With snapping on, you can snap the playhead to a marker. Make sure snapping is on for the following steps.

9   In the Timeline, drag the playhead over the second marker and notice the brown snapping arrow that appears when the playhead snaps to the marker.

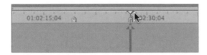

You can also add markers on the fly as you're playing a music track.

10   From the clip 2 marker, play the music track and, as the music is playing, press M on the strong musical downbeat when you hear "(Be)–LIEVE" again. Press M at the final "(Be)–LIEVE" refrain, and once again at the end of the clip.

Marking on the fly is a great way to set markers to several musical beats very quickly. Remember, naming markers isn't required for editing purposes. But if you want to name the markers you created, you have to move the playhead back or forward to each marker and open the Edit Marker window.

11 Press Option-M several times to move the playhead back to the first unnamed marker. Press M to open the Edit Marker window and rename it *clip 3*. Press Shift-M to move the playhead forward to the next marker and rename it. Rename the last marker the same way.

> **TIP** ▶ To go to a marker, you can Control-click in the ruler area and choose a marker from the shortcut menu. And just as you use the Up or Down Arrow keys to move backward or forward to the next clip, you can use Shift with the Up or Down Arrow keys to move backward or forward to a marker.

Now that markers are set to identify music beats, you can use those markers to create In and Out points for new video clips.

12 Move the playhead between the first two markers, and choose Mark > Mark to Markers, or press the shortcut, Control-A.

In the Timeline, an In point is placed on the first marker before the playhead, and an Out point is placed on the first marker after the playhead. Rather than marking an entire clip, you are marking the area between these two markers. With these two marks in the Timeline, you only need one mark in the Viewer to choose source content that will cover this series of beats in the music.

13 In the Browser, display the contents of the Underwater clips in the Clips bin. Open the **uw_push two trainers** clip. You will use this clip from the head so you don't have to set an In point. Edit just the video from this clip as an overwrite edit to the V1 track and play the clip.

NOTE ▶ Don't forget to disconnect the audio source controls to edit just the video.

This clip is edited between the two markers, which represent one musical phrase or series of beats on the music clip. As in other edits, once you've edited the clip into the Timeline, the In and Out marks are removed.

TIP ▶ To undo an edit, perhaps to choose different source content, you can always press Command-Z, which returns you to the edit setup prior to making the edit.

14 Continue to use the Mark to Markers function outlined in step 12 to set edit points for one section of music at a time. Then edit the following three clips in this order:

▶ **uw_propel jump**—Mark when dorsal fin is in view.

▶ **uw_rotations**—From the head of the clip.

▶ **uw_mom and calf jump**—Set an Out point at the splash to backtime this clip.

TIP ▶ You can also add markers to individual clips, which is helpful if you need to move that clip to a different location in the sequence. The markers will be moved along with the clip.

MORE INFO ▶ In Lesson 6, you learn to set markers in clips.

Project Tasks

If you'd like to practice some of the techniques you've learned in editing to music, create a new sequence, edit the **Track 12_believe short.aif** music track to the A1 and A2 tracks, and then edit video-only whale behavior clips to the V1 track. This music track has lyrics, so it's a good opportunity to mark In and Out points around the content of the song. You can also set markers in the song on beats, and edit to those beats.

Copying, Cutting, Pasting, and Positioning

When you edit a text document, you do a lot of copying, cutting, and pasting to get the order of words just right. In Final Cut Pro, you can copy, cut, and paste clips or portions of your sequence in the same way. In order to finish your rough cut, you may need to copy a sound effect to lengthen its duration, or you may want to reuse a beauty shot of a whale jump in your opening. And just as Michelangelo carved his *David* out of a raw block of marble, you may decide to knuckle down and chisel the excess from your own masterpiece.

For some of these changes, you set In and Out points in the Timeline to mark and delete extraneous sections. There are other ways to condense time in a sequence, such as placing clips on top of others, similar to the cutaways you edited earlier in this lesson. There are also special Final Cut Pro shortcuts to cut and paste. Before you begin hacking away, you will create a new version of the current sequence.

NOTE ► If you are editing a broadcast program, the show's timing is critical. Longer-format programs, such as documentaries and films, tend to have more leeway, but you still need to keep an eye on moving the story forward.

1   In the Sequences bin in the Browser, Control-click the *Interviews_v3_cutaways* sequence and choose Duplicate from the shortcut menu. Name the sequence *Interviews_v4_cuts*. Open this sequence in the Timeline.

2   You will be cutting sections out of this sequence, so take note of the current sequence duration in the Canvas Timecode Duration field.

Depending on how you marked your clips, your sequence duration may be shorter or longer than the duration in the image above.

3   Press Shift-Z to see the entire sequence. Then move the playhead to the head of the **_SA_favorite behavior** clip and play it along with the clip that follows it.

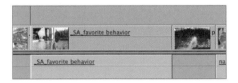

It would make more sense to see Steve jump over the sprayers *as* he's talking about the experience. But rather than go to the Browser and open the source clip into the Viewer, then mark and re-edit this clip, you can simply drag it in the Timeline up to the V2 track and place it over Steve's clip on the V1 track.

4 Move the playhead in the **_SA_favorite behavior** clip to just after Steve says, "…zoom to the bottom of the pool." Drag the **performance_S spray jump** clip up to the V2 track, and then left to snap the head of the clip to the playhead. Play these clips to see how they work together.

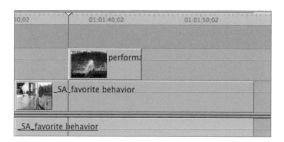

Now you see Steve jumping over the sprayers as you hear him talking about it. The **Applause FX 05.aif** clip was not linked to the clip of Steve jumping, so it did not move along with it.

5 Drag the **Applause FX 05.aif** clip left on its track and snap it to the head of the **performance_S spray jump** clip.

When you begin to mix these audio tracks together, this sound effect may be helpful, but it doesn't cover the entire length of the performance clip. Let's copy the effect.

6 Select the **Applause FX 05.aif** clip and press Command-C to copy it. Position the playhead at the end of the first applause clip, and press Command-V to paste it at this location. Then deselect the second **Applause FX 05.aif** clip.

The same copy and paste shortcuts you've used in other applications—
Command-C to copy, Command-X to cut, and Command-V to paste—
also work in Final Cut Pro on the selected clip or group of clips.

TIP You can also choose these options from the Edit menu, or by
Control-clicking a selected clip and choosing Cut, Copy, or Paste from
the shortcut menu.

However, even though dragging the clip of Steve jumping over the sprayers
to the V2 track helped the story, it left a gap.

7   Play the second half of the **_SA_favorite behavior** clip. To delete this somewhat
redundant section, and the empty space that follows this clip, mark an In
point after Steve says, "…that's just plain fun." Mark an Out point on the last
frame of the gap before the **J pec slaps** clip. Choose Sequence > Ripple
Delete, or press Shift-Delete.

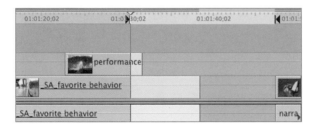

This removes the marked section of the sequence on all highlighted or
selected tracks and pulls up the remaining clips in its place.

TIP You can also use the Forward Delete key on an expanded keyboard to perform a ripple delete.

8 Play the **_SA_favorite behavior** clip again. Let's bring Steve back on camera at the end of this clip saying, "…that's just plain fun." Mark an In point just after he says, "…come down with the whale," and an Out point on the last frame of this clip. If you haven't already done so, zoom into this section of clips.

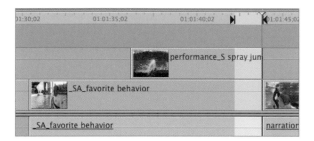

In the Timeline, all the tracks between the two edit points are lighter, indicating they will be involved in the next action.

9 Press Delete.

All the clips on all the highlighted or selected tracks between the two edit points are deleted. This isn't what you want. You actually want to delete only what's on the V2 track.

However, you can't use the source controls to designate which tracks you want to delete or protect. The source controls are used only to edit a source clip from the Viewer *into* a specific Timeline track. Once a clip is already in the Timeline, you have to use different track controls, the Auto Select controls, to make an internal change on a specific track.

10 Press Command-Z to undo the last action. In the Timeline patch panel, toggle off the Auto Select controls for all the tracks you don't want to delete (V1, A1, A2, A5, and A6).

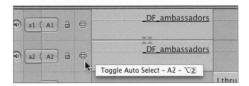

Now look at the area between the marks. Only the V2 clip is lighter, or selected, indicating it is the only track that will be affected in the next action.

11 Press Delete and play this section of clips. Then toggle back on the Auto Select controls for all tracks.

Now you see Steve on the V1 track say, "That's just plain fun." You can use the Auto Select controls anytime you want to remove or include individual Timeline tracks in a specific internal action, such as deleting, copying, and pasting within the Timeline.

TIP ▶ Even though you toggle off these controls for specific functions, it's a good idea to keep them toggled on for all tracks until you need to use them again to control the track selection. To toggle off or on all video or audio tracks but one, Option-click that track's Auto Select control.

In playing this section of clips, you may find that the first line of the narration, along with the video of Julie slapping the whale's flipper, could be a nice introduction if it were repositioned to the head of this sequence. To cut these clips and reposition them, you will use two variations on the cut and paste functions: ripple cut and paste insert.

12 Press Shift-Z to see the entire sequence. Click the **J pec slaps** clip and Command-click the first **narration_2** clip to add it to the selection. To cut these clips and pull up the remaining clips, press Shift-X.

The ripple cut function (Shift-X), like the cut function (Command-X), doesn't delete selected clips. It places them on the computer Clipboard so that you can paste them in the next step. If you had used Command-X to cut the clips, it would have cut the clip but left a gap.

There are two options to pasting cut or copied material. One is to paste the clips at the playhead location using Command-V, which overwrites whatever material may be there. The other is to insert the clips using the paste insert function.

13 Position the playhead at the head of the sequence. Choose Edit > Paste Insert, or press Shift-V, to insert this clip before the **_DS_show concept** clip.

The paste insert function pastes copied or cut material as an insert type of edit. Command-V paste clips as an Overwrite edit.

Project Tasks

There are other opportunities to trim the fat of this sequence or to change the clip placement. For example, if you added the two cutaways over the **_SA_team ideas** clip in the previous project tasks, you may want to delete the duplicates from the V1 track. Remember, to find the length of a group of clips in the sequence, set an In point on the first frame of the first clip in the group, and set an Out point on the last frame of the last clip in the group. As you've seen, you can delete portions of a sequence by marking that group of clips.

TIP If you have a clip selected in the Timeline and press Delete, the selected clip will be deleted, not what's between the In and Out marks. Selected clips override In and Out marks.

Lesson Review

1.   What are the shortcuts for setting In and Out points in the Timeline?

2.   What is the shortcut for marking the duration of a clip in the Timeline?

3.   What does the Auto Select control in the Timeline patch panel determine?

4.   When you mark an area of the Timeline and press Delete, will you leave a gap?

5.   What happens to the marked area of the Timeline when you press Shift-Delete or the Forward Delete key?

6.   On what menu do the lift and ripple delete appear?

7.   What mark is necessary in the Viewer when backtiming a source clip into a marked area in the Timeline?

8.   What is one way to access the Import Folder command?

9.   How do you patch source controls to Timeline tracks?

10. Which video track will you see when there is more than one video clip at the same location in the Timeline?

11. What is a three-point edit?

12. How do you save a Timeline track layout?

13. What marks are left behind after cutting with the Razor Blade tool?

14. What key do you press to add a marker at the playhead location?

15. How do you create In and Out points from Timeline markers?

Answers

1. Press I to set an In point; press O to set an Out point.

2. Position the playhead over the clip in the Timeline and press X to mark the duration of that clip. You can also click the Mark Clip button in the Canvas.

3. If the Auto Select control is toggled on for a track, the clips between the edit points on that track will be highlighted and included in the next action.

4. Pressing Delete alone leaves a gap where the material was edited. (This type of delete is referred to as a *lift*.)

5. Pressing Shift-Delete or Forward-Delete removes both clip and gap within the marked area. This type of delete is referred to as a *ripple delete*.

6. The lift and ripple delete appear on the Sequence menu.

7. The Out point of a source clip in the Viewer is necessary to backtime it into the Timeline edit points.

8. To import a folder, you Control-click in the Browser and choose Import > Folder from the shortcut menu. You can also choose File > Import > Folder.

9. Drag a source control to the desired destination control, or Control-click either the source or destination control and choose the appropriate option from the shortcut menu.

10. You always see the uppermost video track.

11. Using just three edit points to determine location, duration, and content.

12. Click the Track Layout control in the lower-left corner of the Timeline and choose Save Track Layout.

13. Red through edit indicators.

14. The M key. Press M again to open the Edit Marker window.

15. Choose Mark > Mark to Markers, or press the shortcut, Control-A.

Keyboard Shortcuts

B	Selects the Razor Blade tool
Delete	Lifts an item or section from the Timeline and leaves a gap
M	Sets a marker in the Timeline ruler area
MM	Opens the Edit Marker window
X	Marks the full length of a clip
Command-` (grave)	Deletes marker at current playhead location
Control-A	Sets In and Out points at marker locations on either side of the playhead
Option-M	Moves playhead to the previous marker
Option-W	Toggles clip overlays
Option-Command-W	Toggles audio clip waveform displays in the Timeline
Shift-Delete (or Forward Delete)	Removes an item or section from the Timeline and ripples the following edits up the duration of the gap
Shift-M	Moves the playhead to the next marker
Shift-V	Pastes cut or copied material as an insert
Shift-X	Cuts a marked selection and removes the gap
Shift-` (grave)	Relocates the marker forward to the playhead location

Refining the Rough Cut

4

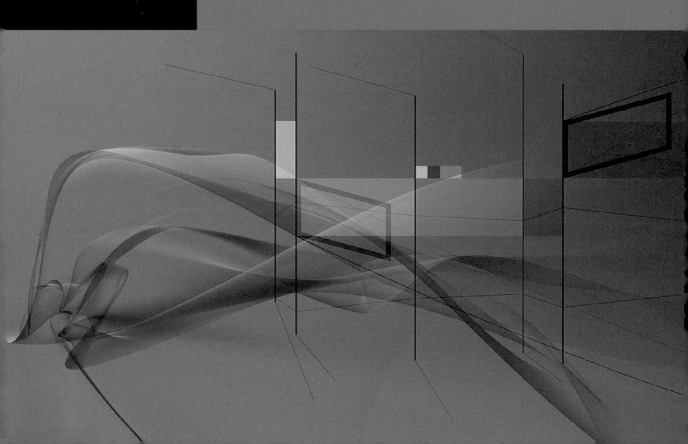

Lesson 4
Trimming to Refine Clip Duration

After you've built a rough cut, as you've done in the past few lessons, you will want to turn your attention to refining your sequences. This refining process is called *trimming*, which simply means making adjustments to the duration and position of clips within a sequence.

In the next three lessons, you'll pursue three goals that will help you refine your rough cut as you refine your Final Cut Pro editing skills. Your first goal, which you will tackle in this lesson, is to fine-tune the length of a single clip, to make it shorter or longer, bringing the sequence to an appropriate length.

The second goal is to adjust how the clips flow together and work in conjunction with each other in a sequence. You can think of this as adjusting your edit points, and you will learn additional trimming techniques and tools for that purpose in Lesson 5. In practice, the trimming techniques used to achieve these two goals are often used in combination during an edit session, but for learning purposes we will focus on each one separately.

Once you've mastered the basic trimming methods, you'll want to move on to the third goal of refining your overall editing process. To do this, you will learn to use several more Final Cut Pro features and techniques in Lesson 6.

As you begin to refine your sequence, you will typically start by trimming to adjust the length of the clips in a sequence. There are several ways to adjust a clip's duration in Final Cut Pro. You can drag an edit point in the Timeline, or you can use the Ripple tool to trim. You can even trim a clip in the Viewer window or use a Razor Blade tool to cut off a portion of a clip.

In this lesson, you will work with different trimming techniques as you refine several real-world rough cuts, adjusting the length of various clips within the sequences.

Preparing a Project for Trimming

In this lesson, you have a new set of footage and a new genre in which to work in addition to the SeaWorld "Believe" project. Since you are refining a sequence, the exercises involve sequences that are already cut together but still have some rough edges, as any rough cut would.

1   Launch Final Cut Pro, and choose File > Open, or press Command-O. Open the **Lesson 4 Project** file from the Lessons folder on your hard drive.

2   Close any other projects that may be open from a previous session by Control-clicking their name tabs in the Browser and choosing Close Tab from the shortcut menu.

3   In the Monk Clips bin in the Browser, double-click the **Monk.mov** clip to open it in the Viewer. To view the clip in a larger window, press Shift-U to recall the larger Viewer layout you saved in an earlier lesson. Then play the edited Monk scene.

This is a QuickTime movie of an edited scene from the NBC Universal television series *Monk*, starring Tony Shalhoub. This scene is from the episode "Mr. Monk and the Actor" and includes a discussion between Mr. Monk and his psychiatrist, Dr. Kroger, played by Stanley Kamel. This is a good example of the dramatic genre, with scripts and actors. The show is shot in super 16mm and transferred to HD video for finishing and delivery. In order to reduce the file size, the clips you will edit were recompressed using the new Apple ProRes 422 codec.

4 Press Option-U to switch to the larger Canvas layout, and play the *Scene from "Monk"* sequence in the Timeline.

TIP ▶ If you no longer have the customized large Canvas window layout, you can resize the interface windows and refer to Lesson 1 for directions to save it.

This is a rough cut of a portion of the finished scene you screened in the Viewer. All the clips are in the right order but need to be trimmed to lengthen or shorten them according to the scripted dialogue. For some clips, you may need to remove an unwanted or duplicated line. For others, you may need to extend the clip to allow a line to be completed.

NOTE ▶ As you trim the rough cut throughout this lesson, you will get closer to the look of the finished version. You will get even closer as you adjust these edit points in other ways in the next lesson.

Since this is a different type of project, let's take a closer look at the clips in the sequence.

5   In the lower-left corner of the Timeline, click the Track Layout controls and choose Show Audio Waveforms from the menu. You can also press the shortcut, Option-Command-W. Then zoom into the head of the sequence.

6   Play the first few clips and watch the audio waveforms to determine which actor's sound is on which audio track. Click the A1 Audible control to toggle off the A1 track and listen to just A2 for a few clips. Then toggle A1 back on, toggle off A2, and listen again. Toggle A2 back on.

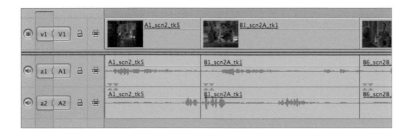

During this shoot, there was one microphone on each actor. The A1 track is the on-mic sound of Dr. Kroger, and the A2 track is the on-mic sound of Mr. Monk. When you listen to just one track at a time, you can hear the off-mic sound of the other actor. But when you listen to them together, the audio sounds full and balanced. You can also see the audio levels of each track in the audio waveforms. Toggling on audio waveforms in the Timeline is a very helpful aid when trimming dialogue or narration clips.

7   Click the video portion of the first clip, the **A1_scn2_tk5** clip. Then deselect it.

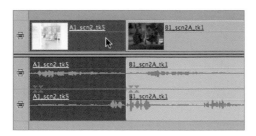

Since there is a link line beneath the clip name, you know that this clip's video and audio tracks are linked together. With linked selection toggled on in the Timeline button bar, selecting either the video or audio tracks will automatically select all tracks of the clip. Similarly, when you trim a linked clip, all tracks of that clip are trimmed at the same time.

Before you begin working in this sequence, let's duplicate it to create your own version.

8   In the Sequences bin in the Browser, Control-click the *Scene from "Monk"* sequence and choose Duplicate from the shortcut menu. Name the new sequence *Monk Rough Cut_v1*, and double-click it to open it in the Timeline.

9   Click the *Scene from "Monk"* sequence tab, and then click the *Monk Rough Cut_v1* sequence tab.

If audio waveforms or other overlays are on when you duplicate a sequence, they will be on or present in the duplicated sequence as well. For now, leave the audio waveforms on in both sequences.

10   Close the *Scene from "Monk"* sequence.

Trimming Overview

If you're new to the concept of trimming, quite simply it's a way to change your mind about where you want a clip's In or Out points to start or stop *after* you've placed the clip in the Timeline. When you trim an edit point, you are lengthening or shortening the clip either at the head or the tail. In most situations, lengthening or shortening a clip in the Timeline affects the length of the entire sequence, because the clips that follow the trimmed clip are often pulled up or pushed forward to accommodate the new clip length.

You can trim a clip in four ways. Look at the graphical display below of these four options and compare the original clip length with the trimmed clips. First, consider the In point at the head of the clip:

Trim the In point to the left, and the clip will begin on an earlier frame. The clip will be longer.

Trim the In point to the right, and the clip will begin on a later frame. The clip will be shorter.

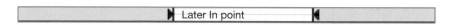

Consider the Out point at the tail of the clip:

Trim the Out point to the left, and the clip will end on an earlier frame. The clip will be shorter.

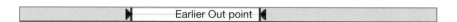

Trim the Out point to the right, and the clip will end on a later frame. The clip will be longer.

When you play a sequence in the Timeline, you are seeing only the marked portion of the clips. However, you still have access to all the frames in the original media file. Remember that the maximum number of frames you can add to lengthen a clip in an outer direction (head or tail) depends on how much material is available in the original media file. The additional frames outside the marked portion of a clip are referred to as *handles*.

Let's continue this introduction to trimming by looking at some of the functions you will use during the trimming process. For these steps, you will trim two clips in the *Monk Rough Cut_v1* sequence using the default Selection tool.

1   In the Timeline, play the last clip in the sequence, **B6_scn2B_tk4**. Then park the playhead after Monk says, "…only twice as much as a normal person."

The playhead location gives you a *target* for where to trim the edit point. This is where you will end this sequence, before Monk starts to discuss Harold Crenshaw.

NOTE ▶ You may notice a light or camera in some of these clips. In a later lesson, you will learn how to resize and reposition these images so the light or camera won't be seen.

2   Move the pointer over the Out point of the last clip in the sequence. When you see the Resize pointer, click the Out point.

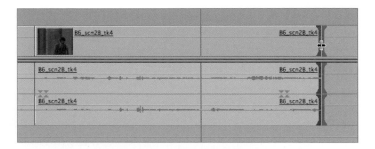

Just the edge of the clip is selected, not the body of the clip. If the entire clip were selected, you would end up moving the clip, not trimming it. The tracks are linked together and linked selection is on, so when you select the Out point, the Out points on all three tracks of this clip become highlighted and can now be trimmed together.

3 Drag the combined edit points left and snap them to the playhead location. Then play the clip.

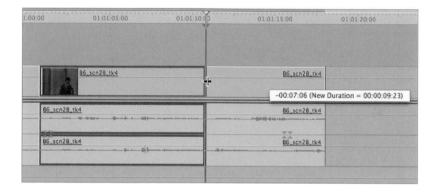

As you drag the Out point to the left, the clip itself remains stationary and just the Out point moves. The clip becomes shorter, and a brown outline appears around it, indicating a new clip length. The new clip duration appears in the information box. Notice that the playhead becomes thicker and snapping arrows appear at the top of the playhead when you snap the edit point to it.

TIP ▶ As you drag an edit point, make sure you always drag through the same track on which you selected the edit point. If you first clicked the V1 edit point, then drag left through the V1 track.

4 Play the first portion of the previous clip, **B1_scn2A_tk1**, until you can identify the place in the A2 track waveform where Monk says, "OK, I'll see you on Wednesday." This time, move the playhead away from the edit point and this area.

In this clip, you want to move the In point to the right so the clip will start later, after the psychiatrist finishes speaking.

5 Click just to the right of the In point at the head of the **B1_scn2A_tk1** clip and drag to the right. Try to align the In point with the beginning of Monk's line, "OK, I'll see you on Wednesday."

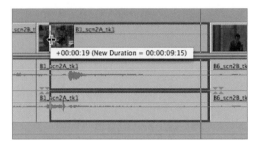

Sometimes, snapping to the playhead is very helpful. Other times, when you are close to an edit point, you may find that snapping confines you as you drag.

6 Press Command-Z to return the In point to its original position. Press N or click the Snapping button in the Timeline button bar to toggle snapping off. Now drag the head of the clip to just before Monk's dialogue, using the waveform as a guide.

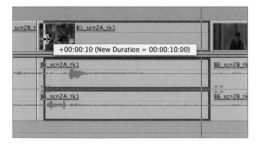

As you drag this In point to the right, it shortens the clip. And with snapping off, you have greater control over where you can stop dragging or trimming.

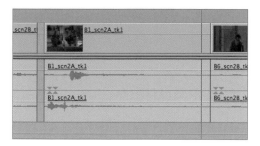

To be even more precise as you trim this clip, you can open it into the Viewer and use the larger waveform display as a reference.

7   Double-click the **B1_scn2A_tk1** clip to open it in the Viewer, and click the Stereo tab. In the scrubber bar, drag the In point left or right to further refine the new In point.

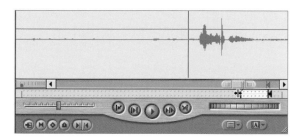

When you position the pointer over the current In point in the scrubber bar, the Resize pointer appears. You can drag the edit point left or right until you reach the end of the media file, or until you bump into a neighboring clip in the sequence. When you do bump into another clip, "Media Limit on V1" appears as a note.

However, trimming this clip by dragging with the Selection tool produces a gap. In the next exercise, you will use the Ripple tool, which removes the gap as you trim.

8   Click the gap and press Delete. Then press N to turn snapping back on.

TIP ▶ One way to gain greater control when snapping is turned on is to zoom into the area you are trimming. With a larger waveform and clip display, you will have more control snapping to a new target location if it's close to the original edit point.

Rippling Edit Points

In Lesson 3, you used the ripple delete function to delete a clip or marked portion of a sequence without leaving a gap. To trim the clips in the Monk sequence, you will use a new tool, the Ripple tool. The Ripple tool can delete a portion of the head or tail of a clip, and ripple the rest of the sequence clips so no gaps remain. The Ripple tool is accessed via the Roll tool, the fourth button from the top in the Tool palette.

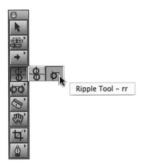

When you use the Ripple tool to trim an edit point, you drag an In or Out point left or right, and all the clips that follow are automatically pushed down or pulled up the length of the trim. If you lengthen a clip, it will push the remaining clips down and lengthen the sequence. If you shorten a clip, it will pull up the remaining clips and shorten the sequence.

1   In the Tool palette, click and hold the Roll tool. When you see the Ripple tool icon, which looks like a single roller, click it. You can also press the keyboard shortcut RR to select this tool.

2 Drag the zoom slider to the left until you see the first few clips of the sequence. Zoom into that area if necessary to see the waveform displays more clearly. Play the first two clips, **A1_scn2_tk5** and **B1_scn2A_tk1**.

A line is duplicated in this rough cut. You will trim off the end of the first clip, where Monk says, "no big deal" for the first time.

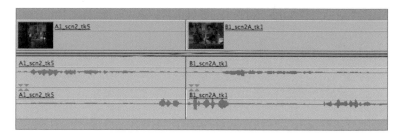

NOTE ▶ Sometimes, assistant editors prepare a sequence for an editor and include additional lines or material from each camera for the editor to consider.

3 Without clicking or dragging, just move your pointer over the first clip, **A1_scn2_tk5**.

The Ripple tool has an *X* on it, indicating that the tool cannot be applied to this area. You can use the Ripple tool only on a clip's In or Out edit point.

4   Move the Ripple tool toward the clip's In point.

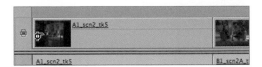

When the Ripple tool gets close to the In point, the X disappears, and the tail of the Ripple icon points right, toward the inside of the clip you will be trimming.

5   Move the Ripple tool to the clip's Out point, and click the inside edge of the Out point.

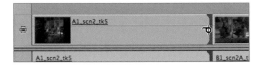

When the Ripple tool is positioned over the Out point, the tail points inward to the left, toward the body of the clip you are trimming. This is a visual clue so you know which clip you are adjusting. When the Out point is correctly selected, just the Out point of this clip is highlighted.

6   Play this clip and stop the playhead just after the psychiatrist says, "…proud of you." Use the Left or Right Arrow keys to finesse the playhead location. Now drag this edit point left to snap to the playhead location.

TIP ▶ If you can't hear the audio scrub as you drag your playhead or use the arrow keys, choose View > Audio Scrubbing and make sure it's checked.

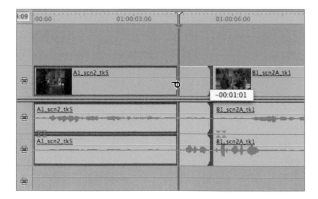

As with the Selection tool, using the Ripple tool drags both the audio and video of the linked clip together. As you drag the edit point, an information box appears with just the trim amount. There is no gap left, and all the clips in the sequence are pulled up by the amount of the trim.

NOTE ▶ As you move forward in these steps, you will be jumping over edit points that need additional trimming and refining. You will come back to those edit points and apply other methods of trimming that are more appropriate for those areas.

7 Play the third clip, **B6_scn2B_tk4**. Park the playhead just before Monk says, "I might even leave my room."

Although the Ripple tool is selected, you can still play clips and navigate the sequence. The Ripple tool is active only when it's in the Timeline track area.

8 Drag this clip's In point to the right, but don't release the mouse.

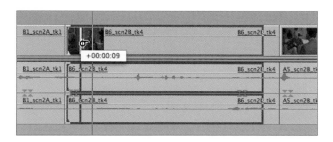

When you use the Ripple tool to drag a clip's edit point to make the clip shorter, the boundary box shortens to display a representative clip length.

When you ripple an edit point, a two-up display appears in the Canvas to help you review or match the action from the Out point of one clip to the In point of the next. The image on the right updates the new In point as you drag. The image on the left displays the last frame of the clip that comes before the one you're trimming. The clip names and source time-codes appear over the clips as a reference.

9   Snap the In point to the playhead and release the mouse. Play the new edit point.

10   Play the fourth clip, **A5_scn2B_tk4**.

You will trim this clip's In point to just before the psychiatrist says, "No." But this time, since it's so clear in the waveform display where the psychiatrist speaks, you don't have to use the playhead as a target for the edit point. The waveform itself can be the target.

11   Move the playhead away from the clip's edit point and press N to turn off snapping. Using the waveform as a guide, drag the In point to just before the psychiatrist says, "No." Play the new edit point.

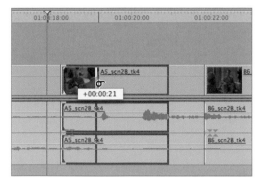

When you can see your target either as an audio cue on the waveform display or visually in the Canvas, you can move directly to it.

Rippling in the Viewer and by the Numbers

The Ripple tool, like other tools in Final Cut Pro, can be used in more than one window. Just as you can set marks in the Viewer and in the Timeline, you can also trim marks in the Viewer and Timeline. The reason this is so helpful is that when you open a sequence clip in the Viewer, you can see the area outside the range of the In and Out points, allowing you to find a target you can't see in the Timeline. In this exercise, you will trim in the Viewer and also trim a selected edit point "by the numbers," specifying a few frames or an amount of time, just as you did to move a clip in the Timeline.

1 Play the second clip in the sequence, **B1_scn2A_tk1**, and focus on the end of the clip, where the psychiatrist says, "Two nights, alone, in a…."

When the clip's Out point stops short of a word or line, in this case the word "hotel," you can't target the trim area in the Timeline. You could trim the Out point a few seconds later to locate where he says "hotel," and then trim back to create a more precise edit point. Or you could open the clip in the Viewer to find where he says, "hotel," or see it displayed in the wave-form, and mark that exact location.

2   Double-click the body or middle of the **B1_scn2A_tk1** clip to open it in the Viewer.

With the Ripple tool selected, you can still double-click a sequence clip to open and edit it in the Viewer. With the clip visible in the Viewer, you can see the In and Out points and play beyond them.

3   Click the Stereo tab and focus on the a1 track. Position the playhead after the psychiatrist says, "alone, in a hotel," just before Monk begins speaking.

4   To see this area in more detail, press Command-+ (plus) to zoom into the waveform at the playhead location.

NOTE ▶ Command-+ (plus) or Command-– (minus) will zoom in or out of a display in any active window. But Option-+ and Option-– will affect *only* the Timeline, no matter which window is active.

As you zoom into the playhead location, the playhead itself gets wider, representing the width of one frame.

NOTE ▶ Depending on the size of your monitor and window layout, your Viewer size may appear different from the image shown here.

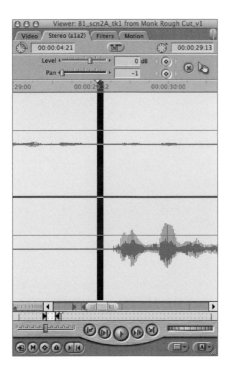

5   Use the Left and Right Arrow keys to finesse the playhead to the correct
    location, and then press O to set a new edit point in the Viewer.

    Because you still have the Ripple tool selected, pressing O resets the Out
    point to the playhead location just as though you dragged the edit point
    there. The clip in the Timeline is now longer, and it ends after the psy-
    chiatrist says, "in a hotel."

    NOTE ▶ You can also drag the edit point in the Viewer scrubber bar
    using the Ripple tool. However, you may not have as much control when
    dragging to a target edit location.

6   Play the edit point between the eighth and ninth clips, **A5_scn2B_tk4** and
    B6_scn2B_tk4.

    It sounds as though the psychiatrist should be saying something after he
    says, "affirmative reflex" and before he says, "big step."

7   To hear the missing phrase, double-click the **B6_scn2B_tk4** clip to open it
     in the Viewer. Play a few seconds before the In point and position the play-
     head after the psychiatrist says, "affirmative reflex," before he says, "and it's
     a very, very big step." Press I to mark a new In point at this location.

8   Using the Ripple tool, click the In point of the second clip, **B1_scn2A_tk1**.
     Zoom into this area and play it.

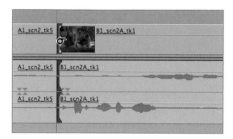

     At the head of this clip on the A2 track, there is a "bump" on the wave-
     form representing a sound. It may or may not be part of Monk's laugh.
     Let's remove it by nudging forward the clip's In point one frame at a time.

9   With the In point selected, press the] (right bracket) key to move the In
     point to the right one frame. Continue making one frame trims until this
     waveform blip is no longer part of the edit. If you go too far, nudge back
     to the left one frame by pressing the [(left bracket) key.

     NOTE ▶ The < and > (angle bracket) keys also adjust selected edit points
     just as the bracket keys do.

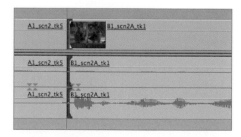

As you trim the clip, you are making individual frame adjustments. You can tell from the waveform when you've successfully removed the blip and when you've gone too far the other way.

TIP ▶ You can press Shift with a bracket key to apply a multi-frame trim size to the trim. You can change this amount (from 1 frame up to 99 frames) in the Editing tab of the User Preferences window.

When you need to nudge more than a few frames, for instance a full second or more, you can select the edit point and type that amount, just as you typed a move duration in the Timeline to move a clip. Let's take a few seconds off the end of a clip that's too long.

10 To change the Out point of the eleventh clip (**B1_scn2A_tk1**), click its Out point with the Ripple tool, and enter *–115*.

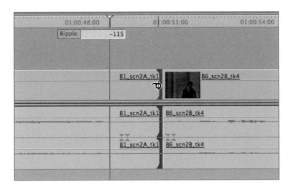

The Ripple trim amount appears in the Timeline beneath the ruler area.

11 Press Return to enter this amount.

The edit point automatically moves to the left 2 seconds.

NOTE ▶ Use the < and > (angle bracket) keys to adjust this edit point and match it to the action of Monk sitting down in the clip that follows.

Project Tasks

To practice using the Ripple tool to trim edit points, trim the following clips. Don't forget to apply 1-frame adjustments to clean up or finesse the edit point when necessary. Remember when you zoom in and out in the Timeline, if an edit point is selected, you will zoom into that edit point, not the playhead location. Press Shift-Command-A to deselect any selection; then you can zoom into the playhead location.

> **NOTE** ▶ You will come back to this sequence later in the lesson to apply other trimming techniques.

1   Press N to turn snapping back on.

2   On the fifth clip's In point (**B6_scn2B_tk4**), remove the psychiatrist's redundant line, "It's your vacation." Start the clip where Monk says, "It's my treat."

3   Clean up the edit points between the sixth and seventh clips (**A5_scn2B_tk4** and **B6_scn2B_tk4**). End the sixth clip with the psychiatrist saying, "actually looking forward to something." And start the seventh with Monk saying, "I am."

4   At the tail of the ninth clip (**B6_scn2B_tk4**), trim off the "ahhh." Trim away some of the extra "dead" space on the head of the tenth clip (**A5_scn2B_tk2**).

Trimming on the V2 Track

Using the Ripple tool is not the only way to trim an edit. As you saw earlier in this lesson, you can also drag an edit point using the default Selection tool. The problem with using the default Selection tool is that you cannot *ripple* the clips that follow, or drag an edit point *into* a neighboring clip.

The solution for this problem, and it's a handy one that many editors use, is to place cutaways on the V2 track, as you did in the "Believe" *Interviews* sequence in the previous lesson. When you edit your clips to the V2 track, you have elbow room to trim edit points by dragging them into empty track territory without having to ripple the clips around them.

1   In the Sequences bin in the Browser, open the *Interviews_v4_linked* sequence and scrub through it to refresh your memory of the clips and their placement.

In this sequence, you edited cutaways to the V2 track. This placement gives you the ability to reposition the clip earlier or later in the sequence. It also gives you more freedom to trim the In or Out using the default Selection tool.

2   Press A to return to the default Selection tool. Make sure snapping is on for these steps.

3   In the Timeline, play the **_SA_team ideas** clip. To change the feel of this section, click in the middle of the **_SA_room discussion** cutaway and drag the entire clip to the left. Snap it to the head of the **_SA_team ideas** clip and play it.

With the cutaway on a separate track, you can move the clip to reposition it, trim it by dragging its edit points, or even turn off track visibility to see what the sequence looks like without it.

4 Control-click the **_SA_room discussion** clip in the sequence. From the shortcut menu, choose Clip Enable.

This shortcut menu provides a long list of functions and changes you can apply to this clip. When you toggle off Clip Enable, it's as though you toggled off the Audible and Visible controls for that one clip. This can be a helpful feature if you want to preview an area of the sequence without a particular clip.

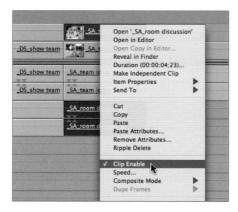

When the clip is disabled and deselected, it appears dark in the Timeline, just as it does when you toggle off the Audible or Visible controls in the Timeline patch panel.

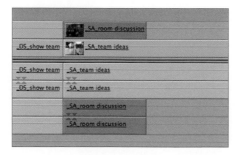

5   Play the **_SA_team ideas** clip to see it without the cutaway above it. Then Control-click the **_SA_room discussion** clip again and choose Clip Enable to toggle the clip back on.

With this clip repositioned to the head of the **_SA_team ideas** clip, you are free to adjust its Out point, and also the In point of the following cutaway on the V2 track. Since the **_KW_at board** cutaway is short, you can lengthen the clip by trimming its In point earlier, to the left.

6   Play the **_SA_team ideas** clip and position the playhead after Steve says, "…in-house staff."

7   On the V2 track, hold the pointer over the In point of the **_KW_at board** clip. When you see the Resize pointer, drag the edit point to the left and snap it to the playhead. As you drag, look at the trim amount and the new clip duration as they are updated in the information box and the two-up display in the Canvas.

When you drag an edit point using the default Selection tool, you see the amount of the trim and the new clip duration in the information box.

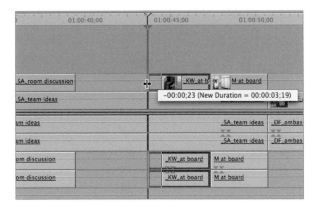

8 Play from this clip into the head of the **_DF_ambassadors** clip. Stop the playhead after David says, "…never tire of it." Click the Out point of the **_MB_behavior board** clip, but don't drag it.

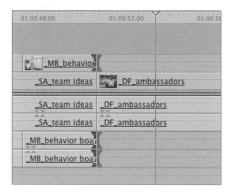

You will cover this first portion of David speaking using a different trimming technique. This time, you won't drag an edit point to the playhead; instead, you will *extend* the edit point to that location. Although it's a different technique, it produces the same result.

9 With the playhead positioned where you want this edit point to be and with the edit point selected, press E, or choose Sequence > Extend Edit. Play these clips.

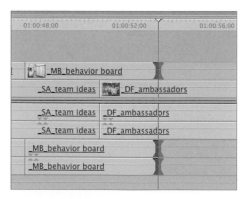

The Out point is trimmed, or extended, to the playhead location. To review, extending an edit point requires that you do three things:

▶   Position the playhead at the target location.

▶   Select the edit point you want to move using the default Selection tool.

▶   Press E, or choose Sequence > Extend Edit.

As with the other trim options you've worked with in this lesson, extending an edit can make a clip longer or shorter.

10   Let's extend the **performance_S spray jump** clip's Out point to the next edit point so it covers the remaining **_SA_favorite behavior** clip. Position the playhead to snap to the head of the **J hugs whale** clip. Select the Out point of the **performance_S spray jump** clip, and press E.

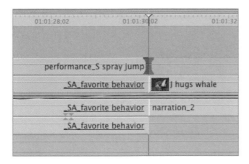

The clip's Out point automatically snaps to the playhead location.

NOTE ▶   You can extend an edit only if you have enough clip material to support the move. If you've placed the playhead out of the clip's range of material, you can't extend the clip to the new location, and no change will be made to that clip.

11 Play the second cutaway in the sequence, **_MM_with trainers**. Try to drag this clip's In point to the left, but don't release the mouse until you see the film strip on the left.

In the Canvas image area, the end-of-clip filmstrip overlay appears on the left side of the image, indicating that you are seeing the first available frame of the clip's media. (When the end-of-clip filmstrip appears on the right side of the image, you are on the last frame of media.) If this overlay appears as you trim, as it does in this clip, it means you cannot trim the clip any further in that direction.

Sometimes, you may want to remove a larger chunk of material from a clip. In the previous lesson, you used the Razor Blade tool to divide a narration track and add video. But you can also divide the clip and delete the unwanted portion.

12 Play the **_DF_ambassadors** clip and stop after David says, "…we have special jobs." Press B to select the Razor Blade tool, and click at the playhead location on one of the clip's tracks.

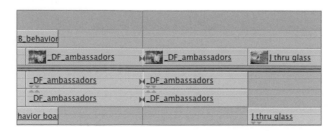

13 Press A to return to the default Selection tool. To delete the second half of
this clip, and ripple the remaining clips forward, select the clip and press
Shift-Delete.

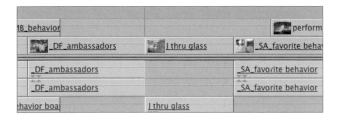

The through edit indicators no longer appear because the material is no
longer continuous from one clip to the next. Using the Razor Blade tool is
a good way to trim and shape clips in a sequence, and especially to pull out
"ums" and "ahhs" or portions of extended answers from nonprofessional
talent. You can also mark an unwanted section and press Shift-Delete to
remove the material between the In and Out points along with the gap.

TIP ▶ If you want to use the Razor Blade tool to cut through all tracks
in a sequence, rather than just one clip's tracks, press BB, or choose the
Razor Blade All tool from the Tool palette.

Trimming One Track of a Linked Clip

Thoughout this lesson, you have worked with clips that have linked tracks. You
click one track and all tracks become selected when you're in the default linked
selection mode. As you've seen, this mode also affects trimming. When you click
one edit point, such as the video Out point, all Out points on all tracks of
that clip become selected. This can be very helpful when you want to change
the Out point of the clip the same amount on all tracks. But sometimes when
editing, you may want to trim just the video track of a clip to be shorter or
longer than the audio, and vice versa.

The reason for this is that when both the audio and video change at the same
time in a sequence, the edit appears "harder" and more abrupt to the viewer.
If one of the tracks cuts first and the other one follows, it softens the effect of

the edit. Offsetting edit points this way is a technique that's used frequently in the refining process.

1   Play the first clip in the *Interviews_v4_linked* sequence.

Currently, both the narration and the whale clip stop at the same time. By staying with the video of the **J pec slaps** clip longer, it will soften the edit point.

You're not ready to drag this edit point just yet. First, you must drag the **J pec slaps** clip up to the V2 track where you will have more room to adjust the Out point. And since you want to work with just one track of this linked clip, you have to toggle off linked selection.

2   In the Timeline button bar, click the Linked Selection button to toggle it off, so it is gray. You can also press Shift-L.

As with snapping, linked selection is on, or active, when the button is green, and off when it is gray.

3   To drag the Out point of this clip over the **_DS_show concept** clip, click the **J pec slaps** clip on the V1 track and drag it up to the V2 track. Hold down Shift as you drag to maintain an exact vertical move upward, without slipping the clip left or right.

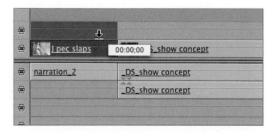

TIP ▶ Whenever you drag a clip, an information box appears, indicating the amount of the move left or right. When moving clips vertically in the Timeline, keep an eye on that box, or use the Shift key, to make sure you aren't moving the clip horizontally at the same time.

4   Click the Out point of the **J pec slaps** clip on the V2 track.

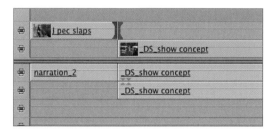

When linked selection is off, you can select and trim a clip's audio or video tracks individually, even if the tracks are linked together.

5   In the **_DS_show concept** clip, move the playhead to the point after David says, "…born from the whale itself." To trim this clip, you can either drag the Out point right and snap it to the playhead, or press E to extend the edit point to the playhead location. Play this clip again.

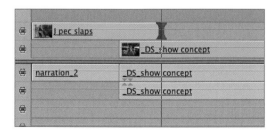

Now, as David says the show is "born from the whale itself," you see the whale behavior.

You can apply this same principle and process to refine some of the edit points in the Monk sequence. Since the clips in the Monk sequence are all linked, the linked selection function must be off for you to trim any one track of a clip independently.

6 In the Timeline, click the *Monk Rough Cut_v1* sequence tab and play the eighth clip, **A5_scn2B_tk4**.

At the head of this clip, the psychiatrist stutters a bit over the first line. With linked selection off, you can trim the In point of just the audio tracks to correct this.

7 Zoom into this clip so you can see the waveform more clearly. Play from the beginning of the clip and stop the playhead where you hear the psychiatrist say the second "you know…" Drag the In point on the audio tracks to snap to the playhead.

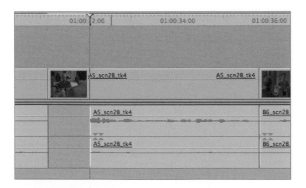

Because the audio tracks are a stereo pair, whenever you trim one track, the other moves the same amount.

8 Play the audio from the new In point. If it needs adjusting, select the audio In point and press the < and > (angle bracket) keys, or the [and] (bracket) keys to nudge the selected edit point right or left until it's as clean as you can make it.

> **NOTE** ▶ Before a show would air with this gap in the audio, sound mixers would edit in ambient room noise to fill in the blank space.

9 In the Timeline, click the Linked Selection button to toggle that function back on.

You can choose to edit with linked selection on or off. For now, and for the purposes of these lessons, keep linked selection on, in its default state.

> **TIP** ▶ To temporarily override linked selection to trim a single track of one clip, press Option and then drag the edit point. You will drag just the audio or video edit point you select.

Project Tasks

If you want to practice trimming techniques, continue working in both the *Monk Rough Cut_v1* and *Interviews_v4_linked* sequences, trimming the current clips. You can also duplicate the original *Scene from "Monk"* sequence to create a new version and trim the clips in a different way.

Lesson Review

1. What does toggling off linked selection in the Timeline do?

2. What does the Ripple tool do when you use it for trimming?

3. What is the keyboard shortcut to select the Ripple tool?

4. What keys can you use as shortcuts to ripple a clip's edit point by a few frames?

5. What is one advantage of trimming a clip in the Viewer?

6. How can you disable a single clip in the sequence?

7. What tools can you use to drag an edit point in the Timeline?

8. What is the keyboard shortcut for extending an edit?

9. What tracks does the Razor Blade tool cut through when you click a clip?

10. How do you drag a clip vertically in the Timeline without moving it horizontally?

11. What is the advantage of editing on the V2 track?

Answers

1. It allows you to select and trim one track of a linked clip.

2. It ripples the trim amount through the unlocked tracks in the sequence.

3. Pressing RR selects the Ripple tool.

4. Use the left and right bracket keys ([and]) and the < and > (angle bracket) keys.

5. You can view the material outside the marked area.

6. Control-click the clip in the sequence and toggle off Clip Enable in the shortcut menu.

7. Use the default Selection tool and the Ripple tool.

8. The E key extends an edit.

9. It cuts through all the tracks of a linked clip when linked selection is on.

10. Hold down the Shift key as you drag.

11. It allows you to lengthen a clip without bumping into a bordering clip on either side.

Keyboard Shortcuts

B	Selects the Razor Blade tool
BB	Selects the Razor Blade All tool
E	Extends an edit
N	Toggles snapping off and on
RR	Selects the Ripple tool
Option-Command-W	Toggles audio waveforms off and on in the Timeline
Shift-L	Toggles linked selection off and on

5

Lesson Files   Lesson 5 Project

Media   Monk and SeaWorld folders

Time   This lesson takes approximately 60 minutes to complete.

Goals   Trim two edit points at the same time

Slip In and Out points

Roll edit points

Extend edit points

Slide a clip

Reposition a clip

Keeping clips in sync

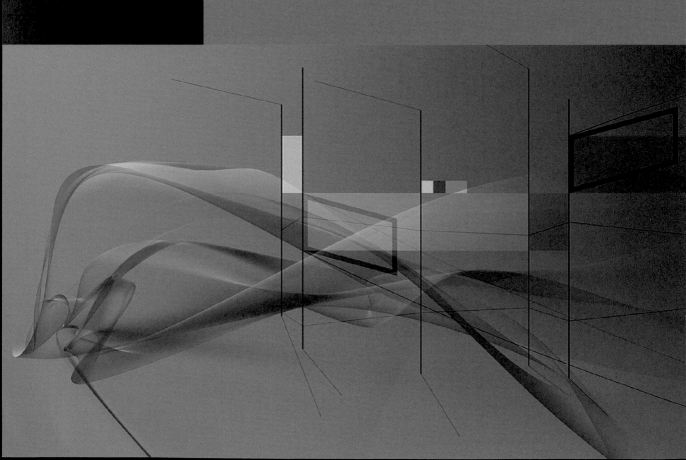

Lesson **5**

Trimming and Adjusting Two Edit Points

In the previous lesson, you used the Ripple tool to trim clips longer or shorter to refine the story, getting you closer to the intended length of your sequence. Now you're ready to polish the clip edit points, clip location, and even clip content without changing the overall length of the sequence. To do this, you will use three Final Cut Pro tools: Slip, Roll, and Slide. You will also use the Selection tool to reposition clips within a sequence.

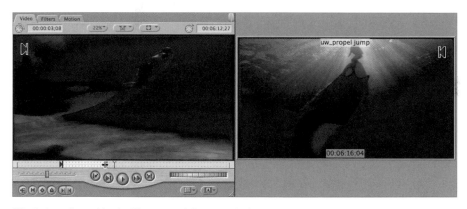

Clip being slipped in the Viewer and Canvas windows

Preparing Your Sequence

As you continue to refine your rough cut, you may want to set up your sequence a little differently and use markers to identify areas that need adjusting. To get started in Lesson 5, you will launch Final Cut Pro and open the project for this lesson. You will work with rough cuts you've built in earlier lessons.

1   Choose File > Open, or press Command-O, then select the **Lesson 5 Project** file from the Lessons folder on your hard drive. Close any other open projects.

   There are several sequences open in the Timeline, all similar to ones you built in earlier lessons. As you learn to use different tools, you will also learn how to apply them to various types of sequences.

2   Click the *Behaviors_v3* sequence tab and play the sequence.

   This sequence, like the other ones in this project, is already the right length, but it needs some polishing to improve how some of the video clips align with the music track. In certain instances, it also needs different clip content.

During the editing process, you might add a marker at an edit point to remind yourself where you need to make a change. There are a few markers already placed in this sequence for that purpose. Some of the markers just have names indicating what action to take, and others have an additional comment.

3   Control-click the Timeline ruler area. From the list of marker names on the bottom of this shortcut menu, choose "include re-entry."

The playhead moves directly to that marker.

4   In the Canvas, click the Play Around Current Frame button, or press the \ (backslash) key.

This engages an automatic function that moves the playhead back a specific number of seconds (called the *pre-roll* time), plays forward through the playhead's original location, continues to play a few more seconds (*post-roll*), and returns the playhead to the original location. Rather than having to position your playhead manually before the edit point, this function lets you see "around" the edit point.

This will be a helpful way to preview edit points throughout this lesson, so let's take a moment to change the pre-roll and post-roll settings to suit your own preferences.

5   Press Option-Q to open the User Preferences window, and click the Editing tab. In the Preview Pre-roll field, enter *2.* (two period) and press Return. Leave the Preview Post-roll at its current setting. Click OK to save this change.

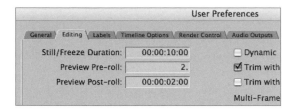

6   Press the \ (backslash) key to preview this edit point with the new pre-roll settings.

In this lesson, you will be working with tools that outline or in some other way mark the clips or edit points you're adjusting. To see those markings more clearly, let's turn off the thumbnail images for the clips in this sequence.

7   Choose Sequence > Settings, or press Command-0, and click the Timeline Options tab. Click the Thumbnail Display pop-up and choose Name. Click OK.

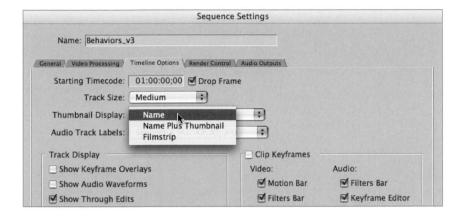

In the Timeline Options tab of the Sequence Settings window, you
can change how the active or current sequence appears in the Timeline.
For example, you can change the track size, toggle off or on the audio
waveforms display and through edit indicators, and even change the
starting timecode of the sequence. In this situation, when you select the
Name option, the thumbnail images no longer appear on the clips in
the sequence. Instead, you see just the name of the clip.

TIP ▶ To display the clip names larger in the Timeline, Control-click in
the Browser's empty gray space and choose Text Size > Medium from the
shortcut menu. This enlarges the text in the Browser as well.

Since you will use a number of different tools and options in this lesson, it
might be helpful to create a new demo sequence in which you can explore
how a tool works before applying it to a sequence

8 To create a backup of the original *Behaviors_v3* sequence for you to return
to if necessary, Control-click that sequence and choose Duplicate from the
shortcut menu. Name it *Behaviors_v3 backup*. Just leave it unopened in the
Sequences bin.

Trimming Two Edit Points

There are three trimming tools in Final Cut Pro that have one thing in common: They always preserve the current sequence length. The three tools—Slip, Roll, and Slide—never change the length of a sequence because they simultaneously change two edit points by equal amounts. You could use the Ripple tool to first trim one edit point, and then the other. But these tools save you time by applying identical trim amounts to two edit points at the same time. One way to organize your thinking around these three tools is to consider the number of clips each tool affects.

> NOTE ▶ The term *edit point* can refer to a single clip's In or Out point, but it can also refer to the juncture between adjoining clips.

Slipping

Slipping trims both the In and Out points in a *single* clip at the same time. As you adjust both the In and Out points together, you *slip* the contents of a clip to the left or right of its original edit points. Clip and sequence durations remain the same, but you will be showing different clip content.

Starting clip content

Content after slipping

Rolling

Rolling affects the edit point between two adjacent clips. It trims the Out point of one clip and the In point of the following clip simultaneously. If you roll left, the first clip will be shorter, and the second clip will be longer. The opposite is true when you roll to the right: The first clip becomes longer, and the adjacent clip becomes shorter. Rolling edit points left or right does not change the overall sequence duration because as one edit point changes, its neighbor compensates for the change.

Edit point selected

Rolling an edit point left

Rolling an edit point right

Sliding

Sliding trims two edit points but involves *three contiguous clips*. You can shift, or *slide*, the middle clip into the one on the left, making the first clip shorter; but the In point of the third clip adjusts to compensate, and the third clip becomes longer. The opposite holds true if you slide the middle clip to the right. The middle clip content remains unchanged, though its position shifts slightly right or left in the Timeline. Taken together, the length of the three clips remains the same.

Starting center clip position

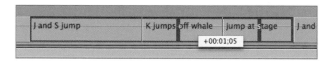

Sliding the center clip left

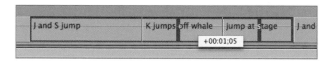

Sliding the center clip right

Slipping One Clip

As you edit, you may find yourself wanting to trim a clip to begin earlier or later, but you don't want to change the clip's current duration. This is when you can use the Slip tool to slip the clip. Should you use that whale jump earlier in the clip? Or that twirl later in the clip? Slipping allows you to trim the In and Out points of a single clip by the same amount at the same time. This lets you select slightly different content without changing the clip length. However, you must have additional material—handles—on either side of the clip to give you some place to go, or you will have no additional frames to slip.

Working with the Slip Tool

When you apply the Slip tool to a clip in the Timeline, you drag *right* to see earlier clip material before the In point or *left* to see later material after the Out point. Think of the clip as your windshield; the additional material to the left or right outside your windshield view makes up your handles.

In the Tool palette, the Slip tool is the fifth tool from the top. To explore how it works, you will copy a clip from one sequence and paste it into the empty *Exploring* sequence.

1   In the Timeline, click the *Behaviors_v3* sequence and select the **K jumps off whale** clip. Press Command-C to copy this clip, then click the *Exploring* sequence tab and press Command-V to paste it. Move the clip to the middle of the Timeline.

Notice that the clip in the *Exploring* sequence appears with a thumbnail image on the clip. When you choose Sequence > Settings, you are making changes only to the sequence that is active when you access the Sequence Settings dialog. If you like, you can change the track display of this sequence to Name.

TIP ▸ You can change the default settings for all new sequences in the User Preferences > Timeline Options tab.

2   In the Tool palette, click the Slip tool, or press S.

When you look closely at the Slip tool, you see what appear to be two Ripple tools facing each other. The two thin vertical lines represent the clip In and Out points. You could think of the Slip tool icon as two edit points on wheels, moving or trimming the edit points in tandem, left or right.

3   In the Timeline, with the Slip tool chosen, click and hold the **K jumps off whale** clip. You may have to zoom in or out of the clip to see the complete outline.

One brown outline appears around the video clip box, and another one appears past the boundaries of the clip. This outer outline indicates graphically how much source material is available for you to draw from on either side while making a slip adjustment. These are your *handles*. Let's slip this clip to see the first portion of its available media.

4   Using the Slip tool, drag right as far as possible, but don't release the mouse. Look at the Canvas two-up display.

In the Canvas, the clip's new In and Out points appear along with the clip name and source timecode. The end-of-clip filmstrip overlay appears in the left frame to indicate that you are currently on the first frame of the clip. You cannot slip the clip any farther to the right. If you drag all the way to the left, you will see the end-of-clip overlay on the right frame.

In the Timeline, an information box appears, showing the amount forward or backward you have slipped the clip.

5   Release the mouse and play the new clip content.

After slipping this clip, you now see from the head of the clip as Katie approaches the platform. But you don't see her jump off the whale. That comes later in the source clip.

Remember to think of the windshield of a car as a metaphor for slipping in the Timeline. The area outside the windshield is the additional media on each end of the source clip, whereas what you see in the windshield is the current clip content. To see media outside the left of the windshield, drag the clip right to pull it into view. To see what content follows the current selection, drag left.

6   To reveal a later action, slip the clip left and focus on the right frame of the Canvas two-up display. When you see Katie jump off the whale, release the clip, and then play it.

As you slip this clip, think about what portion of the clip will work better in the sequence. Is it when Katie jumps off the whale, or when she raises her fist in the air?

7 Slip the **K jumps off whale** clip left until you no longer see the director in the left frame of the two-up display.

The image on the left is the new In point. Slipping the clip so you don't see the director moves the Out point down past Katie raising her fist in the air. You can focus on either the In or the Out point, or both. But however much you slip an edit point in one direction, the opposite edit point is slipped by the same amount in the same direction. In the Timeline, the clip is still the same length.

8 Click the *Behaviors_v3* tab and then slip the **K jumps off whale** clip in that sequence.

In a sequence, the slip media handles appear over the other clips. Since this clip is in between several others, you may find you don't have as much control as you'd like because the Slip tool snaps to other edit points as you drag.

9 Press N to toggle off snapping. Slip this clip again. To gain even greater control as you slip, hold down the Command key as you drag.

> **TIP** Pressing the Command key as you drag increases the precision of your adjustments. You can use the Command key anytime you drag, including when you reposition audio level overlays in the Timeline audio tracks.

Slipping Sequence Clips

There are other ways you can slip a clip. For example, you can enter the number of frames, or even seconds, you want to slip, just as you did with the Ripple or Move tool in previous lessons. In order to use numbers or other shortcuts to slip a clip, the clip must first be selected in the Timeline. Also, once a clip is in the sequence, you can double-click it and make slip adjustments in the Viewer. The Slip tool also provides a very handy way to see a "blueprint" of your sequence clips.

1   In the Timeline, with the Slip tool selected, click and hold the **whale nods head** clip, but don't slip it in either direction.

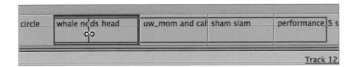

When you select a clip using the Slip tool, you see how much additional media you have, and in which direction, so you know what kind of a slip adjustment you can make—little or big, earlier or later. If you see no handles on one side of a clip, such as in the **whale nods head** clip, you know you can't slip this clip any earlier.

TIP ▶ When you want to change or adjust a particular clip or area of the sequence, it's always a good idea to zoom into that area.

2   Click the **sham slam** clip to see a "blueprint" of its media length, then release the clip.

In the Canvas window, an end-of-film clip overlay appears on both frames of the two-up display, indicating there are no additional media handles to slip this clip at its current length.

Another way to slip a clip is to open it into the Viewer. This option uses the Viewer to display the In point, and the Canvas to display the Out point. You may want to make those windows the same size before opening a clip.

3   If necessary, press Control-U to choose the default Standard window layout. Double-click the last clip in the sequence, **S show open**.

From the edit points in the scrubber bar, you can tell this clip has long media handles. Two rows of sprocket holes appear in the scrubber bar to indicate that this clip is already in the sequence.

4   In the Viewer scrubber bar, move your Slip tool over either the In or Out point. Drag left and watch the Viewer window to see where Steve starts to come out of the water at around 8:45:00. In the Canvas, the Out point should show him sinking back down. Then, release the mouse.

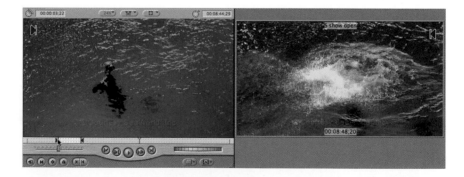

As you drag, both edit points move simultaneously. The first frame of the new clip content appears in the Viewer, and the last frame appears in the Canvas. As you slip a sequence clip in the Viewer, you are actually making that change to the clip in the Timeline.

TIP ▶ You can also open a clip in the Viewer and slip the edit points by pressing Shift and using the default Selection tool.

5   Play the **S show open** clip in the sequence to preview the new clip content.

6   Double-click the **whale nods head** clip to open it in the Viewer. Play past the current Out point to see what other material is available in this clip. Stop the playhead after the whale lifts its tail.

When an Out point is located before an important action, or an In point is later than an action, you can use the Viewer to find the action and slip the edit points to that location.

You may also want to think about whether it would be more helpful to work with snapping on or off as you slip a clip.

7   Using the Slip tool, drag the Out point to the right until the Out point snaps to the playhead. If snapping is off, you can press N *as you drag* to toggle it on. Then release the clip and preview it in the Timeline.

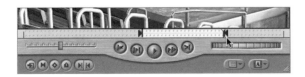

As with rippling and moving, you can also adjust a clip by slipping it a few frames to refine the selection of material. You use the same adjusting keys— < and > or [and]—as you did when adjusting move and trim amounts.

NOTE ▶ Having two sets of adjusting keys on the keyboard can be useful. Sometimes your hand is close to the I and O keys, and reaching to the [and] keys is convenient. Other times you may be using the J-K-L keys and the < and > keys are more convenient.

8   Play the first clip, **S onto stage**.

In this clip, you see Steve start to jump off the whale's back, which is a distracting place to cut. It would be nicer to end this clip before he jumps off.

To nudge or slip this clip by a few frames, you first have to select the clip. Although you can double-click a clip to open it in the Viewer, you can't click a clip to select it without a modifier key.

9   To select the **S onto stage** clip, hold down Shift. When the pointer changes to the default Selection tool, select the clip, then release the Shift key to revert back to the Slip tool.

10 Position the playhead on the last frame of this clip to see the updated frame in the Canvas. Type *1.* (one period) and press Return.

NOTE ▶ Unlike other uses of plus or minus in adjusting a sequence clip, when you slip a clip using numbers, the direction may seem reversed. Adding a minus sign to a number is the same as dragging the clip left with the Slip tool, and therefore choosing later clip content. A plus sign is the equivalent of dragging the clip to the right, or slipping earlier content into the clip.

11 Play the clip. If it needs additional adjusting, use the < and > keys to slip one frame forward or backward, respectively.

Project Tasks

There are several clips in the *Behaviors_v3* sequence that could be improved by slipping clip content. You can slip by dragging in the Timeline, by opening the clip in the Viewer, by entering a slip amount, or by nudging a frame at a time. Don't forget to watch the Canvas two-up display to capture a specific action in the clip. You won't be using this sequence again for this lesson, so you can make whatever changes to it you like.

Rolling Two Edit Points

When you don't like the way one clip cuts to the next —perhaps because the action doesn't match or the edit point doesn't hit on the beat of music or narrator's pause—you may need to think about using the Roll tool. The Roll tool will trim both sides of an edit point at the same time. It will trim the Out point of one clip the same amount it trims the In point of the following clip. This allows you to adjust the edit point earlier or later without changing the overall sequence duration.

> **TIP** ▶ If necessary, zoom into an area of the Timeline in order to see the clip names more clearly.

Working with the Roll Tool

The Roll tool is the fourth tool from the top in the Tool palette. It shares the same position as the Ripple tool. For some projects, especially dramatic scenes and interviews, you might use the Ripple and Roll tools in tandem. You might first apply the Ripple tool to refine a single clip's edit point, and then follow it with the Roll tool to adjust the way that clip's edit point works in conjunction with the clip next to it. To explore how the Roll tool works, you will copy two clips from one sequence and paste them into the empty *Exploring* sequence.

1   To continue adding to the *Exploring* sequence, you will open another version of the *Behaviors* sequence, copy two clips from that sequence and paste them into the *Exploring* sequence. Follow these steps:

▶   Press A to select the default Selection tool.

▶   From the Sequences bin, open the *Behaviors_v4_roll* sequence.

▶   Click the **uw_propel jump** clip and Command-click the **J and L circle** clip next to it.

▶ Press Command-C to copy both clips.

▶ Click the *Exploring* sequence tab.

▶ Position the playhead in an empty area to the right of the **K jumps off whale** clip.

▶ Press Command-V to paste these clips.

▶ Play the two clips.

These two clips appear to have a synchronous relationship. The first clip propels the trainer to the surface from an underwater perspective. The second shows the trainer and whale breaking the surface of the water. If you trim or adjust just the Out of the first clip or just the In of the second, you would throw these clips out of sync.

2   In the Tool palette, select the Roll tool, or press R.

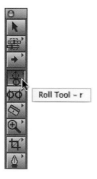

The Roll tool shares the same tool area as the Ripple tool. The Roll icon looks like two Ripple tools adjacent to each other, and it adjusts two sides of an edit point.

3 Click the edit point between the two clips.

Both sides of the edit point become highlighted.

4 Drag the edit point left about 1 second and note the following *before* you release the mouse:

▶ In the Timeline, a brown outline box surrounds both clips. This indicates that these two clips are involved in this adjustment. The outer edges of these boxes will not change, only the edit point in the middle will.

▶ The amount or duration of the roll appears in the information box.

▶ In the Canvas two-up display, the left frame displays the outgoing clip's new Out point along with an Out mark in the frame's upper-right corner. The right frame displays the incoming clip's new In point along with an In mark in its upper-left corner. The clip names and source time-code locations also appear in the Canvas frames.

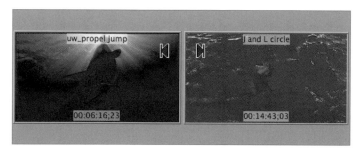

NOTE ▶ When the Caps Lock key is engaged, the two-up display is disabled in the Canvas.

5   Adjust this edit to the left one frame at a time by pressing the < key. Press Shift-< to move it the multi-frame trim size amount. Then play the clips.

In the Canvas, every time you adjust the edit point, you see an update of the first frame of the second clip, which is where the playhead is located. (Like the Slip and Ripple tools, you can also enter a number to roll a specific amount of time.) Because each roll adjustment trims both edit points together the same amount, the clips still appear to be generally in sync.

MORE INFO ▶ This footage was not shot at the same time, and therefore the action doesn't match exactly. In Lesson 6, you will work with and learn to edit multiple camera footage.

In addition to maintaining sync relationships, rolling edit points is very helpful when you want an edit point to hit in a particular place in the sequence, such as on a music beat or at a narrator's cue.

6   Click the *Behaviors_v4_roll* sequence tab. To go to a specific marker location, Control-click in the ruler area and choose "magic moment" from the shortcut menu. Press the \ (backslash) key to hear where the music beat hits on the word "moment."

It would be nice if the edit point of these two clips hit right on this beat of the music.

7   With the Roll tool selected, drag the edit point between the **J thru glass** and **uw_push two trainers** clips to the right until the edit point snaps to the playhead. Play this edit point.

Now the edit point hits on the beat of the music. Let's repeat this process for another music beat. This time, you will snap the edit point directly to the marker.

8   Find the *earth and sky* marker and play the edit point before it. Then move the playhead out of the area. With snapping on, roll the edit point and snap it to the marker. Release the edit point and play the clips.

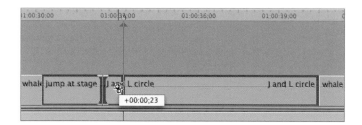

When you snap an edit point to a marker, brown snapping arrows appear beneath the marker in the ruler area as they would if you snapped to the playhead.

NOTE ▶ Since rolling changes the length of each clip, you may need to go back and slip the clip content of the clips after you've rolled the edit point to its target location.

Rolling One Track of a Linked Clip

If you are cutting a sequence of two people talking, such as the *Monk* sequence or an interview between two people, rolling just the *video* edit point of the clips left or right can make the dialogue seem more natural. If you imagine yourself observing a conversation between two people, you often listen to one person speak and, after you *hear* the other person speak, you turn your head to *look* at him. Editors often cut to mimic that behavior. Let's finesse some of the edit points in the *Monk* sequence by offsetting the video edit points.

1   Click the *Monk Rough Cut_v2* sequence tab and play the edit point at the *roll 1* marker, between the **B6_scn2B_tk4** and **A5_scn2B_tk4** clips.

To soften this edit point, you can switch to Dr. Kroger's camera a little later, after the audio edit point.

Because the audio edit point is already where you want it to be, you need to adjust or roll just the video portion. Rather than toggle off linked selection, you will use a shortcut to temporarily override the linked selection status, which will save you a few steps.

2   Position the playhead just as Dr. Kroger says, "…term for this." Hold down the Option key and click the video edit point.

When you Option-click an edit point, just that edit point on that track becomes selected.

NOTE ▶ Option-clicking can also be used with the default Selection tool to select one track of a clip, or with the Ripple tool to trim just one track.

3   Drag the video edit point to snap to the playhead location. Play the edit point.

In the Timeline, the Linked Selection button is still green and has not been toggled off, yet only the video edit point was rolled over to the playhead position.

TIP ▶ Since you will frequently work with linked selection on, it's a good idea to leave it on always and to use the Option key when you need to access just one track.

There's another keyboard shortcut you can apply to the next rolling adjustment. This is a shortcut you used in the previous lesson to extend an edit point. Rather than extend a single edit point to make a clip longer or shorter, here you will extend both sides of the edit point in tandem, exactly as though you used the Roll tool to roll it.

4   Move the playhead to the edit point before the *roll 2* marker and play this area. Position the playhead after Dr. Kroger says, "OK."

In the current edit point, you don't see Monk open his eyes until Dr. Kroger says, "OK." Rolling the edit point will extend the camera angle to include Monk opening his eyes.

5   Option-click the video edit point and press E to extend this edit point to the playhead location.

Since the playhead was parked where you wanted the new edit point to be, pressing E extends, or rolls, the selected edit point to that location.

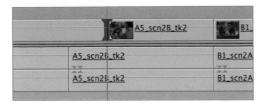

In this sequence, you can also look at how the audio is cut. If one person's audio is taken from two different takes, you may want to roll an edit point so the audio for that person comes entirely from a single take.

6   Move to the *roll 3* marker and play the clip before and the clip under this marker. Press Option-Command-W to turn on the audio waveform display, and play again.

7   Position the playhead to the beginning of Dr. Kroger's line, "But it's your breakthrough…." Find the area where the waveform appears flat and there is no sound.

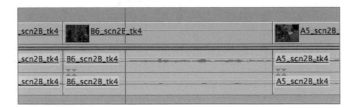

This is a clean audio cut point. Let's roll just the audio track back to this location so Dr. Kroger's on-camera line will be coming entirely from one source clip.

8   Hold down Option (to override linked selection) and click the audio edit point. Press E to extend or roll this edit point back to the playhead. Play the new edit point.

9   Press < or > to finesse the edit location even further.

10 Press Command-S to save your changes.

> **TIP** ▶ You can also use the < and > keys or the bracket keys to extend or roll edit points selected with the default Selection tool.

Project Tasks

Look through the *Monk* sequence and see if you find any other edit points that might be improved if you offset the video from the audio.

> **MORE INFO** ▶ You can double-click an edit point to open the Trim Edit window. This window displays the two clips involved at the edit point. In this window, you can apply both the Ripple and Roll tools. You can learn more about the Trim Edit window in the Final Cut Pro User Manual.

Sliding Clips to Refine Position

If you like a clip's length and content but want to adjust its position—maybe a little to the left or right between its neighbors—then you'll want to use the Slide tool. This third method of adjusting two edit points affects three clips. Sliding the middle clip maintains its content and duration but adjusts its placement between the bordering clips. This alters the duration of the two neighbors but not the overall sequence length.

Sliding is a fine-tuning adjustment that doesn't change the general location of a clip in the sequence, but just finesses its placement. The Slide tool shares the same location as the Slip tool in the Tool palette.

To begin, you will copy and paste three clips into the *Exploring* sequence.

1   In the Timeline, click the *Interviews_v5* sequence, and move to the *narration* marker. Drag a marquee around all three narration clips and the video clips above them. Press Command-C to copy them.

2   In the *Exploring* sequence, position the playhead in an empty area of the Timeline after the existing clips. Press Command-V to paste these clips at this location and play the three clips. Notice how Leslie kisses the whale at the end of the middle clip.

Since the video clips above the narration are not linked to the narration clips, you can adjust them freely without having to toggle off linked selection or use the Option key to override linked selection.

3   To select the Slide tool in the Tool palette, click and hold the Slip tool until the Slide icon appears, then select it, or press SS.

TIP   To better see the brown outlines the Slide function will create, choose Sequence > Settings, click the Timeline Options tab, and choose Name from the Thumbnail Display pop-up menu.

4   Using the Slide tool, click and hold the **L hugging whale** clip. Notice the outlines, then release the clip.

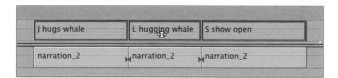

The brown outline boxes appear, this time around all three clips involved with this adjustment. As you slide the middle clip, you will be making the clips on either side longer or shorter.

TIP ▶ Whenever you use narration as a reference point, it's helpful to toggle on audio waveforms. Press Option-Command-W or choose that option from the Layout pop-up menu.

5 Play the first clip, and stop the playhead after the narrator says, "...two worlds." Using the Slide tool, drag the **L hugging whale** clip to the left and snap its In point to the playhead. Before you release the mouse, look at both the clip in the sequence and the two-up display in the Canvas image area.

As you slide the middle clip, the outside edges of the outer two clips do not move; only the inner edges bordering the middle clip move to show how the clips are compensating for the adjustment.

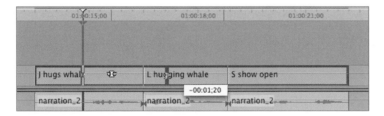

In the Canvas two-up display, the two frames show the new Out point of the first clip and the new In point of the third clip. You can watch these frames as you drag to determine the best position for the clip you are sliding.

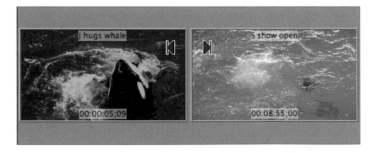

6   Release the mouse, and play these three clips again.

By sliding the middle clip to the left, the outgoing **J hugs whale** clip is shortened at the tail of its clip, and the incoming **S show open** clip is lengthened at the head of its clip. But the **L hugging whale** clip is unchanged except for its position between the two in the sequence.

If you decide you want the first clip to be longer but still don't want to change the middle clip's length, you can slide the middle clip to the right. Let's slide the middle clip to the right over the third narration clip.

7   With the Slide tool, drag the **L hugging whale** clip to the right and snap its In point to the third narration clip edit point. Then, release the mouse and play these clips.

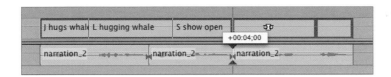

In this situation, you've extended the Out point of the **J hugs whale** clip and shortened the head of the **S show open** clip. The middle clip remains unchanged in length and content, and Leslie still kisses the whale at the end of that clip.

TIP ▶ You can also press Shift to select the clip and enter an amount for a slide, or use the [and] (left and right bracket) keys or the < and > (left and right angle bracket) keys, to make slide adjustments, just as you did with the Slip tool.

8   Click the *Interviews_v5* sequence tab, and slide the **L hugging whale** clip into what you think is its best position.

Dragging Clips to New Locations

In an earlier lesson, you edited several interview clips into a sequence as you began building your rough cut. As is often the case, once you see the assortment of clips in the Timeline, you may start to question if another arrangement of those clips might improve the sequence. Since no new clips are added to the sequence, and you've only made a location change, the overall sequence length remains the same. Repositioning a clip to a new location in your sequence does not require any editing tool other than the default Selection tool and a modifier key.

1   In the Sequences bin, open the *Interviews_v6_repo* sequence, and play it. (Press N if snapping is not on.)

This sequence contains the original on-camera interviews with the key members of SeaWorld's "Believe" team. While the current order of clips has a natural flow, you could rearrange the order of some of the clips to create an alternative version.

For example, moving the **_MB_behavior board** clip into the second clip position would allow viewers to see the different behaviors on the board before hearing Steve talk about them.

2   Press A to choose the default Selection tool.

NOTE ▶ To reposition a clip successfully, you must use precise key combinations at specific times. Follow steps 3 through 5 carefully, and release the mouse only when instructed to do so.

3   Drag the **_MB_behavior board** clip left and snap its In point to the head of the **_SA_team ideas** clip, but don't release the mouse. Press and hold the Option key.

When you press Option, the pointer changes to a hooked downward arrow, indicating that you will be inserting the clip at this point.

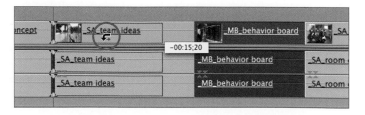

In the Canvas, look at the names of the clips in the two-up display. These are the frames that will appear on either side of this clip when you release the clip as an insert edit.

NOTE ► As you drag a clip through a sequence, if black appears in one of the Canvas two-up frames, you are either at the head or tail of the sequence, or you're over a gap that will be created when you move the clip.

The next step is important for positioning this clip successfully.

4 First release the mouse, and then release the Option key. Play the first few clips to see how the new arrangement works.

The **_MB_behavior board** clip is now the second clip in the sequence. As in other insert edits, the remaining clips in the sequence are pushed down to allow room for the repositioned clip.

In reviewing the remaining clips, you might decide that hearing the trainers described as "ambassadors" would be a better clip to end the sequence rather than Steve talking about his favorite whale behavior.

5   Drag the **_SA_favorite behavior** clip left and snap its In point to the In
point of the **_DF_ambassadors** clip. Press and hold the Option key.
Release the mouse, and then release the Option key. Play the clips in
this configuration.

> **TIP** ▸ Look for the snapping triangles around the edit point to ensure
> you are at the correct location.

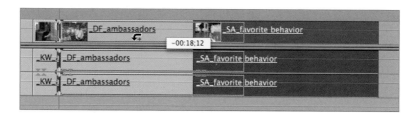

There's another way to drag and reposition a clip, and that's to drag a copy
of the original clip. This leaves the original in its current location but allows
you to drag a copy to a different location and drop it as an overwrite or
insert edit. Since you are really performing two steps in one—copying and
pasting, it's important to think about which step you're performing and
which modifier key you need.

In this sequence, Katie mentions a behavior as she's standing at the
board. You might want to preview how her clip would look following the
_MB_behavior board clip, without changing the original clip's location.

> **TIP** ▸ Dragging a copy of a clip can also be used when you want to
> repeat an action at a different location in the sequence.

6   Adjust the Timeline so you can see the target clip, **_KW_at board**, and the
target clip location, the end of the **_MB_behavior board** clip.

7   First click the **_KW_at board** clip and release the mouse. When you see
the Move tool, press the Option key. When you see the tiny plus sign
next to the Move tool, start dragging left, but don't release the mouse or
the Option key.

You are now dragging a copy of this clip, not the original.

Next, you have to determine whether you want to release this clip as an insert edit (indicated by a right-facing arrow) or an overwrite edit (indicated by a down arrow). Continuing to hold the Option key allows you to insert the clip. Releasing the Option key creates an overwrite edit.

8 To continue, snap the **_KW_at board** clip into position at the head of the **_SA_team ideas** clip. Release the Option key, and you see a downward over-write arrow. Press the Option key again, and the forward insert arrow returns. Release the mouse to insert this clip at this location.

Hold down the Option key to make an insert edit.

Release the Option key to make an overwrite edit.

Now you can preview both areas to see where this clip fits best.

9 For this exercise, click the original clip and press Shift-Delete to remove it from the sequence.

Keeping Linked Clips in Sync

As you continue to trim and adjust your sequence clips during the refining
process, you may slip or trim one track of a clip only to realize that you have
thrown the remaining tracks or other clips out of sync. A simple Command-Z
will undo any step in Final Cut Pro. But there are other options to correct out-
of-sync clips.

1   In the current *Interviews_v6_repo* sequence, double-click the **_KW_at board**
     clip to open it in the Viewer. Play past its current Out point and listen for
     when Katie says, "Kayla…is that Kayla?"

     This is another section of the clip you might use instead of the current
     selection. To choose this clip content, you can slip this clip. But first, let's
     set you up for the fall!

2   Click the Linked Selection button to toggle it off, or press Shift-L.

     If you previously had been adjusting just the video or audio tracks of a
     sequence, linked selection might still be toggled off.

3   To slip to later content, press S, then click the video track of the **_KW_at
     board** clip in the Timeline and drag left about 4:15 seconds. Look at the
     information box to determine that amount of time. Release the clip and
     play it.

When you play this clip, you can clearly see and hear that the video is out
of sync with the audio tracks. However, if it was out of sync only a few
frames, you might not notice it as you watched the clip play in the Canvas.
To warn you of a sync problem, big or small, red out-of-sync indicators
appear on each linked track in the Timeline, indicating the amount you
are out of sync.

If slipping just the video track alone was an oversight, you could press Command-Z to undo the move, turn linked selection back on, and slip all the tracks together at one time. However, you have other choices as well:

▶ Leave the audio where it is, out of sync.

▶ Slip the audio so the portion beneath the video returns to its original location.

▶ Slip the video back to its original location to match the audio.

4 In the A1 track, Control-click the red out-of-sync indicator and choose "Slip into Sync" from the shortcut menu. Make sure you click the red out-of-sync indicator and not the clip itself. Play the clip again.

Now the audio tracks have been slipped so that they match the video, and the red out-of-sync indicators are removed. If you had moved one track of a linked clip, out-of-sync indicators would appear, and you would have the option to move or reposition the tracks back into sync.

TIP Sometimes you may need to purposefully slip a clip's audio out of sync. Rather than stare at the red out-of-sync flags, you can select the tracks and choose Modify > Mark in Sync. The sync flags will be removed.

Lesson Review

1. How can you display a list of markers that are in a sequence?
2. Where can you change the Timeline settings of the active sequence?
3. What two edit points does the Slip tool adjust?
4. What two sets of shortcut keys allow you to adjust edit points one frame at a time?
5. What two edit points does the Roll tool adjust?
6. How do you adjust one track of a linked clip?
7. How many clips are affected when you apply the Slide tool?
8. Is extending two edit points most similar to rolling, slipping, or sliding edit points?
9. What modifier key is essential to reposition a clip in a sequence without overwriting any other material?
10. What does Option-dragging a clip do?
11. If one track of a clip has gotten out of sync with its other tracks, either by being slipped or moved, how do you resync those tracks?

Answers

1. Control-click in the ruler area. The markers appear at the bottom of the shortcut menu.
2. In the Sequence Settings window (Sequence > Settings).
3. The Slip tool adjusts the In and Out points of one clip.
4. The < and > (angle bracket) keys, and the [and] (bracket) keys.
5. The Roll tool adjusts one clip's Out point and the adjacent clip's In point.
6. Toggle off linked selection, or hold down Option before clicking the track.
7. The Slide tool affects three clips.
8. Extending changes an edit point in the same way rolling does.

9. The Option key is used to reposition a clip and move all other clips down in the sequence.

10. Option-dragging creates a copy of a sequence clip and repositions the copy to a different location, leaving the original sequence clip in place.

11. Press Command-Z, or Control-click the red out-of-sync indicators on the tracks you want to adjust and choose either "Slip into Sync" or "Move into Sync."

Keyboard Shortcuts

S	Selects the Slip tool
R	Selects the Roll tool
SS	Selects the Slide tool
E	Extends selected edit points to the playhead location
Drag then Option	Inserts a clip in a new location
\ (backslash)	Plays around the current playhead location
Option-drag	Drags a copy of a clip to a new sequence location
Option-Q	Opens the User Preferences window
[(left bracket) or < (left angle bracket)	Moves the selected edit point or points left in single-frame increments
] (right bracket) or > (right angle bracket)	Moves the selected edit point or points right in single-frame increments
Shift-[or < (left angle bracket)	Moves the selected edit point or points backward the length of the multi-frame duration
Shift-] or > (right angle bracket)	Moves the selected edit point or points forward the length of the multi-frame duration

6

Lesson Files   Lesson 6 Project

Media   Monk and SeaWorld folders

Time   This lesson takes approximately 90 minutes to complete.

Goals   Create subclips

Create subclips using markers

Use markers to sync clips

Change poster frames

Create a storyboard

Replace edits

Edit Multicam

Lesson 6
Refining the Editing Process

The tools you've learned in the previous two lessons helped you trim and refine individual clips or edit points in your sequence. In this lesson, you will learn new ways to organize and refine your overall editing workflow. A workflow is simply a process that develops based on the kind of editing you typically do. Sometimes workflows are influenced by a particular format or the genre you're editing, and sometimes by your hardware configuration. As you continue to develop your skills in Final Cut Pro, your workflow will evolve as you integrate different editing options into your own process.

In this lesson, you will learn new editing options to improve your workflow, including taking one clip and making mini-clips, or *subclips*, from it; using markers to synchronize action; using clips to create storyboards; organizing and editing material shot with multiple cameras; and working with a third type of edit, the replace edit. As you begin to incorporate these strategies and procedures into your workflow, you will add power to your editing sessions.

Preparing the Project

Because this lesson is about different approaches to the editing process, let's open the project in a different way: by double-clicking a Final Cut Pro project file.

1   On your desktop, open a Finder window and navigate to the Lessons folder. To open the **Lesson 6 Project** project file and launch Final Cut Pro at the same time, double-click this project file.

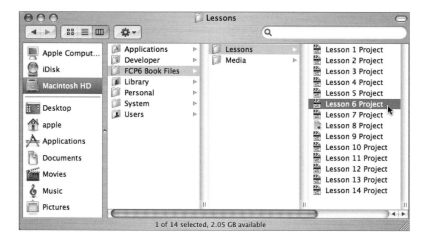

2   In the Browser, look at the contents of the bins.

For this lesson, you will work with both *Monk* and "Believe" footage. All the "Believe" audio and video clips you need for this lesson are in the one bin. The Marked Clips bin will be used for storyboard editing.

3   Click the different sequence tabs in the Timeline.

There are four sequences in the Timeline that are in different states of completion. During this lesson, you will finish these sequences using new methods of editing.

4   If it's not already selected, click the *News Story* sequence tab and play this sequence.

This sequence was created using the storyboard editing process. You will use this process later in this lesson to create a similar sequence.

There are a variety of "Believe" clips in this sequence that you've edited in previous lessons. In this sequence, each clip is cut to a series of beats in the music track. Just as you can integrate different editing techniques into your process, you can combine project elements to create several products for output. With the addition of a news reporter's voice-over, this sequence can be used as a news story.

5   Position the playhead between the sixth and seventh clips in the sequence, **J rises and dives** and **trainer on belly**. Zoom into this location and play these two clips.

You may recognize the content of these two clips as you view them in the Canvas. But when you look at the clips in the Timeline, you won't recognize their names because they are new. These are subclips created from the original master clip, **J and L circle**. You will create subclips in the next exercise.

6   Press Shift-Z to see the entire sequence.

Creating Subclips

When you capture source material, you determine the duration of each clip. You might start and stop your tape and capture several short clips, or specific actions within different clips. Or you might let the tape run and capture a longer clip with several actions. You may even capture an entire tape as a single clip. There are many capturing workflows you can choose to adopt, and each has its own advantages that you will learn more about in Lesson 8.

If you do choose to capture long clips, or the entire tape as one clip, it might become challenging to locate specific actions during the editing process. For example, let's say you're looking for the shot of the trainer riding on the whale's belly. Every time you want to view or edit that action, you first have to find it among all the other actions in the long clip.

Instead, you can create a shorter *subclip* of that one action. When you make a subclip, you create a new clip that stands on its own, has its own unique name, such as *trainer on belly*, and can be accessed directly, as though you originally captured that action as a shorter, separate clip.

> **MORE INFO ▶** When you create a subclip, it becomes its own master clip. In the next lesson, you will learn more about working and editing with master clips.

1   In the Believe Clips bin in the Browser, double-click the **J and L circle** clip to open it in the Viewer. Drag the playhead through this clip to review it.

    The duration of this clip is 1:22:10. During that time, you see the whales perform several behaviors. By breaking this clip into subclips, you can have direct access to each behavior.

    To create a subclip, you mark In and Out points identifying the portion of the clip you want to stand alone. Keep in mind that you're using these marks to create a new clip; you're not setting marks to edit tight around an action. You have to mark a bigger, or *fatter*, portion to create the clip in order to allow for trimming and refining during the editing process.

2   Play toward the end of the **J and L circle** clip and set an In point at about 15:06:00, just before Julie begins to ride on the whale's belly. Set an Out point at the end of the clip. Note the duration of the marked portion.

    Even though you could edit this clip without an Out point, you can't create a subclip without setting both an In and an Out point in the clip.

3   Choose Modify > Make Subclip, or press Command-U.

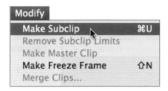

The Browser window becomes active, and a new icon appears under the original clip in the Believe Clips bin. The subclip icon has jagged edges, as if it had been torn or cut from the original clip. It also shares the original clip's name for the moment, but the text box is highlighted, awaiting a name change.

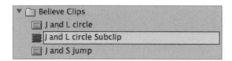

NOTE ▶ If the Make Subclip item is not available in the Modify menu, make sure the Viewer window is active and that you have marked both an In and an Out point in the clip.

4   Rename the subclip *trainer on belly*, and press Return.

When you press Return, this clip is sorted alphabetically among the other clips in this bin.

5   Double-click the new **trainer on belly** clip to open it in the Viewer. Press the End key, then press the Home key to see where this clip stops and starts. Play the clip.

The end-of-clip filmstrips indicate where the media limits are for this subclip, and the Viewer Timecode Duration field displays the distance between the In and Out points you used to create the subclip. With additional material outside the primary action, you can mark a subclip and edit it just like any other clip.

Let's create another subclip in which the whale propels Julie out of the water as she holds on to the whale's rostrum (nose).

6   From the Browser, open the **J and L circle** clip again, and set an In point around 14:41:00. Set an Out point around 14:51:00, about a 10-second duration.

NOTE ▸ You may wonder why the duration reads 10:01 for what appears to be a 10-second duration. When timecode runs at 30 frames per second, 1 second is measured from 00 to 29. When you mark on the next frame, 00, it is one frame beyond an even second.

7   Choose Modify > Make Subclip, or press Command-U. In the Browser, enter *J propelled up* as the new subclip name.

Again, the new subclip is sorted alphabetically with the other clips in this bin.

To contain or organize subclips to stay with their original master clip, you can place them into their own bin.

8 Control-click the Believe Clips bin and choose New Bin from the shortcut menu. Name the new bin *J and L circle SUBCLIPS*.

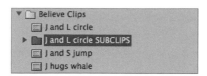

9 Drag the original **J and L circle** clip, and the new **J propelled up** and **trainer on belly** subclips, into the bin. Then display the contents of this bin.

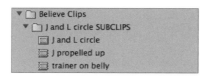

Now any new subclips you create from the **J and L circle** master clip will be placed in this bin.

TIP ▶ After you edit a subclip into a sequence, you cannot lengthen the subclip. You can, however, remove the subclip restrictions you placed on it by selecting the sequence clip and choosing Modify > Remove Subclip Limits. This reverts the clip back to the original master clip length but retains the subclip name.

Project Tasks

There are three more behaviors in the **J and L circle** master clip that may need their own subclips. Find the following actions of Julie, Leslie, and the whales. Mark them, create subclips of them, and rename them as follows:

▶ 14:29:00   *J rises and dives*

▶ 14:52:00   *J push thru water*

▶ 14:02:00   *J and L in circle*

NOTE ▶ It's OK if one subclip overlaps another. Each subclip can be made of any portion of the original master clip.

Adding Markers to Clips

Utilizing markers in a project doesn't stop at identifying a beat of music in the Timeline. You can add markers directly to a clip in the Viewer, which opens up a world of other editing possibilities that will help make your workflow more efficient. There are two specific ways you will use clip markers in these exercises: to create subclips and to align action between two clips.

Converting Markers to Subclips

Just as you do in the Timeline, you can add markers to the clips themselves to denote the location of a particular action. You can then use the clip marker to create a subclip of that action. Unlike the previous exercise, you can convert markers to subclips without setting In and Out points. In fact, you can even add several markers to a clip during your initial capture process, so the clips will come into the Browser with markers already attached and ready to become subclips, which can be a big timesaver.

> **MORE INFO** ▶ In Lesson 8, you'll learn how to add markers to clips during the capture process.

1 Open the **J and L circle** clip into the Viewer. Press Option-X to remove the In and Out marks.

   Since you're familiar with where the whale behaviors are in this clip, you will go through and set markers at these actions. You set markers on a clip in the Viewer just as you did in the Timeline. You also name markers in the same way, by accessing the Edit Marker window.

2 Park the playhead where the first trainer starts to rise out of the water at 13:57:00. Press M to create a marker, and press M again to open the Edit Marker window. Name this marker *J and L in circle*, and click OK.

Unlike the Canvas and Timeline markers, which are green and mark a location in the sequence, the Viewer marker is yellow when the playhead is over it. When you move the playhead away, the Viewer marker is pink.

NOTE ▸ You can apply the same shortcuts you used to delete sequence markers to delete or go to clip markers in the Viewer. Press Command-` (grave) to delete the marker at the playhead location; press Control-` to delete all markers in the clip.

3   In the Browser, click the disclosure triangle next to the **J and L circle** clip.

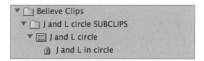

When you add a marker to a clip (or a subclip) in the Viewer, it is attached to the clip and appears as an entry in the Browser. You can rename or delete a marker in the Browser just as you do a clip or sequence. Let's continue adding markers to this clip.

4   Add markers to the following locations in this clip and name each marker as follows:

    ▶   14:29:00   *J rises and dives*

    ▶   14:41:00   *J propelled up*

    ▶   14:52:00   *J push thru water*

    ▶   15:05:00   *trainer on belly*

NOTE ▸ These timecode numbers include additional pad, or handles, before the action you want to use in editing.

You should now have five markers in the Viewer scrubber bar. Each marker represents a start point for a portion of this longer clip.

In the Browser, the five markers are attached to this clip.

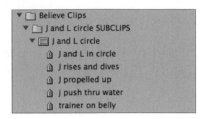

5   In the Browser, double-click the *J and L in circle* marker and play it in the Viewer.

Unlike a subclip that has a specific Out point, this clip begins at the marker location and continues to the next marker in this clip. If the clip had no other markers, it would continue to the end of the clip.

Before you convert these markers into subclips, let's create a new bin to organize them.

6   Control-click the Believe Clips bin and choose New Bin from the shortcut menu. Name this bin *Markers to Subclips*. Drag the **J and L circle** clip into this bin and reveal the bin contents and the markers in the clip.

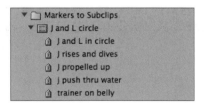

Now when you create subclips from the markers in this clip, they will appear in this bin, as they did when you organized subclips in the previous exercise.

First, let's work with just one marker.

7   Select the *J and L in circle* marker in the Markers to Subclips bin, then choose Modify > Make Subclip.

A new subclip has been created using the marker name followed by the master clip name as a reference.

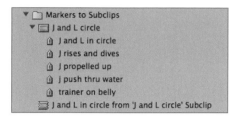

TIP ▸ If you can't see the full name of the new subclip, move the pointer between the Name and Duration column heads. When you see the Resize pointer, drag right.

8   To shorten this subclip name, click its name area and delete *from 'J and L circle' Subclip*. Double-click this new subclip to open it in the Viewer. Play the clip.

This subclip looks the same as the marker clip you opened and viewed.

TIP ▸ You can also use the Edit Marker window to enter a duration for a marker. When you convert a marker that contains a duration into a subclip, the subclip will be the length of the marker duration.

The real power and beauty of converting markers to subclips is that you can convert a group of markers into subclips at one time.

9   Select the other markers in the Markers to Subclips bin, and choose Modify > Make Subclip.

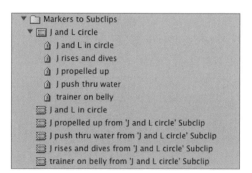

The selected markers are converted to subclips in one command.

NOTE ▶ Some editors prefer to leave the master clip name attached to a subclip as a reference. There are other ways to find a subclip's originating master, which you will learn in Lesson 7. For now, you can remove the master clip reference from these subclips.

Using Markers to Align Actions

There is real power in using markers to edit. Another example of how you can incorporate markers in the editing process is to sync action points between two clips in a sequence. When attached to a clip, a marker will always mark the same frame on that clip no matter where the clip is positioned in the sequence. To use a marker to sync action, you align a clip marker to a sequence marker, or align one clip marker to another clip marker. In the following steps, you will align a trainer's action to a beat of music. But you could also plan an entire sequence around matching actions with music beats or narration cues.

1 Click the *Sync with Markers* sequence tab in the Timeline and play the **Track 8_guitar.aif** clip.

   There is a nice guitar strum in this music track where you could line up or sync a specific whale or trainer activity on the V1 track.

2 Play the **Track 8_guitar.aif** clip from the beginning and stop when you hear the guitar strum, around 1:00:06:00. Click the clip to select it, and press M to set a marker at this location.

With a clip selected in the Timeline, the marker is placed at the playhead location on the selected clip.

3   Drag this clip to the right, then back to the beginning of the sequence. Then deselect it.

When you reposition this clip, the marker moves with it, continuing to reference that guitar strum no matter where the clip is positioned in the sequence. When the clip is deselected, you see a pink marker, as you did in the Viewer.

4   From the Believe Clips bin, open the **J hugs whale** clip. In the Viewer, create a marker at 15:20, where Julie places her hand on the whale's chest. Name this marker *hand on chest*.

This would be a nice action to sync to the guitar strum in the music track. Rather than edit at the marker, let's set an In point earlier on this clip.

5   In the Viewer, press Shift-Left Arrow four times to move the playhead back 4 seconds and press I to set an In point.

Since this clip has music on its audio tracks, you will need to disconnect the a1 and a2 source controls to edit just the video.

6   In the Timeline, disconnect the a1 and a2 source controls, and position the playhead at the head of the sequence. Edit the clip as an overwrite edit.

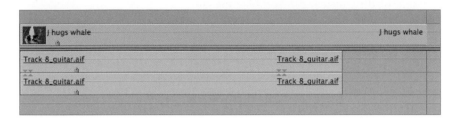

TIP ▶ Make sure snapping is on before you perform the next step.

7   To sync the marker in the **J hugs whale** clip with the marker in the music track, click and hold your pointer directly above the marker in the **J hugs whale** clip, but don't move the clip just yet.

Dragging a clip from a marker makes that marker the active sync point when you snap it to other markers in the Timeline.

8   Drag this clip from its marker over the marker in the music track, and when the markers snap to each other, release the clip.

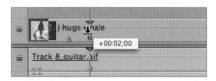

With snapping turned on, the brown snapping arrows appear when you align the markers to each other.

NOTE ▶ You can also snap a clip marker to a sequence marker in the ruler area of the Timeline in the same way.

9   To fit the **J hugs whale** clip to this music track, drag the In point to the left to the beginning of the sequence. Drag the Out point to snap to the end of the music sequence. Play the clip.

Now Julie's hand touches the whale's chest exactly when you hear the guitar strum.

You can also use other editing tools to snap markers to markers. For example, let's say a clip is the correct length, as this one is. If you want to change the clip content in any way, you would have to slip it. Instead of moving the clip by the marker, you can use the Slip tool and slip the marker to a music cue.

10   Move the playhead to 1:00:14:09 and press S to select the Slip tool. Place the Slip tool directly above the *J hugs whale* marker and drag right to snap the marker to the playhead. Play the clip.

NOTE ▸ The trainer touches the whale's chest two times in similar fashion in this clip. With this new adjustment, you will see an earlier touch as well.

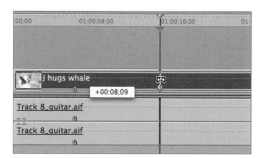

Slipping the video marker to the next music cue gives you another option for this clip. It also allows you to cover the camera bobble toward the end of the clip.

TIP ▶ Since markers are such a powerful editing tool, and they're so easy to create, incorporate them into your workflow frequently to help refine your editing process.

Storyboard Editing

Storyboards are used to explain the flow of a story with pictures or drawings. For example, to explain how a scene will look when it's cut together, an artist sketches intended camera shots and places them side by side as individual frames. This allows the director to imagine more clearly what the film will look like or anticipate problems that may arise during the shoot.

The task of a video editor is no less demanding. To help visualize clip placement in a sequence, you can create your own storyboard in Final Cut Pro using clips in icon view as the visual reference. Storyboard editing is a great tool for certain editing situations. For example, you may know what sound bites you want to use in an interview, but are not sure in what order you want them. Or you may be editing a montage of different whale actions, but want to experiment with the arrangement or order of those shots.

Although storyboard editing is quite simple and requires only a few steps, you must do a little preparation beforehand. For example, you need to arrange clips in a bin using the icon view and change the representative frame for a clip. In its simplest use, you can use storyboard editing to lay out or arrange a group of clips to bring into a sequence into a particular order. Later, you can trim and refine the clips into shape. But you can also take a few extra steps to use the process for a different purpose, such as editing clips to a music track.

1   In the Timeline, click the *Storyboard* sequence tab and play the music track. Then deselect the a1 and a2 source controls, since you will only be editing video.

In this exercise, some of the preparation has been done for you. For example, in order to edit one clip to every four beats of music, clips were selected and marked with a 3:23 duration, the length of one measure of music at the current tempo.

2   In the Browser, close all open bins and double-click the Marked Clips bin to open it as a separate window. Look at the Duration column next to the Name column.

These clips have been marked with the same duration. To use these clips for storyboard editing, you will need to change the bin view to an icon view.

3   Control-click under the Name column and choose "View as Large Icons" from the shortcut menu.

If the bin window is small, you can't see all the clips. Let's make the window larger to accommodate the clip icons and rearrange the clips to fill the window.

4   Drag the lower-right corner of this bin down and to the right. (It's OK if the bin covers other interface windows.) Control-click in the gray bin area and choose Arrange > by Name from the shortcut menu.

Whenever you resize a bin window, you can arrange the clips to fit into that window size.

NOTE ▶ You will recognize a few subclips as part of this group. When you create subclips, you can work with them individually and they can stand alone in this type of layout.

Notice the clip icons associated with each clip. The frame you see representing the clip is called a *poster frame*, just as a movie poster is a visual representation of a film. In some cases, such as the **jump at stage** clip, the poster frame does not represent the clip content as well as it could. You can choose any frame within this clip to use as its poster frame.

NOTE ▶ The default poster frame is the first captured frame of a clip, unless you've marked an In point, in which case that frame becomes the poster frame.

5   Double-click the **jump at stage** clip to open it in the Viewer. In the Viewer, position the playhead when you see the whale in midair. Choose Mark > Set Poster Frame, or press Control-P.

In the Marked Clips bin, the new poster frame for this clip makes it easier to identify in this view.

TIP ▶ You can also use the Scrub tool in the Tool palette (HH) to scrub through a clip in icon view. To set a poster frame with the Scrub tool, locate the frame, press the Control key, release the clip, then release Control.

To use this group of clips to create a storyboard, you must first arrange them in the order you want them to appear in the sequence. Where you position the images in the bin will determine how they eventually line up in the Timeline sequence. Final Cut Pro starts with the first clip at the upper-left corner of the bin and reads across the line. It then drops down to the next row, and so on, like reading a book.

For this exercise, to achieve a specific result, you will arrange the clips according to the following lists. To arrange the clips, you simply drag a clip into position, and when necessary, drag other clips out of the area.

6   Place these clips on the first row of the bin in this order:

▶ **sham slam**

▶ **_SA_favorite behavior**

▶ **performance_S spray jump**

▶ **_MM_with trainers**

▶ **jump at stage**

▶ **J rises and dives**

7   Place these clips on the second row of the bin:

▶ **trainer on belly**

▶ **K jumps off whale**

▶ **S show open**

▶ **performance_2 whales jump**

▶ **whale nods head**

Placing the clips in rows is part of what determines their order in the sequence. The other factor is their height within the row.

8 Place each clip a bit lower than the previous one so that the rows slant slightly down from left to right, as in the following image.

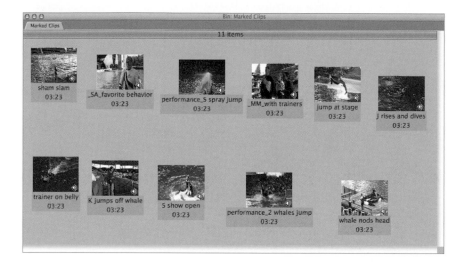

Higher clips, even though they are on the same row, will always go first when you edit the group to the Timeline. Higher-to-lower order overrides left-to-right order.

9 In the Marked Clips bin, press Command-A to select all the video clips.

NOTE ▶ For the next step, you may need to position the Marked Clips bin so that you can also see the Timeline window.

10 Drag the selected clip icons down into the Timeline and snap it to the head of the sequence. When you see the downward overwrite arrow, release the mouse. Play the sequence.

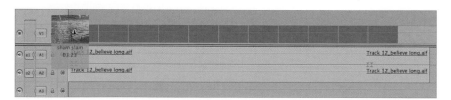

NOTE ▶ Depending on the size of your Timeline, you may not see all of the clips in the window. If you don't, continue with the edit and then press Shift-Z to bring the sequence into full view.

All the clips are positioned in the Timeline just as they were in the Storyboard bin. Only the marked portions are edited.

With the storyboard edit complete, you can refine and finesse the placement of these clips by using your editing tools and markers. For example, there is an orphan beat of music in the middle of the sequence that needs attention, and the end of the sequence needs adjusting as well.

11 Press RR to select the Ripple tool. Click the Out point of the **_MM_with trainers** clip and snap it to the marker to the right of it. Then press A to return to the default Selection tool.

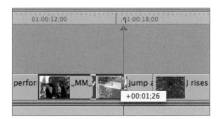

Now the remaining clips also hit on the strong music beat.

You can finesse the end of the sequence in several ways. First, the video clip has to cover the remaining music track. Then you can determine where you want to see the whale lift its tail.

12 Drag the Out point of the **whale nods head** clip to extend it to the end of the music track. To finesse this clip further, slip the "whale's tail up" frame over the music cutoff.

Project Tasks

At the moment, these music and video clips serve as a *promo*, short for promotional material. Promos are used to tease and excite the viewer into watching the entire show. By adding a news reporter's voice-over to this promo, you could repurpose it as a news story, like the one you screened at the beginning of this lesson.

1   From the Believe Clips bin, open the **news voice over** clip and mark an In and Out around the reporter's track.

Like the narration clips, the audio for this clip appears only on the Mono (a1) track.

2   In the Timeline, patch the a1 source control to the A3 track, and make sure the a2 source control is disconnected. Move the playhead to the head of the sequence and click the Overwrite button.

3   Mix the volume levels of the audio tracks so you can clearly hear the reporter's voice above the music.

MORE INFO ▶ In Lesson 10, you will learn about mixing different audio tracks and adding fades for smoother audio transitions.

Replacing Edits

After you've arranged clips in a sequence, either by editing them individually or as a group using the storyboard process, you can replace individual clips by using the replace edit function. This function is very helpful when you're at the stage of your editing process when you like the length and position of each clip in your sequence but want to swap out one clip for another using the original clip's length and location as a reference.

Unlike the overwrite and insert edit functions, the replace edit function does not rely on In and Out points, either in the new clip or in the sequence. It relies solely on the location of the playhead in both the Viewer and the Timeline.

1   In the Timeline, click the *News Story* sequence tab.

This is the sequence you screened at the beginning of the lesson. It is the completed storyboard exercise and includes the news reporter's voice-over.

2   Move the playhead to the first frame of the sixth clip, **J rises and dives**. Zoom into this clip.

Unlike other types of edits where you mark In and Out points in the sequence, here you don't have to use In or Out points to identify clip duration. Identifying the clip with the playhead and using the replace edit function saves these steps for you. Since the clip has a specific length, only that portion of the sequence will be affected.

3   From the Believe Clips bin, open the **performance_costume change** clip, and play it. Scrub through the clip to where all four trainers are lined up and putting on costumes, around 18:33:15.

You will begin using this clip from the playhead location. Remember, with replace edits, you just use the playhead; you don't use In or Out points.

4   Since you want to edit only video, make sure both the a1 and a2 source controls are disconnected. Drag the source clip from the Viewer to the Canvas and into the blue Replace section in the Edit Overlay. Release the mouse, and play the edit.

The entire video portion of the Timeline sequence clip is replaced by source content starting at the Viewer playhead position. In this case, the frame at the Viewer playhead is lined up and edited at the Timeline play-head position.

Let's change where you place this clip, by changing the Timeline playhead to the last frame of the sequence clip.

5   In the Timeline, position the playhead on the last frame of the new **performance_costume change** clip. (Look for the lower-right last-frame overlay in the Canvas.) With the Viewer playhead still on the same frame of the trainers in a line, drag the Viewer image to the Canvas and release it as a replace edit. Play the clip in the Timeline.

Now the Viewer playhead frame (depicting the trainers in a line) is positioned as the last frame in the sequence clip, which is where the Timeline
playhead was located. In this case, rather than replacing from the first
frame forward, the sequence clip is replaced from the last frame backward
to fill the existing clip duration. This is another way to backtime a clip
into position.

If you wanted the action of the trainers to appear in the middle of
the sequence clip, you could position the Timeline playhead at that
location.

6   In the Timeline, position the playhead in the middle of the **performance_
    costume change** clip. In the Viewer, leave the playhead on the current
    frame of the trainers in a line. This time, click the blue Replace button.
    Play the clip in the sequence.

    TIP ▶ If you don't like the edit you made, you can press Command-Z
    to undo the edit, and then readjust your playhead positions and perform
    another replace edit.

    Wherever you want the Viewer frame to be located is where you place the
    Timeline playhead. Let's replace another clip.

7   From the Believe Clips bin, open the **S gives pendant** clip. Move the play-
    head to the beginning of the zoom-out, around 22:05:20.

8   In the Timeline, move the playhead to the first frame of the next clip, **trainer on belly.** Click the Replace button, or press the shortcut key, F11, and play the clip.

In this location, the zoom-out starts at the head of the sequence clip, but it doesn't finish before you cut to another clip. What if you wanted to end the sequence clip where the zoom out ends?

9   In the Timeline, move the playhead to the last frame of the **S gives pendant** clip. Remember to look for the last-frame overlay in the Canvas.

This is where you want the zoom-out to end. This is another example of backtiming a clip using the replace function. The two playheads line up and fill in whatever material is needed back to the In point.

10   In the Viewer, move the playhead to where the zoom-out ends, around 22:13:14. Press F11, and play the clip in the Timeline.

11   Press Command-S to save project changes.

NOTE ▶ If you try to replace the sequence clip with a shorter source clip, or position the playhead in the Viewer too close to the head or tail of the clip, a message will appear saying "Insufficient content for edit."

Using Multicamera Editing

If your production includes the use of multiple cameras shooting the same event, you can utilize Final Cut Pro's *multiclip* feature. Whether you shoot with 2 cameras or 20, this feature allows you to group or sync together all the individual source tapes that recorded an event. Then you can edit a sequence in real time, as if you were cutting it live in a sports production truck or television control room. Several types of productions use this function, including sitcoms, soap operas, reality television, music concerts, and sporting events. Even dramatic television shows, such as *Monk*, shoot some scenes rolling A and B cameras at the same time. With a little creative planning, anyone with a few cameras shooting an event can use this feature as well.

> **NOTE** ▶ With Final Cut Pro's multiclip approach to grouping clips, you can sync and play any set of clips at one time. The material does not have to share the same timecode, be in the same format, or even be shot at the same time or location.

Organizing a Multicamera Editing Workflow

There are really just three stages to working with multicam footage in Final Cut Pro: creating the multiclip, organizing or modifying it, and then editing it. Before you begin, however, there are some important things to consider while shooting and capturing a multicam project that can make this editing process go smoother:

▶ If the production budget allows, add a timecode generator to send the same timecode to each camera or recording device. You can use the timecode as a reference to organize the sources.

▶ If a timecode generator is not an option, record a visual or sound cue, such as a clapboard, an audio pop, or a camera flash before the action begins, or after it ends, to help synchronize the sources.

▶ Assign each camera a number or letter that identifies that camera angle, such as A, B, C, or 1, 2, 3.

▶ Enter the camera angle number or letter during the log and capture process. While this is not a critical step, it can save time organizing the clips during editing.

Creating a Multiclip

When creating a multiclip, you group together a set of clips for the purpose of seeing them play at the same time. Before you actually group the individual clips into a single multiclip, you have to know how you will synchronize the sources. If you recorded the same timecode to all sources, you can skip a few steps and proceed to actually making the multiclip. If you recorded an audio pop, clapboard, flash, or other audiovisual cue, you first have to set an In or Out point at that precise sync reference. If no reference was intentionally recorded, you can still create a multiclip by finding and marking the same cue, dialogue line, or visual reference in all clips.

You can group up to 128 sources or angles into one multiclip and view up to 16 cameras at one time. For this exercise, you will create a multiclip using two clips from the *Monk* footage you've worked with in earlier lessons. These clips do not share the same timecode, but there is a clapboard (slate) at the head of each clip where you can set an In point.

1   In the Browser, close the Believe Clips bin, and open the Monk Clips bin. Double-click the **B6_scn2C_tk2** clip and play the beginning of the clip.

     In this scene, the B camera was focused entirely on Mr. Monk. There is a clapboard/slate at the head of the clip. You will use the visual of the clapboard closing as your sync reference.

2   Find the first frame where the clapboard has completely closed, at 00:00:00:12, and move the playhead back one frame. Mark an In point at this location.

3   Open the **A6_scn2C_tk2** clip. Play the beginning of this clip and listen to the off-camera dialogue between the two actors.

You can hear the same off-camera dialogue on both clips. While the B camera was shooting Mr. Monk, the A camera was shooting Dr. Kroger throughout the scene. Notice that the names of these two clips are identical except for the *A* and *B*, which denote different cameras.

4   To sync this clip at the same clapboard cue, listen for someone off-camera say, "B-mark." Then watch the back of the clapboard for the clapboard to close. Set an In point one frame before it closes, at 00:00:04:01.

TIP ▶ You can also click the Stereo tab to see this frame on the waveform display.

With these two clips marked, Final Cut Pro knows where to start playing them to be in sync.

5   To group these two clips as a multiclip, select them and choose Modify > Make Multiclip. You can also Control-click one of the selected clips and choose Make Multiclip from the shortcut menu.

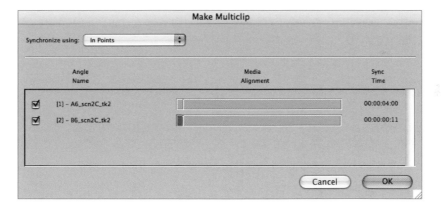

A Make Multiclip window appears, displaying the two clips. If no angle number was entered in the Angle column in the Browser, the clips are placed in alphabetical order, as they are here. The solid blue bars represent the clip content. The gray portion of the bar indicates areas where there is no clip content.

TIP ▶ If you need to group a lot of clips into a multiclip, take the extra step of giving each clip an angle number based on its position in the original shoot. You can enter angle numbers or letters for each clip in the Angle column in the Browser.

6   Click the "Synchronize using" pop-up menu to view the options. You can synchronize these clips by In points, Out points, or Timecode. Choose In Points, which is the default option.

The clips are aligned according to the In points you set on the clapboards. If the clips all had the same timecode, you could skip the steps of marking In points. In that case, you would choose Timecode as the sync option in this window.

TIP ▶ To deselect one of the multiclip angles from the multiclip selection, click the angle check box next to that clip.

7   Click OK.

A multiclip icon appears in the Browser. This icon always represents a group of clips. Notice the name is italicized and begins with the angle 1 clip, **A6_scn2C_tk2**.

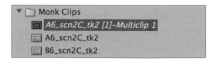

NOTE ► The number following the word *Multiclip* indicates the number of multiclips that have been created in this project as you've been working, not necessarily the number of multiclips currently in the project.

8   Click the name portion of the multiclip. When it becomes highlighted, rename it *Monk*, then press Return.

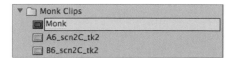

Since the angle and clip name are added automatically, only the name of the multiclip is changed.

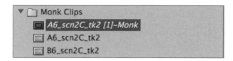

NOTE ► A multiclip can contain any type of clip in the Browser, such as a graphic file or still image. You can also choose a bin and make a multiclip of all the clips in that bin.

Playing and Organizing a Multiclip

Now that you've created a multiclip in the Browser, you can view it, organize it, and arrange your interface to better utilize this process. No matter how many cameras you have in the multiclip group, it's important to organize or modify the multiclip in a way that best represents the original scene or event. That generally means positioning the images in the Viewer to make them appear as though you are watching the scene live. Let's start by playing the multiclip in the Viewer.

1   In the Browser, double-click the **Monk** multiclip to open it in the Viewer.

In the Viewer, both clips are displayed simultaneously according to angle number. You can use all of the play functions and shortcuts in a multiclip that you've used to play other clips.

2   Play the clip from the beginning and watch to see if the clapboards are in sync as you play.

The clips are synchronized according to where you set the In point in each clip.

3   To create a larger Viewer image area, choose Window > Arrange > Two up.

4   Click between the two clips in the Viewer.

By clicking a clip in the Viewer, you are *switching* angles. The selected, or active, angle is highlighted with a blue-green outline.

In the Browser, the angle name and number on the multiclip changes to reflect the active angle, while the name of the multiclip itself, *Monk*, remains constant. The multiclip will reposition itself within the Monk Clips bin according to the current sort order.

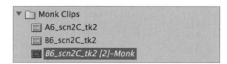

TIP ▶ If at any time you no longer see both multiclip angles in the Viewer, just double-click the multiclip in the Browser to reopen it.

5   In the Viewer, click the View pop-up menu and choose Show Multiclip Overlays.

The multiclip overlay displays each clip's angle number, clip name, and timecode number. It works like other overlays in that you see these only when you scrub through the multiclip, not when you play it.

6   To see Mr. Monk's camera on the left, Command-drag the **B6_scn2C_tk2** clip to the left. Then Command-click it again and drag it back to the right, where he would naturally be if you were watching the scene.

As soon as you begin to drag a clip to a new angle position, the clip in the original angle position moves to allow for the new clip arrangement. When you have a lot of camera angles to organize, you simply Command-drag each clip into whatever position makes the most sense for you.

7   Click the Playhead Sync pop-up menu in the Viewer. Make sure Video + Audio is selected.

When Video + Audio is the active mode, you are switching to the video *and* audio of the clip you select. But when you change the mode to Video, you can switch between just the video sources and take the audio unaltered from one clip. This can reduce audio artifacts, such as pops at the edit points or uneven sound levels between the clips. Since the audio is the same on both of these clips, let's switch the audio to **B6_scn2C_tk2** for the entire scene.

8   Click the **B6_scn2C_tk2** clip. Click the Playhead Sync pop-up menu again, and this time choose Video as the switching mode. Then click the **A6_scn2C_tk2** clip.

The blue-green highlight separates when not in Video + Audio mode. The green highlight stays over the active audio source, and the blue highlight switches to the **A6_scn2C_tk2** clip, indicating it is the active video angle. By leaving the Playhead Sync option on Video, you can switch between just the video of these two clips, and take the audio from just one clip.

Editing a Multiclip

Editing multiclips is a little different from editing single clips. With multiclip editing, you edit the multiclip to the Timeline and *then* make editing choices about when you want to cut to a different angle.

Except for one important difference, editing a multiclip into the Timeline is the same as editing a single clip. You mark your multiclip in the Viewer, position the playhead in the Timeline, and patch the source controls. You can even click the Overwrite or Insert buttons in the Canvas to make the edit. The only difference is that when you manually drag a multiclip to make the edit, either to the Canvas Edit Overlay or directly to the Timeline, you must use the Option key.

1   In the Viewer, play the multiclip from the beginning and set an In point just after you hear the director say, "Action." Then move the playhead toward the end of the multiclip, and set an Out point after Monk says, "That's only twice as much as a normal person."

2   Make sure the **B6_scn2C_tk2** clip is the active audio source and has a green highlight around it. Make sure the **A6_scn2C_tk2** clip is the active video angle.

3   In the Timeline, click the *Monk Multicam* sequence tab. Make sure the playhead is at the beginning of the sequence, and that the video and audio source controls are patched to the V1, A1, and A2 destination tracks.

4   To edit the multiclip into the Timeline, click the red Overwrite button in the Canvas.

   TIP ▶ Hold down the Option key to manually drag the multiclip into the Canvas Edit Overlay or directly into the Timeline.

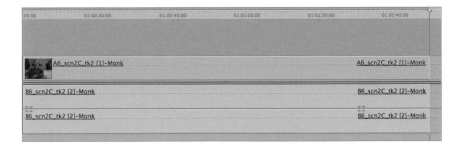

In the Timeline, a stereo audio track appears along with one video track. Multiclips are contained within one video track and two audio tracks in the Timeline. You can see from the names on the different tracks that the audio is from one clip and the video is from another.

5   Play the beginning of the sequence.

When you play the sequence, you see only the active angle, or the top layer, play in the Canvas. To see the other angles play in the Viewer at the same time, you have to change the playhead sync.

NOTE ▶ Although you can double-click the multiclip in the sequence to open it in the Viewer, you still need to perform the following step to see all angles play simultaneously.

6   In the Canvas, click the Playhead Sync pop-up menu and choose Open. (You can also choose View > Playhead Sync Open, or press Shift-Control-O.) Play the multiclip again.

With this option, Final Cut Pro opens the multiclip into the Viewer and keeps it open as you continue editing so you can see all the angles play at once. Notice in the Viewer scrubber bar that the sprocket holes appear as they do when you open a single clip from the Timeline.

7 Without playing the multiclip, click each angle in the Viewer to see it appear in the Canvas.

In the Timeline V1 track, the thumbnail image changes whenever you switch to a different angle, as does the angle name on the clip. However, since the switching mode is set to Video in the Playhead Sync pop-up menu, the audio track doesn't change.

NOTE ▶ In the Timeline, make sure the multiclip is deselected. Anytime the multiclip is selected in the Timeline, many of the multiclip functions are disabled.

Switching from angle to angle is for screening purposes. To change the angle at a certain point in the sequence, you need to cut between angles to create edit points in the multiclip. The way you cut to a different camera, and make a new edit point in the multiclip, is to play the clip and select a different camera *as the multiclip is playing.*

8 In the Timeline, play the sequence, and listen for different cues where you might want to cut from one camera to another.

Just as a director rehearses when to switch between cameras on a production shoot, you will find it helpful to review and rehearse certain edit possibilities, or *cut points,* before actually cutting the scene. For example, the first cut might be after Dr. Kroger says, "I'm very proud of you." The next cut might be after Mr. Monk says, "It's no big deal."

NOTE ► How frequently you cut, or how long you stay with each camera, is a personal choice. Feel free to experiment with your choices in this exercise.

In the next step, you can put on your director's hat and let the footage roll as you cut between the two camera angles in real time. This is often called *cutting on the fly*. To do this, you watch the individual images in the Viewer and click the one you want *when* you want to cut to it. Remember, once you've cut the new edit points, you can also fine-tune them with the Roll tool, as you did in the previous lesson.

9 With the Timeline window active, play from the beginning of the multiclip. After you hear Dr. Kroger say, "I'm very proud of you," click Mr. Monk's clip in the Viewer. Then stop playing and view the edit.

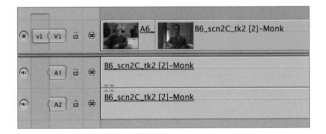

A new clip appears where you cut to the different angle. These clips are still part of the multiclip.

TIP ► To switch to a different angle at this location, place the playhead over the edit and click a different angle in the Viewer.

10 Play the multiclip from this edit point and click each person's image in the Viewer as he begins to speak.

When you click a new angle in the Viewer as the multiclip is playing, you see blue markers appear in the Timeline ruler area at your cut points.

When you stop playing the sequence, these markers become edit points in the multiclip.

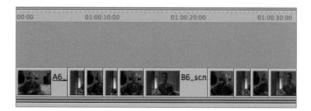

11 Play the new multiclip to see how it looks. If you want to redo the entire take, press Command-Z to remove all the edit points that were created in the most recent take. If you want to adjust one or two of the current edit points, use the Roll tool so the clips will remain in sync.

> **TIP** ▶ If you need to collapse a multiclip into a single clip for output, you can select the clips in the Timeline and choose Modify > Collapse Multiclip(s).

> **MORE INFO** ▶ There are additional ways to switch and cut multiclips that utilize customized keyboards and button bars. You can find these, along with other methods of editing multiclips, in the Final Cut Pro user's manual.

Lesson Review

1. How do you create a subclip?

2. Where can you place a marker?

3. Does snapping affect markers?

4. How do you create a subclip from a marker?

5. What modifier key is used to create a new poster frame?

6. What does the replace edit function do?

7. How should clips be organized in a bin before making a storyboard-type edit?

8. What does it mean when a production is shot multicam?

9. How do you create a multiclip?

10. When creating a multiclip, what are the three ways you can sync clips or angles?

11. What modifier key do you use to modify the arrangement of multiclip angles in the Viewer?

12. What modifier key do you use to drag and drop a multiclip from the Viewer to the Canvas Edit Overlay or directly to the Timeline?

13. What's the difference between switching angles and cutting angles?

14. Can a multiclip in a sequence be collapsed for output as single clips? If so, how?

Answers

1. Set In and Out points in the clip, and choose Modify > Make Subclip.

2. Place markers in the Timeline ruler area or on a selected clip in the Timeline. You can also add markers to a clip in the Viewer.

3. Yes. When snapping is on, you can snap the playhead to markers and snap a clip marker to a sequence marker or other clip marker.

4. Select the marker under the clip in the Browser, and choose Modify > Make Subclip.

5. The Control key is used to create a new poster frame (Control-P).

6. It replaces a sequence clip with a source clip, aligning the two playhead positions.

7. In rows, with each clip in a row appearing slightly lower than the previous clip.

8. Multiple cameras were used to shoot the same action at the same time but from different angles.

9. In the Browser, select the clips you want to include in the multiclip and choose Modify > Make Multiclip, or Control-click a selected clip or bin and choose Make Multiclip from the shortcut menu.

10. In points, Out points, or timecode.

11. The Command key.

12. The Option key.

13. Switching changes the angle you see at the playhead location; cutting makes a new edit point at that location.

14. Yes, you collapse a multiclip by choosing Modify > Collapse Multiclip(s).

Keyboard Shortcuts

Command-U	Makes a subclip
M	Adds a marker
Shift-M	Moves forward to the next marker
Shift–Down Arrow	Moves forward to the next marker
Option-M	Moves backward to the next marker
Shift–Up Arrow	Moves backward to the next marker

Keyboard Shortcuts

Command-` (grave)	When playhead is over the marker, deletes marker in sequence or selected clip
Control-` (grave)	Deletes all markers in sequence or selected clip
Shift-` (grave)	Moves a marker forward to playhead position
Control-P	Resets the poster frame in a clip
Shift-Control-O	With the Multi-camera Editing keyboard layout loaded,changes the Playhead Sync to Open allowing you to see the clips in the Timeline in the Viewer

Supporting the Process

7

Lesson 7
Supporting the Editing Process

As you develop your workflow and editing strategies, Final Cut Pro silently supports you in many ways. Even though much of this support goes on without your knowing it, tapping into the way Final Cut Pro "thinks" can benefit all of your editing projects.

In this lesson, you will go under the hood to learn how Final Cut Pro helps you develop and refine your workflow. You'll learn how to play multiple video formats in one sequence, give clips unique labels, organize and find information in the project, and work with master clips and match frames. You'll also explore ways to reconnect offline media, recall customized layouts or move them to other computer stations, customize the keyboard and button bars, and optimize your user preferences. While these aids don't always affect the look of your finished sequence, they do help you work more effectively.

Reconnecting Media

To start this lesson, you will open the **Lesson 7 Project** file and find that some of the clips in the project are not linked to their media files. Final Cut Pro will always look for a media file in the same location that it was in when you first captured or imported the clip into a project. If a media file has been removed, renamed, or relocated, for example to a different drive, the link back to the clip in the project may be broken, and the clip will go *offline*, meaning it won't play in the project until it's reconnected. When this occurs, Final Cut Pro will ask for your advice on how to proceed.

1   Launch Final Cut Pro by clicking its icon in the Dock. Navigate to the FCP6 Book Files > Lessons folder, and open the **Lesson 7 Project** file.

At some point, a few of the media files for this project were moved to a FireWire drive in order to continue editing at a different computer. They were then moved back to their current location into the Media > Yellow folder. Now Final Cut Pro needs to relink the clips in this project to the media files in their current location.

When Final Cut Pro cannot find the media files that connect to your project clips, three things happen:

▶   An Offline Files window appears, indicating that some files have gone offline. You have the option of reconnecting the files or continuing with them offline. If you select Media Files in the Forget Files section and then click Continue, Final Cut Pro will assume that you don't want to connect the files, and it won't remind you about them in the future.

NOTE ▶ A good time to select the Forget Files option is when you have slimmed down a project by removing some of the unused media files from your hard drive, but haven't yet removed those clips from your project.

▶ In the Browser, the offline clips that do not link back to media files have a red slash over their icons.

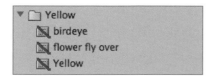

▶ In the Timeline, offline clips appear white with a red and black thumbnail image.

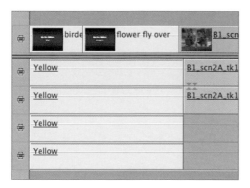

NOTE ▶ When the playhead moves over an offline clip in the Timeline, *Media Offline* appears in the image area of the Canvas along with the clip name.

To view these media files in this lesson, you need to reconnect the clips to the original media files in their current location.

2   In the Offline Files window, click the Reconnect button.

A Reconnect Files window appears. Under the Files To Connect portion of the window, each offline file is listed along with the path to its location before you moved it. If you know where the files are located now, you can select Search Single Location and then navigate to the appropriate location. This will speed up the search, since Final Cut Pro won't have to check all the available hard drives and directories. Leave the Single Search option deselected for now.

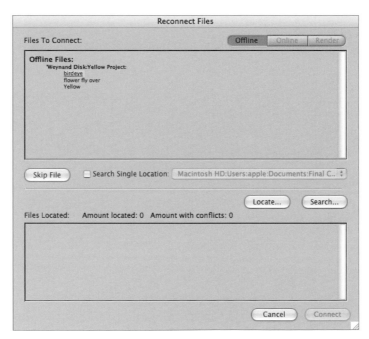

You have two options for finding a missing media file: Locate or Search. Click the Locate button to look for the missing file manually. (Choose this option when the name of the media file has changed, or when you have more than one version of the media file, perhaps in different formats.) Clicking the Search button initiates an automatic search for the file. In this case, since you know exactly where the file is located, you will locate it yourself.

3 Click Locate.

A Reconnect window appears.

4 Navigate to the FCP6 Book Files > Media > Yellow folder. In the Yellow clips column, click the **birdeye** file, and then click Choose.

> **TIP** ▶ If the file you want to relink is dimmed and can't be selected, click the Show pop-up menu in the lower left of the Reconnect window and choose All Files. This will enable you to click any file. Also, you can deselect "Matched Name and Reel Only" if the filename has changed and you'd like to relink to the clip with the new name.

Once found, the clips are listed in the Files Located section along with the file paths to their new locations.

NOTE ▶ If you changed something about your clip—such as reel number, timecode, or number of tracks—a warning will appear. If you are aware of the conflict and know this is the right clip, go ahead and connect to it. When a mismatch does occur, the number of conflicts appears in the lower left of the window and the clip name is italicized.

5   Click Connect.

In the Browser, the red slashes on the offline clips are removed because Final Cut Pro has reconnected these clips to their media files and can play them in the project. In the Timeline, the clip thumbnails are restored, and the Canvas window again displays a frame of the video clip.

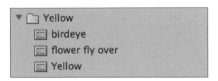

If you change the name of the clip in the Browser, it will still be able to link back to the media file. However, if you rename the media file on the hard drive, you will have to reconnect the project clip.

TIP ▶ To reconnect a clip that is offline, you can also Control-click the clip in the Browser or Timeline and choose Reconnect Media from the shortcut menu.

Playing Multiple Formats

During production, many projects are shot using just one video format, such as HDV, DV, HD, and so on. Other shows may need to incorporate several formats into one project. For example, sports or reality television productions may shoot some of the program in HD and then use DV for smaller *lipstick* cameras, which shoot hard-to-get angles such as the helmet point of view of a skier. Then, they might add older SD (standard definition) material from previous shows that were shot on DigiBeta or Betacam. In this exercise, you will play multiple formats in the same sequence and use two windows to view details about a clip or sequence.

1   In the Timeline, click the *Show Reel* sequence tab and play this sequence.

The *Show Reel* sequence contains footage from three sequences. (Two of the sequences you'll recognize from previous lessons; one is from an upcoming lesson.) Notice the four-track audio clip at the head of the sequence. This was captured from a DigiBeta source tape.

There is one more segment that needs to be added to the *Show Reel* sequence from a fourth set of footage. Let's copy and paste it into this sequence.

NOTE ▸ This is a rough cut of the *Show Reel* sequence. In a later lesson, you will learn to add transitions to move creatively from one segment to the next.

2   Position the playhead at the end of the *Show Reel* sequence. Click the *Commercial_v1_blowup* sequence tab, and press Command-C to copy the marked portion of the sequence.

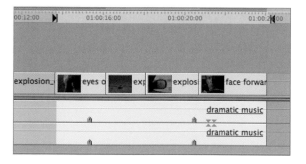

3   Click the *Show Reel* sequence tab, and press Command-V to paste the copied material at the end of the sequence. Then deselect the clips.

Within the *Show Reel* sequence, there are three formats—DVCPRO PAL, HDV, and Apple ProRes 422 —and three frame rates—25, 23.98, and 29.97. Let's take a closer look at the format settings for these clips.

4   In the Timeline, Control-click the **sham slam** clip and from the shortcut menu, choose Item Properties > Format.

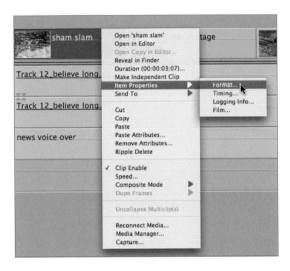

The Item Properties window opens, displaying format information for this clip, including its compressor type, frame or video rate, and frame size (pixel dimensions). From this window, you see this clip was compressed using the HDV 1080i60 format, its video rate is 29.97 frames per second (fps), and its frame size is 1440 x 1080 (pixel and line count, respectively).

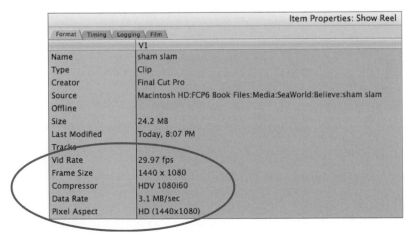

NOTE ▶ In the Item Properties window, the Timing tab displays clip timecode, In and Out locations, and marked duration; the Logging tab contains information that was entered during the capture or editing process; and the Film tab displays film information, if that was the originating format. The keyboard shortcut for opening the Item Properties window is Command-9.

5   To close the Item Properties window, click Cancel. With the *Show Reel* sequence tab active in the Timeline window, choose Sequence > Settings, or press Command-0.

Looking at the QuickTime Video Settings in the lower left of this window, you see the compressor type is HDV 1080i60. Above that, you see the Editing Timebase is 29.97 fps and its frame size is 1440 x 1080. These settings match the clip settings you saw in the Item Properties window.

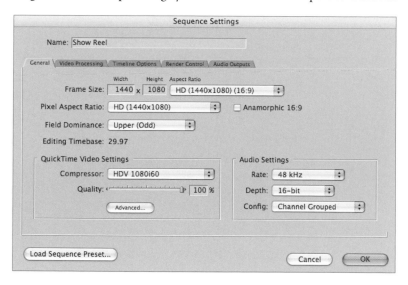

These settings represent the SeaWorld footage, but they don't necessarily represent the other footage in this sequence.

6   Click Cancel to close the Sequence Settings window. In the Timeline, Control-click the first clip, **birdeye**, and from the shortcut menu, choose Item Properties > Format.

This clip is DVCPRO PAL, and its video rate is 25 fps. Its frame size is 720 x 576, smaller than the HD image of the HDV footage. This is why you see black around the image, because it's fitting inside a larger image area.

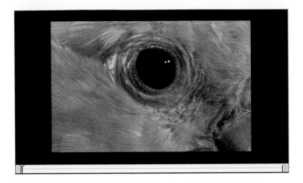

Even though this footage differs from the sequence settings in both frame size and frame rate, Final Cut Pro plays these clips without interruption.

NOTE ▶ You can also Control-click a clip in the Browser to access the Item Properties window for that clip, or choose Edit > Item Properties.

In the previous exercise, you had to reconnect project clips to media files on your hard drive. In the future, if you ever lose track of where a clip is located on your hard drive, just look in the Source line in the Item Properties window.

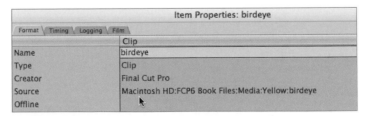

7   Click Cancel to close this window.

To change the settings of an existing sequence, you use the Sequence Settings window. Let's change the current *Show Reel* sequence's starting timecode.

8 Choose Sequence > Settings, and click the Timeline Options tab. In the
Starting Timecode field, enter *2:00:00:00*, for 2 hours. You can also enter
the shortcut *2…* (two period period period).

> **TIP** Every period you add to a timecode or duration entry is read as
> two zeros.

In the Timeline ruler area, notice that the sequence now starts at
2:00:00:00, rather than the default 1:00:00:00. If you had four active
projects and each had its own *Show Reel* sequence, changing the starting
timecode would be a good way to identify or code this sequence.

You can make other changes in this window, such as choosing to see thumbnails on the video tracks and waveforms on the audio clips. These changes
affect the selected or active sequence only. They *will not* affect any new
sequences you create. Those settings are controlled in the Timeline Options
tab of the User Preferences window, which you will work with later in this
lesson.

> **TIP** You can also Control-click a sequence in the Browser and choose
> Settings from the shortcut menu to open the Sequence Settings window.

9 To make the tracks taller in the *Show Reel* sequence, click the Track Size
pop-up menu and choose Medium. Then click OK.

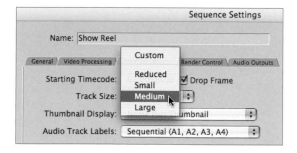

This changes only the tracks in this sequence.

Working with Master Clips

As you delve deeper into Final Cut Pro, you'll find that master clips are the foundation of any Final Cut Pro project, because they provide direct links back to the media files on your hard drive. In an effort to maintain this direct link, Final Cut Pro gives master clip status to a clip when it's the first use of that clip in the project. If you copy and paste that clip from one bin to another, or edit it into a sequence, the copied or edited clip will be an *affiliate* of the master clip, but not a master clip itself.

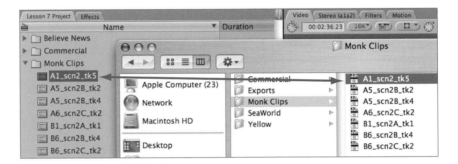

The main purpose of the master clip hierarchy is to *supervise* the naming of the clip. If you rename a master clip, all the affiliates (the other uses of that clip) will be renamed to follow the master clip name. Likewise, if you rename an affiliate, the master clip is changed to give all instances of that clip the same name. This is why making subclips is so valuable.

By creating a subclip, you create a new master clip, and you can change the subclip name without affecting the original master clip name or its affiliates. You can use this master clip naming convention to help track clips in your project. But you can also use it to find or match a frame from the sequence back to its original master clip.

1   In the *Show Reel* sequence in the Timeline, move the playhead to the **sham slam** clip and zoom into this clip. Choose View > Reveal Master Clip, or press Shift-F.

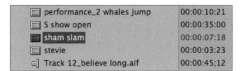

Even though the Believe News bin was closed in the Browser, this function automatically opens the bin where the master clip is located and selects it. This is the clip that was used originally to edit the sequence clip. The sequence clip in the Timeline is an affiliate of this master clip.

2 In the Browser, click in the name area of the **sham slam** clip, and change the name to *whales tails*. In the Timeline, look at this clip in the *Show Reel* sequence, then click the *Believe News* sequence tab and look at the first clip in that sequence.

The clips that were originally named **sham slam** now appear as **whales tails** in both sequences. Whenever you change the name of a master clip, the names of all the affiliate clips throughout the project are also changed.

Once you change a clip name in the project, you can easily change it back to its media file name, even if you don't remember what that was.

3 In the Browser, Control-click the **whales tails** clip, and choose Rename > Clip to Match File Name from the shortcut menu.

The name of the clip is restored, as is its alphabetical position in the bin. (In the same way, you can also change the name of the media file to follow the project clip name. You will learn more about this in Lesson 8.)

NOTE ▶ When you create a subclip, it becomes a master clip because it is the first use of that new clip in the project. If you rename the master clip used to create the subclip, the subclip name will remain unchanged, yet the subclip will still link back to the original master clip media file.

In the previous exercise, you used the Item Properties window to see where a clip was located on your hard drive. Sometimes, it's helpful to go directly to that file location and to see what other files might exist for the project.

4   In the Browser, select the **jump at stage** clip. Choose View > Reveal in Finder.

A Finder window appears on top of the Final Cut Pro interface with the master clip selected. Let's say someone else captured or organized the media files and only imported certain clips. By viewing the files in the Finder window, you can determine whether there are any hidden jewels you can add to your project. You can also use this function to find the master clip that was used to create a subclip.

5   Click in the Browser and select the **trainer on belly** subclip. Choose View > Reveal in Finder. Notice the **J and L circle** clip is selected, then close the Finder window.

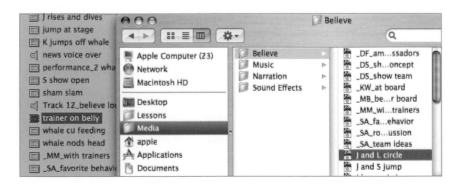

The clip revealed in the Finder window is the **J and L circle** master clip that you used to create this subclip.

The connection back to the media files exists even if there are no master clips in a project. Let's say you copied a sequence from one project to another, but not the clips. Final Cut Pro can easily trace where those original media files are located, and import those as clips into your project so you can continue editing.

6   In the *Show Reel* sequence, position the playhead over the last clip in the sequence, **face forward**. Press Shift-F. When the dialog appears, click OK.

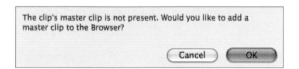

The clip's master clip is not present. Would you like to add a master clip to the Browser?

Cancel   OK

Final Cut Pro imports the master clip into the project. Now you could screen and mark this clip to continue editing.

TIP ▶ To import the master clips for an entire sequence, select the sequence in the Browser and choose Tools > Create Master Clips. A new bin of master clips is imported into the project, which link to the clips in that sequence.

Another time to use master clips is when you want to locate the original frame of a source clip that you used in a sequence clip, or vice versa. This is called finding a *match frame*. For example, you may want to know whether a specific frame from a master clip was used in the edited sequence. You can open the master clip in the Viewer, then ask Final Cut Pro to search for its match in the sequence.

7 In the Timeline, click the *Believe News* sequence tab. From the Browser, open the **whale cu feeding** clip, and move the playhead to the end of the zoom in (about 2:40:56:26). Choose View > Match Frame > Master Clip, or press F.

The playheads in the Timeline and Canvas move to the exact frame that matches the master clip frame in the Viewer.

NOTE ▶ If the frame you identify in the Viewer was not used in the sequence, you will hear a computer beep, and no frame will be displayed in the Canvas.

This matching capability can be very powerful when you want to add back a track of a clip already in the Timeline. For example, in the current *Believe News* sequence, there is no audio for the **K jumps off whale** clip, only video. If you want to add back the sound of Katie screaming "Yes" into the sequence, you first find the clip's matching frame in its master clip.

8 In the Timeline, position the playhead at the first frame of the **K jumps off whale** clip. Press F to search for a matching frame in the master clip.

In the Viewer, the matching master clip appears with In and Out points representing the exact length and content of the video clip. You will use these edit points in the next step to edit the matching length and content of this clip's audio into the sequence at the current playhead position.

9 Patch the a1 and a2 source controls to the A4 and A5 destination tracks. Then disconnect the v1 source control, and click the Overwrite button. Play the clip.

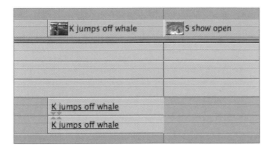

The audio perfectly matches the existing video clip. However, the volume of this clip needs to be lowered.

10 Double-click the A4 track of the **K jumps off whale** clip to load it in the Viewer. Lower the volume level to –20 dB, and play the clip again.

When you double-clicked the audio track, the video was not selected, nor did it open in the Viewer. Although the video and audio match, the clips are not linked because they were edited at different times. You can relink these tracks if you want to maintain their sync throughout the editing process.

11 Select the video track of the **K jumps off whale** clip, and Command-click the audio tracks. Choose Modify > Link.

Now the name of the video clip is underlined, indicating it is linked to the audio clips beneath it.

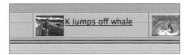

TIP ▶ When you want to find a match frame from the Timeline, the Auto Select controls determine which track you will match. The priority for the Auto Select controls is from V1 up through the total number of video tracks in the sequence, and from A1 down through all the audio tracks. To find a match to tracks other than the V1 track, turn off the Auto Select controls for all tracks leading up to the one you want to match.

Project Tasks

Now that the tracks are patched correctly, take a moment to find and edit the matching audio for the first five clips in the sequence. You can try a different approach to the edit setup. First, position the playhead *anywhere* over the target clip, and press X to mark the clip in the Timeline. Then press F to call up the match frame in the master clip, and click the Overwrite button. Don't forget to adjust the audio volume of each clip so the news reporter's voice-over can be clearly heard.

Logging Information in Browser Columns

In the Item Properties window, you saw that clip information was organized onto different tabs according to topic. You can find this same information in the Browser columns. But unlike the Item Properties window, the Browser columns let you choose how to sort and display the clip information.

Not only can you reposition columns for easier access, you can also hide some columns and show others that are more helpful to you. With more than 65 Browser columns to choose from in the list view, you're sure to quickly and easily find a clip's reel number, scene number, log note, or other information you need to retrieve.

1 In the Browser, close all open bins, and reveal the contents of the Believe News bin. To enlarge the Browser window to see more columns, click the Browser Zoom button.

In the Browser, with the Name column selected, all clips and sequences within a bin are arranged alphabetically, and all bins are arranged alphabetically as well.

The downward arrow on the Name column heading indicates that the column is sorted in ascending order, from A to Z. Also, the Name column is lighter than the other columns, indicating that all the information in the Browser is being sorted by name.

2   To reverse the sort order, click the Name column heading. Then click it again to return to the ascending sort order.

When reversed, the project elements of any column head are sorted in descending order, from high to low, or from Z to A.

You can locate a clip based on specific criteria—such as the type of tracks contained in a clip—simply by re-sorting the information in the Browser by track. For example, let's say you wanted to find just the audio clips in a bin.

3   Click the Tracks column heading.

Now all the clips are organized according to the number and type of tracks contained in each clip. The audio clips are grouped together, and are easy to spot.

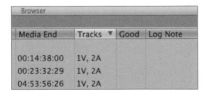

You could also, for example, click the Duration column to sort the clips by length, and find a long clip to place behind the credit roll.

As you edit there may be times when you want to see a note you made about a clip, such as whether it was one of the better clips you captured. You can enter information into certain Browser columns for this purpose.

4 Click the _SA_favorite behavior clip in the Browser. Follow it over to the Good column and click in that column.

When you select a clip in the Browser, the information pertaining to this clip in the other columns turns blue and the clip's row is highlighted with a faint dark bar. This helps you locate the correct line when entering clip information into a field.

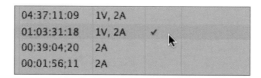

You can log additional information about a clip, for example, by flagging all the clips with a certain subject, during the capture process. If you don't enter information at that stage, you can add it at any time during editing. Let's flag all the clips where we see Steve.

5 On the _SA_favorite behavior clip line, click in the Log Note column. When the text field appears with a blinking cursor, type *steve*.

6   Click the **S show open** clip and Control-click in the Log Note area for that
clip. When you see the shortcut menu, choose steve.

Once you've entered a log note in an editing session, you don't have to
enter it again. You can choose it from the shortcut menu.

It's nice to have these references in the different columns, but not very
helpful if you can't easily see the notes you've made. Although the Name
column is a fixed column, all other columns can be repositioned simply
by dragging the column heading left or right.

7   Drag the Good column to the left and release it just after the Name
column. Then drag the Log Note column and position it to follow the
Good column.

When you drag a column heading, a rectangle appears representing that
column. Adjacent columns shift over to make room for the column you
are moving.

You can also display additional columns that might be helpful at different
stages of editing. For example, if you choose to view bin contents as a list,
you don't have access to clip thumbnails, which are helpful when you first
start working with new material. By adding another column to this view,
you can maintain the list view and see the clip thumbnails at the same time.

8 Control-click the Good column heading. From the shortcut menu, choose Show Thumbnail.

> **NOTE ▶** There are two preset column layouts you can recall at any time: standard columns and logging columns.

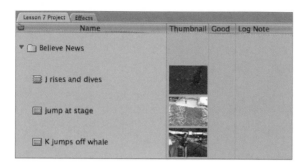

A thumbnail appears next to each clip name. Not only are they a handy visual reference, but you can also scrub through these thumbnails to preview the clip.

> **NOTE ▶** When you add a new column to the Browser layout, it will always appear to the left of the column you Control-click.

9 To scrub through the **jump at stage** clip, drag across the thumbnail image to the right, and then to the left. To reset this clip's poster frame, drag across the thumbnail image to the right until you see the whale in midair, press Control, release the mouse button, and then release the Control key.

If there is a column that you don't feel is useful, you can always hide it to make room for other columns that are more valuable to you.

10 In the Browser columns, Control-click the Label 2 column. From the shortcut menu, choose Hide Column.

That column is removed from the current Browser layout, but it can be retrieved at any time by Control-clicking any column and choosing Show Label 2.

> **NOTE ▶** Later in this lesson, you will learn to save this column layout.

Finding and Labeling Project Items

When you enter clip information into Browser columns, you store this information in the project. But what if you want to find a clip in the Browser or Timeline based on the criteria you entered?

Final Cut Pro's Find function is like that of any other application. Its purpose is to locate clips using names, notes, or various other criteria. The Find function allows you to call up a clip instantly when you want it or when someone else on the production team requests it. You can also color-code your clips and bins to make them easier to identify as you're editing.

1   Press Control-U to return to the Standard window layout. Then close each bin in the Browser to hide its contents.

Closing the bins isn't required for finding items, but it's helpful for demonstrating how the Find function works.

2   Click an empty space in the Browser to deselect everything, then choose Edit > Find, or press Command-F.

A Find window appears in which you can enter the name of the clip or item you want to locate, and the name of the project you want to search.

3   In the Search pop-up menu, choose Project: Lesson 7 Project, if it's not already selected, and in the text field with the blinking cursor enter *sham slam*. Click Find Next, or press Return, to find this clip in this project.

The Believe News bin is automatically opened, and the **sham slam** clip is highlighted.

What if you don't know the clip name but remember entering a log note for it? Previously, you entered log notes for two clips that contained some action with Steve, the whale trainer.

4   Click in the Browser to deselect the **sham slam** clip. Press Command-F to open the Find window again, and type *steve* in the lower-right search field.

5   In the lower left, click the pop-up menu and choose Log Note. Click the Find All button to find all the clips that have *steve* entered as part of their log notes.

A Find Results window opens, listing the clips having the specified criteria, in this case, a log note that includes the word *steve*.

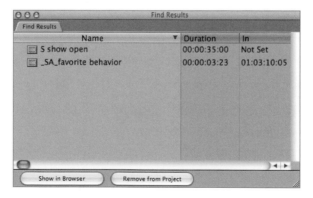

6 Reposition the Find Results window over the Timeline so you can also see the other clips in the Browser. Now press Command-A to select all the clips in the Find Results window.

As soon as you select clips in this window, the same clips are also selected in the Browser window. You can scroll through the Browser to see the other selected clip.

Let's create a new bin for this trainer's clips.

7 In the Browser, press Command-B. Name the new bin *Trainer Clips_Steve*. Drag the two clips from the Find Results window into this new bin.

When you move clips from the Find window to a new bin, you are removing them from their original location—in this case, the Believe News bin.

8 Close the Find Results window.

There is a similar Find function used to search for clips in the Timeline. To access it, the Timeline window must be active. If more than one sequence is open in the Timeline, you also need to choose the sequence you want to search.

9 In the Timeline window, click the *Monk Scene* sequence tab and press Command-F. In the Find in Monk Scene window, enter *B6_scn2B_tk4* in the Find field and click Find All to find all uses of this clip in this sequence.

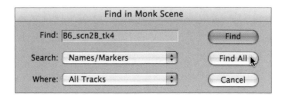

The playhead moves to the first **B6_scn2B_tk4** clip, and highlights the other uses of that clip in the sequence. With these clips selected, you can now modify them as a group, perhaps to adjust their audio levels at the same time, or paste a copied attribute to them, such as an image size or position change. You could even delete them all from the sequence.

Clip names and log notes are useful ways to identify clips. Another way is to use Final Cut Pro labels, which color the clip in the Browser and Timeline. Adding color to your clips and bins is a great way to organize your material because your eye immediately identifies color.

There are two ways to label clips: use the Label column in the Browser, or Control-click the clip icon in the Name column.

10 Press Shift-Command-A to deselect any clips in the Timeline. In the Browser, display the contents of the Monk Scene bin and Control-click the **B6_scn2B_tk4** clip. From the shortcut menu, choose Label > Best Take.

NOTE ▶ You can also select a group of clips and choose a label for the entire group.

In the Timeline, all of the affiliate clips that were edited from this master clip are now labeled with a red highlight over the clip name on each track and the image icon. This provides a quick visual reference to where these clips are in your sequence.

NOTE ▶ In Lesson 12, you will change the size and position of the red-labeled clips to remove the camera from each shot.

11 In the Timeline, click the *Show Reel* sequence tab.

Since there is an affiliate of the **B6_scn2B_tk4** clip in this sequence, it too has the red label.

You can also use a label to organize your material by type.

12 In the Browser, Control-click the Sequences bin and choose Label > B Roll.

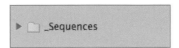

While "B Roll" is not the correct description for this bin, changing the Sequences bin to a different color will make it stand out from the other bins. When you optimize your user preferences later in this lesson, you will learn how to change the descriptions of these labels.

> **TIP** ▶ To remove a label, Control-click the clip or group of selected items and choose Label > None from the shortcut menu. For the moment, leave these labels attached for the next exercise.

Customizing Shortcut Keys and Button Bars

Now that you're getting familiar with Final Cut Pro functions, buttons, and shortcuts, you might ask yourself whether you would redesign the system. Would you give a function another shortcut or use a different modifier key? Would you place a button for a particular function in the Viewer or in the Canvas? You may find there are certain buttons you would like to group together when working with audio, and an entirely different group of buttons you want to use when adding effects.

Although you can't change the actual Final Cut Pro interface, you can change the keyboard shortcuts and add or group together additional buttons to facilitate your personal editing style.

1 To open the keyboard layout map, choose Tools > Keyboard Layout > Customize.

In this window, you see a keyboard with icons on the keys that represent mapped Final Cut Pro functions. To the right of the keyboard is a list of functions or commands organized by menu set and function.

NOTE ▶ The keyboard layout you see represents the computer you are using. A laptop computer, for example, will not display a number pad.

You can access any Final Cut Pro function by pressing a combination of keystrokes. Some keystrokes require one or more modifier keys. The tabs across the top of Keyboard Layout window organize the keyboard short-cuts according to modifier keys—Command, Shift, Option, Control, or a combination of these.

Before you can make changes to this keyboard layout, however, you have to unlock it.

2   In the lower left of this window, click the Lock button to allow changes to the current keyboard layout.

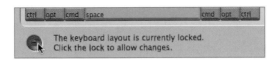

3   In the command list area to the right of the keyboard layout map, drag the blue vertical scroller up and down to see the list of command sets.

The first nine sets contain all the commands in the Final Cut Pro menus. The items that follow are organized by editing function.

4   At the top of the list, click the File Menu disclosure triangle to display the commands in that menu.

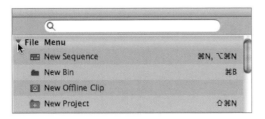

If a command currently has a keyboard shortcut, it is listed to the right of the command. There are a few functions that do not currently have keyboard shortcuts, such as Close Project and Import Folder. Let's create a shortcut for Import Folder.

5   Click the Shift-Command modifier tab in the keyboard layout map.

Since Command-I is the shortcut for Import File, mapping the Import Folder function to the Shift-Command-I key will be easy to remember.

6   Drag the Import Folder name or icon from the command list onto the I key.

The new keyboard shortcut appears on the keyboard layout as well as to the right of the Import Folder command in the command list area. When you choose File from the main menu, you will see the new shortcut appear under File > Import > Folder.

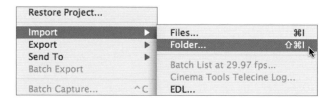

TIP   To reload the default U.S. keyboard layout, choose Tools > Keyboard Layout > Default Layout - U.S.

Although the interface buttons you see in the Viewer and Canvas can't be changed, you can add shortcut buttons to a button bar in the Browser, Viewer, Canvas, and Timeline windows. The Timeline default layout has two buttons; the other windows have only the button tabs with no buttons in between.

Viewer button bar with no buttons

If you edit extensively with your mouse, adding buttons for functions you use frequently can significantly speed up the editing process because you don't have to remember keyboard shortcuts or what menu to choose to access a specific function.

7 Click in the search field at the top of the commands list to open an alphabetized list of commands. In the search field, type *audio*. Scroll through the different audio commands. Then add *scrubbing* to narrow your search to "audio scrubbing."

When you enter a general topic, such as audio, you see numerous commands from which you can choose. When you enter a more specific term, the options decrease.

TIP ▶ After entering a word in the search field, don't press Return. Final Cut Pro will read it as a keystroke and try to search for items that use that keystroke. Also, if you want to return to the main function and command menu, click the X to the right of the search field.

8 Drag the Audio Scrubbing icon into the Viewer window between the two button tabs.

The Audio Scrubbing button is added to the Viewer button bar.

9 Hold the mouse pointer over the new Audio Scrubbing button to reveal the tooltip that identifies it.

10 Use steps 7 and 8 as a guide to add two new buttons in the Browser you can use to create a new bin and a new sequence.

TIP ▶ To remove a button from a window's button bar, Control-click that button and choose Remove > Button, or drag it out of the button bar and release it. Choose Remove > All to remove all the buttons from a window's button bar.

Project Tasks

Now that you know how to customize your button bars, take a moment to think about the functions you've used repeatedly but for which there are no buttons on the interface. Place the new buttons in the window where you will most often use those functions. You can also color code the buttons and group them using spacers.

NOTE ► Before customizing your keyboard layout, keep in mind that the exercises in this book utilize the default Final Cut Pro layout.

1   In the Browser, Control-click the New Bin button and choose Color > Blue from the shortcut menu. Make the New Sequence button green.

2   To add some space between these two buttons, Control-click the button on the left and choose Add Spacer.

You can drag a button from one button bar into another to further customize the button bar layout.

3   When you've finished customizing your button bars, close the Keyboard Layout window.

To prepare for the exercises in Lesson 10, you can create Timeline buttons for the following functions:

►   Show/hide audio level overlays

►   Show/hide waveform display

►   Open the Audio Mixer

TIP ► You can also open the Button List window by choosing Tools > Button List.

Saving and Loading Layouts

You've made many changes to different layouts in this lesson. You've rearranged Browser columns, added buttons to button bars, added new shortcuts to the keyboard layout, and so on. In earlier lessons, you changed window layouts and the layout of Timeline tracks. It would be a real shame if you lost those layouts or moved your project to a different computer and had to customize them all over again.

With a few easy steps, you can save each and every one of the layout decisions you've made and even take your customized layouts with you wherever you edit.

Final Cut Pro organizes saved layouts into individual folders in your Final Cut Pro User Data folder. Although they are organized into separate folders, the way you save each layout is the same.

> **NOTE ▶** Changes you make to Browser or bin columns in a project remain until you change them again or load a previously saved layout. If you create a new project, it will have the default Standard Columns layout.

1   Press Command-H to hide Final Cut Pro. On the desktop, open a Finder window and navigate to Macintosh HD > Users > [User Name] > Library > Preferences > Final Cut Pro User Data.

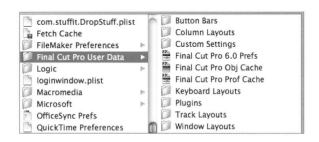

This is where all Final Cut Pro customized layouts, preferences, and even plug-ins for the current user are saved. Although you may not currently see individual folders for each layout category in your computer, when you initiate the Save Layout command, a folder for that category will be created in this location.

NOTE ▶ If another user has been set up on this computer, that user's preferences and layouts will appear when he or she logs in and launches the application.

Let's save some of the layouts you've created in this lesson. Remember, if you found it helpful to change a layout for an editing task on one project, you will probably find it helpful to load and use on another project.

2   In the Dock, click the Final Cut Pro icon to restore the interface. To save the current Browser column layout with the Thumbnail column in view, Control-click any Browser column heading, other than Name, and choose Save Column Layout from the shortcut menu.

A Save window appears with a default layout name and a target save location. In this case, the target is Column Layouts. This folder is created for you automatically in the Final Cut Pro User Data folder specifically to organize bin layouts.

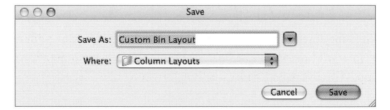

3   In the Save window, rename the layout *thumbnails*, and click Save.

You save window layouts the same way you save column layouts. In Lesson 1 you used the Custom Layout 1 and 2 options to save the "big Viewer" and "big Canvas" layouts. Those options work well when you're editing on one computer. But it doesn't create a backup for you or allow you to use those layouts on a different computer station.

4   Press Shift-U to recall the "big Viewer" window layout. Then choose Window > Arrange > Save Window Layout. In the Save window, name this layout *big Viewer*, and click Save to save it. Repeat the process to save the big Canvas layout.

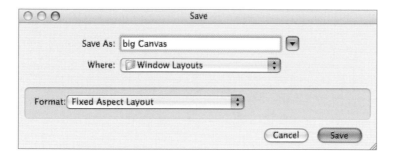

These layouts are saved in the Window Layouts folder.

The Timeline tracks can also be customized to your project's needs. For example, you can minimize or reduce the height of just the audio tracks in your Timeline as you work with your video tracks, or vice versa. In the *Believe News* sequence, enlarging the V1 track will create larger thumbnail images, which might make it easier to identify the clips.

5   In the Timeline, click the *Believe News* sequence tab. Move your pointer over the V1 track boundary line. When you see the Resize pointer, start to drag up. When you get a nice large height you like, release the mouse button.

TIP ▶ Pressing Option as you drag will resize just the video or audio tracks, depending on which track you are dragging. Pressing the Shift key as you drag a track boundary will resize both audio and video tracks to the same customized height.

6 To save this track layout, click the Timeline Layout pop-up. From the pop-up menu, choose Save Track Layout. Name this layout *big video*, and click Save.

This track layout is saved in the Track Layouts folder.

TIP ▶ You can also turn on audio waveforms and audio level overlays and save that as an audio track layout.

7 To save the layout of buttons you recently added to the button bars, Control-click any button bar and choose Save All Button Bars from the shortcut menu. Enter *my buttons* as the layout name and click Save.

This button bar layout is now saved in the Button Bars folder. As you continue to develop and add to the current layouts, you can rename the layouts for specific editing functions, such as screening clips, mixing sound, adding effects, and so on.

TIP ▶ To restore the default button bar layout, Control-click in the Timeline button bar and choose Remove > All / Restore Default from the shortcut menu.

8 To save the keyboard layout, choose Tools > Keyboard Layout > Save Keyboard Layout. Name this layout *my keyboard* and click Save.

This layout is saved in the Keyboard Layouts folder.

Now all the layouts are saved in their appropriate folders in the Final Cut Pro User Data folder. If you change a layout during the course of editing, you can easily recall or load a saved layout.

9 In the Viewer, remove the new button you added by dragging it out of the button bar and releasing it.

As you remove and release a button, you see a puff of smoke, and the button no longer appears in the button bar.

10 To reload the button bar you saved, Control-click any button bar and choose Load All Button Bars from the shortcut menu. In the Choose a File window, select the "my buttons" layout from the Button Bars folder and click Choose.

All the buttons you added are now returned to their saved layouts.

With all the layouts saved that can be saved, you're ready to take your edit-ing on the road, or at least work on another system without having to recreate these same layouts. If you choose to move your project to another computer, all you have to do is transfer the Final Cut Pro User Data folder to a flash drive, navigate to the new computer's Final Cut Pro User Data folder, and place the layouts you want to use in the appropriate folders. If no folder exists, copy the entire folder from your flash drive to the new computer at that location.

TIP ▸ You can save multiple layouts in each category. As you customize or adjust other customized layouts, save that layout as its own unique file. You can also save over an existing layout to update it with additional but-tons, columns, or track options.

Optimizing User Preferences

If you find yourself pressing Command-Z to undo several actions, only to find that the action you really want to retrieve is the 11th undo, which is not avail-able to you, then you will want to take a closer look at the User Preferences in Final Cut Pro. User Preferences is a collection of options that determines how you personally work in any editing session. They cover editing choices such as the number of undos, the number of tracks you want to appear when you create a new sequence, how and when to back up your projects, and so on. User Preferences apply to all open projects and are another way you can harness more power in Final Cut Pro.

MORE INFO ▸ You can find a precise definition of each preference or setting in the Final Cut Pro 6 User Manual.

1   Choose Final Cut Pro > User Preferences, or press Option-Q.

The User Preferences window has six tabs. The General tab is where you choose assorted user preference settings. You will cover the capturing preferences in the next lesson. Other options are covered throughout the book.

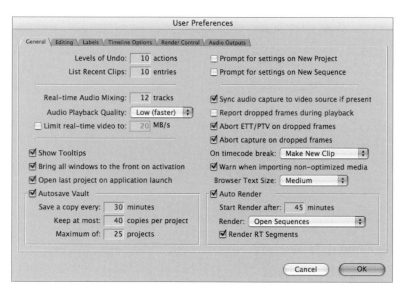

2   In the General tab, click the Levels of Undo field and enter *30*.

Now you can press Command-Z 30 times to get back to a previous editing decision. If you want to see additional clips listed in the Recent Clips pop-up menu in the Viewer, you can change that here as well.

3   In the List Recent Clips field, enter *20*.

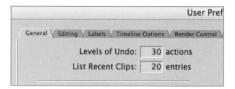

If you forget to save your project frequently throughout your editing sessions, Final Cut Pro will save it for you automatically. In the Autosave Vault section in the lower left of the General tab, you can set how often it saves.

4   In the "Save a copy every ___ minutes" field of the Autosave Vault section, enter *15*.

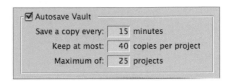

Now Final Cut Pro will automatically save a backup of your project every 15 minutes as you work. You can choose how frequently a project will be saved, how many versions of the project will be saved, and the maximum number of projects saved. When the maximum number of versions is reached, Final Cut Pro moves the oldest version into the Trash before saving the current version. These backup projects are saved at this location on your hard drive: [User Name] > Documents > Final Cut Pro Documents > Autosave Vault.

TIP   As a backup, some editors set their Autosave to a different drive, just in case anything happens to the project files on their primary drive. You will learn to do this in the next lesson.

5   Click the Editing tab. In the upper right of this tab, click the Multi-Frame Trim Size field and type *10*.

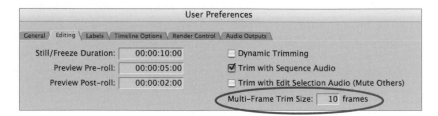

The Editing tab is where you set preferences for certain editing functions, such as previewing pre-roll and post-roll and setting multi-frame trim size. The multi-frame trim size determines how much you nudge an edit point when you use the Shift-< or Shift-> key commands. The default is 5 frames, but you can make it 10 frames or even 1 second. You can also choose a preferred duration for still images you import into your project.

When you applied labels to clips and bins earlier in this lesson, you chose a color or a type of clip. But you can also reassign or rename a label color to better support your project.

6   Click the Labels tab. In the current B Roll field, type *Sequences*.

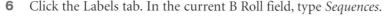

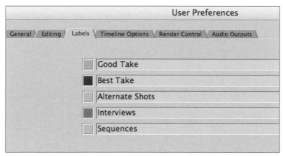

You can rename the color labels anything you want to reflect your project needs. The label colors cannot be changed, only the label names.

Earlier in this lesson, you made changes to existing sequences in the Timeline Options tab of the Sequence Settings window. If you want to make changes to a sequence before it's created—to add additional audio or video tracks automatically, or turn on the audio waveforms display, for example—you do that in the User Preferences Timeline Options tab.

7   Click the Timeline Options tab. In the Default Number of Tracks area, enter *2* for Video tracks and *6* for Audio tracks. Select the Show Audio Waveform checkbox.

Here you choose settings for all new sequences. You can determine a default number of tracks so that each new sequence you create has that track configuration, or choose drop frame or non-drop frame timecode to ensure every new sequence displays that mode. Any changes made here will not affect any *existing* sequences, only new ones.

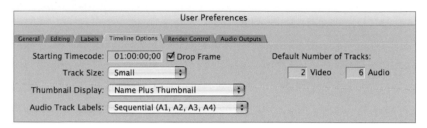

8   Click the Render Control tab.

This is where you enable or disable the most processor-intensive effects in Final Cut Pro.

9   Click the Audio Outputs tab.

Here you can create custom Audio Output configurations. You can use these settings when laying off various audio tracks to tape. For example, if your hardware supports it, you can create an Audio Output configuration that outputs up to 24 distinct tracks at one time.

10   Click OK to accept the user preferences you changed.

NOTE ▶ To revert to the default Final Cut Pro preferences, quit the application, and find the Final Cut Pro 6 Preferences file in the Final Cut Pro User Data folder. Drag this file to the Trash, and reopen FCP.

11   Press Command-S to save your current project. With the Browser or Timeline window active, choose File > Restore Project.

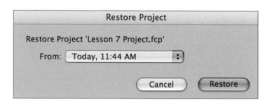

Once a project has been saved in the Autosave Vault, you can restore it to get back to an earlier project version. If you can recall the approximate time you were editing, you can simply restore the project with that time stamp. Restoring a project will automatically close the current project. So make sure to save the current project before initiating this command.

NOTE ▶ If the Autosave time has not elapsed, no choices will be available in Restore Project.

12 Click Cancel to close the Restore Project window. In the Browser, click the Yellow bin disclosure triangle and choose File > Revert Project.

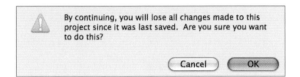

Choosing this option reverts you to the most recently saved version of this project.

13 Click Cancel to close this window. Click OK to revert to the previously saved project.

Lesson Review

1. How do you sort by a column other than the Name column?
2. How do you show a column that you can't currently see in the Browser?
3. How do you search for a clip in the Browser using specific criteria?
4. What determines whether a clip is a master clip in Final Cut Pro?
5. What does it mean when a clip has a red slash through the clip icon?
6. How can you look at the detailed information about a single clip or item?
7. Where are all customized layouts saved on your computer?
8. In what menu can you choose User Preferences?

9. How do you make changes to an existing sequence?

10. How do you find a matching frame to a sequence clip?

11. What is saved in the Autosave Vault?

Answers

1. Click a column heading.

2. Control-click a column heading and choose Show Column from the shortcut menu.

3. Select the Browser window and press Command-F to open the Find window, and choose specific search criteria.

4. A clip is a master clip if it represents the first use of that clip in the project.

5. The clip is offline and disconnected from its media file.

6. Select the clip, and press Command-9 to open the Item Properties window. You can also Control-click the clip and choose Item Properties from the shortcut menu.

7. They are saved at Macintosh HD > Users > [User Name] > Library > Preferences > Final Cut Pro User Data.

8. Choose User Preferences from the Final Cut Pro menu.

9. Make the sequence active in the Timeline, or select it in the Browser, and press Command-0 to open the Sequence Settings window. You can also choose Sequence > Sequence Settings.

10. Position the playhead over the frame of the sequence clip, and press F.

11. Backup copies of your project file.

Keyboard Shortcuts

F	Finds the frame in a sequence that matches the frame displayed in the Viewer, and vice versa
Command-F	Opens the Find window
Shift-F	Selects the master clip in the Browser
Option-Q	Opens User Preferences
Command-9	Opens the Item Properties window
Command-0	Opens the Sequence Settings window

8

Lesson Files   None

Media   Media > Imports; Your own

Time   This lesson takes approximately 60 minutes to complete.

Goals   Connect video sources for capture

Preview and mark source material

Log clips

Choose clip settings

Choose capture presets

Choose capture options

Batch capture clips

Import from nontape sources

Lesson 8
Capturing Footage

It may seem unusual for the first step of the editing process to appear in the middle of this book. The reason is simple. Now that you know how clip information is organized, how subclips are created, how markers are applied, and how you might want to shape your workflow, you can take advantage of the many ways to log and capture clips.

As video technology continues to evolve, editors have the opportunity to work with a variety of video formats. Some of these formats, such as DV, HDV, and DVCPRO HD, can be captured from a source device using a single FireWire connector; however, standard definition (SD) formats—such as DigiBeta and Beta SP—or some high definition (HD) formats, require the use of a third-party capture card. Of course, film is another shooting alternative, but it needs to be transferred to video before it's brought into Final Cut Pro.

Whichever video format option you are using, capturing footage will be your first step in preparing for the editing process. While some decisions must follow the needs of your shooting format, other capturing decisions can be the result of personal preference.

Connecting Sources for Capture

The first step in capturing source material is to connect a capture device to your computer. Final Cut Pro can capture and control footage from a variety of camcorders and decks using just a FireWire cable. You can also capture in some video formats using a third-party capture card or an analog-to-digital converter with FireWire output. Whatever your capture source, have that device running before launching Final Cut Pro. Otherwise, Final Cut Pro may not "see" the device, and you may have to relaunch the software so that it can.

When connecting a standard FireWire device, for example, you might use these steps:

1   If Final Cut Pro is open, save your projects and quit the program.

2   Connect the FireWire cable from the camera to the computer.

4-pin FireWire   6-pin FireWire   9-pin FireWire

FireWire 400, also called IEEE 1394a, has two types of connectors. The smaller 4-pin connector usually attaches to a camera or deck. The larger 6-pin connector goes into your computer's FireWire port. Independent FireWire drives typically use 6-pin-to-6-pin connectors. FireWire 400 transfers data at 400 Mbps. FireWire 800 is a higher-bandwidth version capable of transferring data at up to 800 Mbps and uses 9-pin-to-9-pin connectors. You can also get 9-pin-to-4-pin and 9-pin-to-6-pin cables to work with other FireWire devices.

3   Turn on the camera and switch it to the VTR (video tape recorder) mode. Load the source tape, and cue the footage.

Once you launch Final Cut Pro, you can control the camera from within the application. For now, viewing the tape just confirms you have loaded the right source or reel.

If you are using a third-party capture card, you can follow the manufacturer's instructions to connect the appropriate cables to your VTR and computer.

> **NOTE** ▶ You can also connect your camera or deck to a separate video monitor or television set, or through a VCR, just as you would if you were screening a tape. However, this is not necessary, because you can use the preview image area within the Final Cut Pro Capture function to view your source footage.

Creating a New Project for Capturing

Every new project contains a sequence that uses the default audio and video format settings. Final Cut Pro will automatically change the settings of an active sequence to match those of the footage you're editing.

But what if the first clip you edit doesn't represent the majority of footage you will be editing? For example, you might need to edit a few DV clips at the head of a primarily HD sequence, or vice versa. In this case, to maintain an efficient workflow, it is a good idea to choose specific settings that represent the majority of your footage.

Final Cut Pro makes it easy to choose accurate audio and video settings by providing a list of default presets in the Easy Setup window. These presets include capture settings, sequence settings, device control settings, and output settings. By choosing an Easy Setup preset, you simultaneously load all these settings at one time.

> **NOTE** ▶ The Easy Setup presets apply a group of settings to all *new* sequences and are not attached to a specific project. A single project could contain sequences created with several presets.

After you've connected a capture device, you can launch Final Cut Pro. If you're starting a new project, you can create and save that project so Final Cut Pro knows where to link the captured footage. If you're adding material to an existing project, you can open that project and capture into it.

1   In the Dock, click the Final Cut Pro icon to launch Final Cut Pro.

Any project that was active when you last quit the program will be opened. If you closed all projects before quitting Final Cut Pro, it will launch with a new project called Untitled Project 1.

2   Close any open projects, including any untitled projects that were created automatically.

In Final Cut Pro, project files are containers. A project, itself, does not have settings. The settings for your footage are attached to sequences. To ensure that all new sequences contain the correct settings to match your footage, first choose the appropriate settings, then create a new project.

NOTE ▶ Remember that the Canvas and Timeline windows close when there are no open sequences to display.

3   Choose Final Cut Pro > Easy Setup. In the Easy Setup window, click the Use pop-up menu.

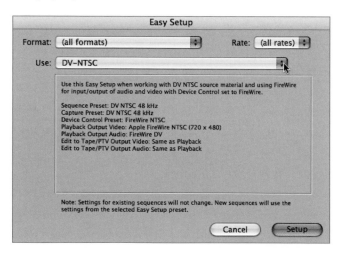

The Easy Setup window contains presets for several media formats. Each preset contains media settings that are appropriate for that format.

Rather than search through this myriad of options, you can limit or filter your search by choosing Format and Rate settings for your footage. This will filter the Use pop-up menu to display only those presets that pertain to your footage format.

4 Click the Format pop-up menu and choose an appropriate format for your media.

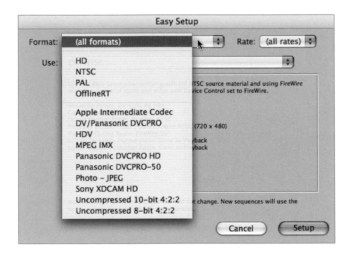

NOTE ▶ If you have loaded additional presets from a third-party company, such as AJA or Blackmagic, those presets will also appear in the Use pop-up menu.

5 Click the Rate pop-up menu and choose the frame rate of your footage.

These choices should follow the specifications of your particular source material.

6   Click the Use pop-up menu again.

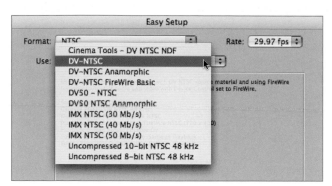

Depending on the format and rate option you chose, the menu items may be greatly reduced, showing only those presets that fall under the two filter categories you chose.

7   Click the Setup button to accept the selected preset.

Now that the correct preset for your footage has been selected, you can create a new project. Since the new project will contain a new sequence, that sequence will contain settings that match the preset you just selected.

8   Choose File > New Project to create a new project.

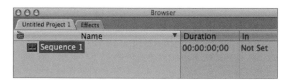

An Untitled Project tab appears in the Browser window along with a default sequence, *Sequence 1*. This sequence contains the settings of the Easy Setup you just selected.

9   To name and save this project, choose File > Save Project As, and type *Lesson 8 Project* as the new name.

Notice that the .fcp extension for this project is not automatically added in the Save As field. If you want the .fcp extension to be part of the name, deselect the "Hide extension" box in the lower-left corner of this window. If you are using a server to store or share a project, it's a good idea to display the extension so the file can be correctly identified.

10 Navigate to the Lessons folder on your hard drive, and click Save to save the project there.

What you are saving is just the project file. It is not where the media will be stored. You will set that destination later in this lesson.

Previewing and Marking Your Source

Once the video source is connected and the project is open and ready, you can control the camera or tape deck using controls in the Final Cut Pro interface. As you screen and preview the material, you can set In and Out points to identify the areas you want to capture. Marking source material for capture is very similar to marking clips for editing. You will learn other approaches to the capture process later in this lesson.

Opening and Sizing the Capture Window

All capturing is done in the Log and Capture window. This window has two main areas: the Preview area on the left, where you screen and mark your source tape, and the Logging tab on the right, where you log information about clips and select where and how you will capture footage.

1 Choose File > Log and Capture, or press Command-8.

The Log and Capture window appears.

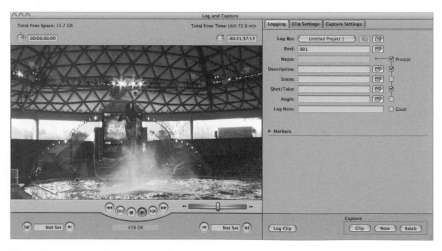

Preview area   Logging tab

NOTE ▶ If you are capturing HDV footage and have selected the HDV Easy Setup preset, you will see a slightly different window. The log and capture options that appear function the same as those in the default window.

The HDV Log and Capture window

If your playback source device is not properly connected to your computer's FireWire port, you may see the following message:

When you click OK, the Log and Capture window will open, but you will only be able to log clips or use a noncontrollable device. If you want to capture from a FireWire device, close the Log and Capture window, turn on the capture device, then reopen the Log and Capture window.

The Preview area of the Log and Capture window defaults to the size of the Canvas window. To change the size of the Log and Capture window, you must first change the size of the Canvas window, or the Viewer and Canvas windows together. However, you can't do this while the Log and Capture window is open.

2   Close the Log and Capture window.

3   To make the Log and Capture window larger, choose Window > Arrange > Two Up, to enlarge the size of the Viewer and Canvas together.

4   Choose File > Log and Capture, or press Command-8, to reopen the window.

A much larger Log and Capture window appears.

Playing the Source Tape

The Preview area of the Log and Capture window is used to screen your source material and mark sections of footage you want to capture. If your capture device is connected via FireWire, or a third-party capture card with a device control cable, you will have direct control of the device. That is, you can play and control the device in the Final Cut Pro interface. If not, you will have to control the device manually.

1   To start viewing the material, make sure you have a source tape in your camera or deck.

Timecode Duration field   Available space and time   Current Timecode field

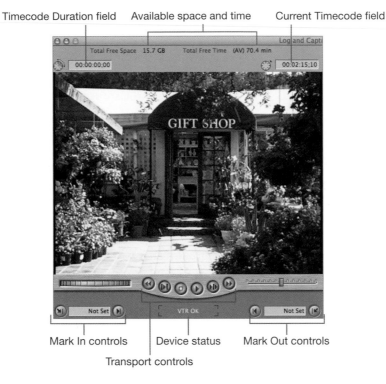

Mark In controls   Device status   Mark Out controls

Transport controls

The Preview area is similar in layout to the Viewer and Canvas windows. It has Timecode Duration and Current Timecode fields above the image area, a set of transport controls below the image area, plus shuttle and jog controls. The marking controls are in the lower-left and lower-right corners of the Preview area. Between the marking controls is a device status area that indicates whether or not you can control the capture device. In addition, the total amount of free hard drive space and the available capture time (for the currently selected format) appears in the upper-middle area of the screen.

2   In the Preview area, click the Play button to play the tape.

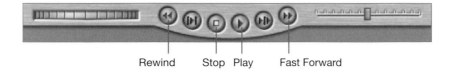

Rewind   Stop Play   Fast Forward

NOTE ▶ When you capture into Final Cut Pro using a FireWire device, you can preview the audio through Final Cut Pro, as you will learn later in this lesson; or you can monitor it through headphones or speakers plugged directly in to the playback device.

3   Click the Stop button to pause the tape, then click it again to stop the tape.

When a tape in a camera or deck is stopped, the tape unwraps from the video heads, but the Preview area displays a freeze frame of the most recent frame played.

TIP ▶ Pausing your tape is more efficient than stopping it completely. But leaving the tape in pause mode too long can damage the tape or cause video dropouts.

4   Press the spacebar to play the tape, and the Play button lights up. Press spacebar again to pause the tape, and the Stop button lights up.

5   Click the Rewind or Fast Forward buttons to move quickly backward or forward. Use the shuttle control, or the J-K-L keys, to scan your footage or zero in on a closer destination.

6   To prepare for the capture process, use the transport controls to cue your source tape to the footage you want to capture.

Marking and Viewing Source Material

Marking a tape source is similar to marking a clip in the Viewer. In fact, you use the same marking controls or shortcut keys (I and O). The primary difference is that when you mark a clip in the Viewer, you place tight marks around the action you want to edit into the sequence. When you capture a clip, you need to capture a few seconds before and after the action. This adds the pad, or handles, to the clip that you can use when adjusting edits in the Timeline.

The Preview area marking controls include Mark In and Mark Out buttons, Go to In Point and Go to Out Point buttons, and timecode fields that display both the In and Out timecode locations you've marked. The marking controls appear at the bottom of the Preview area, as they do in the Viewer.

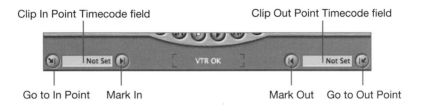

1   If you haven't done so already, play the tape to the section you want to capture. Press the spacebar, or click the Play (or Stop) button, just as the action begins.

There are different approaches to marking footage. You can mark the footage loosely around the action you want to edit, creating editing handles in the process. Or you can mark the action more precisely and add handles afterward. Sometimes, you don't know where the desired action begins until you see it, so mark this clip when you first see the action begin in your footage.

2   Click the Mark In button, or press the I key, to set an In point at the current tape location.

The timecode for your mark appears in the Clip In Point Timecode field. Unlike the Viewer marks, this mark will not appear in the image area, and there is no scrubber bar to scrub to the marks.

NOTE ▶ The specific timecode numbers you see in the images throughout this lesson will not match your own.

Since marking at this point doesn't give you the handles you need to adjust the clip during the editing process, you need to place the In point earlier.

3   To create a 3-second clip handle, click in the Clip In Point Timecode field, enter –3. (minus three period), and press Return.

When you enter this change, a new In point appears that is 3 seconds earlier than the previous mark, giving you a 3-second pad, or handle, before the desired action begins.

NOTE ▶ Remember, you don't need to create extra pad if your original mark allowed for handles prior to the action you want to use.

As you play forward, look for an appropriate place to stop capturing this clip. You can mark a specific location and add handles to the Out point at a later time, for example, +3:00. Since you can more easily anticipate where an action ends than where it begins, you can mark this Out point on the fly as the tape is playing.

4 Press the spacebar, or click the Play button, to move forward to where this portion of the action ends. Allow the tape to continue playing, and after about 3 seconds, press O to set an Out point.

While this technique is not as precise as making an exact change to a mark, you still have enough of a handle to make adjustments as you edit and may have saved yourself a little time in the process. Keep in mind that the marks you set while capturing don't usually have to be frame accurate.

TIP ▸ To mark an In point on the fly, start the tape several seconds before the action begins, play the tape, and start pressing the I key repeatedly until you reach the In point you want, then stop marking. It may be that the previous mark was early enough to include handles. If not, trim back the In point.

Seeing the head and tail of what you will capture can be helpful. But remember, this is a tape source, so moving to the In or Out point will not be as immediate as it is in the Viewer.

5 To verify the In and Out frames, click the Go to In Point or Go to Out Point button to navigate to the In or Out point. You can also use the shortcuts, Shift-I and Shift-O.

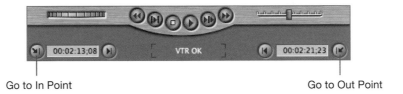

Go to In Point   Go to Out Point

If navigating to the exact In or Out point didn't confirm that your marks were good, you can always play the marked portion.

6 In the Preview area, click the Play In to Out button.

If you need to change a mark, you can mark again to set a new timecode location, or use the marks you have as a reference and trim them backward or forward.

TIP ▶ If timecode was logged during the shoot, you can enter a time-code number and go to that specific location. You may still need to adjust that In point to include handles.

Logging Your Clips

Now that you have marked a source clip, you are ready to log information about that clip. If you look at the Logging tab of the Log and Capture window, you will recognize some of the fields—such as Name, Description, Scene, Angle, and Log Note—because you previously saw them as Browser columns. Information you log at the capture stage also appears in the Browser columns for later reference. Notice, too, there is an area in which you can add markers during the logging process. Before logging a clip, however, it's a good idea to determine the best approach to organizing logged clips in the project.

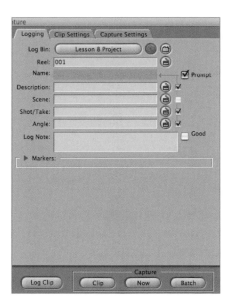

Setting a Log Bin

When you capture a clip, Final Cut Pro needs to know where to place the new clip icons. The actual media files will be saved to your hard drive, but the clip icon linking to that media will be saved to the current project in the Browser. If you want to move quickly, you can capture all the clips into a project tab in the Browser and organize them later. If you want to organize as you capture, you can create a new bin for each category, such as reel/tape number or type of footage. In either case, Final Cut Pro needs to be told where to place the clip icons. This destination is called the *log bin*. You can have only one log bin active at any given time, no matter how many projects you have open.

1   If necessary, position the Browser so you can see both the Capture and Browser windows while doing these steps.

In the Logging tab of the Log and Capture window, the project name, Lesson 8 Project, appears on the long oval Log Bin button.

In the Browser window, a slate icon appears at the upper left of the Name column, indicating that this project is the current logging bin.

At this point, you can capture clips into your project and organize them into bins after capturing them. However, if you want to explore the option of capturing to a new bin, continue with the following steps.

2   In the Logging tab, on the far right of the Log Bin button, click the New Bin button.

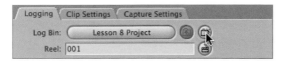

A new bin is created in the current project with the default name Bin 1. The slate icon appears next to this bin in the Browser to identify it as the target location for new clips.

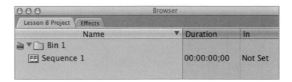

3   In the Logging tab, click the Log Bin button with the new bin name on it.

The new bin opens as a separate window, which allows you to view just the new clips you are capturing without mixing them up with other clips already in your project.

4   Close this window.

5   In the Logging tab, click the Up button.

This takes the Log Bin destination to a higher level, in this case back to the project level. In the Browser, the slate icon is attached once again to the project, not to the bin.

6   In the Browser, rename the new bin *Test Capture*, or any other name that's appropriate for the group of footage you're about to capture.

Let's assign this bin to be the logging bin.

7   In the Browser, Control-click the Test Capture bin, and choose Set Logging Bin from the shortcut menu.

In the Browser, the slate icon now appears to the left of the Test Capture bin.

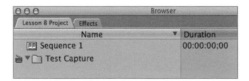

Logging Clip Information

Before you begin entering information about a single clip, consider whether this clip is going to be part of a series of clips taken from this source. If so, you might want to create a clip-naming convention before you begin. For example, dramatic footage, as in *Monk*, uses camera, scene, and take numbers to identify a clip. In the SeaWorld "Believe" project, the interview clips had an underscore before the interview subject's initials, the behavior clips began with the trainer's initials, and the underwater footage began with *uw_*. Unless you're working with a production group that requires a specific naming procedure, you're free to determine your own naming conventions. Just a word of advice: The more consistent you are in the naming stage, especially on a complex project, the easier it will be to find a clip during the editing stage.

Although you don't have to fill every blank, certain logging information is required—such as reel number and clip name—or Final Cut Pro will not capture the clip. You can also add additional logging information after you have captured the clip, as you learned in the preceding lesson.

1 Enter an appropriate reel number or name for your source tape, or you can leave the default 001 reel number if you have just one tape.

Ideally, you should use the same reel name or number that you used when labeling your tapes. That way you will always know from which source tape your clips were captured.

2 Try clicking in the Name field.

The Name field is not for entering information, just displaying it. The name is actually compiled from the four descriptive fields below it that have an active checkmark.

3 In the Description field, enter a description of the clip you want to capture, such as *gift shop ext*, *village ws*, or *boy cu*. Use a name that will help you distinguish between that clip and another while you are editing.

Some clip names include a reference to camera framing, such as *ws* for wide shot, *cu* for close-up, or *ext* for exterior. If you lead with that information, all of the close-ups will be sorted together in the list view in the Browser. That may be helpful, but if it's more helpful to find all the gift shop or boy shots quickly, you should add the camera-framing reference after the topic.

TIP ▶ When naming a clip, don't use the forward slash as part of the name. This may cause capturing errors.

4   Make sure the Description checkbox next to the Slate button is selected, then press Tab or Return.

When selected, the information in the Description field automatically becomes part of the name.

5   If you're working with a script, enter the scene number and press Tab or Return. You might also want to add the descriptive *Sc* before the number.

Not all footage is organized by scene, take, and angle. For many situations, you can leave these fields blank. For now, follow these steps so you can see how to deselect specific clip information in the Name field.

6   In the Shot/Take field, enter *tk 4*, and in the Angle field, enter *cam 2* (for camera 2).

Even though you've entered information in each field, you don't have to use it in the name that identifies the clip. The tiny checkboxes to the right of each field toggle off or on each descriptive entry.

7   Select and deselect the checkboxes next to each line to see how the name changes in the Name area. To use the scene and take numbers as the sole name, check those boxes, and deselect the Description and Angle checkboxes.

Any one, or all four, of the descriptive entries can be included in the full clip name. Keep in mind that the longer a clip name is, the harder it may be to read when edited into a sequence in the Timeline. You might find it more useful to enter the information, but not select the checkboxes to include the information in the name. The information will remain attached to the clip, and you will still have access to it in the Browser columns and through the Find function.

8   Next to the Shot/Take entry, click the Slate button.

Every time you click one of the slates, the next consecutive number is added to the descriptive entry. This is true even if no number was originally entered. To change to another number, click the number to highlight it, and enter a new number. Notice that the *tk* descriptive shortcut remains unchanged.

9   Deselect all the checkboxes except the Description checkbox. In many cases, this will be the primary source of your clip name.

10   Select and deselect the Prompt checkbox. Leave the box selected.

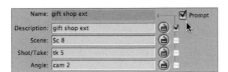

With the Prompt box selected, Final Cut Pro will prompt you to verify the logged information before capturing or logging the clip. This allows you to check it, change it, or add to it before you capture.

TIP ▶ Keep in mind that Final Cut Pro links project clips to media files stored on your hard disk. While you can rename clips and media files, it is always best to use an organized naming convention during the capture process.

11 Enter a log note about the clip, such as *windy shot* or *great catch,* and select the Good checkbox.

After you capture this clip, the log note will appear in the Log Note Browser column, and a checkmark will appear in the Good column. Again, you can enter anything in the Log Note field, but if you're going to take the time to enter something, make sure it's helpful information.

Adding Markers While Logging

Throughout these lessons, you've used markers to identify specific locations in a clip or in the Timeline. You also used markers to create subclips of a longer clip. Depending on your project, you might want to add markers to a clip during the logging process for these same purposes. When you open the captured clip, it will already have markers identifying specific locations.

Some nature editors use this feature quite creatively. For example, say you were given a one-hour tape of a moose grazing in Yellowstone National Park. You capture the entire drama so as not to miss a single twig or leaf. This gives you one clip in the project that you will have to scour for good shots. Rather than working with a single one-hour clip that has no clues as to shot content, you can set markers as you log the clip to denote periods of time or interesting action. When you've finished capturing, you can use the markers to go directly to those references, or better yet, convert them into subclips containing specific actions or periods of time.

1 On the Logging tab, click the disclosure triangle next to Markers to expand the pane.

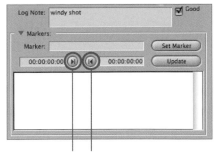

Set Marker In button   Set Marker Out button

2 With an In point selected on your source tape, play the tape from the In point, and click the Set Marker In button wherever you want to place a marker on the clip you are capturing. Then stop the tape.

NOTE ▶ Clicking the Set Marker Out button will create a duration from the In marker to the Out marker.

3 In the Marker field, enter a name for the marker.

Remember, a marker name becomes the name of the clip when you convert markers to subclips.

TIP ▶ If you are capturing interview material, include some of the question or answer in the name as a reference.

4 Click Set Marker.

The timecode designating the marker location appears in the Marker In Point Timecode field. Now you can add another marker to this clip.

If you will be logging that long nature tape, or a talking-heads interview, you can set markers on the fly. Although this process takes a little practice, it's well worth the effort.

5   To set a marker on the fly as you log a tape, follow these steps:

▶ Play the tape and mark an In point.

▶ As the tape is playing, click the Set Marker In button where you want to place a marker.

▶ Type a marker name in the Marker field.

▶ Click the Set Marker button to enter the marker name and location.

▶ Repeat for the next marker as the tape continues to play.

▶ Mark an Out point at the end of the material you want to capture

▶ Choose a capture option (covered later in this lesson).

The list of markers will appear below the marker controls. Once the clip is captured, the markers will be attached to the clip.

Choosing Clip Settings

In the Clip Settings tab, you make selections about *how* you want to capture a clip. Do you want to capture just the video, just the audio, or both? How do you want to capture the audio—as mono tracks or as a stereo pair? How many audio tracks do you want to capture—two or eight? Some of the options in the Clip Settings tab, such as the number of audio tracks you can capture, will depend on the type of deck or source you are using, and whether you are capturing via FireWire or using a capture card.

1   In the Log and Capture window, click the Clip Settings tab.

This tab is divided into Video and Audio sections. Each section has a checkbox to activate it. If you are capturing from a FireWire device, the video controls will be dimmed. If you are working with a capture card, you can use these controls to adjust the incoming video levels of your clip.

If you are capturing HDV, you will see a slightly different Clip Settings tab. In this tab, you have the option to create a new clip wherever you stopped and started your camera while shooting.

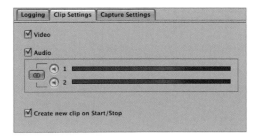

2 To capture the logged clip's audio and video, make sure the Video and Audio boxes are selected. To capture just one or the other, deselect the undesired element.

As you consider these options, keep in mind that audio files are not as large as video files. If you know you're going to use only the audio portion of a section of footage, perhaps for narration or ambient room noise, capture only the audio to reduce the file size and conserve hard drive space. When you know you will use just the video portion of your source material, capture video only so you won't have empty audio tracks attached to the clip.

3 In the Audio area, click the Toggle Stereo/Mono control connecting the two Capture Audio Channel controls (the speaker icons). Click it again to toggle between capturing two audio channels as a stereo pair and capturing them as twin mono channels.

When this option is deselected, as it is in the image above, the audio tracks are *unpaired*, and the audio tracks are captured as separate channels. Capturing audio as mono tracks is helpful when you use two separate mics during recording—perhaps a lavalier or lapel mic for the speaker and a boom mic for room ambience—as opposed to the stereo camera mic. Capturing the audio as twin mono channels gives you control over the individual tracks during editing.

Toggling to the Stereo option will create a connecting bracket around the two audio controls, indicating the tracks will be treated as a stereo pair. As you know, this can be helpful because when you adjust the volume of one track or trim one track, the other track in the stereo pair is automatically adjusted the same way. The two audio tracks will also appear on just one audio tab in the Viewer.

NOTE ▶ After a clip has been edited into the Timeline, you can change two mono tracks into a stereo pair to adjust them simultaneously. Or, you can change a stereo pair into two mono tracks to adjust them separately.

4   Deselect the Stereo option, and click the channel 2 control.

When the stereo option is deselected, you can choose whether you want to capture two mono channels or one individual channel of audio.

NOTE ▶ If you are using a capture card that supports multiple track capture, you can select the number of tracks you want to capture from the Input Channels pop-up menu. Whatever tracks you select appear in the audio track area. Here you can toggle stereo or mono off or on for any set of tracks.

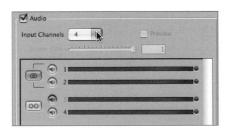

5   To listen to the source audio as you are capturing, select the Preview box.

When the Preview box is selected, you can hear the audio of your source tape as you screen and mark your clips, and also as the clip is captured.

6   If you have color bars at the head of your source tape, click the Video Scopes button to view them.

A Live Waveform Monitor and Vectorscope window appears that displays your incoming source levels. The Waveform Monitor on the left measures the brightness (luminance and black levels) of your incoming video; the Vectorscope on the right measures the color (saturation and hue).

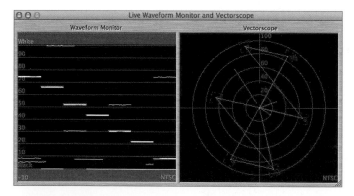

NOTE ▸ Keep in mind that you can view the color bars at the head of a DV tape, but you cannot change them at this point.

7   Close the Live Waveform Monitor and Vectorscope window.

Choosing Capture Settings

Earlier in this lesson, you chose an Easy Setup preset suitable for the footage you were capturing. Those presets settings, along with other system and audio and video settings, ensure that your system is optimized for the most efficient workflow for that format. The parameters of the Easy Setup preset trickle down into other areas of Final Cut Pro as well, including the Capture Settings tab in the Log and Capture window. In this tab, you determine three things: how you will control the playback device, what codec you will use to capture your footage, and where you will store it on your computer or FireWire drive. If you chose an Easy Setup preset for this capture session, some of those settings will already be selected in this tab.

1 In the Log and Capture window, click the Capture Settings tab.

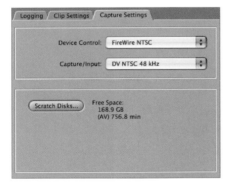

2 From the Device Control pop-up menu, choose FireWire NTSC, FireWire PAL, or another appropriate option.

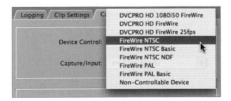

If you are capturing from a device that cannot be controlled through FireWire, choose the appropriate preset, or choose Non-Controllable Device.

3   Click the Capture/Input pop-up menu.

This is where you select the format in which your footage will be captured. You can capture a number of NTSC or PAL formats, including an assortment of options for DV, DVCPRO HD, and HDV. The current option reflects the Easy Setup preset you selected earlier in this lesson. If the type of footage has changed, or if you want to capture using a format other than the Easy Setup preset, choose that codec here.

NOTE ▶ If you are using a third-party capture card, such as the AJA Io or Kona card or the Blackmagic DeckLink card, those options will appear here as well.

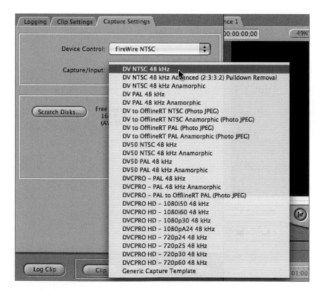

If you shot a lot of footage, or have high-resolution footage, and don't have enough available hard drive space to store it, you can also capture the footage at a lower-quality resolution, which will create smaller media files. The OfflineRT option is often used for this purpose. You can edit your entire project using low-res files. Once the editing is complete, you can recapture just the footage used in your sequence at its full resolution.

MORE INFO ▶ You can read more about this process in the Final Cut Pro User Manual.

4   To select the destination for your captured media, click the Scratch Disks button.

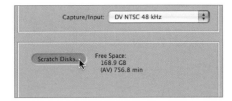

A window opens where you can reset the path to the targeted scratch disk or drive you will use to save your media files. The current scratch disk is listed, along with the amount of currently available free space. You can choose a different scratch disk for audio and video and for render files, which you will create in a later lesson. For now, capture them all to one destination.

TIP ▶ If one scratch disk isn't large enough for your media-capturing needs, you can target up to 12 separate scratch disks. When the primary disk is full, the capturing continues on the disk with the most available space. This is very helpful when working with long-format projects or high-resolution footage.

MORE INFO ▶ To learn about how much disk space you need for your project, refer to the section on "Calculating Hard Disk Space Requirements" in the Final Cut Pro User Manual.

TIP ▶ To save other types of files—such as the backup files in the Autosave Vault—to separate locations, click the Set button and choose a destination.

When you set the scratch disk, Final Cut Pro automatically creates folders in that location for each type of file. As those files are captured or created, it automatically places files in those folders. The default location for the scratch disk is Macintosh HD > Users > [User Name] > Documents > Final Cut Pro Documents. Let's take a look at those capture folders.

5   Press Command-H to hide Final Cut Pro, and double-click the Macintosh HD icon, or press Shift-Command-N, to create a new Finder window. Navigate to Macintosh HD > Users > [User Name] > Documents > Final Cut Pro Documents.

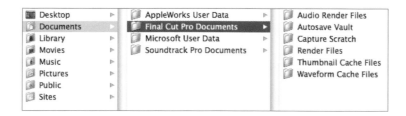

When you capture in a different project, a folder with that project name is created in the Capture Scratch folder, and the media files you capture are placed there. If you don't change the default scratch disk location, all the organizational work of correctly placing captured footage, render files, and backup project files saved in the Autosave Vault will be done for you, project by project.

6   If you do want to change the currently selected scratch disk—to target a FireWire drive for example—click Set.

A file browser appears, in which you can select a different scratch disk.

7   Navigate to where you want to save your captured files, and click Choose, then click OK in the Scratch Disks window.

When you set a new scratch disk, Final Cut Pro creates the same set of folders in that location as are in the default scratch disk location.

TIP ▸ Although the Final Cut Pro default is to capture media files to your internal hard drive, digital media files make your hard drive work harder. For optimal performance of your software and operating system, capture media files to a separate drive.

There's another settings window where you can change the scratch disk, just as you do in the Capture Settings tab.

8   Choose Final Cut Pro > System Settings, or press Shift-Q.

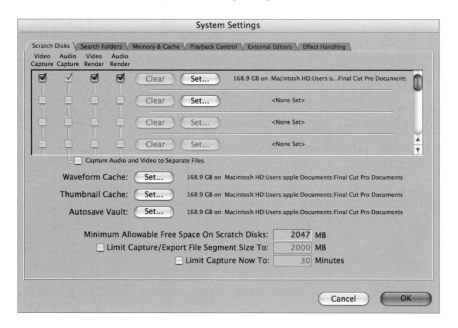

The first tab of this window shows the same scratch disk information that appears if you click the Scratch Disks button in the Capture Settings tab. You can set the scratch disk in either location. If the desired scratch disk is set in the System Settings window, and you are not changing it, you do not have to select it in the Capture Settings tab. Notice that this window also follows the Easy Setup preset that you chose earlier in this lesson.

9   Click Cancel, then choose Final Cut Pro > Audio/Video Settings, or press Command-Option-Q.

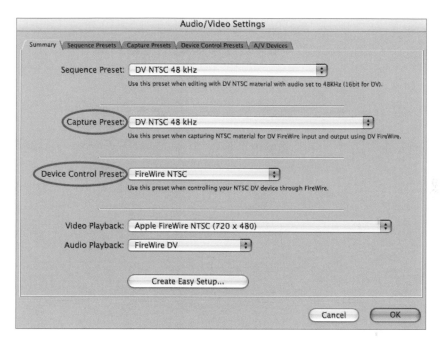

In this window, you can select the device control and capture presets. If they are correctly selected, the same settings will appear in the Device Control and Capture/Input pop-up menus of the Capture Settings tab. Here, too, the settings follow and reflect the Easy Setup preset you chose earlier.

TIP ▸ As you move through the capture setup stage, it doesn't matter in which order you proceed. You can change your settings first, and then move on to logging your clips, or log and then choose your settings. But you must choose the appropriate settings before starting to capture clips.

Choosing Capture Options

Now that you've chosen the right capture settings, targeted a scratch disk to contain the media files, and created a logging bin to organize the captured clips in the project, you're ready to choose which of the three capture options you want to use. The lower portion of the Logging tab area has three Capture buttons—Clip, Now, and Batch—and a Log Clip button. These buttons appear regardless of which tab is selected in the Log and Capture window. Each of the capture options converts footage from your tape source into computer media files. The Log Clip button builds a list to be captured later using batch capture. Although all the capture options create media clips, each performs the process differently.

> **MORE INFO** ▶ If you're capturing a project that originated on film, you may want to track the relationship between the keycode of the film frames and the timecode of the video you are capturing. You can refer to the Apple Cinema Tools User Manual for more information.

There are several ways to approach the capture process. In some situations, you may want to enter detailed information for a clip and then capture it before going on to the next clip. In other situations, you may want to log information about all of your clips, and capture them as a group. Other times, working with footage that doesn't have timecode, you won't be able to log any information. Sometimes you can choose to capture an entire tape and let Final Cut Pro automatically create the clips based on where the tape stopped and started.

Capturing a Clip

The most direct way to capture is to mark a clip in the Preview area of the Log and Capture window, enter the logging information for the clip, and click the

Capture Clip option. This gives you one new media file, complete with logged notes and markers, based on the In and Out points you set. Capturing clip by clip is a stop-and-start process. You mark a clip, log it, then capture it. Mark, log, and capture; mark, log, and capture. A good time to use this approach is when you have only a few clips to capture from one source, such as a stock footage shot, or a few cutaways from B-roll footage.

1   Mark a new clip from your source footage, or use the clip you marked in previous exercise steps.

2   Enter or amend the logging information.

3   In the Capture area of the Logging tab, click the Capture Clip button.

If you selected the Prompt checkbox next to the Name field, the Log Clip dialog appears. This is a good double-check to ensure all the logging information is correct before you actually capture the clip.

TIP   If you do not want to be prompted for your log information each time you click the Capture Clip button, deselect the Prompt checkbox in the Logging tab.

4 If necessary, make changes to the clip log information, then click OK.

When capturing begins, a window displays the material you are capturing. Don't worry if the image seems jagged at this point. The display during capturing does not reflect the quality of the captured clip.

GIFT SHOP

Batch Capture – NOW CAPTURING (press 'ESC' to abort)
Capturing File: gift shop exu (00:00:08:16) – Item 1 of 1
Remaining to capture on 001: 00:00:08:16

NOTE ▶ If you are capturing HDV footage, the audio and video may appear to be out of sync. This is apparent only during the capture process. The final clip will capture in sync.

Capturing Now

When you want to capture footage from a source that Final Cut Pro can't control, or that doesn't have timecode, you use Capture Now. With this option, you log information, but you don't enter timecode In and Out points or markers. You can use this option when you do not have FireWire control over a source device, such as a nondigital camera. And since this process does not include a pre-roll to cue to a location, you can use it to capture the first few frames on a tape. You can also use this function to capture an entire tape at one time. Many editors use this approach because it's much easier to find specific shots or material in a clip after it's been captured.

1   In the Logging tab, enter the next clip name and, if necessary, a new reel number.

This is an important step. If you don't name the clip before you start the Capture Now process, Final Cut Pro will give the clip a default name.

TIP ▶ To change the name of a media file to reflect the name of the project clip, select the clip in the Browser, and choose Modify > Rename > File to Match Clip.

2   Cue the source tape about 10 seconds before the action begins that you want to capture.

This is a less exact method of capturing than the Capture Clip option, so make sure you give yourself adequate pad before and after the action.

3   Play the tape from that point.

4   Click the Capture Now button.

Make sure you give yourself a few extra seconds past the last action before continuing with the next step.

5   Press the Escape key to stop capturing.

6   To limit the amount of time you automatically capture in one stretch, click the Capture Settings tab and then click the Scratch Disks button.

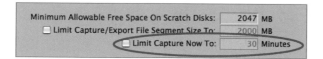

At the bottom of this tab is an option to limit the Capture Now process to a specified amount of time. When selected, the default time is 30 minutes. To activate this option, select the Limit Capture Now To checkbox and enter an amount of capture time. Click OK.

NOTE ▶ When using Capture Now, you can easily capture long pieces of material without realizing how large a file you are creating. Remember that 5 minutes of DV media will consume about 1 GB of hard drive storage space.

If you shot with a DV format (DV, DVCAM, DVCPRO, DVCPRO 50, or DVCPRO HD) and stopped and started the camera at different times, you can use the DV Start/Stop Detect function to streamline your work-flow. It can be used to create subclips from long clips captured in either the Capture Clip or Capture Now mode.

TIP ▶ To practice DV Start/Stop Detect, you can import the **pond life** file from the Media > Imports folder, and then continue with step 7 .

7   To apply DV Start/Stop Detect, follow these steps:

▶ Capture the long clip, and then open it in the Viewer.

▶ Choose Mark > DV Start/Stop Detect. Final Cut Pro will scan the clip looking for breaks in time when you stopped and started the camera.

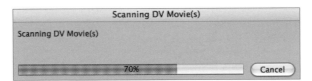

▶ Markers will appear on the clip wherever the original tape was stopped and started during recording.

▶ In the Browser, select a marker, and choose Modify > Make Subclip. A new subclip is created from the location of this marker to the next marker.

▶ To create subclips of all the individual markers, drag all the markers attached to this clip into a new bin. This creates individual subclips with durations from one marker, or shot, to the next.

Logging Clips and Batch Capturing

The third capture option provides an efficient alternative to the mark-log-capture workflow. This approach separates the decision-making process (what to capture and what to name it) from the hardware process (cueing up the tape, playing it forward in real time, and converting the tape selection into a media file). The first step is to mark and log the clips you want to capture, then instruct Final Cut Pro to capture the entire list, or *batch*, of clips you've marked. You don't have to be present while the clips are being captured. As long as the mark points can be found on tape, FCP captures the clips automatically.

1   Mark a new section of footage, and enter the information in the Logging tab as you did before, but do not click a Capture button.

2   Click the Log Clip button, or press the keyboard shortcut, F2.

   NOTE ▶ To use the F2 shortcut to log a clip, make sure that key has not been assigned to an Exposé function in System Preferences.

   If the Prompt box was selected in the Logging tab, the Log Clip dialog will open, reminding you of your logging information. Click OK.

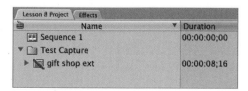

A new clip appears in the log bin just as any other clip would, except this one has a red diagonal line over it to indicate the clip is *offline*. This means the clip information is there, but not the media content, because the media has not yet been captured. Because it has a marker attached, you see a disclosure triangle next to the clip name.

3   Mark another portion of footage, and log the clip information in the Logging tab.

4   Click the Log Clip button again, or press F2.

Continuing this process creates a cumulative list of every clip you log, each with a red line through it indicating that it is offline media.

NOTE ▶ The red offline media line can also indicate that a clip in the project has lost its connection to its media file because the file was moved, renamed, or deleted.

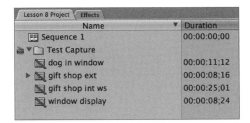

After you've logged several clips, you may realize that you made a mistake entering logging information for one or more clips. For example, you may have had both audio and video selected when you wanted to capture only audio, or you really wanted to capture the clips as a stereo pair, rather than mono tracks.

5   To change the track information of a logged clip before capturing it, select the clip in the Browser and choose Modify > Clip Settings. Make the changes, and click OK.

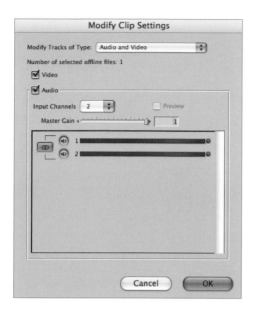

TIP ▶ You can also select a group of offline clips, choose Modify > Clip Settings, and make changes to the selected group at one time.

When you have completed logging all the clips you want to capture, and made any necessary changes to them, you can capture them all at once using batch capture. If you want to capture all of the clips in the current logging bin, you can skip the next step. If you want to capture only some of the offline clips, you must select them.

6   In the Test Capture bin, select the logged clips you want to capture.

7   In the Log and Capture window, click the Capture Batch button.

TIP To access the Batch Capture dialog when clips are selected, you can also Control-click a selected clip in the Browser and choose Batch Capture, choose File > Batch Capture, or press Control-C.

The Batch Capture dialog opens. This is where you choose what you're going to capture and how.

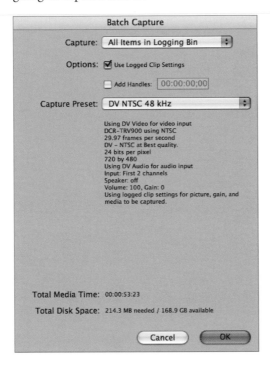

There are four options in the Batch Capture dialog:

▶ Capture—Click the pop-up menu to choose which clips you want to capture (All Items in Logging Bin, Offline Items in Logging Bin, or Selected Items in Logging Bin).

NOTE ▶ These options will change depending on which clips are selected in the Browser. Before making a selection, make sure you read the options carefully.

▶ Options: Use Logged Clip Settings—Select this box to capture the clips with all the settings that were present when you originally logged the clips.

▶ Options: Add Handles—Select this box to add additional handles to the current logged clip only if you did not allow for handles while first previewing and marking the clips.

▶ Capture Preset—If you want to capture the selected clips using a preset different from the one the clips were logged with, choose that preset from this pop-up menu.

At the bottom of the Batch Capture dialog, calculations appear based on the capture settings you select.

8 Make the appropriate selections, and click OK.

The Insert Reel window appears, indicating that you are ready to capture. This window lists the source reel number, the total amount of clip time, and the number of clips.

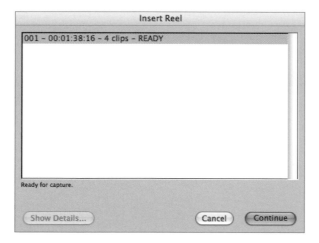

9   Click Continue.

Using all of your logged information, Final Cut Pro seeks out each clip on the specified reel and creates the QuickTime media file necessary for editing. You will see the material you are capturing in a capture screen.

When all clips on that reel have been captured, the Insert Reel window opens again, indicating the number of clips remaining to be captured. If all clips were successfully captured, there should be 0 clips and the status should be "DONE."

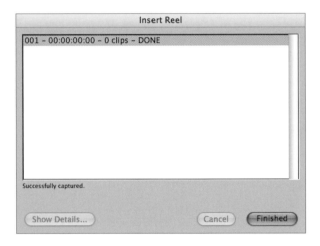

10   When all of the clips are captured, click Finished.

If your list contains footage from another reel or tape, Final Cut Pro will prompt you to change reels and continue. When batch capture is completed, each of the selected clips in the logging bin will have footage connected to them, and the red lines will be gone.

Setting Capture Preferences

The General tab of User Preferences contains options that relate to capturing. Certain user preferences will affect how you capture video. Some of these preferences help you troubleshoot or work around problematic video, while others smooth the capturing process. Let's take a look at four of these options.

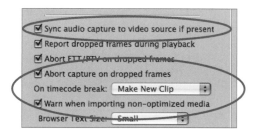

▶ Sync audio capture to video source if present—This option ensures sync for audio captured from a genlocked audio deck.

▶ Abort capture on dropped frames—If Final Cut Pro notices any frames of video being dropped or left out while capturing your source material, it will stop the capture process and report the dropped frames. You will lose all the media captured up to that point.

▶ On timecode break—If there is a break in the source-tape timecode, you have the option to make Final Cut Pro do one of three things: start a new clip at the timecode break, abort the capture process, or warn you that there was a timecode break after capturing is over.

▶ Warn when importing non-optimized media—Final Cut Pro will always optimize media files when capturing. On the rare occasion that it can't optimize a media file for multiple-stream real-time playback, it will warn you if this option is selected. Unless you are editing with multiple uncompressed video streams that demand maximum media file performance, you can usually leave the files as they are and continue editing normally. If you are working with standard definition DV captured in Final Cut Pro, your files are already optimized.

> **TIP** ▶ Try capturing using the default User Preferences settings. If you have problems with dropped frames or timecode breaks, deselect one or more of the options and try again.

Acquiring Other Media

As new technologies develop, so do the possibilities of recording and capturing media. Newer tapeless formats include Panasonic's P2 solid-state acquisition, Sony's XDCAM optical disc recording, and Focus Enhancements' Direct To Edit FireStore recorders. Although capturing from tape is a real-time process, these options convert your footage to digital files as you shoot. Rather than capture the footage as you do with tape sources, you *ingest* the digital files into your project and begin editing immediately. You can even edit in the foreground while you capture, or ingest, in the background.

When these options are connected via FireWire to your computer, Final Cut Pro recognizes them. You use a Log and Transfer window to enter log information and transfer these clips into your project.

> **MORE INFO** ▶ For detailed steps to import these media options, see the Final Cut Pro User Manual or go to www.apple.com/finalcutstudio/ resources.

Lesson Review

1. Before you can capture footage, what is the first thing you must do?

2. Marking clips for capture is similar to marking clips while editing. True or false?

3. You can enter a variety of clip information in the Logging tab. Give an example of logging information that appears in the Browser columns.

4. When you choose a capture preset, what settings do you want it to match?

5. What are the three capture modes you can use to capture footage?

6. What is a scratch disk?

7. How can you save time using the Batch Capture mode?

8. Where do you modify your logged clip settings?

9. You can choose only your computer hard drive as a scratch disk. True or false?

10. What other settings window contains the scratch disk information like that on the Capture Settings tab?

11. What other settings window contains the device control information like that on the Capture Settings tab?

Answers

1. You must connect your source device via a FireWire cable or third-party capture card.

2. True.

3. Log note, good take, scene number, take number, angle number, clip name.

4. Your source footage settings. If you have a variety of footage, it should match whatever format represents the majority of clips or the highest quality, depending upon the project and your hardware.

5. Capture Clip, Capture Now, and Batch Capture.

6. The target destination for your captured media files.

7. With the Batch Capture mode, you can log individual clips then capture them together at the same time.

8. Modify logged clip settings in the Modify Clip Settings dialog, which you access from the Modify menu.

9. False. You can set your computer hard drive or an external FireWire drive as your scratch disk, where the media files will be saved.

10. The System Settings window.

11. The Audio/Video Settings window.

Keyboard Shortcuts

Spacebar	Plays and stops the tape
Command-8	Opens Log and Capture window
Shift-Q	Opens System Settings window
Option-Q	Opens User Preferences
Command-Option-Q	Opens Audio/Video Settings window
Control-C	Batch captures selected items
Escape key	Stops capture process
F2	Logs a clip in the Browser without capturing media

Completing the Cut

9

Lesson **9**
Applying Transitions

The next stage of the editing process is completing the sequence. Completing the sequence does not mean that you're ready to ship the final product; but it does mean that you're wrapping up the big things such as mixing together audio tracks, adding transitions to smooth edit points, and creating text for a title or for identifying the show's host or guests. Without completing these essential tasks, your sequence just won't be ready for prime-time viewing.

In the next three lessons, you will focus on each of these aspects: adding transitions, mixing sound, and creating titles. Add some special effects, and you are only a few short steps from your final output.

This lesson covers transitions. Transitions add variety to your video by changing how you move from one clip to the next. They can be used to fix an abrupt audio or video edit or to create a certain visual style for your sequence.

This lesson explores ways to apply a variety of transition effects to video and audio edit points. You will learn how to render effects and how to choose the best settings to see the maximum number of effects in real time.

A page peel is one type of video transition that can be applied to an edit point between two clips.

Evaluating Project Needs

Not every project requires transitions. Some of the world's greatest films are created with nothing more than a fade-in or a fade-out at the head and tail of the film. Part of your job as an editor is to determine whether or not transitions will improve your sequence and, if so, to choose the appropriate ones. This decision could be based on the style of the show or series. For example, dramatic material, such as *Monk*, typically cuts from one shot to the next, and transitions aren't required, whereas content cut to music, such as the *Believe Behaviors* sequence, typically uses transitions.

In this lesson, you will work with PAL footage. Although NTSC is the video standard used in North America, PAL is the video standard used in Europe and other parts of the world. PAL has a different frame rate (25 fps) than NTSC (29.97 fps), and also has more scan lines that produce a slightly higher image resolution than comparable NTSC SD or DV formats. Final Cut Pro can work with any format and will change the sequence settings automatically when you edit the first clip of a sequence into the Timeline. In this project, that sequence has already been created and edited for you, so you can focus on applying transitions.

> **NOTE ▶** Although you will work with new footage in this lesson, the *Believe Behaviors* sequence is included so that you can apply what you learn in this lesson to that sequence as well.

1   Choose File > Open, or press Command-O, and select the **Lesson 9 Project** file from the Lessons folder on your hard drive. Then close any other open projects.

2   In the Timeline, play the *Yellow Cuts* sequence.

This sequence was created from a series of televised interstitials (shorts between programs) titled *Living Colour*, and this episode is all about yellow. The entire series of five-minute interstitials was produced by the British Broadcasting Company (BBC) using footage excerpted from its long-form programming. It was originally shot on multiple formats, with each clip coming from individual productions. That's why there is black at the top and bottom of the image area: to conform the different formats to one size. It was mastered on PAL DigiBeta and captured for this project using the DVCPRO PAL codec.

Let's take a look at the original source clip, and how this project is organized around it.

3   In the Browser, display the contents of the Yellow bin, and then the Clips bin. Double-click the **Living_Colour_Yellow** clip to open it in the Viewer and play the first 30 seconds of this clip.

This edited piece was captured as one clip. There are four audio tracks: Two tracks are for mixed narration, music, and sound effects, and two are for music and effects (M&E) without narration. The M&E tracks are often separated from the narration tracks on finished programs to allow other countries to record narrations in their own languages but still use the original music and effects as background.

In order to repurpose this five-minute piece into something shorter, subclips were created using images and narration sound bites and edited into a sequence. In the Browser, the subclips appear beneath the **Living_Colour_Yellow** clip. This clip has also been given a red label to make it easy to distinguish it from the subclips.

TIP   To make a clip appear at the top of the alphabetical list, add a space in front of the clip name.

4   Display the contents of the Audio bin, and then the Narration bin. Open the **grabs attention** clip and play it to hear the original narration subclip.

Like the video clips, subclips were created from the two mixed narration tracks and named according to what the narrator was saying. In the Audio bin, the **Narration_1-2_Stereo.aif** master clip appears above the subclips and also has a red label. This is just one way to organize this material.

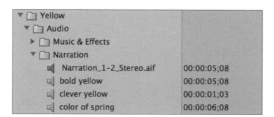

5   Close the Yellow bin. Click the Timeline to make it active.

Since a sequence has already been created, you won't need to access these clips during this lesson. You may, however, want to change your Timeline layout to better view the clip icons in the sequence.

6   Press Option-+ (plus) a few times to zoom in until you can read the names on the first two clips in the sequence. To increase the height of just the V1 track, drag the V1 boundary line up and release it.

Zooming in and changing the height of the tracks helps you to view the sequence as if it were a storyboard. This will make it easier to work with clips that you didn't edit.

7   Look at the first clip in the sequence, **beetle on flower (80%)**.

The clips in the original "Living Colour: Yellow" program were very short. In order to apply transitions between each clip in the *Yellow Cuts* sequence, each subclip was slowed down so it would play longer and have handles to use for transitions. The percentage next to the clip name indicates the speed at which the clip is playing; this clip is playing at 80% of its normal speed. You will learn to change the speed of clips in Lesson 12.

In the Timeline, notice the green bar above the ruler area. This is the video render bar, and its color indicates the render status of a clip. Green means the clip will play in real time with its current effect, which is the speed change. You will learn more about rendering later in this lesson.

8   To save a copy of the original *Yellow Cuts* sequence to use throughout this lesson, duplicate it in the Browser, and rename it *Yellow Cuts Backup*.

Unlike creating a new sequence version and changing it as you did in an earlier lesson, a backup simply remains unchanged in your project in case you need to return to the original.

Understanding Transitions

Whether or not you've ever applied a transition to your own sequence, you've probably seen a million of them on television and in films and intuitively know what they are. A transition is an effect applied to the edit point between two clips in a sequence. Instead of cutting from one clip to the next and making an immediate change, a transition creates a change over time from the outgoing clip to the incoming clip.

Several types of transitions can be applied in Final Cut Pro. One type of transition used frequently is a *cross dissolve*, a video transition that mixes video from the outgoing clip to the incoming clip at the edit point. As one clip fades out, the other clip fades in. This mixing process utilizes the handles of one or both clips that make up the transition. In audio, this process is called a *cross fade*: the end of one audio clip fades out while the beginning of the next one fades in.

Viewing Transition Options

Final Cut Pro organizes its effects into two categories: transitions and filters. (Filters will be covered in Lesson 13.) You can choose a transition effect from one of two places: the Effects menu or the Effects tab in the Browser. Each place contains the same set of transition effects organized in separate Video and Audio Transition bins.

1   In the Browser, select the Effects tab. If this tab is in icon view, Control-click in the gray area and choose View As List from the shortcut menu.

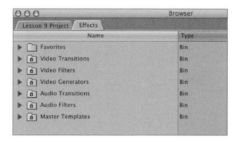

The Effects tab has seven bins. Three bins contain video effects, two contain audio effects, and two can be used to store and organize your favorite effects and apply a Motion template. In this lesson, you will use just the Video Transitions and Audio Transitions bins.

2   Display the contents of the Audio Transitions bin.

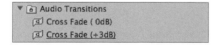

This folder contains two audio cross fades: 0dB and +3dB. A 0 dB cross fade has a slight dip in the audio level at the midpoint of the transition. The +3 dB cross fade is designed to produce a fade without having this dip in the middle. The +3dB cross fade is underlined, meaning it is the default transition.

3   Click the disclosure triangle next to the Audio Transitions bin to hide its contents. Then display the contents of the Video Transitions bin.

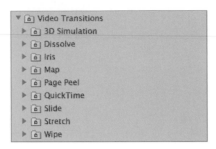

There are nine bins of video transitions, each with its own set of transition styles and parameters.

4   Click the disclosure triangle next to the Dissolve bin to display its contents.

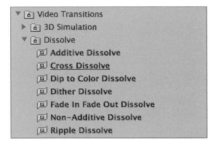

Different dissolve transitions appear here, including the underlined Cross Dissolve, which is the default video transition. Notice too that the Dissolve transitions are in boldface type, which means they can be played in real time (RT), or normal play speed, after you apply them.

5   Choose the Effects menu.

Six of the Effects bin titles appear here, including Favorites, Video Transitions, Video Filters, Audio Transitions and Filters, and Master Templates.

6   From the Effects menu, choose Video Transitions > Dissolve.

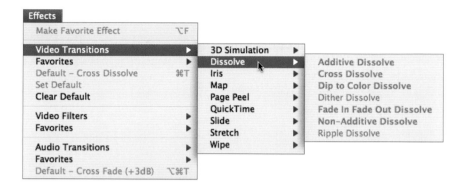

The same dissolve options appear here, although currently dimmed, that appear on the Effects tab in the Browser.

Although you can choose any transition from either location, there is additional information in the Effects tab that might come in handy as you edit.

7   Click in the Browser window and then click the Zoom button to expand the window. Drag the Length column heading to the left to place it next to the Name column.

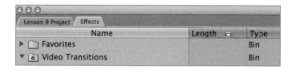

All audio and video transitions have a default 1-second duration. Changing the length in this column changes the default duration of a specific transition.

TIP ▶ Control-clicking in the Name column, and choosing Only Show My Preferred Effects from the Browser shortcut menu, allows you to display only those transitions you prefer to use.

For the steps in this lesson, you will not be screening source footage, just viewing the sequence.

8   Press Option-U to return the windows to their larger Canvas layout.

Applying Transitions

The ways you apply a transition are a little like the automatic and manual approaches to editing you used in Lesson 2. The manual approach is to drag a transition from the Effects tab and drop it over an edit point in the Timeline. This approach relies on your own eye and judgment to place the effect correctly. The automatic approach makes use of the Effects menu, but you first must target the edit point so Final Cut Pro knows where to place the transition you select. You apply audio and video transitions the same way.

While there are a variety of video transitions to explore, in this exercise you will focus on the process of applying a transition using dissolves.

> **TIP** ▶ Make sure snapping is on throughout this lesson, and whenever necessary, zoom into the Timeline so you can more easily identify clips and transitions.

1   In the Timeline, play the first two clips: **beetle on flower** and **bee cu**. Then click the video edit point between them to select it.

> **NOTE** ▶ Your V1 video track may appear taller than those pictured in the images in this lesson.

By selecting the edit point between these two clips, you are giving Final Cut Pro a target location to place the transition you choose from the Effects menu.

2   Choose Effects > Video Transitions > Dissolves > Cross Dissolve. Play the new dissolve transition.

The **beetle on flower** clip fades out as the **bee cu** clip fades in. Since the default length for all transitions is 1 second, this is a 1-second dissolve centered over the edit point. Handles for each clip extend out to either side of the edit point. Notice that the transition name appears on the icon between the two clips. The dark upward and downward shading represents the handle portion of each clip fading in and out.

NOTE ▶ A 1-second dissolve in PAL footage consists of 25 frames. The dissolve is divided over the edit point as 12 frames on the outgoing clip side, and 13 frames on the incoming clip side. When you're working with 29.97 fps NTSC footage, the dissolve is evenly split with 15 frames on either side of the edit point.

Another way to target an edit point is to position the playhead directly on it, and another way to choose the Cross Dissolve from the Effects menu is to choose the most recently applied effect.

3   Press the Up or Down Arrow to move the playhead to the next edit point between the **bee cu** and **daisy bee** clips. This time, choose Effects > Last – Cross Dissolve.

TIP ▶ You can also press the V key to move the playhead to the nearest edit point in either direction.

To apply a transition manually, you must view both the target edit point in the Timeline and the transition you want to apply in the Effects tab. As you drag the transition from the Effects tab, you are dragging the transition icon. When you place the icon over an edit point, it is colored dark brown to indicate how it will be placed. You have the option of releasing the transition centered on the edit point, or to the left or right of it.

4   In the Timeline, make sure you can see the next transition between the **daisy bee** and the **bee in pollen** clips. From the Effects tab, drag the Cross Dissolve icon into the Timeline over this edit point and position the pointer so the transition icon is even on both sides, then release the mouse. Play this transition.

> **NOTE** ▶ Most cross dissolves are centered over the edit point. If a clip does not have enough handles to allow for a transition, you can realign the transition to either end or start on the edit point.

Since the cross dissolve is the default video transition, you can also apply it using a keyboard shortcut. Using a shortcut is an automatic approach and requires that you target the edit point, as you do when you choose a menu option.

5   Select the next edit point in the sequence between the **bee in pollen** and **candle flame** clips. Press Command-T to add the default video transition, and play the transition.

In this sequence, audio edits were made to create a narration track that is different from the original. Sometimes the music or sound effects change abruptly as one audio clip cuts to another. In editing, the emphasis is often placed on the video portion of a sequence. However, if the audio clips in your sequence are jarring as you cut from one to the next, viewers will notice it immediately. To smooth these edit points, you can apply an audio cross fade.

6   Press Shift-Z to see the entire sequence. Find the eighth audio clip, **yellow and black,** and zoom into that clip. Play this clip and the next two that follow it.

The **warning sound** clip is abrupt at the edit points on either side of it. Applying an audio cross fade at these locations will help smooth these edits.

7 Select the edit point between the **yellow and black** and **warning sound** clips. Choose Effects > Audio Transitions > Cross Fade (+3dB), and play the transition.

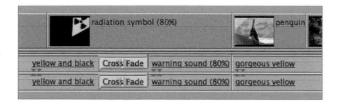

All video and audio transition icons look alike except for the transition name that appears on it. Since the audio clips are stereo pairs, the cross fade is applied to both audio tracks at the same time, and the abrupt cut is smoothed considerably.

You can also use a keyboard shortcut to apply an audio cross fade. As with the video shortcuts, you must first target the edit point.

8 Select the next edit point, between the **warning sound** and **gorgeous yellow** clips. Press Option-Command-T, and play this transition.

When a clip is used in its entirety in the sequence, there aren't enough clip handles to extend past the clip to create a transition. To remedy this, you can position, or *align*, a transition to end or start on an edit point. A good trick for determining how long a clip's media handles are is to click the clip with the Slip tool. You will see the handles extend on either side of the clip as part of the brown clip outline.

9 Play the edit point above the **yellow and black** audio clip, between the **snakes in water** and **radiation symbol** video clips. Press S to select the Slip tool, and click and hold the **radiation symbol** clip.

In the Canvas, you see the end-of-clip overlays in the left and right frames, indicating that there are no handles in this clip. This means there is no media at the head of the clip to mix with the outgoing clip before the edit point. In this situation, you can start the transition to begin at the edit point, instead of centering on the edit point. This extends the outgoing clip past the edit point for the full length of the transition.

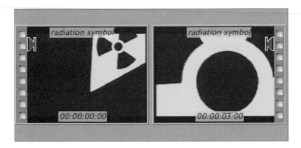

10 Press A to return to the default Selection tool. From the Effects tab, drag the Dip to Color Dissolve icon to the right side of the edit point between the **snakes in water** and **radiation symbol** clips, but don't release the mouse.

When a transition icon is aligned on the right side of the edit point, you see the full length of the dissolve appear over that clip.

11 Release the transition on the right side of the edit point, and play the transition.

This transition starts at the edit point and dips to black as it transitions from one clip to the next. Since this is a different type of transition from a cross dissolve, you see a different name on the transition icon.

NOTE ► This type of transition can be modified to dip to any color. You will make those modifications later in this lesson.

Start On Edit is one of three transition alignments you can choose, along with End On Edit and Center On Edit. The End On Edit alignment is used when an outgoing clip has no extra media to extend past the edit point.

NOTE ► If you try to center a dissolve on an edit point that doesn't have enough handles, you will end up with a one-frame transition.

12 To complete this yellow and black section, apply a Dip to Color Dissolve transition to the previous edit point between the **sunflower** and **snakes in water** clips. Use any method you like.

When you add a transition to a clip at the beginning of the sequence, the clip will transition from black instead of from another clip.

13 In the Timeline, press Home to move the playhead to the head of the sequence. Choose Effects > Video Transitions > Dissolves > Cross Dissolves, and play the new transition.

The **beetle on flower** clip fades up from black. You can also use this approach to fade out a clip at the end of a sequence.

Project Tasks

You will add an assortment of video transitions throughout this lesson. For now, play the sequence and add an audio cross fade to any audio edit point you feel is too abrupt.

TIP You can add buttons for Add Video Transition and Add Audio Transition to the Timeline button bar. Using buttons requires that you first target the edit point by positioning the playhead over it or by selecting it.

Modifying and Copying Transitions

When you find a transition that's just right in one location, you may decide to apply it to several other edit points. Rather than reapply a new transition each time, you can simply copy and paste the one that's already in the Timeline. You can even copy a transition from one sequence in a project to another sequence in a different project. Once it is applied, you can easily modify a transition to give it a longer or shorter duration. You can also reassign a different transition to be the default. There is a handy way to add a transition to a group of clips in the Timeline at one time.

1 Play the section of clips and transitions between the **beetle on flower** and **candle flame** clips. If necessary, zoom into this section to see the clip names.

 Like all other transitions, these cross dissolves have a default duration of 1 second. Since these are all fairly short clips, let's shorten the transitions so we get from one clip to the next more quickly.

2 Move the pointer over either edge of the Cross Dissolve icon between the **beetle on flower** and the **bee cu** clips. When the pointer changes to a Resize pointer, drag the edge away from the edit point as far as possible, but don't release the mouse.

 An information box indicates how much the transition has been lengthened, along with the new duration.

In the Canvas, you see an end-of-clip overlay in the right frame, indicating that you've reached this clip's media limit. A transition will only drag outward as far as there is clip material to support it. If you cannot drag any farther, either you have reached the limit of one or both of the clip's media, or you've reached the next edit point or transition in the Timeline.

NOTE ▶ You may have noticed that the clip information in the Canvas overlays appears in italics to denote that a speed change is applied to these clips.

3   Drag the edge of the icon back toward the edit point until you've reached a new duration of 15 frames. Release the mouse, and play the transition.

TIP ▶ When dragging a transition inward to reduce its duration, turning snapping off temporarily will give you greater control, as will zooming in to that area of the Timeline.

Another way to change the length of a transition is to enter a specific duration amount.

4   Control-click one side of the Cross Dissolve icon between the **bee cu** and **daisy bee** clips, but not on the actual edit point directly between the two clips.

A shortcut menu appears with options to adjust this transition. Here you can choose a different transition alignment. You can also use the copy and paste functions to copy and paste a transition. If you know the specific length of transition you want, you can simply enter it.

TIP ▸ Always click to the side of the actual edit point to select the transition icon. If you click in the middle, the edit point itself will be selected, and a different shortcut menu will appear.

5   Choose Duration from the shortcut menu. When the small Duration window appears, enter *15* for a new 15-frame duration. Press Return to enter the number, then press Return again, or click OK, to close the window. Play the new transition.

NOTE ▸ You can also enter the total number of frames. For example, since this tape's source frame rate was 25 frames per second, you can enter *50* to represent 2 seconds. If you are editing in NTSC, you would enter *60* frames for 2 seconds.

Notice that the 15-frame transition icon does not appear as wide as the 1-second transition icons. The width of each transition icon in the Timeline also represents its length.

Often, you'll choose a transition that you can use repeatedly throughout the sequence in order to create or maintain a certain style. If you know you want to apply a specific transition other than the Cross Dissolve, you can make that transition the default video transition. You can also change the default transition length. Let's use the Cube Spin to transition in and out of the next group of clips.

6 In the Effects tab in the Browser, close the Dissolve transition bin and display the contents of the 3D Simulation transitions. To make the Cube Spin the default transition, Control-click the Cube Spin icon and choose Set Default Transition from the shortcut menu.

Once set, the default transition line appears under the transition name. Any transition can be the default transition, but there can only be one default video transition and one default audio transition at a time. Now let's change the default transition length.

7 If necessary, expand the Browser window to see the Length column, or make the Name column narrower. Click in the Length column for the Cube Spin transition and enter *20*, to create a 20-frame default transition.

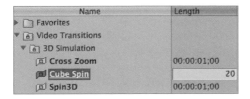

When you apply this transition in the next step, its duration, or length, will be 20 frames. Because the Cube Spin transition is the new default, you can use the keyboard shortcut to apply it to an edit point.

8 In the Timeline, select the edit point between the **candle flame** clip and the **bee between flowers** clip. Press Command-T to apply the new default transition at this location. Then play the transition.

The name of this transition appears on the transition icon.

TIP When you change the length of a transition in the Timeline, and then apply a different transition to that same edit point, the new transition will take on the length of the previous transition.

Let's use a different approach to apply this default transition to the end of this section of quick cuts.

9 Control-click the edit point between the **daisy opens** and **sunset savanna** clips. From the shortcut menu, choose Add Transition 'Cube Spin.'

TIP You can also apply a default transition by choosing Effects > Default – [Transition Name].

Once a transition is already in the Timeline, you can copy and paste that transition to a different edit point. Let's apply a Page Peel transition and then copy and paste it to another edit point.

10 Click once on the edit point between the **sunset savanna** and **sea anemone** clips to select the transition. Choose Effects > Video Transitions > Page Peel > Page Peel, and play this transition.

Some transitions have additional parameters that can be modified. In the Page Peel transition, you can change the curl direction, angle, and so on. You will learn to make parameter changes in the next exercise.

NOTE ▶ Depending on your computer's processing power, Final Cut Pro may not be able to play every frame of a transition, and some may stutter a bit as they play in the sequence. You can render these later in this lesson.

11 In the Timeline, select the Page Peel icon and press Command-C to copy it. You can also Control-click the transition and choose Copy from the shortcut menu. Then deselect the transition icon.

There are three ways to paste copied transitions. In the next step, you will try one method, press Command-Z to undo that paste, and then try a different method.

12 Position the playhead directly on the edit point between the **sea anemone** and **birdeye** clips. Try each of the following methods to paste the Page Peel transition you copied in the previous step. Then play this group of clips.

▶ Press Command-V to paste the copied transition to the target edit point. Press Command-Z to undo that paste.

▶ Control-click the edit point and choose Paste from the shortcut menu. Press Command-Z to undo that paste.

▶ Select the original Page Peel transition, then hold down Option and drag a copy of the transition. Release the copy over the target edit point.

You can always press Command-Z to undo a step and return to a previous transition, or return the edit point to a simple cut.

TIP ▶ To delete a group of transitions at one time, Command-click the transitions and press Delete.

Project Tasks

There is another helpful trick that could save you valuable time as you complete your sequence. You may find that a group of clips should all have the same transition and the same transition length. Rather than create a default transition and apply it to each individual edit point, you can add it to a group of clips at one time using an edit option from the Canvas Edit Overlay.

1 Position the playhead at the beginning of the **petals, pollen, perfume** audio clip.

This audio track underlies three video clips. It would be nice to add the same transition to each of these video clips at one time. The first step is to set the default transition and length.

2   In the Effects tab in the Browser, display the contents of the Dissolve bin, and select the Cross Dissolve transition. Choose Effects > Set Default. In the Length column, enter *15* as the default duration for this transition.

3   In the Timeline, select the following three clips: **yellow field, flowers in breeze, blossom opening.**

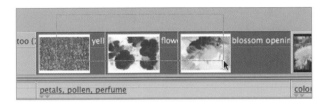

You are going to re-edit these three clips back to their current location using the Overwrite with Transition option in the Canvas Edit overlay. While you can use this option to edit a single clip into a sequence and simultaneously give it the default transition, you can also use it to re-edit clips from the sequence back into the sequence, either at the same location or a different one. When re-edited, each clip will have a default transition at the head of the clip.

4   Drag the selected clips up into the Canvas and release them onto the red Overwrite with Transition option (striped).

In the Timeline, the clips reappear at the original location (based on the playhead location) and each clip has a default 15-frame cross dissolve.

TIP For practice, you can add a default transition to each edit point in the *Believe Behaviors* sequence by following the steps in this project task. Keep in mind that if there are not enough handles to cover the length of a transition, a shorter transition will be applied.

Using the Transition Editor

As with other Final Cut Pro functions, there are typically several ways to achieve the same end result when adjusting transitions. Most of the time, if you need to adjust a transition's length quickly, you will make changes directly to the transition in the Timeline, as you did in the previous exercise. An alternative way to change transitions is to open the Transition Editor, which will appear as a tab over the Viewer window. The Transition Editor displays a graphical representation of the components and parameters of a single transition. In this window, you can make several changes to the transition without having to access a menu.

1 In the Timeline, move the playhead to the fifth clip in the sequence, **candle flame**, and zoom into that area. Make sure no other clips or transition icons are selected or you will zoom into those selected items.

At the head of this clip is a Cross Dissolve transition. At the tail is a Cube Spin transition. Let's take a closer look at the cross dissolve in the Transition Editor.

2   At the head of the **candle flame** clip, Control-click one side of the Cross Dissolve icon, and choose Open 'Cross Dissolve' from the shortcut menu. You can also double-click one side of the icon.

> **NOTE** ▶ If you accidentally double-click the middle of the transition over the edit point, the Trim Edit window will open. To close it, click the Close button or, in the Timeline, click in a gray area above a video track as though you were deselecting a clip.

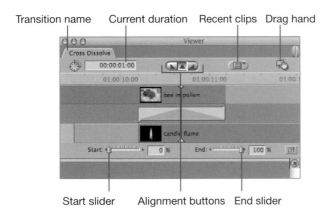

The Transition Editor opens in the Viewer with a graphic representation of the current transition. You have already adjusted or selected some of the options that appear here, such as duration and alignment.

> **TIP** ▶ If your window layout is still on the larger Canvas display, you may want to press Control-U to return to the Standard layout, to see a larger Transition Editor.

3   In the Transition Editor, click the End On Edit alignment button (on the right) and then the Start On Edit alignment button (on the left). Then click the Center On Edit button (in the center).

The graphic representation of the dissolve in the Transition Editor changes, as does the transition on the edit point in the Timeline.

4   Click in the Duration field and type *50*, then press Tab, Return, or Enter.

Since this footage is PAL and the video frame rate is 25 frames per second, entering *50* in the Duration field creates a 2-second transition.

5   In the Transition Editor, move the pointer over the transition icon.

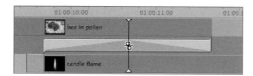

The pointer turns into the Roll tool, allowing you to adjust or roll the edit point left or right to improve the timing of the edit without changing the transition. Notice the light blue area on the outer edge of each clip. This represents the clip's handles.

6   Drag the transition icon right and look at the Canvas two-up display. When you see the bee fly out of frame, release the mouse, and play the transition.

In the Timeline, the edit point and transition appear later in the sequence.

NOTE ▶ The Start and End percentages beneath the graphic display are typically used for wipes or other types of transitions in which you want the wipe pattern to begin at a midpoint from its original starting location.

In the previous exercise, you copied a transition from one edit point and pasted it to another. You can also drag a transition from the Transition Editor to a different edit point.

7   In the upper-right corner of the Transition Editor window, drag the drag hand icon to the previous edit point between the **daisy bee** and **bee in pollen** clips.

Applying a transition from the Transition Editor replaces whichever transition was on an edit point with all the current transition parameters displayed in the Transition Editor. If there aren't enough handles to apply the current transition length (2:00), as in this edit point, a transition is applied to the maximum extent of the handles.

Let's make changes to another dissolve type of transition: the Dip to Color Dissolve transition you added later in the sequence. To move directly to that transition, you can use the Find function.

8   Click in the Timeline and press Command-F to open the Find window. In the Find field, type *dip to color*, and click Find.

The playhead moves directly to the first Dip to Color Dissolve transition in the sequence. In the Canvas, you see the yellow sunflower, which is the first frame of the transition.

TIP ▶ You can also use the Timeline Find function to find all transitions with the same name. When all of the named transitions are selected, you can delete them, or you can replace all of them at one time by choosing a new transition from the Effects menu.

9   Control-click the Dip to Color icon and choose Open 'Dip to Color Dissolve' from the shortcut menu, or you can select the transition and press Return.

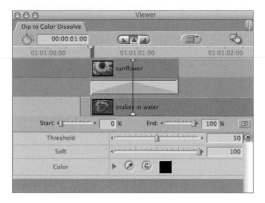

This dissolve has a few more parameters than the default Cross Dissolve transition, including color controls where you can choose the color that a clip dips to during the transition.

10 In the Transition Editor, click the Select Color eyedropper in the color controls.

11 Move the eyedropper into the Canvas window and click one of the yellow sunflower petals.

In the color controls, the color picker changes from the default black to the color you clicked in the Canvas.

TIP ▶ To search or preview different colors before selecting one, select the eyedropper, and click and drag around the Canvas image area without releasing the mouse. The color picker will reflect whatever color the eyedropper picks up. When you see the color you want, release the mouse.

Changing Transition Parameters

Dissolves are the simplest types of transitions. When you apply a more complex transition with several parameters, such as a page peel or cube spin, it becomes necessary to modify these parameters in the Transition Editor. The more complex a transition is, the more parameters you can adjust. Once you've adjusted a transition to your liking, you can save it as a favorite transition and apply it to other edit points. As you work with complex transitions, you will find that most of them can play in real time; but some may have to be *rendered*, which you will learn to do in the next exercise.

TIP ▶ To make sure you see as many real-time effects as possible, click the RT pop-up menu in the Timeline and choose Unlimited RT from the shortcut menu. Click the RT pop-up menu again, and make sure you see a checkmark next to Dynamic in both places that it appears. You will learn more about these options in the next exercise.

1   Move the playhead to the previous edit point between the **paint on canvas** and **sunflower** clips. Choose Effects > Video Transitions > Iris > Oval Iris. Play this transition, then reposition the playhead over the edit point.

Parking the playhead on the transition allows you to make adjustments in the Transition Editor while viewing them in the Canvas. Make sure you do this in the following steps before you make changes.

2 To open this transition, double-click one side of the transition icon, but not on the edit point itself.

Under the transition graphic display, there are additional parameters that can be controlled or adjusted using a slider or numerical-entry box. Some parameters in other effects use pop-up menus. Most parameters are self-explanatory after you've changed the parameter values and looked at the effect in the Canvas.

NOTE ▶ Clicking the tiny triangle at the end of each slider will change the numerical value of that parameter by single increments.

3 Experiment with the different settings for this transition as you view the results in the Canvas window. When you are through making changes, click the red X Reset button to return to the default settings for this effect, and make sure the playhead is once again positioned on the edit point.

Many transitions, including this Oval Iris effect, have a border you can adjust to be thin or thick. When the border value is 0, you see a hard edge. When the value is greater than 0, a border color appears.

4   To create a thin border, type *3* in the Border entry field, and press Tab.

Rather than use the default black border, let's select a border color from one of the Final Cut Pro color pickers.

5   Click the black color picker in the color controls. In the Colors window, if a color wheel appears, and it's black, drag the control on the vertical slider all the way up to see the brightest colors.

TIP ▶ You can resize the Colors window by dragging the lower-right corner.

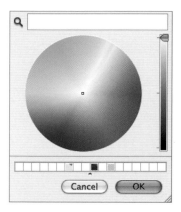

At the top of the Colors window are icons representing five color-picking layouts: Color Wheel, Color Sliders, Color Palettes, Image Palettes, and Crayons.

6   Click each icon to see how that option displays color choices. Then click the Color Wheel icon, and drag your pointer around inside the color wheel.

As you move over a color, that color appears in the horizontal color well above the color wheel.

To the left of the color well is a magnifying glass. This tool is similar to the eyedropper you used in the previous exercise in that it can select a color from an image in the Canvas. It differs in that it magnifies the colors so you can see exactly what color you're picking before you click it.

7   Click the magnifying glass next to the color well. In the Canvas, position it over the brown outer circle of the sunflower's black eye, and click.

In the Colors window, the color well changes to reflect your most recent selection.

Many television shows, networks, and companies repeatedly use a favorite color for borders, text, backgrounds, and other elements, as part of a show style. If you think you might use this particular color in a different transition elsewhere in your sequence, you can store it in the color palette.

NOTE ▶ This is the OS X Colors window, so the saved color will be available for use on other projects or applications on the same computer.

8 Click in the color well and drag down into the color palette beneath the color wheel. Release the color onto one of the squares. Then click OK.

> **TIP** ▸ By dragging down on the color palette, you can expose additional squares that can be used to store favorite colors.

The border is now the same color brown you picked from the sunflower image.

> **TIP** ▸ To make changes to an existing color in the Transition Editor, click the triangle next to the Select Color eyedropper. Drag the S (Saturation) and B (Brightness) sliders to adjust the color. Don't drag the H (Hue) slider, or you will change the original color you picked.

Since the transition is round, and the sunflower is round, it would be nice if the transition were centered directly over the sunflower as it transitions from this clip to the next.

9 In the Center parameter in the Transition Editor, click the crosshair button. Move the pointer into the Canvas window and click in the middle of the brown eye of the sunflower. (The red crosshair icon in the image represents the current center location.) Play the transition.

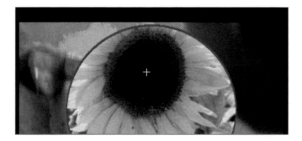

The Oval Iris transition now begins over the brown eye of the sunflower.

Now that you've customized this transition, you may want to save it in the Favorites bin to use again. Before you save this transition, make sure you can see the Favorites bin in the Effects tab in the Browser.

10 In the Effects tab, click the disclosure triangle next to the Favorites bin to display its contents.

Unless you have added your own favorite effects to this bin, it will be empty.

11 Click the Viewer window, and choose Effects > Make Favorite, or press Option-F. You can also drag the drag hand icon to the Favorites bin and release the mouse when the bin becomes highlighted.

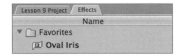

In the Favorites folder, a new Oval Iris transition with all of your changes appears. You can rename any favorite effect to reflect some parameter you changed, such as *oval brown border*.

Project Tasks

In a previous exercise, you applied Cube Spin and Page Peel transitions. Using what you've learned from these Transition Editor exercises, find those transitions, open them, adjust their parameters, and save them as favorites.

Previewing and Rendering Effects

Final Cut Pro can play multiple streams, or layers of effects, in real time. How the transitions are played back, however, depends on your computer hardware and video format, as well as some option settings that you can choose. You sometimes have to give up either image quality or a consistent frame rate to see all the effects play together. Or you may have to preview, or *render*, the transition.

Rendering processes a selected item in the sequence—in this case the transition between two clips—and creates a separate clip. That clip is stored in the Render Files folder on the designated scratch disk and played back in the sequence as a separate but invisible clip—meaning that it does not appear in the Browser or the Timeline.

A render bar in the Timeline displays a color for each effect that indicates whether or not it needs to be rendered. As you applied transitions throughout this lesson, you were probably aware of the changing colors on the render bar.

1   In the upper left of the Timeline under the sequence tabs, click the RT pop-up, but don't release the mouse.

You have been working in Unlimited RT. This setting tells Final Cut Pro to do what it has to do to play as many effects as possible in real time, even if it has to drop out some of the effect parameters, or not play every frame. The other option is Safe RT. This option tells Final Cut Pro to play an effect only if it can do so without dropping frames.

NOTE ▶ It's acceptable to drop an occasional frame while previewing and playing effects. When you are ready to output your sequence in a later lesson, you will change these settings to achieve the highest quality without dropping frames.

2   In the Timeline, press Shift-Z and scan the ruler area for any yellow or orange bars. Choose Safe RT from the RT pop-up menu, and release the mouse. Now see if any appear.

3   Click the RT pop-up again and look at the quality settings under Playback Video Quality and Playback Frame Rate.

The lower the quality and frame rate, the more effects Final Cut Pro will be able to play in real time. Choosing Dynamic will ensure that at any given moment you will have the best possible quality at the best possible frame rate while maximizing the number of effects that will play in real time.

The more complex the effects are, the lower the quality will be, so your computer will still be able to play the effect in real time. When there are fewer demands on your computer, Final Cut Pro will use a higher video quality and frame rate.

4 In the Timeline, zoom into the first Cube Spin transition, between the **candle flame** and **bee between flowers** clips.

Video render status region

Audio render status region

The colored line above the transition is a render bar. The render bar actually contains two thin regions. The upper region represents video, the lower region represents audio. A render bar can appear in the ruler area above a transition, or above the body of a clip when a speed or filter type effect has been applied. When no effects have been applied, as is the case for the audio clips, no render bars appear.

NOTE ▸ You will see render lines above the bodies of clips in this sequence because their speed was adjusted.

Different colored lines can appear in the render bar, indicating the status or capability of Final Cut Pro to play this effect in real time given the current RT settings. The render status of an effect will depend on the speed of the computer you are using. The status of an effect may be one of the following:

▶ Red   Needs to be rendered to play in real time.

▶ Orange   Exceeds the computer's real-time playback capabilities, but can still play if Unlimited RT is selected, although it may drop frames.

▶ Yellow   Transition can play in real time but may approximate
                 certain attributes.

▶ Green   Will play in real time but not at full quality.

▶ Dark green   Capable of real-time playback and output with no ren-
                 dering required.

▶ Steel gray   Material has been rendered.

▶ Dark gray   No rendering is required.

5 Move the playhead to before the Cube Spin transition and play it.

The outgoing clip plays at normal play speed until it gets to the transition,
when *Unrendered* appears in the Canvas image area for the duration of the
transition. With the Safe RT option, Final Cut Pro doesn't even try to play
this effect in real time. Yet there is a way to preview this effect.

NOTE ▶ Your playback results may vary depending upon the processing
power of your Mac.

6 Drag the playhead back before the transition once again. This time, press
Option-P. You can also press Option-\ (backslash) or choose Mark > Play >
Every Frame.

The clip plays at normal play speed until the playhead reaches the transition. At that point, the play speed slows down to process the transition,
then picks up again when it has passed the transition area. When Final

Cut Pro can't play all the effects, even set to the Unlimited RT option, previewing is a good way to get a sense of the effect without rendering it.

> **TIP** If you use Option-P a lot, you might consider adding that function, Play Every Frame, to the Timeline or Canvas button bars.

7 This time, drag the playhead manually through the transition area to see unrendered transition frames. Use the Left and Right Arrow keys to move through it frame by frame.

This is somewhat like scrubbing an effect. But to see this effect play in real time at Safe RT, you must render it. There are three render options:

▶ Render Selection   Select one or more effects and render the selected items.

▶ Render All   Render all items that need rendering.

▶ Render Only   Render only those items that are of a specific render status color.

8 Click the Sequence menu and look at each of the three Render options.

9 In the Timeline, click the Cube Spin transition once. To render it, choose Sequence > Render Selection, but don't release the mouse.

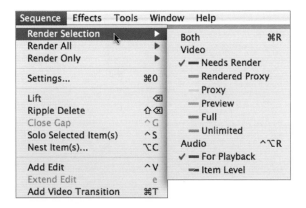

In the Render Selection submenu, the different render status colors appear. If the render color that is above the cube spin in the Timeline is not checked in this menu, your effect will not be rendered.

10 Make sure you see a checkmark next to the red render bar, or whatever color appears in your Timeline, and choose Sequence > Render Selection > Video, or press Command-R.

A window appears with a render progress bar. When rendering is complete, a blue render status line appears above the transition, indicating it has been rendered.

NOTE ▶ If a transition has already been rendered, changing its duration or any other aspect will require it to be rendered again.

11 In the Timeline, click the RT pop-up and choose Unlimited RT.

This is the best option to choose when trying out different effects.

TIP ▶ To change the scratch disk designation where render files are saved, press Shift-Q to open the System Settings window.

Project Tasks

You can continue to work with transitions in this sequence, or you can open the *Believe Behaviors* sequence and apply new transitions to it.

Lesson Review

1. From what two places can you choose a transition effect?
2. When you use the automatic approach to applying a transition, what must you do first?
3. What are three ways to change the duration of a transition in the Timeline?
4. What are the three ways a transition can be aligned to an edit point?
5. How can Command-C and Command-V be used on transitions?
6. How do you open the Transition Editor?
7. How are more-complex transitions different from dissolves?
8. What RT setting should you choose when you want to preview as many effects in your sequence as possible?
9. In what three ways can you save a favorite transition?
10. How do you set a new default transition?

Answers

1. Choose transition effects from the Effects tab in the Browser and the Effects menu.
2. Before applying a transition from the Effects menu, you must target the edit point.
3. Drag the edge of the transition icon; Control-click the transition icon, choose Duration from the shortcut menu, and enter an amount in the Duration window; or open the Transition Editor, and change it in the Duration field.
4. Use Center On Edit, Start On Edit, and End On Edit.
5. Selecting a transition and pressing Command-C copies the transition. Moving the playhead to the target edit point and pressing Command-V pastes the copied transition.
6. Either Control-click one side of the transition icon and choose Open [type of transition] from the shortcut menu, or double-click one side of the icon in a sequence clip.

7. They have additional parameters, such as border width and color, that can be adjusted in the Transition Editor.

8. Choose Unlimited RT and Dynamic.

9. From the Transition Editor, drag the drag hand icon to the Effects tab and release it in the Favorites bin; choose Effects > Make Favorite; or press Option-F.

10. Control-click the transition in the Effects tab and choose Set Default Transition from the shortcut menu.

Keyboard Shortcuts

Command-T	Applies default video transition
Option-Command-T	Applies default audio transition
Command-C	Copies a selected transition
Command-V	Pastes a copied transition
Option-P	Previews a transition (Play Every Frame command)
Command-R	Renders a selected transition
Option-R	Renders all transitions in the Timeline
Shift-Q	Opens System Settings window
Option-F	Saves a favorite transition

10

Lesson 10
Mixing Audio Tracks

Another aspect of completing your sequence is mixing the different audio tracks into one balanced, overall sound. In Final Cut Pro, you can work with up to 99 tracks of audio in one sequence.

In this lesson, you will add additional tracks to the Timeline, edit music and sound effects, and blend these tracks together with interview clips to create a final mix. You'll also apply additional Timeline controls to help manage and preview audio clips, and work with two separate tools for mixing audio and recording your own voice-over.

Audio controls and waveform displays in the Timeline

Preparing the Project for Mixing

Before you dive into mixing audio tracks, you should take a moment to evaluate the current status of the audio in your sequence. Are there enough sound effects? Would a different music track improve the piece? Would the addition of audio transitions help smooth out any rough edges? Once you determine what's needed, you can import additional audio clips to complete the sequence. You can also add tracks to the sequence in preparation for the new audio clips.

1 In the Lessons folder on your hard drive, open the **Lesson 10 Project** file. In the Timeline, play the *Believe Mix_v1* sequence.

This promo was cut together using "Believe" interview and behavior clips. In many of the behavior clips, rehearsal music was mixed in with sounds of the whales in the water. Since a new music track is going to be added, these clips were edited as video-only clips, so the different music tracks wouldn't compete. There was no audio attached to the original underwater whale clips. However, these video clips might benefit from some sound effects.

2 In the Browser, display the contents of the Sound Effects bin. Open the **Scuba Breathing.aif** clip and play a few breaths of it.

Sometimes, you edit a sound effect to match a specific action in your sequence, such as a door slam or a balloon pop. Other times, you just need an ambient sound to give an image some depth. This scuba sound effect might add some fullness to the underwater clips.

▶ **Working with Soundtrack Pro 2**

The effects in the Sound Effects bin were all exported from Soundtrack Pro. In that program, you can search for additional music or sound effect files to use in this or other sequences, and export those sound effects as individual clips for use in Final Cut Pro. Or, you can add scoring markers to a sequence in Final Cut Pro, identifying where you want certain sound effects to occur. You can then export that sequence from FCP, import it into Soundtrack Pro, and add music or sound effects clips at those scoring markers. The royalty-free music loops and sound effects files in Soundtrack Pro provide an excellent way to complete the sound of a project. You can also send a sequence to Soundtrack Pro to clean up audio pops and make other changes or corrections.

3   Open the **Water Lake 1.aif** clip and play a few seconds of it. Then lower the volume to –21 dB, and play it again.

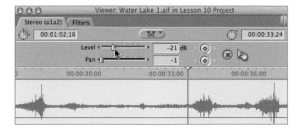

Some effects sound outrageously unrealistic when they are at full volume. But when you lower the volume, they sound more believable. With this clip's volume lowered, it can double for a whale splashing sound.

TIP ▶ When you lower the volume of a master clip in the Browser, every time you edit that clip into a sequence it will already be at a rough mix level.

4   From the Music bin, open the **Track 8_guitar.aif** clip and play about 20 seconds of it.

This is the music track you will use to help dramatize the promo. Since you already have interview sound bites in the sequence, you will have to raise and lower the volume of this clip so you can hear the on-camera individuals when they speak. This is sometimes referred to as *animating* the volume levels. In this lesson, you will learn two different ways to animate volume.

Before you edit these new clips, you need to add additional audio tracks to the sequence. You need at least two tracks for sound effects and two tracks for the music score. Rather than add these tracks individually, you can add them all at one time.

5   Click the Timeline, and choose Sequence > Insert Tracks.

An Insert Tracks window opens in which you can choose the type of tracks you want to insert as well as the number and location. You can insert tracks after the last track or before the base, or lowest, track number. Even though the Insert Video Tracks checkbox is selected, the number of tracks is set to 0 by default, so no new video tracks will be inserted.

TIP ▸ You can access the Delete Tracks window by choosing Sequence > Delete Tracks. Here you can delete all unused video or audio tracks at the same time.

6 In the Insert Tracks window, enter *4* in the Insert Audio Tracks field. Leave the default After Last Track selected, and click OK.

> **TIP** If you want to add additional sound effects clips, or preview alternative music tracks, you can always insert more tracks.

Whenever you work closely with audio in the Timeline, it's a good idea to display the audio level overlays to help you adjust volume, and to view the audio waveforms as a visual reference to clip content. Let's toggle on those functions using keyboard shortcuts.

7 Press Option-W to toggle on the audio level overlays, and press Option-Command-W to toggle on audio waveforms in the Timeline. To make the audio waveforms easier to read, press Shift-T to toggle to a taller Timeline track.

> **TIP** If you added audio buttons in the Lesson 7 project tasks, you can click those to toggle these functions off and on.

With audio waveforms toggled on, you can take a closer look at the clips in the sequence. One thing to look for is whether there are any "dead" audio tracks. Sometimes an audio clip is captured as a stereo pair, but audio is recorded on only one track. Having an additional track of dead audio in the sequence can be misleading since it doesn't accurately represent the clip.

Look at the clips in the Timeline. The **narration 2** clip has no audio waveform on the A2 portion of this clip, yet there is a stereo pair indicator attaching the two clips together. You can unlink the stereo pair clip and remove the empty track of the clip.

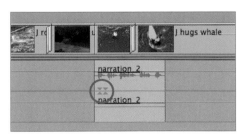

8   Select the **narration 2** clip. Choose Modify > Stereo Pair, or press Option-L. Deselect the clip.

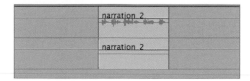

The stereo pair indicator no longer appears. You can toggle off or on the stereo pair status of any clip. This allows you to remove the dead audio from the clip, or to change the volume on each track independently when, for instance, two separate microphones were used for recording.

9   Select the **narration 2** clip on the A2 track, and press Delete.

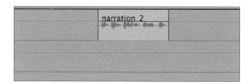

TIP ▶   If you want to boost the audio for a single mono clip, you can copy and paste the clip beneath itself, select both audio clips and make them a stereo pair.

10 Play the **narration 2** clip and look at the Audio meters.

This mono clip plays in the left audio channel only. Typically, you'll want the narration or voice-over to be heard in both channels. To direct this audio to both channels, you can pan it to the center by choosing that option from the Modify menu in the Viewer Audio tab, or using a keyboard shortcut.

11 In the Timeline, select the **narration 2** clip, and choose Modify > Audio > Pan Center, or press Control-. (period). Play the clip again.

Now the single mono track of audio is panned to the center and heard through both channels.

NOTE ▶ If you double-click this clip to open it in the Viewer, you will see a Pan setting of 0, which represents center. To pan a mono audio track left, enter *−1* in the Pan field, and to pan it right, enter *1*. With a stereo clip, *−1* indicates the left and right audio channels will be heard in the left and right speakers, respectively; *1* indicates that the left and right channels will be reversed.

Editing and Organizing Audio Effects

The most important aspect of organizing audio tracks is to edit similar types of clips in the same or neighboring tracks. This will make them easier to modify. There are ways in which you can select, monitor, and modify all the clips on a single track. Placing all of the sound effects on one track, the dialogue on another track, and music on still another, and so on, will make it much easier to modify them.

Some editors like to edit their sound effects beneath the video clips they support, and place the music clips on the lowest tracks. Others prefer placing the music tracks beneath the dialogue or interview clips to view them as a reference when mixing the volume levels. You can experiment to see what works best for you and your sequence. Just be consistent with the tracks you choose when editing similar clips in any given sequence. To edit and organize the sound effects in this exercise, you will use editing techniques different from those you learned in previous lessons.

1 With the **Track 8_guitar.aif** clip in the Viewer, drag the drag hand icon down into the Timeline into the A5 and A6 tracks, and release the clip at the head of the sequence as an overwrite edit. Play some of this music track in the sequence.

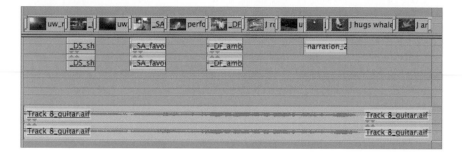

You might be able to complete some sequences by simply mixing a music clip into the existing audio sources. Other sequences might require several music sources. And others, like this one, require sound effects to add some atmosphere to the whale behavior shots.

2   Move the playhead back to the head of the sequence. Patch the audio source controls to the A3 and A4 tracks.

Since the A3 and A4 tracks are empty, you don't have to worry about over-writing any other material.

3   In the Viewer, click the Recent Clips pop-up menu and choose the **Scuba Breathing.aif** clip. Lower the volume to –10 dB. Mark an In point just before the sound begins, and edit this entire clip as an overwrite edit.

NOTE ▶ As you edit sound effects, it's helpful to lower the volume to a background level, even though you may need to readjust that level when you mix it with other clips in the sequence.

There are three underwater whale clips in this sequence. The first two, toward the beginning of the sequence, are now supported by this scuba sound effect. Later in this lesson, you will animate the volume so you don't hear the scuba sound while the individuals are speaking. Let's split off a portion of this sound effect and reposition it under the third underwater clip.

4   Position the playhead over the middle of the **_SA_favorite behavior**
clip. Press B to select the Razor Blade tool, snap it to the playhead in
the A3 or A4 track, and click to create a new edit point in the **Scuba
Breathing.aif** clip.

When sound effects are more generic, such as this one, it's easy to work
with them in the Timeline. You can copy and paste them, or razor blade
and reposition them, and they will still sound pretty good.

5   Press A to return to the default Selection tool, and drag the second **Scuba
Breathing.aif** clip to the right beneath the **uw_propel jump** clip (before the
narration 2 clip). To allow room for effects on either side of this clip, drag
the In and Out points to match the length of the **uw_propel jump** clip.

An easy way to add a new sound effect is to mark the length of the corre-
sponding video clip in the Timeline.

6   In the Timeline, move the playhead over the previous clip, **J rotations**, and
press X to mark the length of this clip. From the Viewer Recent Clips pop-up
menu, choose **Water Lake 1.aif**, and edit this clip as an overwrite edit.

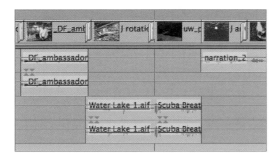

Although this clip does not appear to be long in the Timeline, it has plenty of media handles so that you can later add a transition at the beginning or end of the clip. To add this sound effect to the remaining video clips, you can drag a copy of it and trim it longer.

7   Select the **Water Lake 1.aif** clip. Press Option and drag the clip right. Snap the new clip's In point to the end of the **Scuba Breathing.aif** clip. Release the Option key, then release the clip as an overwrite edit.

To trim this clip's Out point to the end of the sequence, you could drag the edit point right and snap it to the other clips' Out points. Or you can extend it using Extend edit.

8   Snap the playhead to the end of the sequence, select the **Water Lake 1.aif** clip's Out point, and press E.

Project Tasks

Sometimes, you have to work a little to make an effect sound realistic. When you play the **performance_S spray jump** in the Timeline, you see that the peak moment is midway in the clip when Steve jumps out of the water and over the spray. This is where a big crowd cheer should be. You will have to alter an applause clip to make this happen.

1   From the Sound Effects bin in the Browser, open the **Arena Crowd Cheer.aif** clip. Play until after the crowd roar settles down, then mark an In point and enter a 5-second duration for this clip. Lower the volume to −15 dB.

2   In the Timeline, position the playhead at the head of the **performance_S spray jump** clip, and edit the **Arena Crowd Cheer.aif** clip as an overwrite edit.

3   In the Timeline, position the playhead where Steve is out of the water and at the top of the spray.

4   In the Viewer, mark an In point in the **Arena Crowd Cheer.aif** clip a few frames into the crowd roar, and create a 6-second duration. Edit this clip as an overwrite edit.

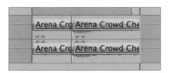

Now it sounds as though the crowd is responding to Steve's jump.

TIP ▶ For a more complex sound mix, you can insert new tracks, and add additional effects beneath the current ones. To insert a new track between two existing tracks, in the Timeline patch panel Control-click the track that you want the new track to follow, and choose Add Track.

Monitoring and Adjusting Audio Levels

After you've prepared your sequence, adding sound effects and music, you can set the relative audio level for each clip in the sequence. You begin by monitoring and setting the levels for the highest priority tracks—those tracks that must be heard above all others. Often, those are the clips with sync sound, dialogue, or narration.

In this exercise, you will use another set of Timeline track controls, audio controls, to monitor individual tracks. You'll also select all the clips on one track and adjust the volume for a group of selected clips.

TIP Before you begin monitoring audio levels, set your computer to a comfortable sound level.

1 Move the playhead to the beginning of the sequence. In the lower left of the Timeline, click the Audio Controls button, which is represented by a speaker icon.

This expands the audio controls area of your Timeline window to reveal the Mute and Solo buttons. The Mute buttons are the speaker icons on the left, and the Solo buttons are the headphone icons on the right. When you solo a track, you hear just that track and no others. This is a good way to isolate a track when setting its volume. When you mute a track, you don't hear it at all.

▶ **Setting Decibel Levels**

In digital audio, no part of the *overall* audio signal of the *combined* tracks may exceed 0 dB (decibels), or the sound will be clipped and distorted. This differs from analog audio, which uses a different dB scale and often averages sounds at around 0 dB. In order not to exceed the 0 dB level for all tracks, you set the primary audio tracks—such as dialogue and narration—well below that level, perhaps between –12 dB and –6 dB. You might set the music volume to –15 or –18. These settings allow you to combine the sound clips with an overall level well below the 0 dB peaking level, at about –6 to –3 dB. If, however, adding the additional audio tracks causes the volume to peak, you have to adjust your mix accordingly.

2 To hear how the music plays alone against the video, click the A5 and A6
Solo buttons, and play the sequence. As the sequence is playing, click the
A1 and A2 Solo buttons to add the sync sound to the mix.

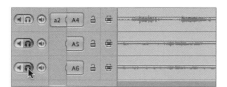

Clicking a Solo button isolates that track while simultaneously muting all
the other tracks. When you click the Audible control (the green button
next to the Solo button) as the sequence is playing, it stops the sequence.
When you click a Solo or Mute button, it adds or drops that track from
the preview without interrupting the sequence playback.

3 Toggle off the Solo buttons for the A5 and A6 music tracks. Play the
sequence again and look at the audio meters as you play just the A1
and A2 tracks.

The audio levels of these clips are fairly close. However, some of the sync
sound and narration clips are a little below –12 dB, and other clips are a
little above –12 dB. To give these clips a more uniform level, you can apply
a new function in Final Cut Pro 6 that normalizes the audio to a specific
dB level.

Since you will want to modify all the clips on the A1 and A2 tracks, select
them all using yet another selection tool.

4 To select all the clips on the A1 and A2 tracks, press T to choose the Select
Tracks Forward tool, the third tool in the Tool palette. Click the **_DS_show
concept** clip on the A1 track.

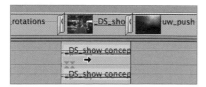

There are five track selection tools in the Tool palette, and each one either selects clips located before or after the place you click, or it selects all the tracks. With the current clips selected, you can modify them as a group.

5 Choose Modify > Audio > Apply Normalization Gain. In the Apply Normalization Gain window, enter –6 in the "Normalize to" dBFS field, and click OK.

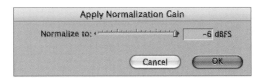

In this window, the dB level is referred to as dBFS. This stands for *decibels full scale*, and it means that the current highest volume of each clip will be raised to the level you entered. When you play these clips again, they will peak at –6 dB in the audio meters.

NOTE ▶ In this situation, Final Cut Pro applies an audio filter to the clip that boosts the volume level, or *gain*. If you double-click one of the filtered clips, and click the Filters tab in the Viewer, you can see the specific gain adjustment. You will work with filters in a later lesson.

6 Press A to return to the default Selection tool. Play the A1 and A2 clips again and notice the change in the audio meters.

Now the sync sound and narration clips sound a little more robust.

Let's evaluate the volume level of the sound effects in conjunction with the music track.

7 Click the A1 and A2 Solo buttons to remove the sync sound from the mix, and toggle on the A3–A6 Solo buttons. Play the music and effects together.

NOTE ▶ In many productions, music and effects are mixed together for final output, while the narration or dialogue remains on a separate track.

The current volume level of the breathing effect is a little high and distracting.

8   In the first **Scuba Breathing.aif** clip, drag the audio level overlay down to −16 dB. Play this clip again with the music.

> **TIP** ▸ For greater control as you drag an audio level overlay, press the Command key. You can also double-click a clip to open it in the Viewer and enter a volume adjustment in the Level field.

If you use an effect several times in the same sequence, you may very likely want to play all uses of that effect at the same volume level. Rather than change the volume of each clip individually, you can copy and paste levels from one clip to another.

9   In the Timeline, select the first **Scuba Breathing.aif** clip. Press Command-C to copy the clip.

When you copy a clip, you copy everything about it, including the audio levels. Since you have another **Scuba Breathing.aif** clip later in the sequence, you can paste just the volume level from the first effect to the next.

10   Control-click the second **Scuba Breathing.aif** clip in the sequence. From the shortcut menu, choose Paste Attributes. In the Paste Attributes window, under the Audio Attributes column on the right, select the Levels checkbox. Watch the pink audio level overlay in the clip as you click OK.

You can also modify the levels of more than one clip at a time. You do this by selecting the clips you want to change, and then modifying the overall gain or volume for the selected clips.

11 Play the first **Water Lake 1.aif** clip in the sequence.

With the music playing up full, it's a little hard to hear the sound effect at its current volume level. You will need to raise the volume on both of the **Water Lake 1.aif** clips in the sequence by the same amount, so let's adjust the clip levels at the same time.

12 Select the first **Water Lake 1.aif** clip, and Command-click the second clip to add it to the selection. Choose Modify > Levels. In the Gain Adjust window, enter 6 as the dB level in the "Adjust gain by" field. Watch the audio level overlays in the Timeline as you click OK. Play the clips again.

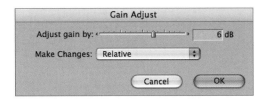

In the Gain Adjust window, you are not entering a specific or absolute dB value. This is a relative adjustment. By entering 6, you are raising the volume 6 dB from its current level. Since both clips were selected, you raised the volume on both clips at the same time by the same amount.

Now let's focus on how the music mixes with the sync sound. At full volume, the music overpowers the individuals talking, so you will adjust the music volume to create an optimum mix level. For music, that is typically around –15 dB or even –18 dB, depending on whether the music genre is a soft ballad or driving hard rock.

NOTE ▶ In the next exercise, you will raise and lower the sound level within the music clip, allowing you to fade it up to a fuller level when the individuals aren't speaking.

13 Solo the A1, A2, A5, and A6 audio tracks. Play the **_DS_show open** clip with the music track. Bring the music volume down to about −15 dB so it doesn't overpower the sync sound clips.

> **TIP** ▶ You can modify the music volume on the fly as you play other sequence clips by using a mouse with a scrolling wheel or ball. Double-click a clip to open it in the Viewer, position the mouse pointer over the Levels slider, and rotate the scroll wheel up and down as the sequence plays.

Project Tasks

To complete adjusting levels in this sequence, listen to the crowd cheer sound effects under the **performance_S spray jump** video clip. Solo the sound effect with the music clip, and adjust the effect to an appropriate mix level. You can also add cross fades to sound effects to smooth some of the more abrupt edit points.

Applying Transitions to Fade Volume

You've now finished the lion's share of audio mixing, which is to set the audio levels for individual clips at their appropriate mix levels. Sometimes that may be enough to complete the sound mix for a project. In this sequence, however, the music track was lowered to a mix level with the sync sound clips, leaving other sections in the sequence with a weak music level. By changing the music to rise and fall around the sync sound clips, you can create a dynamic feeling to this soundtrack.

There are two ways to change, or *animate,* the sound levels. One method involves adding an edit point and an audio cross fade where you want to change an audio level. The other method, which you will learn in the next exercise, uses keyframes. To ensure you're working with all the volume changes made in the previous exercises, you will open a new sequence with those changes already applied.

1 In the Sequences bin in the Browser, open the *Believe Mix_v2_blade* sequence.

> **NOTE** ▶ If you made all of the changes in the previous exercises, you can continue working in that sequence.

For this exercise, you don't need to evaluate audio levels or clip content, so you can turn off the audio waveforms. Since you will be focusing on the music and sync sound clips, you can mute the A3 and A4 sound effects tracks.

2   In the *Believe Mix_v2_blade* sequence in the Timeline, press Option-Command-W to turn off the waveform displays. Make sure no Solo buttons are toggled on and then click the Mute buttons for the A3 and A4 tracks. If you added the Show/Hide Waveform display button, you can click it to toggle the display off.

NOTE ▶ Another reason to turn off the audio waveforms when you don't need them is that they use additional RAM, just like video thumbnails.

One way to animate the music volume is to divide the music track into separate clips, then change the volume within each new music clip.

3   Move the playhead to snap to the In point of the **_DS_show concept** clip. Press B to select the Razor Blade tool, and click the A5 track at the play-head location. Press A to return to the default Selection tool.

A new edit point is added to the music clip, creating two separate clips.

4   To change the volume of the first **Track 8_guitar.aif** clip, drag the audio level overlay up to 0 dB. Play through the edit point to hear the change in volume.

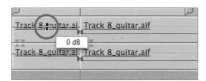

This successfully gives you two different levels, but cutting from one audio level to another makes for an abrupt transition. Applying a cross fade would help smooth the fade from one audio level to the next.

5   Select the edit point between the first two music clips, and press Option-Command-T to add the default audio cross fade between these two clips. Play the edit point again.

NOTE ▶ If you hear beeps as you play these clips, change the Real-time Audio Mixing to 10 tracks in the General tab of User Preferences.

To proceed with the razor blade and cross fade approach, you would repeat steps 3 through 5, adding edit points, changing the clip volume, and applying cross fades. But first, let's change the Timeline track display so the A1 and A5 tracks appear on top of each other. This will make it easier to see where you need to create the new edit points.

6   In the far right of the Timeline, at the audio/video divider, drag the lower
    thumb tab in the vertical scroll bar down until just the A1 track is in the
    static region. Now drag the blue scroller down to scroll through the remain-
    ing tracks until the A5 track is as close as possible to the static A1 track.

NOTE ► Depending on the screen resolution and the size of your Timeline
window, the blue scroller may not appear. To make the tracks taller, either
resize the Timeline or press Shift-T.

7   Press B to select the Razor Blade tool. In the A5 track, snap the razor
    blade to the **_DS_show concept** clip's Out point, and click to create a new
    edit point. Create edit points at the head and tail of each sync sound and
    narration clip in this sequence.

8   On the clips where the sync sound is *not* present, raise the volume to 0 dB.
    Apply the default cross fade at each edit point, and play the sequence.

Project Tasks

There are a few tricks you've already learned that can help streamline this process even further. To apply them, open the *Believe Mix_v3_keyframes* sequence, duplicate it, and work in that copy.

▶   To change the volume of all the clips that are *not* beneath a sync sound or narration clip, select those clips and choose Modify > Levels. Enter *0 dB*, choose Absolute from the Make Changes pop-up menu, and click OK.

▶   To apply a cross fade to each edit point at one time, position the playhead at the head of the sequence, and patch the a1 and a2 source controls to the A5 and A6 destination tracks. Select the clips and drag them into the Canvas Edit Overlay, then drop them into the Overwrite with Transition section (see "Modifying and Copying Transitions" in Lesson 9).

> **TIP**▶   To finesse individual cross fades, you can roll the edit point left or right, and change the cross fade length.

Setting Keyframes to Change Volume

Another way to raise and lower the music volume is to set a *keyframe* where you want to change the audio level. A keyframe identifies the frame in a clip where you want to animate a change, any change. In this lesson, it's volume. By setting a keyframe directly on the audio level overlay, you are giving a precise command as to when and how the audio should change.

> **NOTE** ▶   All keyframes in this exercise will be added to the **Track 8_ guitar.aif** music clip.

1   From the Sequences bin in the Browser, open the *Believe Mix_v3_keyframes* sequence.

This sequence has a static A1 track so you can see the music next to the sync sound clips.

TIP If you want to return to the normal Timeline track display without a static region, drag the lower thumb tab of the static region up and release it.

To raise the volume before the first sync sound clip, you need to set two keyframes around that edit point on the music audio level overlay.

2   As a visual guide, move the playhead to the In point of the **_DS_show concept** clip, and press P to select the Pen tool. Move the pointer into the **Track 8_guitar.aif** clip and over the pink audio level overlay *before* the playhead.

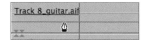

The tool looks like a pen only when the pointer is over the clip's audio level overlay.

3   Click the Pen tool before the playhead position. Make sure you click *on* the audio level overlay.

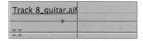

A pink diamond, or keyframe, appears on both tracks of the stereo music clip at the playhead position. This first keyframe establishes or secures the point where you want to begin fading the audio.

TIP ▶ To delete a keyframe, press PP to select the Pen Delete tool and click a keyframe, or Control-click a keyframe and choose Clear from the shortcut menu.

4 Move the Pen tool to the right of the playhead and again click the audio level overlay of the **Track 8_guitar.aif** clip.

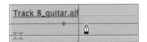

Although you haven't changed the volume yet, this is the location in the clip where you want the fade to stop and level off. With two keyframes in place, you can now adjust an audio level overlay to create an audio fade.

5 Press A to return to the default Selection tool. Move the pointer over the audio level overlay to the left of the keyframes. When you see the Resize pointer, drag up to 0 dB and release it. Play the audio fade.

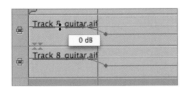

The audio volume stays constant until the playhead reaches a keyframe. At that point, the audio volume begins to change in the direction of the next keyframe, in this case dropping to a lower volume level.

NOTE ▶ You can think of keyframes as thumbtacks or push pins that hold a rubber band in place, allowing you to drag the other side up or down.

After David stops talking, let's add two more keyframes to fade the audio from its "down under" volume to an "up full" volume. This time, you will use the default Selection tool and the Option key to access the Pen tool.

6   Position the pointer on the pink audio level overlay of the music clip just before the Out point of the **_DS_show concept** clip. Press the Option key, and when you see the Pen tool, click the audio level overlay. Set a second keyframe just past the Out point of the **_DS_show concept** clip using the same method.

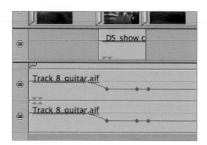

TIP When you press the Option key and move your pointer over an existing keyframe, the pointer changes to the Pen Delete tool.

Before adjusting the level, you can set another two keyframes to limit the fade to a specific area.

7   Set two keyframes around the In point of the **_SA_favorite behavior** clip. With four keyframes in place, drag the audio level overlay up between the middle two keyframes to 0 dB. Play this section of the sequence.

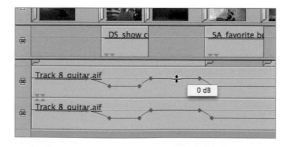

Once a keyframe has been placed on an audio level overlay, it can be raised or lowered to alter the volume at that location. It can also be repositioned left or right to change where the fade starts or stops.

TIP ▶ It may be helpful to turn off snapping for the next step.

8   Play the last portion of the music clip, then zoom into it to make that area larger. Option-click the audio level overlay under the last video edit point. Option-click again about halfway to the music clip's Out point.

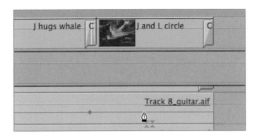

When you set a keyframe directly on the edge of a clip, it can be difficult to access. Setting it well inside the clip gives you greater control as you position the keyframe into place.

9   Move the pointer over the second keyframe. When the pointer changes to a crosshair, drag the keyframe down until you see *–inf dB* (infinity dB) in the information box. Then, drag the keyframe toward the right corner of the clip, staying inside the clip's edge. Play the clip.

NOTE ▶ The crosshair is not a selectable tool. It is a part of the Pen and Select tools and allows you to move a keyframe.

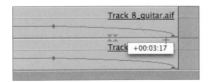

As you drag a keyframe up and down or left and right, an information box appears, displaying the distance and direction you've moved the keyframe from its original position, or the dB level change. You can also make these changes in the Viewer.

10 Double-click the **Track 8_guitar.aif** clip, and drag the zoom slider to the right to move to the end of this clip. Using the audio waveform as a guide, drag the second keyframe left or right to position it where the music ends.

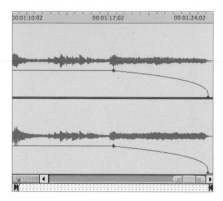

The Viewer's waveform display is much larger than that of a sequence clip, which can make it easier to fine-tune keyframe placement. You can also add new keyframes here.

TIP You can set keyframes in the Viewer's Audio tab before editing a clip to the Timeline.

Project Tasks

Continue adding keyframes to animate the music volume around the sync sound clips. You can also animate the **Scuba Breathing.aif** clip under the two sync sound clips so you don't hear the scuba sound while someone is talking. To smooth the other sound effects' edit points, you can apply cross fades or add keyframes to fade them in and out.

Using the Audio Mixer

Now that you understand how to set keyframes and manually mix audio in the Timeline, you're ready to mix tracks in real time using the Audio Mixer tool. There are several ways to access the Audio Mixer. One is to select the Audio Mixer window layout, which incorporates the Audio Mixer into the interface. Another is to choose Tools > Audio Mixer. This opens the Audio Mixer as a separate window that you can place wherever you like. Before you create a new mix, let's explore the Audio Mixer tool.

1   Click the Timeline to make that window active, and choose Tools > Audio Mixer, or press Option-6. Drag this new window to the left over the Browser window area.

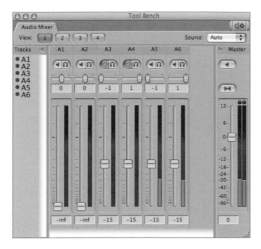

When you open the Audio Mixer, it appears within the Tool Bench window as a tab. There are six audio tracks currently represented in the Audio Mixer—the same number of tracks you have in your sequence. If the active sequence had 20 audio tracks, 20 tracks would appear in the Audio Mixer.

TIP If you are working with several tracks and don't want to see them all at one time, you can hide a track by clicking its Track Visibility control.

2 In the Audio Mixer, make sure the Record Audio Keyframes button in the upper-right button bar is deselected so that no keyframes will be created while you practice.

3 In the Audio Mixer, click the A3 and A4 Mute buttons to return these sound effects into the mix.

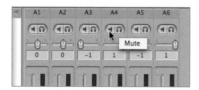

The Mute and Solo buttons in the Audio Mixer work interchangeably with those in the audio controls in the Timeline.

4 In the Timeline, play the sequence from the beginning, but watch the faders in the Audio Mixer.

The track faders move in response to the keyframes and sound levels you set in these clips. Rather than raising or lowering the audio level overlay in the Timeline, you can use these faders to adjust the audio level.

5 Move the playhead over the **_SA_favorite behavior** clip and look at the position of the clip's audio level overlay. In the Audio Mixer, drag the A1 fader down to about –20 dB and release the fader. Look again at the clip's audio level overlay in the Timeline. Then press Command-Z to undo this change.

NOTE ▶ When changing volume on a stereo pair, dragging one fader adjusts the volume on both tracks in tandem.

Changing the volume of a clip in the Audio Mixer changes the audio level overlay on the clip in the Timeline. In the Audio Mixer, the dB level in the field below the fader changes to reflect how much you have raised or lowered the sound from its original 0 dB level. You can also enter a value in a field and press Return, which will move the fader to that level.

Once the individual mix levels are set for each track, you can adjust the overall output level for your sequence by using the Master fader on the far right of the Audio Mixer window. You can also mute all tracks at once using the Master Mute button.

6   If the Master area is not open, click its disclosure triangle.

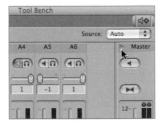

7   Play the sequence from the beginning, and as it plays, look at the Master audio meters. Drag the Master fader up to raise the overall volume level or drag it down to lower it.

While you never want to exceed 0 dB, you typically aim for a lower final output level, such as –6 dB, to ensure the sequence will play back within a safe range in any situation, on different systems, and all equipment. The levels in the Master fader reflect the output levels of the active sequence. When you change the level in a sequence using the Master fader, that output level will remain until you change it again.

NOTE ▶ Any changes made to the Master fader will affect the level of the mix as it's played back or output to tape. For this lesson, you will focus on balancing or mixing the individual tracks, and not outputting them to tape.

In a moment, you will automatically add a new set of keyframes to the **Track 8_guitar.aif** clip. To do this, you need to start with a clean slate: a music track that is at 0 dB and has no keyframes.

8   Control-click the **Track 8_guitar.aif** clip and choose Remove Attributes from the shortcut menu. In the Remove Attributes window, make sure Levels is selected under the Audio Attributes column, and click OK.

    All the keyframes are removed from this clip and the audio level overlay is returned to a 0 dB level.

9   In the Audio Mixer button bar, click the Record Audio Keyframes button to toggle it on.

With this option on, any adjustments you make by dragging a track fader *while the sequence is playing* will automatically add keyframes to the clip in the Timeline.

Since the Audio Mixer works in real time, take a moment to think about the process. First, you will begin to play the sequence, then click and hold the A5 (or A6) fader control and watch the playhead move in the sequence. As the playhead approaches the first sync sound clip, drag the A5 fader down (to about –15 dB) while David is speaking, then back up to its original 0 dB level after he finishes talking. You can continue holding the fader button as you repeat the process for the second dialogue section. Or you can release it between adjustments.

10 Follow these steps to create a live mix:

▶ Move the playhead to the head of the sequence, and press the spacebar to begin playing. Then click and hold the A5 fader.

▶ As the playhead approaches the first sync sound clip, drag the A5 fader down so you can clearly hear David but still hear the music in the background. If you want to, you can release the mouse at that level or continue to hold it.

▶ At the end of the first sync sound clip, drag the A5 fader back up to its original level.

▶ Keep watching the playhead, and as it approaches the second sync sound clip, drag the A5 fader down and under again, then up full.

▶ Continue dragging down and up around each sync sound clip. When the sequence is finished playing, release the mouse.

In the Timeline, keyframes appear to identify peaks in the music clip where you raised and lowered the faders. To adjust your mix, you can raise or lower these keyframes, reposition them, delete them, or manually add new ones as you did in a previous exercise.

NOTE ▶ In the Editing tab of User Preferences, you can choose a different level of automatic keyframing, either more or less sensitive to your fader movements. Start with the current default, which is the middle level.

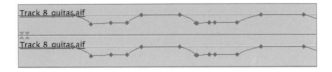

The Audio Mixer is a powerful tool. Using it to set keyframes automatically may require practice before you achieve the desired results. Keep in mind that setting keyframes automatically isn't right for every project. It's most helpful when you have one long audio source, such as music or a sound effect, that continues through a portion of your sequence. Sometimes, manually controlling the individual keyframes—with the Pen tool, for example—may give you the best result.

Recording a Narration Track

As you move your project toward completion, you may find you're still missing a narration track. Perhaps you were given a written script for the narration, but the news reporter or narrator hasn't gotten into the studio to record it. The problem is that you now need the audio track for timing purposes or for seeing how the narration fits your video. The solution may be to record your own unofficial narration, which is sometimes referred to as a *scratch track*.

To record a voice-over in Final Cut Pro, you can use a digital camera or some other audio recording device, such as a USB microphone or an internal microphone on a laptop computer. All of these devices will create a new clip directly in the Timeline. To create a voice-over clip in the current sequence, you can use the Voice Over tool. To prepare for the new scratch track, you first disable the current narration clip and set In and Out points in the Timeline for a new voice-over.

> **NOTE ►** If you are using an external microphone or camera mic, connect the device to your computer.

1   In the Timeline, Control-click the **narration_2** clip and, from the shortcut menu, choose Clip Enable to toggle off visibility for this one clip.

You will now record your own version of the narration script in this same location. To mark this area, you need to set In and Out points.

2   Move the playhead to the beginning of the **J and L circle** clip. Press I to create an In point. In the Canvas Timecode Duration field, enter *12.* (12 period) to create a 12-second duration, and press Return.

These In and Out points will create a clip somewhat longer than the original narration to give you some extra pad as you record.

NOTE ▶ If there are no In and Out points, the voice-over clip begins recording at the playhead location and continues until the end of the sequence.

3   To open the Voice Over tool, choose Tools > Voice Over.

If Final Cut Pro does not detect a recording device, a warning window appears. If Final Cut Pro detects a microphone source, the Voice Over tool appears as a tab in the Tool Bench window. Notice that the Audio Mixer tab is still open in the Tool Bench window.

The Voice Over tool is divided into four areas: Status, Audio File, Input, and Headphones. The first step is to specify the track where you want the new narration. The target track appears in the Audio File area.

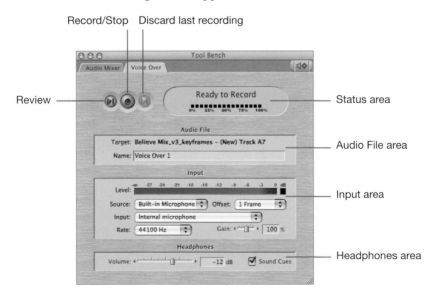

When you record a voice-over, Final Cut Pro places a new audio clip on the A2 track at the marked location. If a clip is already in that location on that track, the new audio clip is placed on the track beneath it. If no track exists, Final Cut Pro will automatically create a new track for the clip.

NOTE ▶ Audio recordings made using the Voice Over tool are saved as media files in your project's Capture Scratch folder.

4   In the Timeline, drag the a2 source control to the A6 destination control and note the new target information in the Audio File area.

The Voice Over tool will always target the track beneath the lowest patched track.

TIP ▶ If you don't see an a2 source control in the Timeline patch panel, Control-click in the track area and choose Reset Panel from the shortcut menu. You can also open a clip with two tracks of audio into the Viewer.

With the a2 source control patched to the A6 destination track, the target for the new voice-over is A7. Although it doesn't currently exist, Final Cut Pro will automatically create this track after you record the voice-over. Since the Voice Over function records only one channel of audio, or mono audio, it needs only one track.

5   In the Audio File area, enter *scratch narration* as the name for this voice-over track.

6 In the Input area, choose the correct source from the Source pop-up menu. If it's DV, choose 48000 Hz from the Rate pop-up menu and 3 Frames from the Offset pop-up menu.

Final Cut Pro will display a default Input configuration based on the audio recording device it detects. A recording offset amount is included as one of the default settings. If your device does not support 48000 Hz, you won't see that as an option.

7 Start talking to set the Gain recording level in the Input area.

> **TIP** ▶ If you use headphones for this process, you can listen to the other audio tracks in the sequence as you record the narration, without recording those audio tracks.

8 Deselect the Sound Cues checkbox.

When the checkbox is selected, you will hear sound beeps as a cue during the 5-second countdown before recording, and once again prior to the Out point. If you're not using headphones, however, the beeps will be picked up and recorded as part of your clip. Instead, you can deselect Sound Cues and watch the Starting countdown in the Status area to see when recording begins and ends.

Before you begin, look for the Ready to Record signal in the Status area. Here's what will happen. You will click the Record button. The playhead will immediately jump backward for the pre-roll, while the Ready to Record window will turn yellow and count down from five. It will then turn red and begin recording. When you are finished reading the narration lines, click the black Stop button.

9   Click the Record button, and record the following lines:

"Two worlds. Two different species—trying to bridge the gap between them. And how do you bridge that gap? You believe."

The recording ends at the Out point. In the Timeline, the new voice-over clip appears on the new A7 track between the previous In and Out marks.

> **TIP** If you want to stop a recording in process, or if you don't have an Out point, click the Stop button. You can also click the Discard Last Recording button to discard an unwanted track. This step cannot be undone.

10   Play back the clip by clicking the Review button or by playing the sequence in the Timeline. Close the Voice Over tool.

Each time you record a new version, or *take*, a new clip is placed in another track in the Timeline and labeled with the next highest take number. These different takes, or versions, are actually QuickTime movies that are stored in your project's Capture Scratch folder.

Importing CD Tracks

Almost all projects are enhanced by the addition of a music track, and CDs make a handy delivery system for these tracks. You may be using a CD from a stock music or sound effects library, a CD of a *temp track* your director handed you, or something off your personal music shelf. Using CDs as a source of additional audio tracks is convenient, but there will most likely be a discrepancy between the quality of your CD and your primary audio sources. There are steps you can take, however, to remedy this.

Standard CD audio is recorded at a 44.1 kilohertz (kHz) *sampling rate*, whereas high-quality audio for video—including DV, XDCAM, HD, and so on—is recorded at 48.0 kHz. Although Final Cut Pro will play a CD track in the Timeline without rendering it, it would be better to convert the CD tracks to 48.0 kHz so the sampling rate of the CD tracks will match the sampling rate of the audio tracks from your video source. In the following image, the audio clip on the right displays a green bar in the upper portion of each track, indicating that it doesn't match the sequence settings of 48.0 kHz. In this lesson, you will load your own CD and convert it to 48.0 kHz.

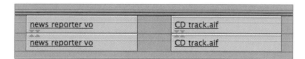

NOTE ▶ In digital audio, a sampling rate represents the number of times each second that a sample is taken from an audio source to create a good representation of that sound. The more samples taken, the more accurately the audio is represented in digital form. Audio sample rates are measured in Hertz and written as *Hertz* (Hz) or *kilohertz* (kHz), such as 48000 Hz or 48.0 kHz.

1   In the Browser, press Command-B to create a new bin. Name the bin *CD Tracks*.

2   Select the bin, and choose File > Batch Export.

An Export Queue window opens with the empty bin selected. This window is a portal for exporting or converting a group of clips at one time. Although you will learn other exporting options in later lessons, for now you will use this window to convert your own CD tracks to 48.0 kHz.

3   Arrange your interface so you can see the Export Queue window and the desktop. Insert your own CD into the computer. Open a Finder window, and drag several audio tracks from the CD into the Final Cut Pro Export Queue window and drop them into the CD Tracks bin.

NOTE ► It may be that your computer is set to import tracks directly into iTunes when it detects a CD. If an iTunes dialog opens, close it, along with the iTunes interface, and open the CD in your desktop Finder window.

4   With the CD Tracks bin selected, click the Settings button.

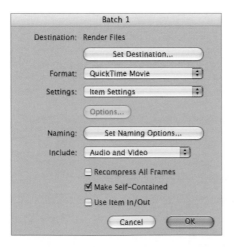

A Batch window appears with several options.

5 Click the Set Destination button, and select a location where you want to save the new music tracks. Click Choose.

6 Click the Format pop-up, and from the menu choose AIFF as the file type.

7 Click the Options button. When the Sound Settings window appears, change the Rate to *48.0* either by entering it in the Rate field or by clicking the lower arrow to the right of the field and choosing 48.000 from the pop-up menu. Click OK.

8 Leave the other settings in the Batch window at their defaults and click OK. In the Export Queue window, click the Export button.

An Export Queue progress bar appears, indicating that the CD tracks with the current settings are being exported to the selected destination. When this process is complete, you can import those tracks into the project and edit them into your sequences.

Project Tasks

Use Clip Enable to disable the music track in the *Believe Mix_v3_keyframes* sequence and import into the project one of the CD tracks you just converted. Mix this new sound track into the sequence.

Lesson Review

1. What button do you click in the Timeline to display the Mute and Solo buttons?
2. What result do you get when you click the Solo button on a track?
3. How can you add several tracks to the Timeline at one time?
4. How do you make the audio level overlay appear on clips in the Timeline?
5. When would you turn on audio waveforms in the Timeline?
6. What tool do you use to set a keyframe on the audio level overlay?

7. How can the Pen tool be accessed without selecting it from the Tool palette?

8. How do you reposition a keyframe or change its volume level?

9. How can you paste just the audio level from one clip to another?

10. On what menu do you find the Audio Mixer?

11. To mix tracks in real time and automatically create keyframes on a clip, what must you do in the Audio Mixer?

12. What tool do you use to record your own voice-over, and where do you access it?

13. When you want to use CD audio tracks in your sequence, what can you do to convert them to 48 kHz?

14. What two functions under the Modify menu help to change audio levels, and in what way?

Answers

1. The Audio Controls button in the lower left of the Timeline.

2. That track becomes the only audible track as you play the sequence.

3. Choose Sequence > Insert Tracks.

4. Press Option-W, or click the Clip Overlays control in the lower left of the Timeline, next to the Track Height control.

5. When you want a visual representation of a clip's audio signals to evaluate or to edit audio clips.

6. The Pen tool, or you can Option-click it with the default Selection tool.

7. Press Option and move the pointer over the audio level overlay on a Timeline clip. The Pen tool appears on the overlay line.

8. Drag left and right to change its position and up and down to change its volume level.

9. Copy the clip that has the desired audio level and paste just the audio levels using the Paste Attributes function.

10. The Tools menu.

11. In the Audio Mixer button bar, click the Record Audio Keyframes button to toggle it on. Then play the sequence and adjust the clip volume by dragging its track fader.

12. The Voice Over tool, found on the Tools menu.

13. Drag the tracks into the Export Queue window, and change the settings to 48 kHz. Export with these settings.

14. Modify > Levels brings up the Gain Adjust window where you can raise or lower volume for all selected clips. Modify > Audio > Apply Normalization Gain resets the decibel level of the clip.

Keyboard Shortcuts

Option-W	Toggles audio level overlays on and off in the Timeline
Option-Command-W	Toggles waveforms on and off in the Timeline
P	Selects the Pen tool
PP	Selects the Pen Delete tool
Option-6	Opens the Audio Mixer
Option-0	Opens the Voice Over tool
Control-. (period)	Pans a selected clip's audio to the center

11

Lesson Files   Lesson 11 Project

Media   Monk and Yellow folders

Time   This lesson takes approximately 90 minutes to complete.

Goals   Add color bars and slugs

Create, edit, and animate text clips

Superimpose a title

Create a lower third

Work with Boris text

Add color mattes and render effects

Build a composite title

Prepare graphic images for editing

Add Motion templates

Creating Titles

All projects, from the simplest to the most complex, will seem more complete when you add text, titles, and graphics. But in Final Cut Pro you don't need to capture or import text clips. Titles—along with other items such as color mattes, color bars, and other effects—can be generated within Final Cut Pro and accessed whenever you need them.

In this lesson, you add text to existing sequences using several methods, including some that generate preformatted text or animate the text automatically. You will also create a *show open* by editing one sequence into another sequence, compositing clips, and adding effects. In addition, you can apply a Motion template to your project to create a more sophisticated look.

Preparing a Project for Titles

There are a few things you can do to streamline the process of adding text to a sequence. You can import a reference clip that contains a style you want to copy. You can place all the text clips onto one track so they can be toggled off or on together. And, if your project is being broadcast, you can turn on an overlay to ensure that your titles fit within a "safety zone" so they can be seen on any television monitor.

1   Open the **Lesson 11 Project** file, and close any other open projects.

2   Press Control-U to return to the default Standard layout. In the Timeline, play the first few clips of the *Monk_v3_titles* sequence.

     This is the edited *Monk* sequence you worked with in earlier lessons.

3   In the Browser, display the contents of the Monk Clips bin, and open the **Monk.mov** clip. Play the first portion of this clip to see the credit sequence.

This is a QuickTime movie of the scene that aired. It begins with a slate that identifies the scene and episode. Since this is the first scene after the opening tease, the title of the episode and several credits appear over the clips of Mr. Monk and Dr. Kroger. Notice that each credit shares the same font style. They have lowercased first names, all capitalized last names, and all capitalized but smaller-sized character names or show credits, such as editor, producer, and so on. Later in this lesson, you will create your own version of a few of these titles.

4   In the Viewer, move the playhead to the head of the clip, and press Shift-M to move forward to the first marker. Press Shift-M again, or Shift–Up Arrow, to move to the next marker, and the next.

Markers have been placed on frames containing titles that you will recreate in your own sequence. You can use these markers as a reference for spelling names and reviewing text style.

5   With the Viewer window active, choose View > Show Title Safe. And play the first portion of this clip again.

Title safe boundary   Action safe boundary

Two rectangular boxes appear as overlays in the Viewer. The inner box represents the title safe boundary, and the outer box represents the action safe boundary. The recorded frame size of broadcast video is actually larger than the viewable area of a television monitor. When text is positioned within the title safe boundary, you can be sure the text will be seen on any television monitor when the show is broadcast. Likewise, when an important action within a clip appears within the action safe boundary, you can be sure that action will be seen by the home viewer. You will work with the action safe boundary in the next lesson.

TIP ▶ If the Show Overlays command is not selected in the View menu, the title safe boundary will not appear. Make sure that both Show Overlays and Show Title Safe are selected.

There is another way to access the title safe boundary, and other overlays as well.

6   In the Viewer, click the View pop-up menu button, and choose Show Title Safe.

This View pop-up menu contains several of the same items you find in the View menu, but in a more convenient location. The Canvas window also has a View pop-up menu button. Since you will be using the Canvas to edit new text clips, let's turn on the title safe boundary for that window.

7   In the Canvas, click the View pop-up menu button and choose Show Title Safe.

When you edit text clips, you use the Viewer window to enter text changes. When a text clip is loaded into the Viewer, you will lose your reference to the **Monk.mov** clip. Let's open that clip in a separate Viewer window so you can have access to it throughout the lesson.

8   In the Browser, Control-click the **Monk.mov** clip and choose Open in New Viewer from the shortcut menu. Reposition this new Viewer window over the Browser window, and move the playhead to the first marker in the clip.

Now you can continue editing and refer to the **Monk.mov** clip as necessary.

Working with Video Generators

The clips you have used so far were captured from source material or imported from other files. But Final Cut Pro can internally create certain clips via *generators*. These generated items include color bars and tone, which are used as color references; slugs to fill a space with black; color mattes and gradients to create vivid backgrounds; and text. Some generated items stand alone, such as color bars at the head of a sequence; some items can be used in conjunction with other video clips.

When selected, most generated items appear in the Viewer with a length of 2 minutes and a marked 10-second default duration. All generated items are video-only except for color bars and tone. You can choose video generators from one of two places, in the Viewer or in the Browser Effects tab.

1   In the Timeline, position the playhead at the head of the sequence.

    If someone else on the production team needs to review the sequence, you will want to add some *leader* material before the scene begins that identifies what's coming. You will also want to include a color reference so viewers can properly set up their monitors.

2   In the lower-right corner of the Viewer, click the Generator pop-up button and look at the different generator categories.

3   Choose Bars and Tone > Bars and Tone (HD 1080i60) from the pop-up menu. Play a few seconds of this clip.

    NOTE ▶ Generated items can also be chosen from the Effects tab, which you will use later in this lesson.

    The **Bars and Tone** clip includes video bars and two tracks of –12 dB tone. All generated items are given a default 10-second duration, which you can change in the User Preferences Editing tab (in the Still/Freeze Duration field).

4   In the Viewer Timecode Duration field, enter 5. (5 period), and press
Return. Insert this clip at the head of the sequence.

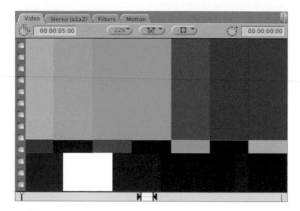

To identify your sequence, let's add a slate after the color bars. You can
create a slate using the basic Text generator.

5   Click the Generator pop-up again, and choose Text > Text from the
pop-up menu.

In the Viewer, the words *SAMPLE TEXT* appear over the image area. This is a default text line. To modify this text clip, and to see the changes at the same time, you will first edit the clip into the sequence.

NOTE ▸ Editing the generic **Text** clip to the Timeline is an important step in your workflow. Not only can you see the changes in the Canvas as you modify the text, but you preserve those changes as well. If you were to open a clip in the Viewer over a generic **Text** clip, you would lose your changes.

6   In the Viewer Timecode Duration field, enter *5.* (5 period), and press Return. Insert this clip after the **Bars and Tone** clip, and zoom into the clip in the Timeline.

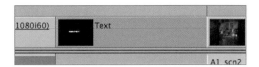

All generated text items appear in the Timeline as purple clips, with the specific type of text as the name of the clip—in this case it's the basic "Text." To make changes to this clip, you open it as you would any other clip in a sequence.

7   In the Timeline, position the playhead over the new **Text** clip to see it in the Canvas, then double-click it to open it in the Viewer. Click the Controls tab.

NOTE ▸ When you select a clip in the Timeline, a cyan outline appears around the edge of the clip in the Canvas. When the title safe boundary is visible, you see three rectangles. To hide the outer box, you can deselect the clip in the Timeline.

A Controls tab is present in the Viewer for most generated items. Note the attributes you can modify, such as font, size, style, and alignment. Scroll down to look at the other attributes, then scroll up to the Text parameter.

8 Click in the Text field, and when *Sample Text* is highlighted, type *"Mr. Monk and the Actor,"* and press Tab to see the new text in the Canvas window.

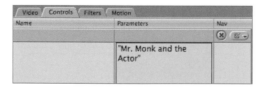

Slates may be very simple one-line introductions to a sequence, or they may include a variety of information such as show name, episode name or number, editor, director, or producer.

9 In the Viewer, click at the end of the text line, and press Return to move the cursor to the next line. Continue entering the slate information. You can use the following as a guide, or refer to the **Monk.mov** clip.

"Mr. Monk and the Actor"

starring Tony Shalhoub

with Stanley Kamel

Edited by Scott Boyd

Version 3_titles

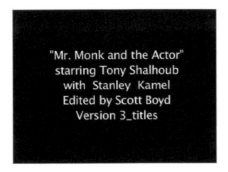

As you continue to add more lines of text, the text begins to move off-screen in the Canvas and out of the title safe area. There's plenty of room for the text in the Canvas image area; you just have to reposition the text higher.

10 In the Viewer, scroll down to the Origin parameter, and click the Point Select (crosshair) button. In the Canvas, click and drag the crosshair up to reposition the center of the text higher.

NOTE ▶ You can reset parameters to their default status by clicking the red X Reset button in the upper-right corner of the Controls tab.

11 To add more distance between the individual lines, change the Leading to 10.

Typically, you follow a slate with a few seconds of black or a countdown of some kind, signaling the start of the sequence. In Final Cut Pro, you can edit a generated item called a *slug* to create black video and two tracks of empty audio. Let's add a few seconds of black after this slate.

TIP ▶ You can also use slugs to hold the place of a clip in a sequence, such as footage that hasn't been captured or a graphic that hasn't yet been completed.

12 In the Viewer Video tab, click the Generator pop-up and choose Slug from the pop-up menu.

13 In the Viewer Timecode Duration field, enter *2.* (2 period), and press Return. Insert this clip at the end of the **Text** clip, and play the first few clips of this sequence.

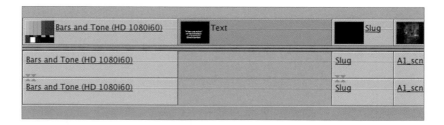

Adding a Lower Third

Final Cut Pro offers more than one kind of text, each with its own set of parameters. Some of the generated text items are preformatted for specific purposes—such as the lower third, which most often identifies a person, place, or thing. For example, when you watch a television news story, you know the reporter's name and location by the text in the lower third of the screen, which appears over the introductory shot. The Final Cut Pro **Lower 3rd** clip automatically creates two lines of text information within the title safe boundary in the lower left of the image area.

To keep the text clips organized in this sequence, you will edit them all to the V2 track. But rather than target the V2 track directly, you will use a different type of edit to *superimpose* the text over an existing clip in the Timeline.

1   In the **Monk.mov** clip, press Shift-M or Option-M to move the Viewer playhead to the episode title marker.

For this show, the lower third format was used for the opening credits, as well as the name of the episode. Although you won't mimic these titles exactly, you will follow the style closely.

2   In the Viewer, click the Generator pop-up menu and choose Text > Lower 3rd.

In the Viewer, a new text clip appears with two default lines of sample text. As you did with the basic **Text** clip, you will edit this clip into the Timeline and then open it up in the Viewer to see the changes as you make them.

Since you want this clip to appear over a specific clip on the V1 track, you can use the superimpose edit. With this type of edit, Final Cut Pro uses the Timeline playhead and the v1 source control to identify a clip's track, duration, and position in the sequence. It then places the new clip on the track directly above the reference clip, matching its length and position.

3   In the Timeline, position the playhead anywhere over the second *Monk* clip, **B1_scn2A_tk1**. Make sure the v1 source control is targeting the V1 track.

With the V1 track targeted, and the playhead over the sequence clip, Final Cut Pro knows to use this clip as a reference when editing the new text clip.

4   In the Viewer, drag the **Lower 3rd** clip into the Canvas window, and drop it over the Superimpose section in the Edit Overlay.

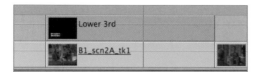

Final Cut Pro automatically superimposes the clip directly above the targeted track with the same length and location as the reference clip.

In the Canvas, you see that the two lines of lower third text fit neatly within the title safe area over the background clip.

Although you may sometimes want text to stand alone over black, such as with the slate, you will often want it to appear over an image. All text clips in Final Cut Pro contain an *alpha channel* that drops away, or makes transparent, the nontext portion of the text clip and allows you to superimpose just the text over any background image.

5   In the Timeline, double-click the **Lower 3rd** clip to open it in the Viewer, and click the Controls tab.

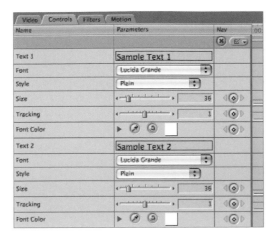

With this clip, there are two separate areas where you can make changes to each line of text.

6   Click in the Text 1 field, and enter *mr. MONK*. Make the font Gill Sans, change the Style to Bold, leave the default Size at 36, and change the Tracking to 3. In the Text 2 field, enter *and the Actor*, and give it the same style attributes as Text 1. Play the clip.

While superimposing this clip saved a few editing steps, you may not want the title to remain visible this long. You can easily change the clip length, and add a default cross dissolve to smooth out the edit point. Let's start this text clip 2 seconds later.

7   In the Timeline, select the In point of the **Lower 3rd** clip, and press 2. (two period), and press Return. Then press Command-T to add a default cross dissolve.

With a transition added, and the clip length shortened, the title looks more professional and closer to the original that aired.

The only thing missing from this title is a drop shadow. In Final Cut Pro, the drop shadow function appears in the Viewer on the Motion tab because, even though not every clip is a text clip, every clip can have a drop shadow. Since every clip has a Motion tab, drop shadow appears on this tab.

MORE INFO ► You will work more with Motion parameters in Lesson 12.

8   In the Viewer, click the Motion tab, then select the Drop Shadow checkbox. Click the disclosure triangle to reveal its parameters.

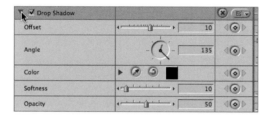

When you toggle on Drop Shadow, the shadow appears behind the text in the Canvas. However, the default Drop Shadow attributes don't match those used in the *Monk* episode.

9   In the Drop Shadow parameters, click in the Offset field and enter *1.5*. Change the Angle to 150, the Softness to 0, and the Opacity to 100.

The opacity of an image ranges from completely solid or opaque (100%) to completely transparent or invisible (0%). As a rule of thumb, the more opaque and crisp a shadow is, the closer the text seems to the background; the more transparent and soft the shadow, the farther the text seems from the background image.

TIP ► When you adjust parameters for your own project, you may want to explore options such as lowering opacity and increasing softness.

10 To see the next title in the **Monk.mov** clip, press Shift-M to move to the next marker, where you see the credit for guest star Susan Ward.

Since Tony Shalhoub is credited during the opening of the show, you will use this actor's credit as a reference. Notice how this lower third credit follows the same general style as the previous lower third clip. Rather than edit a whole new text clip from scratch, you can open the first lower third clip and superimpose it over the next *Monk* clip.

11 In the Timeline, double-click the **Lower 3rd** clip, and position the Timeline playhead to the next clip, **B6_scn2B_tk4**. In the Viewer, drag the **Lower 3rd** clip into the Canvas and drop it as a superimpose edit.

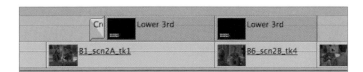

12 Move the playhead to the second **Lower 3rd** clip, and double-click it. Click the Controls tab, if necessary. Click the Text 1 field and enter *STARRING*, and change the Text 1 font size to 26. In the Text 2 field, enter *tony SHALHOUB*. Press Tab.

TIP ▶ In the Lower 3rd controls, you can add a solid background behind the text to help the text stand out against a lighter image. When you choose Solid from the Background parameter, you can change the color of the background and adjust its opacity.

Applying a Boris Title

If you don't find the options you need in the Text generator, you can try another category of text generators—called Boris—in the Generator pop-up menu. Boris contains an advanced set of text generators that provide great flexibility and high-quality output. The Boris submenu lists four text generators. Unlike the text options previously covered in this lesson, these access a separate window, offering a wider variety of parameters, including 3D control of individual characters (Title 3D). The Boris text options, which are part of the Final Cut Pro installation, allow you to make a number of style choices as well.

1   In the Timeline, move the playhead to the middle of the next *Monk* clip, **A5_scn2B_tk4**. In the **Monk.mov** reference clip, press Shift-M to move to the next marker.

Three lines were used to create Stanley Kamel's credit. Since the lower third text clips are preformatted to have only two lines and appear in the lower left of the frame, you have to use a different Text generator to create this credit. While you can enter several lines in the basic **Text** clip, you can't change the font size or style on individual lines as they appear in this credit.

2   In the Viewer, click the Video tab, and then click the Generator pop-up menu and choose Boris > Title 3D. Drag this clip into the Canvas and release it as a superimpose edit.

3   In the Timeline, double-click the clip to open it in the Viewer, and then click the Controls tab. In the Text Entry and Style field, click the Title 3D (Click for options) box.

In the Boris Title 3D options, you don't enter text information in the Controls tab; instead, you use a separate window.

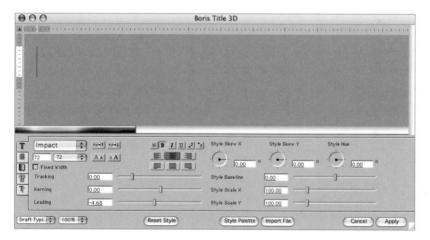

A large window opens with several small tabs running vertically down the left side of the window. The tabs are Text Style, Text Wrap, Text Fill, Edge Style, and Shadow Type. Next to some of the items are tiny checkboxes for toggling them on and off.

4   With the first tab selected, type the information as it appears in the **Monk.mov** clip. In the large gray text area, drag over the text to select it all, or press Command-A.

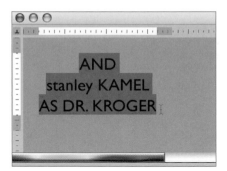

The goal is to follow the same general style with this clip as with the other lower third clips, but it will appear in the lower-right area of the image and, of course, include the third line. Some of the changes will be made to all of the text, and some to individual lines.

5 Change the attributes of this clip as follows:

▶ Click the Right Justify button to justify the text on the right side of the image.

▶ Click the Font pop-up and choose Gill Sans.

▶ Click in the Font Size field, and enter *26*.

▶ Deselect the text, and select just the middle line.

▶ Click the Font Size pop-up and choose 36.

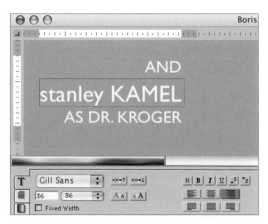

TIP ▶ In the Boris Title 3D window, you can even change individual letters. Just select the letters, words, or lines you want to change, and adjust those parameters. Only the text you select will be modified.

6   In the lower-right corner of the Boris Title 3D window, click Apply.

In the Canvas, the text style appears as it should, but it isn't placed in the lower-right corner of the title safe area.

7   In the Controls tab, click the crosshair button in the Position X/Y parameter. In the Canvas, click in the center of the text (close to the current red center crosshair) and drag down and to the right to position the text just inside the title safe area.

Since you've already set the correct drop shadow parameters in an earlier text clip, you can simply copy that clip and paste the drop shadow attributes to this clip.

8   Select the first **Lower 3rd** clip and press Command-C to copy it. Control-click the **Title 3D** clip and choose Paste Attributes from the shortcut menu. In the Paste Attributes window, make sure Drop Shadow is selected, and click OK.

Project Tasks

The Boris Title 3D text window offers numerous ways to change text parameters, including several preset text styles. If you want to edit another Boris Title 3D clip into the sequence, and explore some of the preset styles, continue with the following steps:

1   At the end of the sequence, create a Boris **Title 3D** clip on the V2 track. Enter *stay tuned for more* as the first line of the text, and enter *MONK* as the second line.

2   Highlight the first line and format the font and size as Arial and 32, respectively. Highlight the second line, *MONK*, and make it a different font and size, such as Impact and 48.

3   Click the Style Palette button, and at the top of the Style Palette window, choose the Gradient tab to view that category of options. Below the tabs, click the Category pop-up menu and choose Straight.GRD. Double-click Dawn, then click Apply.

Creating a Credit Roll

At the beginning of the *Monk* episode, as in many other television shows, each credit is displayed on the screen one name at a time. If you want to create the type of credit roll you often see at the end of a feature film, you use the Final Cut Pro animated Scrolling Text generator. This text generator automatically rolls the text up from the bottom of the image and off at the top.

1   In the Timeline, position the playhead in the middle of the last *Monk* clip in the sequence, **B6_scn2B_tk4**. To superimpose a text clip over this clip, patch the v1 source control to the V1 destination track.

2   In the Viewer, click the Video tab, then click the Generator pop-up menu and choose Text > Scrolling Text. To superimpose this clip, press the super-impose edit shortcut, F12, or click the Superimpose button in the Canvas window.

> **TIP** ▶ You can choose to make any of the Canvas Edit Overlay options appear as the third edit button in the Canvas. Click and hold the arrow next to the blue Replace button, and select the purple Superimpose button to make it the default third edit button for this sequence.

3   In the Timeline, double-click the **Scrolling Text** clip to open it in the Viewer, and click the Controls tab.

Since the credits will roll up and off the screen, if the playhead is parked at the end or beginning of the clip, you won't see the text. With the playhead in the middle of the clip, you can see the text as you enter it.

4   In the Text field, enter the following information, including the asterisks between the credit and person's name, and press Return after each line. Press Tab after the last line to see the text update in the Canvas:

*Producer*Anthony Santa Croce*

*Co-Producer*Scott Collins*

*Editor*Scott Boyd*

Final Cut Pro creates two columns separated by a gap where the asterisks were entered. As you can see, you will have to make additional changes to improve the text's appearance within the title safe area.

NOTE ▶ It may seem intuitive to place a space before and after the asterisks, but it is not necessary and will not create the desired effect.

5   Drag the scroller down to the lower Controls parameters. Make the Size 24 and change the Leading to 120%. Adjust the Gap Width to 4% to reduce the distance between the two columns. Play this clip in the Timeline.

The clip is programmed to animate the scroll for the full length of the clip. If you want the fade to move faster, you shorten the clip.

6   Drag the In point of the **Scrolling Text** clip to the right 5 seconds. Play this clip again.

The shortened clip plays more quickly. You can also set the Fade Size parameter to fade the credits in and out as they appear on and off the screen.

7 In the Fade Size parameter, enter a Fade Size of *15%*, and play the clip again.

Text clips can be rendered just like other effects. If the text clip isn't playing smoothly on your computer, you can select it and render it.

8 Select the **Scrolling Text** clip, and press Command-R to render it.

> **TIP** ▸ Make sure the render status color is selected in the Sequences > Render Selection menu before rendering.

Opacity is another parameter that can be changed on any clip. It determines how transparent an image is. A clip can be completely transparent, completely solid, or any percentage in between. Opacity can be changed in any sequence clip by dragging an opacity overlay, which is similar to the audio level overlay on an audio clip.

9 In the Timeline, click the Clip Overlays control. In the **Scrolling Text** clip, drag the opacity overlay down to 75%. Play the clip again.

Since opacity can be changed on any clip, that parameter appears in the Motion tab just above Drop Shadow. If you click the Motion tab and click the Opacity disclosure triangle, you see that the percentage is 75% there as well.

NOTE ▶ There are two other animated text generators you can experiment with on your own: Crawl and Typewriter. Crawl reveals text moving horizontally across the screen from the left or right. You may have seen weather warnings broadcast this way. The Typewriter text generator reveals one letter at a time until the full text is revealed, as if a typewriter were typing the text.

Adding Mattes and Other Generated Items

There are many more video generators than just text, including color mattes; shapes; and render items, such as gradient, noise, and lens flare. You can use a color matte as a simple color background behind text or behind another image that has been resized or cropped. When you combine a render effect on top of a color matte, you may find that you have created a show open. In this exercise, you build a background to use as a show open for the BBC "Living Colour: Yellow" project, and choose generated items from the Effects tab in the Browser.

1   In the **Monk.mov** Viewer window, click the Close button. In the Browser, open the *Yellow Open_START* and *Yellow Cuts* sequences. Click the *Yellow Cuts* sequence tab to make it active.

2   In the Browser, click the Effects tab, and click the disclosure triangle next to the Video Generators bin. Then click the disclosure triangle next to the Matte bin.

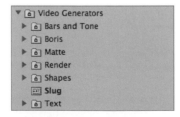

NOTE ▶ Bolded text options will play in real time.

Like transitions, the video-generated items are organized into bins. The Matte bin contains two types of color mattes. The icon that represents these generated items is a frame of color bars. When you edit generated items from the Effects tab, you can drag them from the Browser directly into the Timeline, or open them in the Viewer.

3   Double-click the **Color** clip to open it in the Viewer, and click the Controls tab. In the Color controls, click the Select Color eyedropper and in the Canvas, click a bright yellow area anywhere in the image.

You choose colors for color mattes just as you choose colors for transition effects. You can also use this approach to pick a color for text.

4   In the Timeline, click the *Yellow Open_START* sequence tab, and edit the yellow **Color** clip onto the V1 track at the head of the sequence.

With the color matte on the V1 track, you can add other elements on top of it. For example, there are animated render effects that could liven up the static yellow background. Let's take a look at a few render items.

5   From the Video Generators folder in the Effects bin, open and play each of the following render items in the Viewer: **Caustics**, **Clouds**, **Lens Flare**, **Membrane**, **Noise** (second one), and **Swirly**.

Each of these items creates some pattern or movement that could be used in conjunction with a background image or color matte.

Since generated items have a 10-second marked duration, you can drag the clip directly from the Effects tab into the Timeline, or you can edit it from the Viewer as an overwrite or superimpose edit.

6   Edit the **Membrane** clip into the *Yellow Open_START* sequence directly above the **Color** clip on the V2 track. Play the clip.

As with text clips, this render effect has an alpha channel that drops out the black portion of the image when combined with other clips.

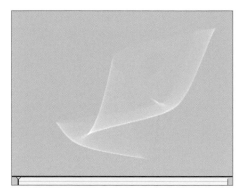

7   In the Effects tab, open the Text bin. Edit the basic **Text** clip onto the V3 track at the head of the sequence, over the other two clips.

8   Double-click the new **Text** clip to open it in the Viewer. In the Controls tab Text field, enter *Living Colour: Yellow.* Change the Style to Bold, and the Tracking to 2.

9   To give this text a drop shadow, click the Motion tab, and click the Drop Shadow checkbox. Change the Offset to 2, the Softness to 0, and the Opacity to 80. Play the clip in the Timeline.

TIP If you like a particular drop shadow that you used on another clip and want to be consistent throughout your project, you can copy that clip, and paste the Drop Shadow attribute to the text clip.

Project Tasks

The render video generators have a somewhat free-form appeal to them. By changing just a few parameters, you can create an entirely different effect. Take a moment to explore the possibilities of the Membrane effect by opening it in the Viewer and changing the speed and other parameters. You can also change its color to black. To make the membrane pattern appear boxlike, enter the settings from the image below:

Speed	0.05
Start 1	-2
Start 2	-1
Start 3	0
Start 4	1
End 1	2
End 2	1
End 3	0
End 4	2
Offset	1
Brightness	10
Color	

Building a Composite Opening Title

Opening titles range from simple white against black to multiple layers of text over a background of color or other images. Because all text clips have alpha channels that make the nontext areas transparent, you can place one text clip on top of another in the Timeline to create a *composite* image in which several text clips are visible at the same time. In this exercise, you will add another text clip to the current show open, then edit this sequence of clips into the *Yellow Cuts* sequence.

1   From the Effects bin, drag the basic **Text** clip into the Timeline and edit it as an overwrite edit on the V4 track above the other clips. Double-click the V4 **Text** clip to open it in the Viewer.

Since the default position of the **Text** clip is center screen, you currently see this text directly over the V3 **Text** clip. Let's move it into its own position so you can see it as you make changes.

2   In the Controls tab, click the Origin Select Point (crosshair) button. In the Canvas, drag the text into the upper-right corner within the title safe area.

3   In the Controls tab, click the color picker. In the Colors window, drag the Brightness slider down to black, and click OK. In the Text field, enter

warming. Change the Font to Geneva, the font Size to 40, the Alignment to right, and the Tracking to 15. If necessary, reposition the text to appear just inside the upper-right title safe area.

At the moment, this black text overpowers the actual title. You can choose a softer, more opaque color, or you can adjust the clip's opacity to make it more transparent.

4   In the lower left of the Timeline window, click the Clip Overlays control, or press Option-W. On the V4 **Text** clip, drag the opacity overlay on the V4 **Text** clip down to about 40%.

As the clip becomes more transparent, the background shows through the dark text, making it appear softer.

NOTE ▶ In the project tasks that follow this exercise, you will add additional words from the Yellow narration track and place them in different parts of the image.

To animate a parameter over time, you can add keyframes as you did when adjusting audio volume. As with audio keyframes, you set one keyframe for a starting position and one for an ending position. Let's animate the size of the main title by setting keyframes in the Viewer. First, you have to make the Viewer wider to see the *keyframe graph* area.

NOTE ▶ Depending on your screen resolution, you may already see the Viewer keyframe graph area in your interface.

5   In the Timeline, drag the Viewer window to the left over the Browser. Drag the right side of the Viewer window to the right to reveal the keyframe graph area.

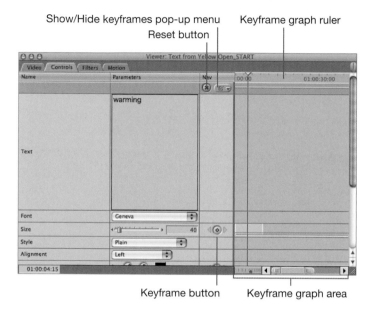

Show/Hide keyframes pop-up menu   Keyframe graph ruler
Reset button

Keyframe button   Keyframe graph area

The keyframe graph area, which is often hidden from view, contains a Timeline-like area where you can set keyframes at specific locations in time.

6   In the Timeline, position the playhead in the middle of the stack of clips. Double-click the V3 **Text** clip. In the Controls tab, click the Size Keyframe button.

In the Size controls, when you click the Keyframe button, a green keyframe is added to mark the size of this clip at this point in time.

7   In the Timeline, move the playhead to the beginning of this clip. In the Controls tab, enter *0* in the Size field. Play the clip in the Timeline.

After you set the first keyframe, if you move the playhead to a different location, or timecode position, and change the Size parameter, a second keyframe is automatically created to mark the change in size from the first keyframe.

With the opening almost set, you might want to see how it looks in the *Yellow Cuts* sequence. You have a few options to do this. You can copy the set of clips and paste them into the sequence. Or you can simply edit this sequence into the *Yellow Cuts* sequence. When you edit one sequence into another, it *nests* the clips together as if they were one clip, which makes a stack of clips like this one easier to handle and view. Before you reset the window layout to see the Browser, you can save this wide Viewer layout to use for other times when you need to set keyframes.

8   Choose Window > Arrange > Save Window Layout. In the Save window, enter *wide Viewer* for the name, and click Save.

9   Press Control-U to return the windows to their Standard layout. In the Timeline, click the *Yellow Cuts* sequence tab. In the Browser, click the Lesson 11 Project tab.

10   To edit the *Yellow Open_START* sequence, drag the sequence icon from the Browser into the *Yellow Cuts* sequence and snap it to the head of the sequence. Release this clip as an insert edit. Play the new title.

NOTE ▸ You can also drag a sequence into the Viewer and edit it into another sequence as an overwrite or insert edit. Or you can mark a portion of a sequence and edit just that portion.

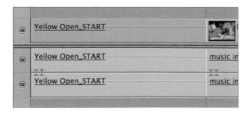

In the Timeline, the sequence appears as a single clip. Notice the altered colors of the video and audio tracks. Although it's one clip, all of the clips that were used to create the show open still appear in the Canvas.

Once you've nested a group of clips into another sequence, you can make changes to the individual clips by opening the nest. These changes are automatically updated in the sequence that contains the nest. For example, if you wanted to see only the primary *Living Colour: Yellow* title appear in the show open, and not the *warming* text, you can toggle off visibility for the V4 track.

To return to the original sequence with the clip layers, you double-click the nested clip.

11 In the *Yellow Open_START* sequence, click the V4 Track Visibility control to toggle off visibility for that track. Then click the *Yellow Cuts* sequence tab and play the first clip again.

With the V4 track toggled off in the *Yellow Open_START* sequence, you no longer see the *warming* text in the *Yellow Cuts* sequence.

Project Tasks

To continue working with the yellow title, add three new text clips. Change the text to read *bold* on one clip, *strong* on another, and *gorgeous* on yet another clip. Then modify the parameters so each text clip looks different. You can change the opacity of each of the additional text clips, or copy the *warming* text clip and paste the Opacity attribute to the other three clips. You can also shorten the different word clips and add transitions to fade them in and out over time.

NOTE ▶ To see one version of this completed title, open and view the *Yellow Open_FINISHED* sequence in the Browser.

Using Master Templates

Also included in the Final Cut Pro generated items is a set of master templates that were created in the Final Cut Studio 2 Motion application. The master templates contain 15 design concepts, each with its own set of animated templates you can use for opens, lower thirds, backgrounds, bumpers, and so on. You edit these templates into a sequence as you would any other generated text item, and change the text of the template in the text fields of the Controls tab. You can even add an image to the template by dragging it into a drop zone.

To change or alter a template design, you can open the template in the Motion application, or send the clip to Motion and make the changes there. In Motion, you can change the primary color scheme or make other changes to the template design. When changed in Motion, those new attributes are also changed and updated in all uses of that template in the Final Cut Pro sequence.

1   Click the *Yellow Cuts* sequence tab and move the playhead to the end of the *Yellow Cuts* sequence.

2   In the Viewer Video tab, click the Generator pop-up and choose Master Templates > Travel > Travel – Lower Third.PAL. Edit this clip at the end of the sequence as an overwrite edit, and play the clip.

   This animated graphics clip is sized and positioned to be used as a lower third. In the next step, you will replace the sample text with text for this sequence. You could place this clip over a background image, and that image would show through the black portion of the lower third template.

3   Double-click the clip to open it in the Viewer, and click the Controls tab. In the Title Information Here field, enter *For More Living Colour*. In the Subtitle Information Here field, enter *www.bbcmotiongallery.com*. Press Tab and play the clip in the Timeline.

Working with Graphics

Final Cut Pro can import many types of graphic files, such as TIFF, JPEG, and so on. You can import a single-layer graphic file or a multilayered graphic file created in Adobe Photoshop. When importing a multilayered file, it appears in Final Cut Pro as a sequence icon, which allows you to edit each layer separately within Final Cut Pro. You import and work with graphics just as you would work with other clips, but there are a few key things to keep in mind to make your graphics look their best.

Before you edit a graphic file into your sequence, be aware that a video-based pixel aspect ratio is different from a graphic file's ratio because computers and graphics programs display square pixels, whereas digital video uses nonsquare pixels. If you create a graphic of a circle and import it into Final Cut Pro, the output of that file will not look perfectly round. To be absolutely accurate, and to please those clients who use circles in their logos, you need to prepare your graphic files to accommodate this pixel difference.

While a full discussion of importing graphics is beyond the scope of this book, the following steps outline a common image preparation workflow that applies to both single-layer and multilayer graphics.

> **NOTE** ▶ When you're working with graphics in video, the dpi (dots per inch) settings are irrelevant. A 300 dpi image will look the same as a 72 dpi image. The pixel dimensions of an image—such as 1440 x 1080 or 720 x 480—determine the resolution of the video image.

1 In your graphics application, begin with a file image size that is 720 x 540 pixels for DV-NTSC or 768 x 576 for DV-PAL. These represent the square-pixel dimensions you should use in any still-image graphic program.

2 When you have completed the graphic, save a copy of it, and change the image size to 720 x 480 for NTSC or 720 x 576 for PAL.

3 Without making changes to the 720 x 480 (720 x 576 for PAL) file, import it into Final Cut Pro.

The image will look as it did in the original version of your graphic file.

> **MORE INFO** ▶ The Final Cut Pro User Manual contains a chart of additional graphic format conversions.

Lesson Review

1. From what two places can you choose a generated item such as text?
2. What tab in the Viewer do you select to make changes to text clips?
3. When you superimpose an edit over a V1 clip, to what track should the source control be patched for the superimposed clip to be placed on V2?
4. What type of generated text identifies a person, place, or thing?
5. Under what menu can you find the Show Title Safe option?
6. What generated item is used as a color and sound reference at the head of a sequence?
7. Where can you find the Drop Shadow attribute?

8. In what text generator does a separate window appear for making text changes?

9. What automated text generator is often used for credit rolls?

10. How can you adjust a clip's opacity?

11. When you choose a color for a color matte, you can pick a color only from the Colors window. True or false?

12. What is it called when you edit one sequence inside another?

13. What category of generated items can you use to apply a Motion template?

Answers

1. Choose from the Browser Effects tab or from the Generator pop-up menu in the Video tab in the Viewer.

2. The Controls tab.

3. The V1 track.

4. A lower third.

5. The View menu, and the View pop-up in the Viewer and Canvas.

6. Bars and tone.

7. In the Motion tab in the Viewer.

8. The Boris Text generator.

9. The Scrolling Text generator.

10. Drag the opacity overlay on a video clip in the Timeline, or open a clip in the Viewer and change the Opacity parameter in the Motion tab.

11. False. You can use the Select Color eyedropper to pick a color from any clip in any open sequence.

12. Nesting.

13. Master templates.

Adding Effects
and Finishing

12

Lesson **12**
Changing Motion Properties

There's something quite satisfying about chiseling a precise sequence from a relatively rough chunk of media files, completing it by adding music, titles, and transitions; and then finishing and preparing the sequence for delivery to a client, the web, or the world.

The really fun part of that completion process is adding the refinements and embellishments that make a sequence sparkle and shine. In the next two lessons, you will explore two approaches to adding effects and finessing a sequence—changing the motion properties and adding filters. In the final lesson, you will learn to output and export a finished sequence.

This lesson teaches how to change the motion properties of a clip, such as manipulating the speed at which a clip plays, or modifying its size and position on the screen.

Motion properties can be changed to alter the style or look of a clip and give it added visual appeal. These changes might include combining clips to create a multi-frame or split-screen image. Or you may change the motion properties as a matter of function, perhaps by removing a camera or microphone from a shot. In the following exercises, you will change clip speed, create a freeze frame, and fit a clip of one length into the sequence space of a different length using the fit to fill edit. Then, you'll resize and reposition clips by stacking them on top of each other to create a split-screen effect, and use keyframes to animate motion properties over time.

Evaluating a Project

Changing the motion properties of a clip in a sequence may not be your first intention. For example, in the "Living Colour: Yellow" project, the subclips were too short to add transitions. Once the clips were slowed down, they became longer, creating longer handles that allowed you to add transitions between the clips. In this case, the original "Yellow" subclips weren't wrong, but they weren't functioning in a way that gave you many alternatives. Let's evaluate three other sequences that have different needs.

1   From the Lessons folder on your hard drive, open the **Lesson 12 Project** file, and close any other open projects.

2   In the Timeline, click the *Monk* sequence tab and move the playhead to any clip with a red label. Notice the camera in the right portion of the image.

This show is shot in 16:9 aspect ratio, or widescreen video format, but airs in 4:3 aspect ratio. Even though a portion of the clip's left and right edges is cropped for the broadcast version, that camera is still prominent and might be seen in the red-labeled clips. To correct this shot, you can make it a little larger, and reposition it in the frame so you don't see the camera in the final version.

3   Play the *Commercial_v2_multiframe* sequence.

This footage is from a branded-content piece intended to promote and feature a specific automotive brand. The directorial vision of this piece was to create all of the elements of a great drama without shooting an entire film. These elements refer to a narrative without explaining it, leaving interpretation and detail to the viewer's imagination. It was produced by coreaudiovisual, and was shot in HD at 23.98 fps, and captured using the DVCPRO HD codec.

4   Press A to return to the default Selection tool. Play the *Commercial_v1_blowup* sequence.

You may recognize several of the shots from the *Commercial_v2_multiframe* sequence. In this sequence, rather than creating a multiframe effect, a different style was created by reversing direction, changing the speed of some of the clips, and adding freeze frames.

By applying motion property changes to the car sequences, a little sparkle was visibly added to those projects. In contrast, when motion property changes are made primarily to correct a clip, as they were in the *Monk* sequence, the modifications are often unnoticeable.

TIP ▶ In the Timeline, click the RT pop-up menu and choose Unlimited RT and Dynamic to see the highest number of speed changes in real time.

Changing Speed Properties

Changing clip speed in Final Cut Pro is a very easy task, and one you can perform to address either a style or a function issue.

Let's say you shot a car being blown up from three different angles. Slowing down the explosion could make those few fiery seconds seem much more dramatic. In the "Believe" project perhaps the best video shot falls short of covering a portion of the reporter's voice-over. Slowing down a whale behavior clip lengthens it, making for an easy fix. Both of these shots benefit in different ways from the same motion slowdown.

If your cameraperson shot a zoom-out of someone's face, but you really want to see a zoom-in, you can change the clip to play in reverse. You can also use a type of edit—called *fit to fill*—that will automatically change the speed of a clip to fit into an existing space in the sequence. You will apply all of these techniques in the following exercise.

1   In the Browser, open the *Commercial_v1_START* sequence, and play it.

These are the same clips you saw in the finished version of this sequence. However, the original speed of these clips has not yet been changed and, therefore, don't cover the music track. Slowing some of the video clips and adding freeze frames will extend the video to cover the music track. First, start by reversing the direction of camera zoom.

2 In the Timeline, click the *Commercial_v1_START* sequence tab. Play the **face forward** clip under the *reverse* marker.

One way you can alter a clip is simply to reverse its direction. If this shot is played in reverse, it zooms into the man's face as the music builds to a climax, which makes it more dramatic.

3 To reverse this clip, select it, and choose Modify > Speed, or press Command-J.

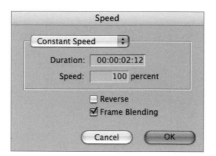

A Speed dialog opens with options for total clip duration, clip speed, reverse direction, and frame blending.

NOTE ▶ When playing a clip at a slower speed, you sometimes see a strobe or stuttering effect. Frame blending helps minimize this effect, which is why it's selected as a default option.

4 Select the Reverse checkbox, and click OK. Play this clip again. Then zoom into the clip in the Timeline.

The clip plays at the same speed, but in reverse direction. Notice the *(–100%)* next to the clip name. The minus indicates this clip is playing in reverse, and the 100% indicates it's playing at 100 percent of its normal speed.

There are two explosion shots in this sequence. It might make the footage more dramatic if you slow down the second explosion, after the man opens his eyes, as if he were reliving what he saw.

5 Move the playhead to the end of the second **Text** clip, and play the explosion scene that follows it. Select the second explosion clip, **explosion_ws**, and press Command-J. In the Speed dialog, enter *50* in the Speed percent field, and click OK. Play these clips again.

Slowing this clip to 50% makes it twice as long and ripples the remaining clips in the Timeline, extending the video portion of the entire sequence. Notice the *(50%)* reference next to the clip name to indicate the adjusted clip speed.

TIP ▶ You can also modify the speed of an audio clip, which is helpful if you need to increase the length of a sound effect, or make a music track sound peppier.

When you change clip speed to play faster, the clip becomes shorter in the Timeline. If you want to change clip speed, but not change the overall sequence length, you can mark the clip before making the speed change, then trim it back to its original length.

6 Move the playhead over the **road lines** clip, and press X to mark its current length. Select the clip and press Command-J. In the Speed dialog, enter *150* in the Speed percent field, and click OK. Play the clip.

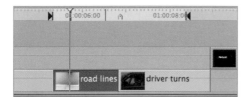

In this situation, the clips are rippled the other way, shortening the sequence length. Using the marks you set in the Timeline as a reference, you can trim this clip back to its original length. This will give you twice as much footage in the same amount of space.

7 Press RR to select the Ripple tool. Drag the Out point of the **road lines** clip to snap to the Out point.

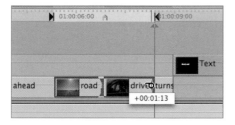

After you apply a speed change to a sequence clip, you can trim or even slip it because the entire clip, including handles, is at the same speed.

TIP You can also change the speed of a master clip in the Viewer before you make an edit. Keep in mind that this will alter the master clip. You can always return a master clip to its original speed by changing its value to 100 in the Speed dialog.

8 Press A to return to the default selection tool, and press Option-X to remove the In and Out points.

Another way you can change clip speed is to edit a clip of one length into a sequence space of a different length. To do this, you use the fit to fill edit.

9 Move the playhead to the head of the **explosion in mirror** clip, and press X to mark this clip length. Play this clip, and then press F to load the master clip into the Viewer.

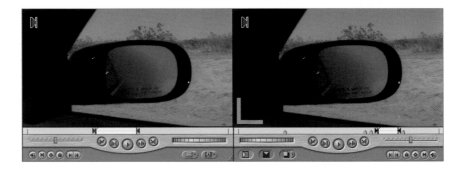

It would be nice to use a longer drive-by segment, to see more action in the rearview mirror, without changing the length of the sequence. You can do this by making a fit to fill edit. The fit to fill edit takes the source content between its In and Out points and changes the speed so it fits (or fills) the duration between the sequence's In and Out points.

10 In the Viewer, play between the current In and Out marks. Then drag the playhead toward the end of the clip to when the car appears at a further distance, at around 22:06:01:10. Mark an Out point at this location.

The duration of this source clip is about 7:10, whereas the duration of the clip in the Timeline is only 2:20. Using the fit to fill edit, Final Cut Pro will speed up the longer source clip to fit the entire 7:10 length into the 2:20 marked duration of the sequence.

11 Drag the clip from the Viewer to the Canvas. Release the clip in the Edit Overlay on the Fit to Fill section. Play the new edit in the Timeline.

TIP ▶ To use fit to fill to cover several clips in a sequence, set an In and an Out point around the clips or area you want to fill, then mark and edit your source clip as a fit to fill edit.

Project Tasks

To practice using the fit to fill edit, open the *Believe News* sequence and mark a segment of the reporter's voice-over. Then, open a whale behavior clip (from the Believe Clips bin) and mark a specific action. Use the fit to fill edit to edit the whale action over the reporter's sound bite. You can experiment with opening a master clip from the Browser and changing the speed or direction of a clip in the Viewer. Then, mark and edit just the portion of that clip you want to use.

MORE INFO ▶ You can also create variable speed changes on a clip by setting keyframes in the Viewer Motion tab or the Timeline, or by using the Time Remap tool. Learn more about variable speed changes in Michael Wohl's *Final Cut Pro: Beyond the Basics*, part of the Apple Pro Training Series.

Creating a Freeze Frame

Another way to modify the speed of a clip is to stop the motion altogether and freeze a specific frame. This technique is applied frequently in television shows to freeze a shot before fading to black and going to commercial. While that's a style choice, freezing a shot can also help fix a problem by extending a too-short clip, for example, or keeping the audience from knowing that on the frame after the freeze, the camera fell off the tripod. In video, a freeze frame is actually created by repeating one frame over and over for a specific length of time. This process is handled automatically by Final Cut Pro. Freeze frames can be created in the Timeline or in the Viewer.

1   In the Commercial Clips bin in the Browser, open the **explosion_cu** clip and move the playhead to the marker named *freeze frame*. To create a freeze frame at this location, choose Modify > Make Freeze Frame, or press Shift-N.

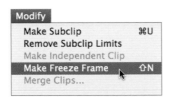

A separate clip is created in the Viewer with a total length of 2 minutes and a marked default duration of 10 seconds. Notice the freeze frame name contains the timecode number where the freeze was created.

You can now mark and edit this freeze frame into a sequence, as you would any other clip.

When you create a freeze frame, it is only temporarily held in the Viewer until you open a different clip. If you want to save a freeze frame to edit later, you have to create a separate clip of it by dragging the frame from the Viewer to the Browser.

2   In the Browser, Control-click the Commercial Clips bin and choose New Bin from the shortcut menu. Name this bin *Freeze Frames*, and click its disclosure triangle to see its contents.

3   Drag the **explosion_cu 23:00:26:05** freeze frame image from the Viewer into the Freeze Frames bin you created in the Browser.

The freeze frame appears as a graphic icon, also used to represent other graphic files such as TIFF or JPEG images. This freeze frame is now its own master clip, which you can use throughout the editing process.

TIP To see the thumbnail images of these freeze frames, open the Freeze Frame bin and change it to icon view.

4   Repeat the process of creating a freeze and saving it (in steps 1 and 3) for the **car on dirt road** clip.

TIP If you anticipate creating a lot of freeze frame images and want them to be of a specific length, you can change the default Still/Freeze Duration in the Editing tab of User Preferences.

Oftentimes, you only think about creating a freeze after a clip has been edited into the sequence. Sometimes, you create a sequence freeze frame to stand alone, and other times you may want a clip to play and *then* freeze action on a specific frame. Let's create this *run-and-freeze* effect by freezing a frame in the **explosion_cu** clip. As in the Viewer, you begin by positioning the playhead over the frame you want to freeze.

5   Drag the Timeline playhead to the middle of the **explosion_ws** clip. You can use the *freeze frame* marker over the clip as a general reference. Choose Modify > Make Freeze Frame, or press Shift-N.

A 2-minute freeze frame appears in the Viewer with a 10-second marked duration, just as it did in the previous steps. To create a run-and-freeze effect, this freeze frame must be edited back into the sequence exactly where it was created.

6   In the Timeline, set an In point at the playhead location where you created the freeze, and set an Out point on the last frame of the **explosion_ws** clip.

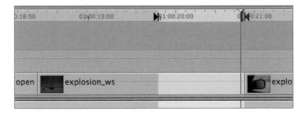

7   Click the Overwrite button. Play the clip, and then zoom into this area.

Freeze frame clips in the sequence appear in a slightly different shade of blue to distinguish them from normal clips. The name of the freeze frame clip is the sequence name and location, since it was created from that frame in the sequence. This freeze captures a dramatic moment.

You can add a freeze frame at the end of a clip to extend the length of the clip, or to capture a certain facial expression to end the scene.

8   Move the playhead to the end of the audio fade at the end of the sequence, and press O to set an Out point. Move the playhead to the last frame of the **face forward** clip, and press I to set an In point.

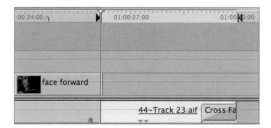

In this situation, you want the last frame of this man's facial expression to hold and continue until the end of the sequence.

9   Choose Modify > Make Freeze Frame to create a freeze frame of this frame. Click the Overwrite button to edit the freeze frame in the Viewer back into the sequence. Play the new edit.

Project Tasks

There are two types of run-and-freeze effects you can create. In the previous exercise, you created a run-and-freeze effect by editing a freeze frame to stop action in a clip and to extend its length. The other type of run-and-freeze effect involves inserting just a few seconds of a freeze into a clip, which splits the clip at the freeze frame location. This creates a *run-freeze-run* effect, which stops the action, and then returns to the remainder of the clip to finish playing. You can practice creating a run-freeze-run effect in the *Believe News* sequence.

1   In the *Believe News* sequence, position the playhead on the frame you want to freeze, perhaps the **jump at stage** or the **performance_2 whales jump** clip when the whale is in midair.

2   Choose Modify > Make Freeze Frame. In the Viewer, change the freeze frame duration to 2 seconds.

3   Press Shift-F5 to lock all the Timeline audio tracks.

4   Insert this freeze, and play the effect.

TIP▶ You can also use the Razor Blade tool to divide a clip into different segments, and then change the speed of each segment. With this approach, you can slow down an action or speed it up in increments.

Changing Clip Size and Position

In Final Cut Pro, every clip in your project has a set of default built-in motion parameters, such as size, position, crop, rotate, and so on, all of which can be changed and even animated. You can adjust these parameters to create a visual style or to correct a problem. The most basic reason to change a clip's size and position is to help erase a shooting error. For example, as you saw earlier in this lesson, there is one particular *Monk* camera angle in which you see the camera in the image. Blowing up that image slightly and repositioning it will solve the problem. In this exercise, you will explore the Size and Center parameters, and access the Image+Wireframe mode to adjust these parameters directly on the image in the Canvas.

1   In the Timeline, click the *Monk* sequence tab, and move the playhead to the first red labeled clip, **B6_scn2B_tk4**. Double-click the clip to open it in the Viewer, and click the Motion tab.

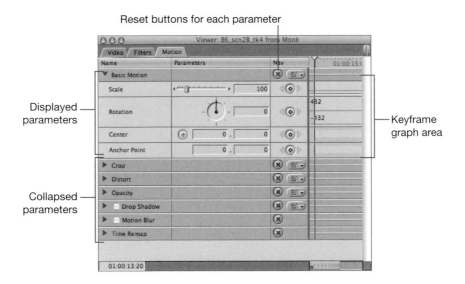

The Motion tab contains several motion attributes, which can be accessed by clicking their disclosure triangles. Within the set of Basic Motion attributes are controls to resize (Scale) and reposition (Center) an image, rotate it, and change how the rotation occurs (Anchor Point).

Before you adjust this image, there are two aids you can access in the Canvas window—the title safe boundaries and the Zoom pop-up—that will help you accurately position the image.

2 In the Timeline, deselect the **B6_scn2B_tk4** clip. In the Canvas, click the View pop-up menu and choose Show Title Safe.

The outer box is the action safe boundary. If seeing something in an image is important, such as a hand gesture or set decoration, make sure it's included within this boundary. In this case, you will use the action safe boundary as a reference for what not to include in this image.

3 In the Canvas window, click the Zoom pop-up, and choose 25% from the pop-up menu.

Zoom pop-up   Zoom pop-up menu

NOTE ▶ If the original percentage amount displayed on the Zoom pop-up button was less than 30%, you won't see much, or any, change. You can access the saved large Canvas window layout, or adjust the size of the Canvas so the zoom percentage is at least 30%. Then change it to 25%.

By zooming out of this image, you can see the image area as well as the space around it. Everything within the image area is visible when you output a sequence.

4   In the Motion tab, drag the Scale slider to the left to make the image smaller.

Making the image smaller reveals black behind it, which will become part of your final image output if the clip remains this size.

5   Drag the Scale slider right until you see only half of the camera in the Canvas image, where the scale is at about 117. In the Timeline, select the **B6_scn2B_tk4** clip.

TIP ▸ It's very important not to increase the size of an image too much. A slight adjustment under 20% is generally OK. With low-resolution footage, or with a greater increase in size, you will start to see pixilation in the image.

In the Canvas, you see the clip's turquoise border outside the image area. Like a photo behind a matte, you can now reposition this clip up or down, and left or right, and still fill the image area. The Center parameter controls the position of the image on the screen. Before you change the position of this image, notice that the default Center settings are 0 pixels horizontal (left field) and 0 pixels vertical (right field).

6   In the Viewer, click the Center point control (crosshair) and move the pointer into the Canvas. Click the center of the image and drag right until the camera is outside the action safe boundary, and then drag down until Mr. Monk's head is within the action safe boundary. Then look at the Center parameter values in the Viewer.

If you move a clip horizontally to the right of center, you will see a positive number. If you move a clip to the left past center, you will see a negative number. The second field represents vertical movement—upward movement shows as a negative number, and downward movement shows as a positive.

To refine this clip's size and position using a more manual approach, you will resize and reposition the clip image in the Canvas. But first, let's reset the Basic Motion attributes to their default settings.

7   In the Basic Motion attributes line, click the red Reset button.

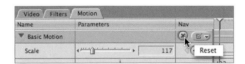

All of the Basic Motion attributes return to their default settings.

8   In the Canvas, click the View pop-up menu and choose Image+Wireframe. You can also choose View > Image+Wireframe, or press W with either the Timeline or Canvas window active.

A large white X appears corner to corner over the image area, and a number appears at the center point, indicating the clip's track number. With this mode selected, you can change several motion parameters by dragging specific areas of the image in the Canvas.

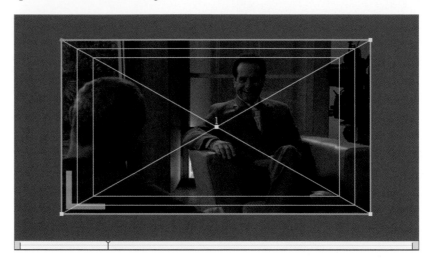

9   In the Canvas, move your pointer over any one of the four corner points of the wireframe. When the pointer changes to a crosshair, drag it outward until the camera is only half visible.

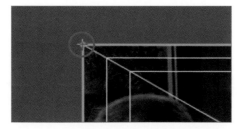

Dragging any corner handle outward resizes the image larger; dragging inward resizes the image smaller.

10 Move the pointer into the Canvas image area. When you see the Move pointer, drag the image to optimize its position inside the action safe boundary.

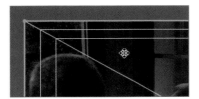

The adjustment corrected this image. However, there are several other red-labeled clips that have the same problem. In fact, each of these clips is from the same master clip that covered the entire scene from this angle. Since the framing in the other clips is the same, you can copy the corrected clip and paste the motion attributes to all the other clips at the same time.

11 Select the **B6_scn2B_tk4** clip, if it's not already selected, and press Command-C. Move the playhead to the next red-labeled clip, and select it. Then, Command-click all the other red-labeled clips. Control-click one of the selected clips and choose Paste Attributes from the shortcut menu.

Since the motion attributes were changed in the copied clip, they become selectable in this window.

12 Select the Basic Motion checkbox, and click OK.

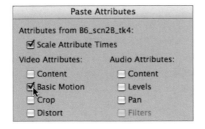

The selected clips' sizes and positions are all adjusted to match those of the first clip you changed.

TIP ▶ Another approach to a correction of this type is to resize and reposition the master clip before you begin editing. Then, every use of that master clip will already have the size and position correction.

13 To display the full image in the Canvas, click the Zoom pop-up, and choose Fit to Window from the pop-up menu. You can also press Shift-Z.

> **NOTE** ▶ In the Zoom pop-up menu, the default Fit to Window setting will always fit the entire clip image in the Canvas window regardless of how you change the window size. Like zooming in or out of the Timeline, changing the percentage in the Zoom pop-up menu does not change the actual scale of the image.

Building a Split Screen

Placing two images on the screen at the same time is a practice that's been around since the early days of film, when two people were shown talking on the phone in the same frame. You can easily create this split-screen or multi-frame effect in Final Cut Pro by adjusting the sizes and positions of the clips involved. And you don't have to limit yourself to just two clips. You can literally fill the screen with smaller images to create a show open. Or you can arrange three or four clips on the screen to show what different characters are doing at the same time. In this exercise, you will use the Motion tab and Image+Wireframe mode to size, reposition, and crop three images. You will also change the Canvas background to help you arrange the clips evenly.

> **NOTE** ▶ To review the multi-frame effect, you can play the *Commercial_v2_multiframe* sequence in the Timeline.

1 In the Viewer, click the View pop-up menu and choose Image+Wireframe. Click the View pop-up menu again and choose Show Title Safe.

You can turn these options off or on as needed for individual sequences.

2 From the Sequences bin, open the *Commercial_v2_START* sequence. Play the first stack of three clips in the sequence, then position the playhead on the first frame of the stack. Double-click the V3 **explosion_ws** clip, and click the Motion tab in the Viewer.

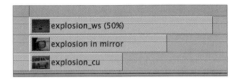

TIP ▶ Continue to reset the playhead to the head of this clip stack. This will ensure that you see the same frame as a reference in the Canvas as you make adjustments.

In this stack of clips, you can see only the clip on the highest track. To create a mixture or blend of these clips, you can lower the opacity of the upper clip, making it somewhat transparent, which allows the image beneath it to show through.

NOTE ▶ There are additional clips that follow in this sequence. You will use those in the project tasks at the end of this exercise.

3 In the Motion tab, click the disclosure triangle next to the Opacity parameter. Drag the slider left to about 50%. Play these clips again.

With the V3 clip at 50% opacity, you can see the V2 clip beneath it, creating a blend of these two images.

TIP ▶ To add the V1 clip to the mix, you would reduce the opacity of the V2 clip. You can also adjust opacity by turning on clip overlays and dragging the opacity overlays on the clips in the Timeline.

4 Click the Opacity Reset button to return opacity to its default state, and click the disclosure triangle. You can also press Command-Z to undo the last motion adjustment.

Another way to combine two or more images is to make the upper image smaller, allowing the clip beneath to be seen.

5 In the Motion tab, enter *50* in the Scale field, and press Tab. Now play the three clips.

TIP If you want to place a clip in each quarter of the image area, you can scale down each of the four clips by 50%. Although it may not be intuitive, scaling down by 50% does create a quarter-screen image, because it reduces the dimensions of each image side by half.

With the V3 image made smaller, you can see the V2 clip in the image area behind the V3 clip. Placing one picture over another in this way is referred to as a *picture-in-picture* effect, or PIP. Some television sets use this feature to allow you to watch two channels at the same time.

6 In the Canvas, drag the V3 **explosion_ws** clip wireframe into the lower-left corner and position the car headlights just above and inside the title safe boundary.

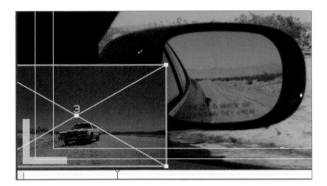

7   In the Timeline, double-click the V2 **explosion in mirror** clip. In the Motion tab, enter *50* in the Scale field, and press Tab. Then drag this clip into the upper-left corner of the Canvas and position the mirror just inside the title safe boundary. Play these clips again.

TIP ▸ When you want one clip to match another clip's size, it's always better to enter a specific amount in the Scale field rather than to adjust the wireframe manually.

With the V2 and V3 clips resized, you can see the V1 clip beneath them. Let's change the scale of the V1 clip.

8   In the Timeline, double-click the V1 **explosion_cu** clip. In the Motion tab, enter *65* in the Scale field, and press Tab. Drag the image to the right until you create some black space between it and the other images. Play these clips.

> **TIP** ▶ You can also double-click a clip in the Canvas window to open it in the Viewer.

In typical Hollywood style, you now see three different views of the car being blown up. There is a lot of finessing you can do to improve this set of clips. One thing you can do is crop the nonessential portions of each image.

9   In the Tool palette, click the Crop tool (the eighth tool), or press C. In the Canvas, click the **explosion_ws** clip in the lower left.

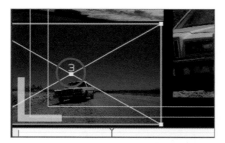

The *3* just above the wireframe center point indicates that the selected clip is on the V3 track. This is a helpful aid to ensure you're making adjustments to the correct clip.

10 In the Canvas, move the pointer over the right edge of the V3 image. When the Crop tool appears, drag left toward the car. Drag the top crop line down toward the car. Play the clip and make any other cropping adjustments you feel are helpful.

> **NOTE** ▶ When you crop the side of an image, the outer clip boundary box remains to indicate the full clip size and location.

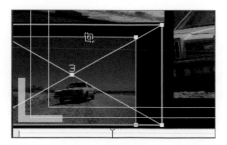

With the non-essential portion of this clip cropped out, you have room to make the image a little larger. Keep in mind, every time you finesse one image, you may have to adjust another. One way to keep the clips aligned is to change the background in the Canvas.

11 With the Canvas window active, choose View > Background > Checkerboard 1. You can also click the View pop-up, and choose Checkerboard 1 from the pop-up menu.

The background behind the images changes from the default black to a checkerboard pattern. You can use the lines in this checkerboard pattern to position the clips evenly.

12 Adjust the size and position of each image in this stack, cropping when necessary, so there are two rows of checkerboard boxes between each of the clips. Here are a few tips to try as you make your adjustments:

▶ If you want to drag an image in a straight line horizontally or vertically, press Shift as you drag.

▶ To make minor position changes in the Canvas, press Option while pressing the Left, Right, Up, or Down Arrow keys to move the selected image in those directions.

▶ Zoom into the Canvas window to see the checkerboard more closely.

▶ Press H for the Hand tool, and drag the zoomed-in Canvas display to your area of focus. This will not reposition a clip, only the display.

▶ Press Shift-Z to fit the entire image in the Canvas window.

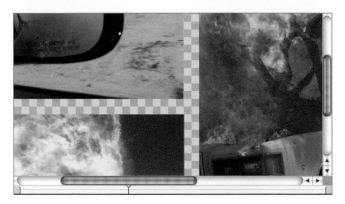

TIP ▶ You can zoom into the Canvas image by choosing a higher percentage in the View pop-up menu; press Command-+ (plus); or press Z and click with the Zoom tool.

Even when you select the checkerboard background, you will see the default black background when you play or output the sequence.

Project Tasks

Now that you've set up a multi-frame image, you can conform the remaining clips in this sequence to play within those same size and position specifications. To do this, you copy a clip on one track, and then paste the Basic Motion and Crop attributes to the remaining clips on the same track. Then all the clips on that track will play within the current image's specifications.

NOTE ▶ The concept for this sequence is that the driver shots are on the V1 track, the car and road shots are on V2, and the female character is on V3. Seeing these shots at the same time helps tell more of the story than the single track of clips in the *Commercial_v1_blowup* sequence.

1 On the V3 track, copy the **explosion_ws** clip.

2   Select the two remaining clips on the V3 track. Control-click one of them and choose Paste Attributes from the shortcut menu. Select the Basic Motion and Crop boxes, then click OK.

3   Drag the two V3 clips left and snap them to the tail of the **explosion_ws** clip.

4   Repeat these steps for the V1 and V2 tracks.

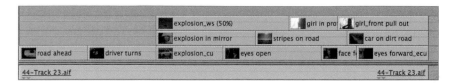

5   Press A to return to the default Selection tool, and play the finished sequence.

> **NOTE ▶** You can refer to the finished *Commercial_v2_multiframe* sequence in the Timeline to see these changes.

Animating Motion Parameters

In addition to changing motion parameters, you can also set keyframes to animate motion parameters over time. A good use of this is to animate text to move on- and off-screen, or to rotate text as it moves into its final resting position. You can also animate images in the same way. Animating a motion parameter requires at least two keyframes. You set one keyframe to identify the starting size or position of a clip. Then you move the playhead to a different timecode location and change that parameter. A new keyframe is automatically added.

> **TIP ▶** Whenever you open a clip from the Timeline in the following steps, click the Motion tab to access those parameters.

1   In the Timeline, click the *Yellow* sequence tab, and double-click the **Yellow Open** nested clip at the head of the sequence. Play the *Yellow Open_NEST* sequence.

When you double-click a nested sequence, that sequence opens as a tab in the Timeline. Here you can make changes to the individual layers, and those changes will automatically be updated in the parent sequence.

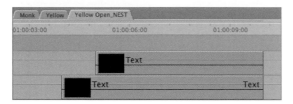

You will set keyframes in the V3 text, *Living Colour: Yellow*, to rotate it as it zooms in to its full size and position. But first, you will expand the Viewer window to see the keyframe area.

2   To use the wide Viewer layout you saved in the previous lesson, choose Window > Arrange > Load Window Layout. In the Choose a File dialog, select wide Viewer and click Choose.

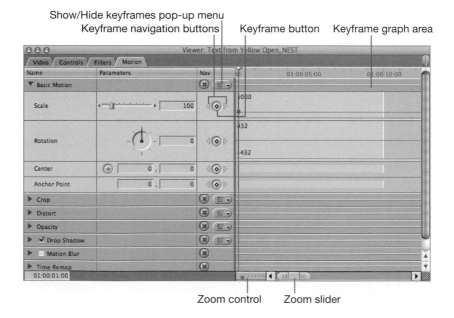

Each Basic Motion parameter has a Keyframe button to set keyframes, and a keyframe graph where individual keyframes appear. The playhead moves in tandem with the Timeline playhead, and a zoom control and zoom slider help to focus on a specific area. The brighter portion of the graph represents the length of the sequence clip. You can zoom into that area so it is prominent in the keyframe graph.

NOTE ▶ For this exercise, always keep the highlighted or brighter portion of the keyframe graph, which represents the clip length, in full view.

In the Canvas, you don't see the text because it was resized to 0 (zero) in the previous lesson. To rotate this text onto the screen, you need to set a starting keyframe at this location.

TIP ▶ It's very important to change text size only in the Viewer Controls tab. When you adjust the Size parameter there, the text remains vector-based, and the quality remains high. When you enlarge text using the Scale slider in the Motion tab, the text becomes pixilated.

3 In the Rotation controls, click the Keyframe button.

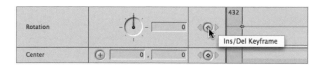

A diamond-shaped keyframe is added to the green keyframe graph at this location. This sets the beginning angle for this clip.

TIP ▶ To enlarge the keyframe graph for a parameter, move the pointer over the bottom portion of the parameter boundary line and when the pointer turns into the Resize pointer, drag it down.

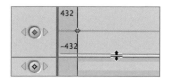

With a starting point set, you now indicate how much rotation, or how many circular rotations, you want the text to complete before coming to a stop at the new playhead location. This is measured in degrees of a circle.

NOTE ▶ Make sure Image+Wireframe is chosen for the following steps.

4   In the Timeline, move the playhead to the beginning of the V4 **Text** clip. Rotate the V3 clip 360 degrees to the right using one of the following methods:

▶   In the Rotation controls, drag the dial control to the right one full rotation

▶   In the Rotation controls, enter 360 degrees in the Rotation field, and press Tab.

▶   In the Canvas, position the pointer over any one of the V3 **Text** clip's turquoise side handles. When you see the circular Rotate pointer, drag to the right, as though you were turning the steering wheel of a car, until the image has gone one full rotation, or 360 degrees.

5   Play the rotation changes.

On the Rotation keyframe graph, a new keyframe has been added automatically. When the playhead is directly over a keyframe, the diamond on the Keyframe button is solid green. The arrows next to the Keyframe button are keyframe navigation buttons, which become solid when there is a keyframe to which you can move forward or backward. You can also press Shift-K to move forward to a keyframe and Option-K to move backward to a keyframe.

NOTE ▸ Rotating an image involves two motion parameters: Rotate and Anchor Point. The *anchor point* is simply the point around which an image is rotated. The default anchor point is the center point of the image.

Let's animate the V4 "warming" **Text** clip to move onto the screen. You will position the clip off-screen to set a starting keyframe, then move it onscreen to its final destination.

TIP ▸ If you don't see any gray around the Canvas image area, change the zoom to a lower percentage.

6 In the Timeline, double-click the V4 **Text** clip. In the Canvas, drag the selected text off-screen to the right, until you no longer see the *w* of *warming*. Press Shift as you drag to ensure the text will move along a straight horizontal line.

7 In the Motion tab, click the Center parameter Keyframe button.

In the Canvas, the center point becomes green, indicating that there is a keyframe at this location.

With the first keyframe set, you have a sort of tracking system in place. Whenever a parameter has a keyframe, a change to that parameter at any other location in the clip will automatically create another keyframe to indicate or track the change from the previous keyframe.

TIP ▶ Remember, keyframes mark an action at a specific timecode location, and the placement of the playhead determines that location.

8   In the Timeline, move the playhead to the head of the V5 **Text** clip. In the Canvas, press Shift and drag the V4 image to the left until the *warming* text is in frame, completely within the title safe boundary.

As you drag, you see tic marks stretch from the first keyframe to the second. This is the *motion path* of this clip, which represents the clip's movement over time.

Often, when you've already finessed a clip into its ending position, you set that keyframe first, then reposition the clip to the starting point. Let's animate the V5 "strong" **Text** clip by first setting its ending keyframe.

9   In the Timeline, move the playhead to the head of the V6 **Text** clip, where the *strong* text will come to a stop. Double-click the V5 **Text** clip. In the Motion tab, click the Keyframe button for the Center parameter.

10   Move the playhead back to the head of the V5 **Text** clip. In the Canvas, drag the V5 image to the left, until you no longer see the *g* in *strong*. Press Shift to move the clip along a straight horizontal line. Play the clip.

Depending on your computer, the clips in your sequence may become sluggish as you change the motion parameters and add additional effects. There is a Final Cut Pro tool you can use to preview effects or composite images in real time without rendering them.

11   Choose Tools > QuickView, or press Option-8. In the QuickView window, adjust the Range slider to 10 seconds. Click the Play button.

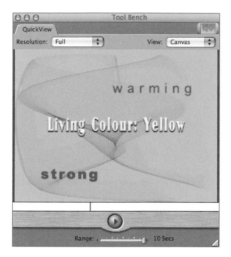

The QuickView will play slowly through the clips and cache the frames to your computer's RAM within the specified range. After caching the frames, it plays the clips in real time. You can also use this tool when you're zoomed into an image to see how the final composition plays without changing the zoom level of the Canvas.

12   Click the *Yellow* sequence tab and play the entire open in the sequence.

> **TIP** ▸ If you want to delete a keyframe, move the playhead to that frame in the keyframe graph and click the Keyframe button. The diamond on the Keyframe button is no longer solid green; it becomes hollow. You can also Control-click the keyframe and choose Clear from the shortcut menu.

Project Tasks

To continue working with motion keyframes, add Center keyframes to the V6 and V7 clips by following steps 6 and 7 in the previous exercise. You can then add dissolves, or Opacity keyframes, at the head of each text clip to have the word fade in as it's moving onscreen.

TIP ▶ To save a specific set of keyframes as a favorite, select the clip in the Timeline and choose Effects > Make Favorite Motion, or press Control-F. The motion will be saved in the Effects Favorites bin in the Browser. You can then drag this effect onto any clip in the Timeline.

Lesson Review

1. From what menu do you select Speed?
2. How can you tell if the speed of a sequence clip has been changed?
3. What type of edit can change clip speed automatically as you edit it into the Timeline?
4. When you create a freeze frame, does a new freeze frame clip appear in the Browser automatically?
5. Where do you access motion parameters?
6. How can you change motion parameters directly in the Canvas?
7. How can motion attributes be copied and pasted?
8. Where are motion keyframes set and adjusted?
9. What is a motion path?
10. What tool do you use to hide unnecessary portions of an image?
11. How is rotation measured in the Motion tab?

Answers

1. From the Modify menu.

2. A speed percentage will appear next to the sequence clip name.

3. A fit to fill edit.

4. No, but you can drag the freeze frame image from the Viewer to the Browser if you like.

5. In the Motion tab.

6. Choose Image+Wireframe from the Canvas View pop-up menu.

7. Copy the clip and access the Paste Attributes window.

8. In the Motion tab keyframe graph area.

9. The path a clip moves along between two or more keyframes.

10. The Crop tool.

11. In degrees.

Keyboard Shortcuts

C	Selects the Crop tool
Command-J	Opens the Speed dialog
Shift-K	Moves forward to next keyframe
Option-K	Moves backward to previous keyframe
Shift-N	Creates freeze frame from playhead position
W	Toggles among Image, Image+Wireframe, and Wireframe modes
Option-8	Opens the QuickView tool
Shift-F5	Locks or unlocks all audio tracks in a sequence

13

Lesson Files   Lesson 13 Project

Media   Yellow, Commercial, and SeaWorld folders

Time   This lesson takes approximately 60 minutes to complete.

Goals   Apply audio and video filters

View and modify filters

Apply filters for image correction

Apply filters to multiple clips

Use tools to adjust filters

Animate filters using keyframes

Lesson 13
Applying Filters

In Final Cut Pro, effects are divided into two groups: transitions and filters. Unlike transitions, which are applied to the edit point between two clips, filters are applied to the content, or body, of a clip. Filters are like rose-colored glasses. When you put them on, you see things differently. Some filters create magical illusions, transforming images into a kaleidoscope of colors or a dizzying array of lights. Other filters conceal their magic—correcting the color of an image or changing the direction someone is facing—so that most viewers don't even know a filter was applied.

Like motion effects, filters serve both style and function. In this lesson, you will apply filters to create visual magic and to correct or improve some aspect of the image. You'll also share filters with other clips and animate them over time.

This image has been mirrored so that one side reflects the other.

Evaluating a Project for Effects

Typically, you'll add filters during the finishing stage of your project, sometimes to make images stand out visually, and other times to correct an image. In the following exercises, filters are added to three completed sequences to refine their look and sound. Let's start by examining some before-and-after examples.

1 Open the **Lesson 13 Project** file in the Lessons folder on your hard drive, and close any other open projects.

2 In the Timeline, click the *1-Yellow_START* sequence tab, and play the sequence.

This sequence was created from the "Living Colour: Yellow" project. You will use this sequence to apply filters, and give each clip a different visual style.

TIP To play back as many real-time effects as possible, click the RT pop-up menu in the Timeline and choose Unlimited RT and Dynamic.

3 Play the *1-Yellow_FINISHED* sequence.

The filters in this sequence are fanciful and bring some fun to the images. Adding a different filter to each clip in this situation is a good way to preview filter effects.

4   In the Timeline, play the *2-Commercial_FINISHED* sequence.

In this sequence, function, not style, rules. The producer wanted to repurpose the footage so the commercial could air in countries where you drive on the right side of the road. If you hadn't worked with the original footage, you wouldn't know a filter had been added to flop these clips.

Though the filters were added for different reasons in each sequence, all of the filters were applied in exactly the same way.

Before you begin applying filters, let's create a backup of the *1-Yellow_ START* sequence so you can use it again later in this lesson.

5   In the Browser, duplicate the *1-Yellow_START* sequence.

Applying and Viewing Video Filters

If you're comfortable applying transitions, then you already know how to apply a filter. You can drag a filter from the Video Filters bin in the Effects tab and apply it directly to a clip in the Timeline. Or, you can select, or target, the clip in the Timeline, and choose a filter from the Effects menu. Filters are applied in the Viewer or the Timeline.

In this exercise, to acquaint you with some of the filters used to create style, you will apply a different filter to each clip in the *1-Yellow_START* sequence. Each of these filters can be modified, as you'll learn in the next exercise.

> **TIP** ▶ Additional filters from Apple's Motion application are accessible in the Effects menu and the Effects tab. To see only the Final Cut Pro filters you need for this lesson, choose Effects > Effect Availability > Only Recommended Effects.

1   In the Timeline, click the *1-Yellow_START* sequence tab, and move the playhead to the first clip, **beetle on flower**. Select this clip.

As with placing transitions, selecting a clip targets it, and parking the playhead on the clip allows you to see in the Canvas how that clip is changed as you apply or modify a filter.

2   Choose Effects > Video Filters, and scroll your pointer through some of the categories in the submenu.

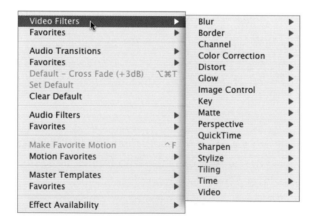

Each filter has a submenu. From the names of the filter categories, you can anticipate that some filters might add an interesting visual effect to a clip, whereas others might be used to correct images. Let's apply a Kaleidoscope filter to the selected clip.

3   Choose Effects > Video Filters > Tiling > Kaleidoscope, and play the clip.

> **NOTE ▶** When you apply a filter in the Timeline, you are not changing the master clip in the Browser or the media file on your hard drive; you are changing only the sequence clip.

This filter turns the yellow, purple, and black **beetle on flower** clip into an interesting kaleidoscopic image, which could even be used as the background for a title.

Look at the Timeline ruler area. If an orange render bar appears above this clip, the clip will play in real time but may drop frames along the way. If the render bar is red, the clip must be rendered to play in real time. You can also press Option-P to preview the effect, but not in real time.

> **NOTE ▶** Clicking the Audible or Track Visibility controls to disable tracks in the Timeline will delete any render files for that track.

4   Move the playhead to the third clip, **bee cu**, and select it. Choose Effects > Video Filters > Distort. Look at some of the Distort filter options, then choose the Insect Eye filter. Play the clip.

You might choose a Distort filter in many situations. You could create the illusion of an earthquake, or create a ripple in a calm lake. The Insect Eye filter creates a pattern over the image suggesting the way an insect sees.

Now let's add a filter by dragging it from the Effects tab.

5   Move the playhead to the fifth clip, **daisy opens**. In the Browser, click the Effects tab, display the contents of the Video Filters bin, and then display the Video bin contents.

NOTE ▶ All filter icons look the same regardless of how a specific filter affects a clip.

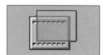

6 Drag the Viewfinder filter to the fifth clip in the sequence, **daisy opens**, but don't release the mouse yet.

When you use the drag-and-drop approach to applying a filter, you see a brown selection outline around the entire clip.

7 Release the mouse, and play the clip.

This filter creates the illusion that you are recording the image on a DV camera.

Filters can be copied and pasted from one clip to another, and applied to a group of clips at one time. Let's apply the same filter to a group of three yellow paint clips.

8 Select the three yellow paint clips above the **grabs attention** audio clip. In the Effects tab, close the Video bin, and display the Glow filters. Drag the Bloom filter into the sequence and release it onto any one of the selected clips. Play these clips.

Now these three clips have the same visual style, or treatment.

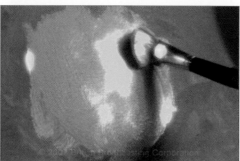

Filters can be added to any type of clip, including text and graphics.

9 Select the **Text** clip at the end of the sequence. Choose Effects > Video Filters > Video > Blink. Play the clip.

The Blink filter causes an image to blink on and off for a specified number of frames. You will adjust these parameters in the next exercise to make the image stay on longer.

NOTE ▶ If there were no clip on the V1 track beneath the **Text** clip, you would just see the black of the empty image area when the text blinked off.

Project Tasks

Continue applying video filters to the remaining clips in the sequence by following the guide below. You can use either the Effects tab drag-and-drop approach, or select the clip and choose the filter from the Effects menu.

- ▶ **bird on branch**—Perspective > Flop
- ▶ **bird in breeze**—Perspective > Mirror
- ▶ **volcano**—Distort > Earthquake
- ▶ **sunrise**—Stylize > Replicate

TIP ▶ You can also target a clip by positioning the playhead over the clip in the Timeline.

Viewing and Modifying Filter Parameters

Every filter has a set of parameters you can modify to fine-tune the effect. These parameters appear in the Viewer within the Filters tab. Here you can modify parameters, delete the filter, toggle it off or on (to compare the clip with and without the effect), or save it as a favorite. You can also specify the priority of filters, which can change the overall look of the clip. But before you can make any of these changes, you need to open the clip from the Timeline into the Viewer.

1   In the *1-Yellow_START* sequence, play the **Text** clip at the end of the sequence. Then use the Left and Right Arrow keys to count how many frames the text stays on, and how many frames it stays off as it blinks.

   NOTE ▶ If you didn't complete the Project Tasks at the end of the previous exercise, you can continue working in the *1-Yellow_FINISHED* sequence in the Timeline.

2   Double-click the **Text** clip to open it in the Viewer, and click the Filters tab.

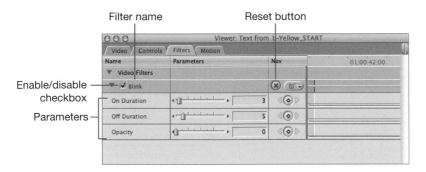

The Blink filter has a default On Duration of 3 frames, and an Off Duration of 5 frames. Let's make the text stay on longer.

All filter parameters have default settings. You modify filter parameter settings as you modified motion effects settings, using sliders, dial controls, and numerical fields. In addition, some filters use color pickers for color selection.

3 In the On Duration field, enter *10*, and press Tab or Return. Play the clip again.

Now the text stays on for 10 frames, and blinks off for 5.

NOTE ▶ With the Filters tab active in the Viewer, you can double-click another clip, and that clip will open with the Filters tab selected.

4 Move the playhead to the **beetle on flower** clip, and double-click it to open it in the Viewer. Explore the Kaleidoscope filter parameters by first adjusting the Segment Angle and then the Offset Angle. Then click the red Reset button to return the filter to its default settings.

TIP ▶ You can position your mouse pointer over a dial control and rotate the mouse scroll wheel or ball up and down to change the angle.

You might modify a filter's parameters for one project differently than you would for another project. Sometimes, just experimenting with a filter's parameters is a good way to become familiar with how you might use it in other projects. Let's explore a few more filters you've applied.

5 Double-click the **daisy opens** clip. Explore this filter by changing the mode, font, size, and color of the text.

To see the clip with or without a filter added, you can toggle the filter off and on.

6 Move the playhead to the **bee cu** clip, and open it in the Viewer. Deselect and select the Insect Eye filter checkbox to toggle the filter off and on. To see one interesting version of this filter, change the Size to 80, and the Border to 8, then play the clip.

Toggling a filter off does not delete it from the clip. It simply allows you to view the clip before and after the filter.

You can apply several filters to one clip to create a special effect. How they affect the image depends on the parameter settings and the order in which they are applied.

7   To add an additional filter to this clip, choose Effects > Video Filters > Blur > Gaussian Blur. Change the Amount to *15*.

The first filter applied always appears at the top of the filter list, followed by the other filters in the order in which they were applied. When you add one filter after another, there is a cumulative effect in which the most recent filter affects not only the clip, but any other filters added before it.

8   Select the checkbox for each filter separately to see how it is affecting the image, then select the checkbox for both filters. Click the disclosure triangle for each filter to hide its parameters.

When you hide each filter's parameters, you can see at a glance which filters you've applied and in what order.

TIP ▶ A good way to sample or "shop" for the best filter is to apply several filters to a clip, then enable them one at a time to see how each looks in the Canvas.

Since the Gaussian Blur filter was applied after the Insect Eye filter, the entire image is blurred, including the insect eye pattern. For a different result, you can change the order of these filters.

9   Drag the Gaussian Blur filter name up above Insect Eye. When a dark bar appears above Insect Eye, release the mouse.

When the Gaussian Blur filter is positioned above the Insect Eye filter, the blur is applied to the original image only, not the Insect Eye effect, and the insect eye pattern is not blurred.

To preview filter changes on the fly, you can open the QuickView tool, which you used in Lesson 12 to change motion parameters.

10 In the Timeline, press X to mark the length of the **bee cu** clip. Choose Tools > QuickView, or press Option-8, and drag the Tool Bench window over the Browser. Click the QuickView tab, and click the Play button.

> **NOTE ▶** Marking an area of the Timeline creates a range of material that the QuickView tool plays. It will continue to play this section in a loop until you click Play again to stop it.

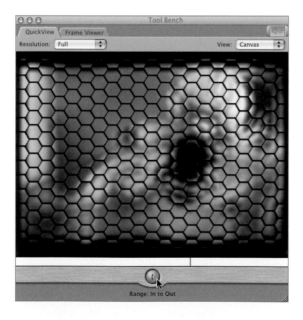

As you preview the effect in the QuickView tab, you can enable and disable individual filters in the Viewer Filters tab to see what suits your clip and what doesn't. You can even make changes to filter parameters as the

QuickView tool plays the clip. This is a helpful way to preview filters that may require rendering or don't play every frame.

11 Close the Tool Bench window, and press Command-S to save your changes.

Before you leave this sequence, take a moment to try the different ways to delete one or more filters. You can press Command-Z to bring back a deleted filter.

To delete a single filter, do one of the following:

▶   Click its name in the Filters tab and press Delete.

▶   Control-click the filter name and choose Cut from the shortcut menu.

To remove all video filters from a clip:

▶   Click Video Filters to select them, and press Delete.

Project Tasks

There are other ways you can work with filters. You can copy and paste a filter from one clip to another, and even to another sequence. In this exercise, you will copy a clip from the current sequence, and paste its filter attributes to several clips in the *2-Commercial_START* sequence.

1   In the current sequence, copy the **bird on branch** clip, to which you applied the Flop filter in an earlier exercise.

2   From the Browser, open the *2-Commercial_START* sequence, and select the five clips located under a marker: **road ahead**, **driver turns**, **eyes open**, **face forward**, and the last freeze-frame clip in the sequence.

3   Control-click one of the selected clips, and choose Paste Attributes from the shortcut menu. Click Filters, and click OK. Play the sequence.

By pasting the single copied filter to all of the selected clips, you flopped all of those images at one time, and created the sense that the driver is driving on the opposite side of the road (and sitting on the opposite side of the car).

Applying Audio Filters

Once the audio tracks of your sequence are mixed together, they often go unnoticed until the final output. But there will be times when you need to improve or correct a clip's sound or add an audio effect before putting the project to bed. In this exercise, you will apply two filters to one clip; one filter will improve the clip's volume level, and another will create the illusion of someone speaking in a stadium. Audio filters are applied just like video filters, by dragging them from the Effects tab, or choosing them from the Effects menu.

1   From the Sequences bin, open the *3-Believe_START* sequence. Play this sequence and focus on the volume level of the **news voice over** clip.

   The level of this clip could be raised—perhaps another few dB—to bring it up to a solid –12 dB level. You could change the volume by dragging the audio level overlay, as you have in other lessons, or you could modify it by applying a Gain filter.

2   In the Timeline, select the **news voice over** clip. Choose Effects > Audio Filters > Final Cut Pro > Gain. Double-click the clip to open it in the Viewer, and click the Filters tab.

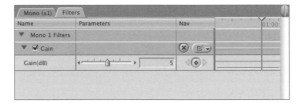

3   Adjust the Gain slider a little at a time until the newscaster's voice level is at a consistent –12 dB in the Audio meters, an increase of about 5 dB.

   TIP ▶ To change the audio level as the clip plays, place the pointer over the Gain(dB) slider and rotate the mouse scroll button.

   In an earlier lesson, you modified a clip by choosing the Apply Normalization Gain command in the Modify > Audio menu. When you choose this option,

Final Cut Pro automatically adds a Gain filter to adjust the volume of the clip. In this step, you are manually applying this same filter.

TIP ▶ If a clip's audio was recorded very low, and raising the audio level overlay to the highest level doesn't give you the desired volume, you can apply the Gain filter to increase the volume further.

Since almost all of the clips in this sequence were shot in the Shamu Stadium at SeaWorld San Antonio, let's make the newscaster's voice sound like she's in the stadium talking to a crowd by applying the Reverberation filter. You'll drag this audio filter from the Effects tab.

4 In the Browser, click the Effects tab, and display the contents of the Audio Filters folder, then display the contents of the Final Cut Pro audio filters. Drag the Reverberation filter into the Viewer Filters tab.

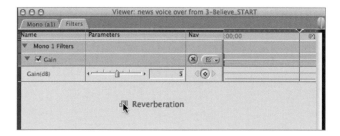

The audio filter icon looks like a speaker with a filter overlay. When the clip you want to apply a filter to is open in the Viewer, you can drag a filter from the Effects tab directly into the Viewer.

The Reverberation filter is added to this clip, beneath the Gain filter. The new filter has four parameters. Let's choose a different type of reverberation from the Type pop-up menu.

5 Play the **news voice over** audio clip in the Timeline. As the clip is playing, click the Type pop-up menu and select a different reverb type. You can continue to choose different types as the clip is playing to audition the effect of each reverb.

While these reverb types get you closer to a believable effect, they don't sound convincing without modifying other parameters. For the next step, make the changes without playing the clip.

6 Click the Type pop-up menu and choose Hall (Medium). Drag the Effect Mix down to 25, and play the clip again.

The music track on A1 and A2 was taken from a CD of the "Believe" show's music. You can give the music a more "live" feel, as though it were playing behind the newscaster in the stadium, by applying the modified Reverberation filter from the **news voice over** clip to that music track.

7 To hear the music track by itself, click the A3 Audible control to toggle off that track.

8 From the Viewer Filters tab, drag the Reverberation filter down into the *3-Believe_START* sequence and onto the **Track 12_believe long.aif** clip. When you see the clip's outline appear, release the filter and play the clip.

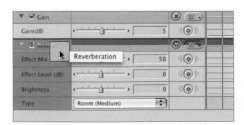

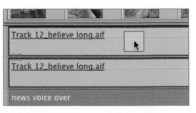

Dragging Reverberation filter from Viewer Filters tab

Releasing filter on Timeline clip

TIP ▶ If applying an audio filter to a clip causes a red audio render line to appear in the Timeline ruler area, open User Preferences, and in the General tab, change Real-time Audio Mixing to 12 tracks. If the red line is still present, raise that number, or render the clip.

In many filters, you can adjust the amount of effect you want to blend with the original clip, where 0 provides no effect, and 100 provides the maximum effect possible. Let's add more reverb to this music track by changing the effect mix.

9 Double-click the **Track 12_believe long.aif** clip, and in the Filters tab, change the Effect Mix to 50. Play the clip again. Then click the A3 Audible control to return the voice-over to the mix.

TIP ▶ You can apply the same filter to a stack of clips at the same play-head location, such as the reporter's voice-over and the music track. Just position the playhead over the clips, and choose the filter. The effect is added to all clips on all tracks at that location, unless Autoselect has been turned off for a specific track.

If you think you might want to apply this modified filter to other CD clips in other sequences, you can save this filter as a favorite.

10 From the Filters tab, drag the Reverberation filter name into the Effects tab and release it in the Favorites bin. Open the bin and rename the audio filter *stadium music*.

If you've applied more than one filter to a clip, such as the **news voice over** clip, you can save the filters as a set.

11 In the Timeline, select the **news voice over** clip. Choose Effects > Make Favorite Effect, or press Option-F.

▼ ☐ Favorites
   ▶ ☐ 3-Believe_START (Filters)

When more than one filter is applied to a clip, all the filters are saved together in a bin and given the sequence name. You can drag this bin to any clip or group of clips if you want to apply the entire set of filters.

NOTE ▶ If individual filters are selected in the Filters tab when you choose Effects > Make Favorite Effect, they will appear as individual filters in the Favorites bin.

Using a Color Correction Filter

While some productions may have the time to set and adjust lights, which will ensure a high-quality video image, others must shoot on the fly with very little, if any, camera setup or lighting support. In these situations, you often have to capture the existing footage and worry about improving the video quality later or, as they say, "fix it in post." There are several video filters that can help correct a clip's color or otherwise improve its look. These filters can change the color balance of an image, adjust the luminance and black levels, add more color, or take color away. Before you make color adjustments to a clip, let's review a few basic color principles.

Understanding Color Basics

Video is an additive color system, meaning that all colors added together will create white. So your reference to white is very important. For example, if you white balance your camera for indoor lighting, and then shoot outdoors, the outdoor footage won't be color balanced because the camera's indoor reference to white will not match the white in the outdoor scene. If your white balance is off, the overall balance of colors in the image will be off as well.

Another aspect of color correction is the *hue* of the image. Hue is the color itself, sometimes represented by a name but most often represented by a number on a 360-degree color wheel. Each color appears at a different location around the wheel. For instance, the three primary colors in video are red, green, and blue, and they fall at 0 degrees, 120 degrees, and 240 degrees.

Some color wheels display more than just the hue. They also reflect the *saturation* of a color. Saturation is the amount of color, or *chroma,* in an image. For all colors, 0 percent saturation shows the color as white. If red is fully saturated at 100 percent, decrease the saturation to 50 percent and you will get rose. Decrease it to 25 percent and you will get pink. Each of these colors is part of the red family in that they share the same hue but not the same level of saturation.

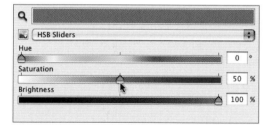

The *brightness,* or *luminance,* of an image is the amount of lightness or darkness present. A 100 percent value is the highest or brightest level, whereas a 0 percent value is black, regardless of the hue or saturation.

Using the Color Corrector 3-Way Filter

In Final Cut Pro, there are several filters you can apply to correct or adjust the color in an image, each offering a different approach to get the same result. For example, you could choose the Image Control > Proc Amp filter, with parameters similar to the controls on a professional videotape recorder (VTR). Also from the Image Control category, you could choose Brightness and Contrast, or Levels, to adjust those aspects of your clip.

However, Final Cut Pro includes a general, all-purpose filter you can use to color correct an image, and it is a real-time effect: the Color Corrector 3-way filter. In these exercises, to understand how to apply a color-correcting filter, you will perform a basic white balance correction by changing the yellow tint in one of the SeaWorld clips.

> **NOTE ▶** Color correcting a video image is a comprehensive subject. For high-level professional color correction, you can send a clip or sequence to Apple's newest application, Color, which is part of Final Cut Studio 2.

1   In the *3-Believe_START* sequence, move the playhead to the *correct color* marker. Double-click the **_MB_behavior board_2** clip to open it into the Viewer. Click the Filters tab.

    The source clip has a yellowish tint. It appears that the camera was not white balanced prior to shooting this material, or that the lighting for the shoot was hard to control.

2   Choose Effects > Video Filters > Color Correction > Color Corrector 3-way.

    The Color Corrector 3-way filter appears in the Filters tab, but the parameter details are not in view. Instead, you see a button named Visual and a separate tab called Color Corrector 3-way.

3 Click the disclosure triangle next to the Color Corrector 3-way checkbox, and drag the vertical scroller down to see all the parameters. Then click the disclosure triangle again to hide those parameters.

These parameters control the color of an image, but there is a much easier approach—a more *visual* approach.

4 Click the Visual button next to the Color Corrector 3-way name, or click the Color Corrector 3-way tab.

Although this filter is very complex and has lots of parameters, it also has a streamlined visual interface. Working within the visual interface lets you focus on the look of the image without getting distracted by the numbers you saw in the numeric interface.

In the visual display, the Color Corrector 3-way filter has three Color Balance controls—Blacks, Mids, and Whites—which modify the color balance in those ranges. The sliders beneath the Balance controls set the brightness levels in the image pixels within each range. The Sat (saturation) slider beneath the Balance controls increases or decreases the amount of color in the image.

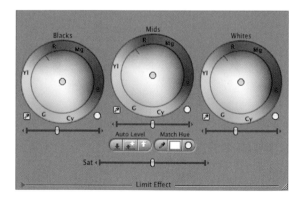

TIP Adjusting the Mids slider is a good way to bring out more detail in an image that is too dark or underexposed, or to remove the washed-out effect of an overexposed image.

One way to improve the color of the **_MB_behavior board_2** clip is to reset (or redefine) what true white is in the clip's image.

5 Under the Whites Balance control, click the small Select Auto-balance Color button (the eyedropper).

With the eyedropper, you can select a new white reference from the image in the Canvas. The whiteboard that Mark refers to in the clip will make a good reference to true white.

6 In the Canvas, click in a blank area of the white board.

Clicking a white area in the Canvas image with the eyedropper rebalances all the colors and resets the colors in the image as though the white you clicked was true white. Look at the Whites Balance control. The indicator in the center of the wheel has moved away from yellow and toward blue.

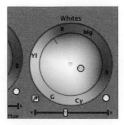

7   Select and deselect the enable checkbox so you can see the image with and without the Color Corrector 3-way filter enabled. Leave the filter enabled.

Just changing the white balance for this image has improved it considerably. Sometimes, when you're adjusting a clip's color, you may simultaneously want to compare the image with and without the filter applied. You can use the Frame Viewer tool to do this.

8   Choose Tools > Frame Viewer, or press Option-7. When the tool opens in the Tool Bench window, reposition the window over the Browser.

NOTE ▶ The Tool Bench window is placed over the Viewer or at the last position it was used in the interface. Note that you may not see the same image pictured above.

The Frame Viewer displays a clip in a before-and-after, split-screen configuration. You can choose what you want to see on each side of the frame and easily compare one clip to another or compare one clip with and without its applied filters.

9   In the lower left of the window, click the Frame Viewer pop-up menu, and choose Current Frame if it's not already selected. Click the pop-up on the right side, and choose Current w/o Filters.

In this view, you see the color-corrected classroom image on the left and the original, uncorrected image on the right.

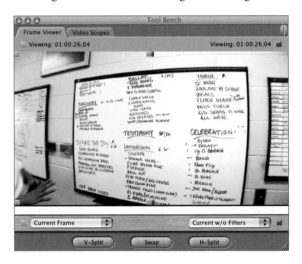

NOTE ▶ You click the V-Split (Vertical), Swap, or H-Split (Horizontal) buttons to divide the frame differently or swap the images. You can also choose Tools > Video Scopes, or press Option-9, to see the image displayed on a video scope.

MORE INFO ▶ In Lesson 14, you will use video scopes to measure the video signal.

Since the color filter change was so effective on this clip, you can save the filter as a favorite to use on other yellowish clips in this project that were shot in the same room under the same circumstances.

10 Close the Tool Bench window. In the Viewer, drag the Drag Filter icon to the Effects tab and release it in the Favorites bin. Rename this filter *yellow board*.

TIP You can apply the Color Corrector 3-way filter with these settings to a different clip in this or another sequence, as you did earlier in this lesson. With this filter, however, you drag from the Drag Filter icon to the target clip.

Project Tasks

The luminance of a clip is often divided into three areas, representing the darker pixels, the midrange pixels, and the brighter pixels in the image. The sliders beneath the Color Balance controls in the Color Corrector 3-way tab are used to adjust these groups of luminance levels. If you need to raise the brightness on someone's face, you can often create that change by raising the mids level. You may be able to improve some of the clips in this sequence by applying the Color Corrector 3-way filter, and adjusting the Mids slider to raise the brightness of that range.

1 Apply the Color Corrector 3-way filter to the **performance_2 whales jump** clip. To make the audience a little lighter, drag the Mids slider to right.

2 Apply the same filter to the **K jumps off whale** clip, and raise this clip's saturation level.

TIP ▶ When making adjustments in the Color Balance controls, press the Command key as you drag to move the balance control indicator faster. To reset a Color Balance control to its default setting, click the Reset button on the lower right of the wheel.

Animating Filters

If you want to change a filter parameter over time, you can animate that parameter by adding keyframes, just as you did when animating motion parameters. Sometimes animating filters supports a visual style you're creating, and sometimes it modifies a correction that a shot needs. For example, you may have a clip that doesn't require color correction throughout the entire clip, but does require correction at the end or beginning. You can animate the color correction to start in one location and stop or change at a different location.

In the *2-Commercial_FINISHED* sequence, you will add filters and animate some of the parameters in order to begin and end the sequence on a black-and-white shot. Television programs often use this style when going in and out of commercial breaks. There are several ways you can animate filters, and you will use two approaches in this exercise.

1   In the Timeline, click the *2-Commercial_FINISHED* sequence tab, and double-click the **road ahead** clip to open it in the Viewer. Choose Effects > Video Filters > Image Control > Desaturate. If necessary, click the Filters tab.

In the Canvas, you see a black-and-white image. This is the result of lowering the saturation of this clip to 0 or, rather, raising the Desaturate value to 100. It would be nice if the color came back to the image once the title clip on the V2 track ended.

2 In the Timeline, move the playhead to the first marker in the **Track 1.aif** music track.

This is where you begin to return the color to the image, and where you will place your first keyframe. Notice the pink marker in the Viewer Filters tab. Both clip and Timeline markers appear here as a reference.

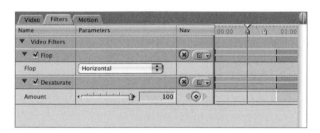

TIP ▶ When adding keyframes in the Viewer, you can expand the window to see more of the keyframe graph area, as you did when setting motion keyframes. You can also zoom into the area and increase the height of an individual parameter graph.

3 Click the Keyframe button for the Amount parameter. Press Shift–Right Arrow to move the playhead forward 1 second. Drag the Amount slider to its center position, 0, and play the clip.

Since you have a starting keyframe, changing the value at a different timecode location automatically adds a new keyframe. Now the clip's color saturation changes over time.

In the keyframe graph of the Filters tab, notice the blue keyframe references on the Desaturate checkbox line. These blue keyframes provide an additional reference should you need to add keyframes to other filters at the same locations. Let's add a blur to this image and use the blue keyframes as a reference to place additional keyframes.

4   Click the disclosure triangle next to the Desaturate checkbox to hide its parameters. Choose Effects > Video Filters > Blur > Gaussian Blur. Change the Radius amount to 30, and play the clip.

5   In the Filters tab, move the playhead to the first blue keyframe, and click the Keyframe button for the Gaussian Blur Radius parameter. Then reposition the playhead to the second blue keyframe, and change the Radius to 0. Play the new opening.

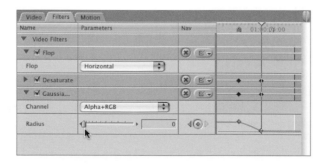

Now you can see the combined visual effect of the image coming into focus and color at the same time.

You can also animate a filter using the Razor Blade tool. After you divide a clip, you can apply a filter to one of the clip segments, and apply a transition to dissolve between the segments. Let's desaturate the freeze frame at the end of the sequence using this approach.

6 Play the last two driving clips in the sequence. Position the playhead about 1 second past the head of the freeze frame clip, **2-Commercial_FINISHED**. Press B to select the Razor Blade tool, and click at the playhead location.

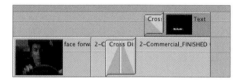

When you divide a clip, you can apply a filter to one of the divided portions.

7 Press A to select the default Selection tool, and select the freeze frame clip *after* the cut point. Choose Effects > Video Filters > Image Control > Desaturate. Play these clips again.

8 Select the edit point between the two freeze frame clips, and choose Effects > Video Transitions > Dissolves > Cross Dissolves. If that dissolve is still the default video transition, you can just press Command-T.

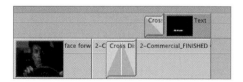

While this may not work for all filters, it might be an easy way to animate some of them.

Project Tasks

In addition to the filters you've already applied in this lesson, there are other filters that add a border around an image, and still others that key out a color or mask a portion of the image. When you apply a Matte or Key filter to an image, the image below it is revealed, creating a composite effect. To experiment with a matte-type filter, let's create a yellow matte over the *1-Yellow_START copy* sequence.

> **NOTE ▶** To see how a matte effect was used in the "Living Colour: Yellow" project, import Media > Yellow > **Living_Colour_Yellow_DV** and play the show open.

1   From the Browser, open the *1-Yellow_START copy* sequence. In the Viewer, click the Generator pop-up menu and choose Matte > Color. Click the Controls tab and give this matte a bright yellow color, using a yellow from the first clip in the sequence.

2   Superimpose the **Color** clip over the first clip in the sequence. Drag the clip up to create a V3 track, and then drag its Out point to the end of the sequence so the **Color** clip covers all the clips. Double-click the **Color** clip to open it in the Viewer.

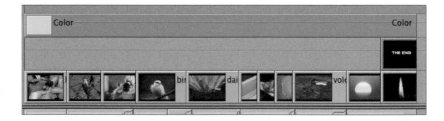

In order to see the V1 images, you have to mask a portion of the **Color** clip. To do this, you will add a Mask Shape filter to the Color clip, which

will mask or matte a portion of the image based either on the shape you
choose, or on the inverse of that shape.

3   Choose Effects > Video Filters > Matte > Mask Shape. In the Mask Shape
filter parameters, leave the Shape to the default Rectangle, enter *65* in the
Horizontal and Vertical Scale fields, and select the Invert checkbox to invert
the mask. Play the sequence.

Now you can see all the images in the sequence appear through the
inverted yellow mask shape. You can apply the Mask Shape filter to
any clip.

You can also use the Mask Shape filter to create a binocular mask effect.
For this, you apply two Mask Shape filters to a black **Color** clip, change
the mask shape type to oval, adjust the parameters to make the shape
round, and then position each mask on opposite sides of the image area.
You can also add a Mask Feather filter to feather the edges of any mask.

TIP ▶ To give a sequence with a 4:3 aspect ratio a widescreen appearance, you can nest the clips in the sequence and apply the widescreen
matte from the Matte filters category.

Lesson Review

1. What two ways can you apply a video or audio filter?
2. What is the procedure to view and modify filters for sequence clips?
3. How do you delete one or all filters in the Filters tab?
4. What real-time filter do you use to change the hue, saturation, and brightness of an image?
5. What tool provides a split-screen before-and-after comparison of a filter?
6. Where do you modify filter parameters?
7. How do you apply a filter from one clip to another clip? To several clips?
8. How do you add filter keyframes in the Viewer?
9. Name one type of filter that can create a composite effect in which two images appear at one time.

Answers

1. You can drag a filter from the Effects tab to the clip in the Timeline, or you can identify the clip by selecting it (or moving the playhead over it) and choosing a filter from the Effects menu.
2. Position the playhead over the clip in the Timeline. Open the clip in the Viewer, and click the Filters tab. To change the priority of a filter, drag the filter name above or below another filter. To disable the filter, click the enable checkbox to deselect it.
3. Click the filter name, and press Delete. To delete all video filters, click Video Filters, and press Delete.
4. The Color Corrector 3-way filter.
5. The Frame Viewer.
6. In the Filters tab.

7. You can drag the filter name from the Filters tab to another clip in the Timeline. To copy a filter to several clips at once, select those clips before dragging the filter. You can also use the Paste Attributes option.

8. Position the playhead where you want to start or end a filter change, and click a parameter Keyframe button. Reposition the playhead, and change that parameter.

9. The Matte or Key filters can create composite effects.

Keyboard Shortcuts

Option-7	Opens Frame Viewer tool
Option-8	Opens the QuickView tool
Option-9	Opens Video Scopes tool
Option-P	Previews an effect

14

Lesson Files	Lesson 14 Project
Media	SeaWorld > Believe folder
Time	This lesson takes approximately 60 minutes to complete.
Goals	Detect audio peaks
	Adjust video levels for broadcast
	Understand file formats
	Export a QuickTime movie
	Export using QuickTime conversion
	Output a sequence to tape
	Create a timecode window burn
	Back up a project

Lesson 14
Finishing and Outputting

After making all of your creative and editorial decisions, and completing and finessing your sequence, you're finally ready to send your master-piece out into the world. There are two ways you might do this. One way is to export the sequence as a digital file that you can use on the web, for DVD authoring, or other file delivery destinations. The other way to deliver your sequence is to output it to tape for broadcast or screening, or just to archive it for posterity. You might also need to export a file for use by other departments, such as a still frame for graphics, or just the audio tracks for an audio postproduction company.

Even if your project will only be viewed on a computer or an in-house system, you should make sure that the audio and video conform to specific broadcast standards. Once you've created the output tapes or files, you will also want to back up or archive the elements so you can retrieve or recreate them if the need should ever arise.

Preparing the Project for Finishing

Since this lesson is about fixing and outputting a completed sequence, you will work with a sequence you completed in an earlier lesson.

1 Open the **Lesson 14 Project** file, and close any other open projects.

This "Believe" interview sequence was copied from Lesson 10, pasted into a new project, and named Lesson 14 Project. The clips in the sequence still link to the original media files, as they did in the earlier project. You will make your final adjustments on these sequence clips. But if you should need the master clips in this project, perhaps to replace an image or to refer back to the sound level of the original media file, you can easily have Final Cut Pro create a new set of master clips inside this project.

2 In the Browser, select the *Believe Output* sequence, and choose Tools > Create Master Clips. In the Browser, click the disclosure triangle for this new bin.

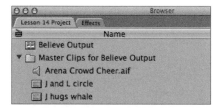

3 Double-click the **J and L circle** clip to open it in the Viewer. Then double-click some of the other clips in this bin.

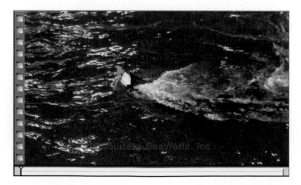

All the audio and video clips used in the *Believe Output* sequence appear as master clips in the new bin.

4   In the Timeline, play the first four video clips of the *Believe Output* sequence.

While the sequence may sound and look good, it's impossible to know whether it satisfies broadcast standards simply by listening and looking. In order to verify that the audio in this sequence is not peaking anywhere—and thereby *clipping* the audio—and that the video is within FCC regulations, you will rely on two tools: the Audio Mixer and Video Scopes.

Rather than open a new window to find a place for the tools in the interface, let's use a preset window layout.

5   Choose Window > Arrange > Audio Mixing. Then choose Tools > Video Scopes to add the scopes to the Tool Bench. Click the Audio Mixer tab to make it active.

6   To maximize the Timeline area, drag the boundary line between the Browser and Timeline to the left. With the Timeline window active, press Shift-Z to see the entire sequence.

You're now ready to make final corrections to this sequence. Let's start by correcting the audio.

Detecting Audio Peaks

For any given project, you may have corralled tracks from a variety of audio sources, such as narration recorded in a studio, ambient sound recorded in the field, sound on tape, and music tracks from CDs. You could have mixed those tracks to your liking, but you still need to do a final sweep of the sequence to see if there are any audio levels that need correction.

As discussed previously, audio levels that peak too high can become distorted. The one absolute rule is never to allow the audio to peak over 0 dB and cause clipping. Final Cut Pro can help you pinpoint exactly where the audio may be peaking over 0 dB in your sequence by placing a marker in the Timeline at each peak.

1   In the Timeline, play the first half of the sequence again. In the Audio Mixer, watch the clipping indicators in the Master audio meters to see if any peaks occur in these clips.

    While you can use the standard audio meters to monitor audio, the Master audio meters in the Audio Mixer extend above 0 dB, which help you determine how much change may be necessary.

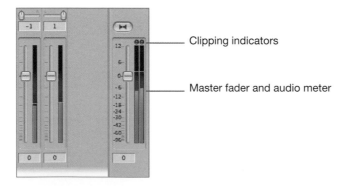

Clipping indicators

Master fader and audio meter

    When audio peaks over 0dB in the Timeline, a red clipping indicator lights up on one or both audio meters, depending on which track peaked. The indicator remains lit until you stop playing the sequence.

NOTE ▸ After a sequence is mixed, there may be times when the volume of a clip is readjusted, or when an additional sound effect is added at the last minute. While these may be minor, they can impact the overall sound level of that group of clips.

Although these indicators tell you there was an audio peak, they don't pinpoint exactly where it occurred in the sequence. Final Cut Pro can detect the peak for you.

2   In the Timeline, press Shift-Command-A to make sure no clips are selected. Then choose Mark > Audio Peaks > Mark.

A progress bar appears while Final Cut Pro examines the sequence.

When the detection is complete, markers are placed in the Timeline ruler area wherever audio peaks occur in the sequence. If the peak is sustained for more than an instant, a long marker—or a marker with a duration—appears over the clip to indicate the length of the peaking audio.

3   Move the playhead to the first audio peak marker. (Press Shift-M to move the playhead forward, or Option-M to move backward.) Then zoom in to get a better view.

Each audio peak marker is given the name *Audio Peak*, along with a sequential number that identifies the specific peak or peak area. When the playhead is over an audio peak marker, its name is displayed in the Canvas.

4 Press Shift-M a few times to move the playhead to the next area of audio peak markers over the **_DF_ambassadors** clip.

Audio meters reflect the levels of the combined audio tracks in the sequence. You have to identify which individual tracks are causing the peaking. Since the first set of markers is isolated above the **_SA_favorite behavior** clip, and the second set is isolated above the **_DF_ambassadors** clip, let's start by modifying those two clips.

> **TIP** If you have the master clips in the Browser, you can open a questionable clip to double-check its original volume level.

5 Select the **_SA_favorite behavior** clip and Command-click the **_DF_ ambassadors** clip to add it to the selection.

6 To see the audio level overlays on the clips, press Option-W to toggle them on. Then choose Modify > Levels, or press Option-Command-L.

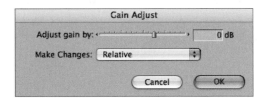

7 In the Gain Adjust dialog, in the "Adjust gain by" field, enter *–3* dB, and leave the Make Changes pop-up menu set to Relative. Click OK. Watch the audio meters as you play through these two clips.

These clips no longer cause the audio to peak above 0 dB.

8 To clear the audio peak markers from the Timeline, deselect the sequence clips, and choose Mark > Audio Peaks > Clear, or press Control-` (grave).

> **TIP** If you've changed the peak levels and want to reassess whether there are still audio peaks, you should once more choose Mark > Audio Peaks > Mark. Remember to deselect all clips before choosing this option to check the entire sequence.

Now that you've corrected the audio peaks, you can take another look at the overall volume level of the sequence. If you're trying to stay within a particular output level, such as –12 dB, you can adjust that level using the Master fader. The Master fader controls the output level of your entire mix while you're playing back the sequence, outputting it to tape, or exporting it as a movie file. It does not affect the audio levels of individual clips.

NOTE ▶ If you are delivering your project to a sound company for additional work, make sure you identify and implement any additional requirements for audio levels or other standards that company may have. Audio requirements can vary among facilities.

Currently, the sequence plays at a little over –6 dB. Television has a limited audio dynamic range and cannot exceed –6 dB for most broadcast standards. Since there are peaks in this sequence beyond that level, let's lower the volume of all the tracks by about –3 dB, down to –9 dB.

9   In the Master audio meters, drag the Master fader down to about –9 dB. You can also enter –9 in the audio level field beneath the meters, and press Tab. Play the sequence again and look at the audio meters.

By finding and correcting audio peaks in this sequence, and changing the overall audio level to an optimum level, you've successfully prepared the audio portion of this sequence for output.

NOTE ▶ The Track Visibility controls (buttons with the speaker icon) in the Timeline turn tracks on and off in the computer processor. Tracks turned off using this method will not be included on output. Solo and Mute buttons affect audio only during playback, and will not exclude tracks during output.

Adjusting Video Levels for Broadcast

Like the audio tracks in a project, the video you captured may also have come from multiple sources. Some footage may have been shot indoors, some outside at night, and some outside in the bright sunlight. Just as you monitor audio for peaks, so you must do the same for video. One of the most common problems with video levels is that the whites of an image, or the luminance levels, are sometimes too bright. The FCC mandates that no video to be broadcast can have a luminance level over 100 IRE, which is considered to be *broadcast safe*.

NOTE ▶ IRE is a unit of measurement in video named for the organization that created it—the Institute of Radio Engineers.

If video luminance does go over 100 IRE, the video level is clipped during broadcast. This can cause audio interference or noise in the signal. Some networks or facilities may reject the tape and choose not to air it at all. Final Cut Pro has a tool called Range Check that will check both the luminance (brightness) and chrominance (color saturation) values of a clip to determine whether they are within a broadcast safe range. When you find clips that are not within broadcast specifications, you can apply the Broadcast Safe filter to correct them.

NOTE ▶ Luminance and chrominance are often abbreviated as *luma* and *chroma*.

1 In the Timeline, move the playhead to the middle of the first clip in the sequence, **uw_rotations**.

2   In the Tool Bench, click the Video Scopes tab, then click the Layout pop-up menu and choose Waveform.

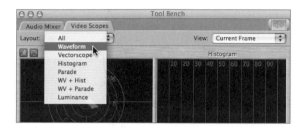

The Waveform Monitor enables you to see the luminance values of the current frame. Broadcast standards specify a maximum luminance level for any video. This is represented in the Waveform Monitor as 100%.

3   Move the pointer up and down over the Waveform Monitor.

A yellow horizontal line follows the movement of the pointer, and a number in the upper-right corner displays the luma percentage of the current pointer location in the scope.

4   To check the luma level of the current clip, make the Timeline active and choose View > Range Check > Excess Luma, or press Control-Z.

When you toggle on Range Check, each clip in the sequence will appear with one of three symbols that indicate whether the luminance level of that clip is within legal range for broadcast use. For the current clip, a green circle and a checkmark appear in the Canvas, indicating that the luminance levels for that frame are below 90 percent and are broadcast safe.

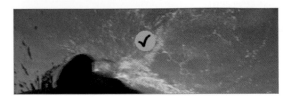

5   Move the playhead to the middle of the second clip in the sequence, the **_DS_show concept** clip.

An in-range icon appears with a checkmark and an upward arrow, indicating that some luma levels are between 90 and 100 percent. The affected areas are indicated by green zebra stripes. Although it's reaching the upper limit of the broadcast safe range, this is still acceptable video.

6   Move the playhead to the middle of the **_SA_favorite behavior** clip.

A yellow warning icon appears, indicating that some luminance levels are above 100 percent. Red zebra stripes show the areas of the image that are above 100 percent. The Waveform Monitor shows by how much those luminance values exceed 100 percent.

You can see that this frame needs correcting, but what about the frames of this clip that follow?

7   Play this clip for a few seconds, then stop and press Option-P to see the range check warning appear on every frame of the clip.

> **TIP** ▶ The range check symbol appears only when the clip is not playing, unless you access the Play Every Frame option by pressing Option-P, or choosing Mark > Play > Every Frame. With that option selected, the range check display remains on the screen and updates each frame. This is a good way to double-check individual frames in suspect clips throughout the sequence.

Final Cut Pro has numerous correction filters you can apply to improve a clip. One filter has a specific job—to reduce the luminance level of a clip so that it is broadcast safe.

8   In the Timeline, select the **_SA_favorite behavior** clip, and choose Effects > Video Filters > Color Correction > Broadcast Safe. Double-click the clip to open it in the Viewer, and click the Filters tab to see the filter parameters.

> **NOTE** ▶ If you have already applied a Color Corrector 3-way filter to a clip, and the luminance levels are out of range, you can try reducing the white level to bring the levels back into range.

With the Broadcast Safe filter applied to this clip, the red zebra stripes in the Canvas turn to green, and the Waveform Monitor shows that the luminance levels have been limited to 100 percent.

TIP ▶ If you have an entire sequence with problem luminance levels, you could apply the Broadcast Safe filter to all of the clips; but rather than apply it to each clip individually, you can nest the sequence clips and apply a Broadcast Safe filter to the nest.

Project Tasks

Move the playhead to each clip in the sequence to see if any other clips exceed the acceptable range. If you find any that do, apply the Broadcast Safe filter to correct it. When you've finished, choose View > Range Check > Off, and press Control-U to return to the default Standard window layout.

Exporting QuickTime Files

When you think about exporting your sequence, you should first ask how and where the output file will be used. For example, if you are creating a file to post on the Internet, you'll use a different codec than if you are creating a DVD.

Final Cut Pro utilizes QuickTime as its standard media format to view, create, import, and export media files. As a multiplatform, multimedia file format, QuickTime can handle many kinds of media, including video, sound, animation, graphics, text, and music. There are two commands you use to export QuickTime files in Final Cut Pro. One allows you to export a clip or sequence as a QuickTime movie. The other allows you to convert a file using a variety of QuickTime-compatible file types.

Exporting a QuickTime Movie

The most basic way to export content from Final Cut Pro is to use the QuickTime Movie option. With this option, you can output a clip, a sequence, or a marked portion of a sequence using current or preset sequence settings. By using the current settings, you create a QuickTime file at the same settings and quality as your clips and sequences; no extra media compression is performed. This allows Final Cut Pro to export your clips quickly with virtually no quality loss. This is a good choice when you want a full-quality version of your sequence to archive or to import into another application, for example, when you want to burn a DVD. You can also include markers for use in other applications, such as Soundtrack Pro and DVD Studio Pro.

You can export a sequence or a clip from the Viewer or the Timeline. You can also export from the Browser, as long as you first select the item you want to export.

To export an entire sequence, make sure there are no marks in the Timeline. To export a portion of a sequence, mark that portion or the clip itself. Let's mark a portion of the active sequence.

1   In the *Believe Output* sequence, set an In point at 1:00:59:06, and an Out point at the end of the sequence.

2   Choose File > Export > QuickTime Movie.

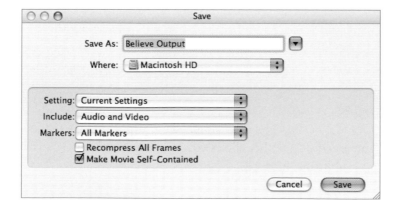

A Save window opens with a name for this sequence automatically entered in the Save As field.

3 Add *_HDV* to the end of the filename. Navigate to the FCP6 Book Files > Media folder, and select the Exports folder as the destination for the new media file.

TIP ▶ Adding *HDV* or some other descriptive text to your files during exporting will help you remember which settings were used for that file. It's especially helpful when comparing compression settings.

4 Make sure the Setting pop-up menu is set to Current Settings, the Include pop-up menu is set to Audio and Video, and the Markers pop-up menu is set to None.

When you choose Current Settings, you are using the current settings of the clip or sequence to create the new file.

NOTE ▶ In Markers pop-up menu, you can select markers that may have been created for a DVD or Soundtrack Pro audio project.

5 Make sure the Recompress All Frames box is deselected.

When selected, this option recompresses all frames in the selected export item. This can introduce additional compression artifacts into the file and increase the export time. If Final Cut Pro ever has trouble processing certain frames in your clips, exporting them with this option selected may be a good troubleshooting technique.

6 Make sure the Make Movie Self-Contained box is selected.

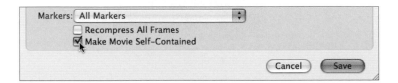

There are two types of QuickTime movies:

▶   Self-contained—A self-contained QuickTime movie can play on any computer because it contains all of the media (not just the clip links) that are in the clip or sequence. A self-contained movie will have a larger file size because the media files are contained within the movie.

▶   Not self-contained—You can play these movies on your computer, and even use them to create a DVD. However, you can't play them on another computer unless that system has all of the source media files on its hard drive.

7   Click Save.

A window appears, showing the exporting progress. When audio files are exported, the process can be so quick that no window appears.

After exporting, you can view the movie at the desktop level.

8   Press Command-H to hide Final Cut Pro. In a column view Finder window, navigate to the FCP6 Book Files > Media > Exports folder, and click the **Believe Output_HDV** clip. In the Preview column, click the Play button to screen the clip. You may want to expand the column to see a larger image area.

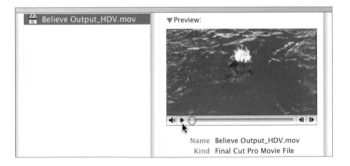

9 In the Finder window, double-click the **Believe Output_HDV** clip.

Because you created this clip with Final Cut Pro settings, it opens within the application in a separate Viewer-like window.

10 In this window, click the Stereo tab, and play the clip.

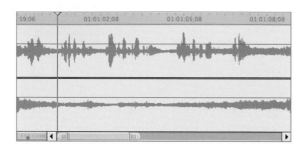

The multiple tracks of audio in the original sequence have been combined into one stereo pair in this clip.

11 Close the **Believe Output_HDV** clip window.

Even though you viewed the clip in Final Cut Pro, you haven't imported it, so it doesn't appear in the Browser. Once you do import the clip into a project, you can view and edit it as you would any other clip.

Exporting Using QuickTime Conversion

The QuickTime Movie export function works in many situations when you want to use preset sequence settings. But there are times when you need to export to a specific file type—perhaps to an audio file such as AIFF, a file you can play on the web, or a still image in TIFF or JPEG format.

In Final Cut Pro, you have numerous file type options for exporting your finished sequence and there is always more than one way to configure export settings. Preparing media for digital distribution is a constant compromise between quality and performance—the higher the data rate, the higher the quality but the slower the performance, depending on your computer's processing power. Through trial and error, you can decide for yourself the correct balance of the two, based on your distribution medium and your intended audience.

NOTE ▶ Several video sources in this book were originally shot in HD but had to be recompressed to another codec to reduce file size and maintain quality. For example, the *Monk* and Commercial clips were originally captured as DVCPRO HD files, and those files were recompressed using the Apple ProRes 422 codec. The "Living Colour: Yellow" footage was first captured from a DigiBeta tape as an uncompressed 10-bit file. But that five-minute file's size was 8.25 GB. To reduce the file size, the uncompressed file was recompressed using DVCPRO PAL, which reduced the file size to 1.2 GB.

In this exercise, you will export a movie for the web using the QuickTime H.264 compressor.

NOTE ▶ The H.264 compressor is a good choice for high-quality playback and small file size. However, it's not a good choice for creating clips to edit because the compression scheme used in this codec creates only one full frame about every 15 frames.

1   Click the Timeline to make it the active window. You can use the existing In and Out marks for this exercise.

2   Choose File > Export > Using QuickTime Conversion.

A Save window opens with the name for this sequence automatically entered in the Save As field, along with the QuickTime suffix, .mov.

3 In the Save As field, add *_H264-web* to the filename. If it's not already the destination, navigate to the Media > Exports folder as the destination for this file.

4 Click the Format pop-up menu and look at the export options.

This is where you choose the type of file you want to create. If you want to export just the audio of your sequence, you might choose AIFF as the format type. If you want to export a video frame as a still image, you would select Still Image. You can export a movie in a format that plays on cell phones (3G), an iPod or Apple TV (iPod/AppleTV), or a Windows-based computer (AVI).

5 From the Format pop-up menu, choose AIFF. Then click the Options button. Look at the Sound Settings window, then click Cancel.

Within each format are options that further define how you will export your file. For example, with AIFF chosen as the format type, clicking the Options button opens a Sound Settings window, where you can choose to export the file as Mono, or Stereo, and so on. Depending on the format type, different options will appear.

TIP If you want to export a still image or freeze frame from interlaced video, you can add a De-Interlace filter to it to reduce any flickering or shaking in the image. This filter is also useful when outputting a QuickTime movie for computer playback, since computer screens display lines progressively.

To export the marked sequence as a QuickTime movie, you must choose that format type.

6 From the Format pop-up menu, choose QuickTime Movie. Then click the Options button.

The Movie Settings window opens, displaying the current settings for Video, Sound, and Internet Streaming.

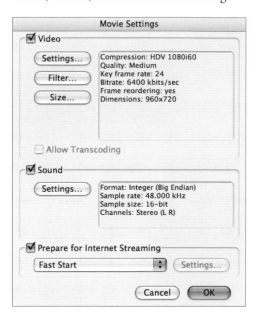

7 In the Video section, click the Settings button.

The Standard Video Compression Settings dialog opens, displaying the current compression settings.

8 From the Compression Type pop-up menu, choose H.264, if it's not already chosen. In the Motion section, change the frame rate to 15 fps; in the Data Rate section, restrict it to 400 kbits/sec; in the Compressor section, select the "Faster encode (Single-pass)" radio button. Leave the other settings at their default values. Click OK.

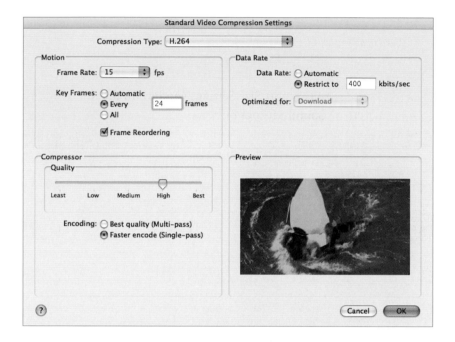

NOTE ► This is just one example of settings you could use to prepare a file for the web. Before you choose settings for your own project, you may need to experiment with different options to get the best quality at the smallest file size.

9 In the Movie Settings window, click the Size button. When the Export Size Settings dialog appears, choose Custom from the Dimensions pop-up menu. Enter a custom size of 480 x 270.

NOTE ▶ This movie has a widescreen aspect ratio. For a 4:3 DV format, you might use the standard 320 x 240 pixel dimension. This would be a good option for posting a vlog (video blog) on the web.

10 Click OK to close the Export Size Settings window. In the Movie Settings window, click the Sound Settings button.

Since this movie will be posted on the web, you don't need the highest-quality audio. Audio doesn't take up as much space as video, but it can still affect the performance of a web movie.

11 In the Sound Settings dialog, click the Channels pop-up menu and choose Mono. Click the Rate pop-up menu and choose 32.000 kHz. Click OK.

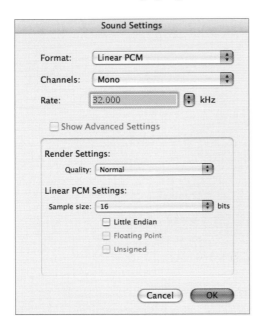

12 In the Save window, click Save.

Because QuickTime conversion is processor intensive, it may take some time for Final Cut Pro to finish exporting your video.

13 When the export is complete, press Command-H to hide Final Cut Pro. Navigate to the Media > Exports folder, and double-click the `Believe Output_H264-web` file. Play it in the QuickTime window.

Since this movie was created using QuickTime conversion and not Final Cut Pro presets, the movie opens in QuickTime Player, rather than in the Final Cut Pro interface.

14 In the Finder window, compare the file size of the two movies you exported. Then, in the Dock, click the Final Cut Pro icon to return to the application.

The QuickTime conversion movie isn't as high quality as the QuickTime movie that used Final Cut Pro sequence settings. But the difference in file size is significant. As you choose your export options, always keep in mind the purpose and destination of your movie file and you will get the best results for that purpose.

> **TIP** ▸ You can export a sequence to use as a reference in Soundtrack Pro or LiveType. In these applications, you can create a music score for the sequence and add 32-bit animated titles. Choose these export options from the File menu.

> **MORE INFO** ▸ You can also send a clip or sequence to a different Final Cut Studio application to make changes to it, and then import it back to Final Cut Pro to continue editing. This is referred to as "round-tripping," and is covered in the APTS book *Final Cut Pro: Beyond the Basics*.

Outputting to Tape

Final Cut Pro can export to a wide variety of tape formats. Through a FireWire connection, it can output to DV, DVCPRO, HDV, and DVCPRO HD. With additional hardware, it can output to other tape formats from VHS to DigiBeta. You will usually record a master copy of your sequence to the same tape format you started with or to the required delivery format; but you may also want to make a viewing copy in another tape format, such as DV or VHS.

When you output a sequence to tape, you generally want to lead the sequence with color bars and tone, a slate of what's to come, and possibly a countdown to indicate when the sequence will begin to play. This is collectively called *leader material*, which you added to a sequence in an earlier lesson.

> **NOTE ▶** Before you begin outputting, make sure your recording device is properly connected to your computer and turned on.

As with exporting files, you can output the entire sequence or just a section of the sequence as defined by In and Out points in the Timeline.

There are three ways to output your sequence to tape:

▶ Manually recording the sequence

▶ Using the Print to Video command

▶ Using the Edit to Tape command

The first two methods, manual recording and Print to Video, are available when using any FireWire recording device. The third method, Edit to Tape, is available only when using devices that Final Cut Pro can control remotely.

Recording Manually

The easiest way to output to tape is simply to start the connected recording device—camera or deck—and play the sequence while the device records. This is referred to as *manual recording*. You use this option when you want to make a quick dub to tape.

Though this output method is the simplest, it is also the least precise. It is very much a "what you see is what you get" proposition. To record manually, you should have any preprogram or leader material edited into your sequence in the Timeline. And you should also mix down your audio and render any unrendered video.

1   From the Browser, open the *Output Manual* sequence. Look at the **Slug** clips at the head and tail of this sequence.

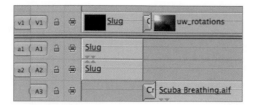

When you output a sequence manually, it's good to have at least 5 seconds of black at the head and tail of a sequence. This is because you need to start your recording device and allow it to come up to speed before you play the sequence. The frame on which the playhead is parked as the tape begins recording will appear as a freeze frame until you start playing the sequence. When the playhead reaches the last frame of the sequence, it will freeze on that final frame. Having a slug of black before your sequence begins and after it ends will ensure that no frame of the sequence is used as the starting or ending freeze frame.

Next, you want to make sure the sequence is playing back the highest-quality images.

2   In the Timeline, click the RT pop-up menu, and make sure you see a checkmark next to these settings: Safe RT, High (under Playback Video Quality), and Full (under Playback Frame Rate). You may have to click the RT pop-up menu to choose each option.

3   If there are red, yellow, or orange render bars in the Timeline ruler area, choose Sequence > Render All, and make sure the same render level colors that appear in the Timeline ruler area are selected in the Sequence > Render All menu. Press Option-R to render everything in the Timeline.

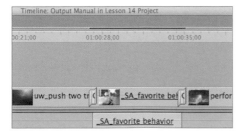

4   Cue up your recording device, and begin recording.

5   After at least 5 seconds, play the sequence.

> **NOTE ▶** If you want the sequence to repeat, choose Loop Playback in the View menu. The amount of black you want to play between the looped sequences is determined by the slug edit at the tail and head of each sequence.

6   When the sequence has finished playing, continue recording a few seconds, and then stop the recording device.

Printing to Video

The second output option combines the convenience of manual recording with some automation. Rather than edit the leader material at the head of your sequence, you can choose it from a checklist before outputting to tape. During the output process, Final Cut Pro will automatically generate these items as though they were clips in your sequence. This is a good method to use when you want to save time and take advantage of the automatic leader options, but don't have a device that can be controlled remotely using timecode.

Also, you don't have to render your sequence. The Print to Video command automatically renders and plays your sequence at high quality even if the Timeline playback settings are set to Low Quality or Dynamic.

NOTE ▶ To output HDV material to tape, you would use the Print to Video option.

1 Click the *Believe Output* sequence tab, or open a sequence you want to output.

2 Press Option-X to remove the In and Out points from the sequence.

3 Choose File > "Print to Video," or press Control-M.

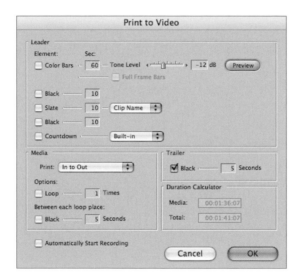

There are four areas in this dialog: the Leader, Media, Trailer, and Duration Calculator areas. In each area, select a checkbox to include that option in the output or choose an option from the pop-up menus. You can also enter a specific amount of time for some items.

4 In the Leader area, select the Color Bars checkbox, and change the duration to 10 seconds.

NOTE ▶ Generally, you record from 10 to 60 seconds of color bars, depending on the sequence's intended use and delivery requirements.

5   Select all the checkboxes in the Leader area. For a sample output, shorten the Black durations to 2 and Slate to 5.

6   In the Slate pop-up menu, choose Text. In the field that appears to the right, type *Believe Output version 1*.

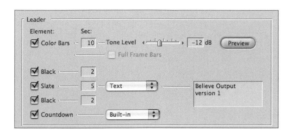

TIP ▶ You can also create your own slate with graphics and a company logo. To use a personal slate, from the Slate pop-up menu, choose File, and click the folder button to the right to navigate to the file.

7   In the upper-right corner of the Print to Video dialog, click the Preview button to test the audio level going into your recording device.

When you click the Preview button, Final Cut Pro emits a tone that you can use as a reference for setting audio output levels.

8   If the level is not high enough, adjust it using the dB slider. When you're finished adjusting the tone, click Stop in the dialog.

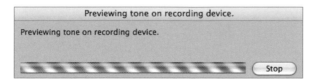

9   In the Media area, choose Entire Media from the Print pop-up menu to output the entire Timeline contents, and select Loop.

> **TIP** ▶ If your sequence is short, such as a promo, commercial, or music video, use the Loop option to loop it several times so that you won't have to rewind the tape to see it again.

10   In the Trailer area, select Black, and change the duration to 10 seconds.

11   Look at the Duration Calculator to see how long the total output will be, and make sure the tape you have selected is long enough.

12   Click OK.

A progress bar appears as Final Cut Pro renders files and mixes down audio to prepare the sequence for output.

> **TIP** ▶ Keep in mind that this mixdown is temporary and available for only one printing. If you decide to print the sequence again to make another copy, Final Cut Pro has to do another mixdown. To create a render file of the mixdown to use for additional outputs, choose Render Only > Mixdown.

When Final Cut Pro is ready to play back the sequence and any additional elements, a message will appear telling you to begin recording.

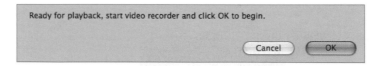

13   Start recording on your recording device, and after about 5 seconds, click OK to start the playback of your sequence and elements.

Editing to Tape

The third way you can output your sequence to tape is the Edit to Tape method. It is similar to Print to Video in that the same leader and other options are available for you to select and include with the output. The primary difference is that the Edit to Tape window also has transport buttons for controlling the deck, and you can set an In point where you want to begin recording your sequence. Depending on the recording device you're using, you can also set an Out point if you want to stop recording at a certain location on the tape. You can also choose to output just audio or video.

1   With the Timeline active, choose File > Edit to Tape.

If you do not have a controllable device connected, a warning will appear.

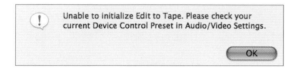

If the device is properly connected, the Edit to Tape window opens.

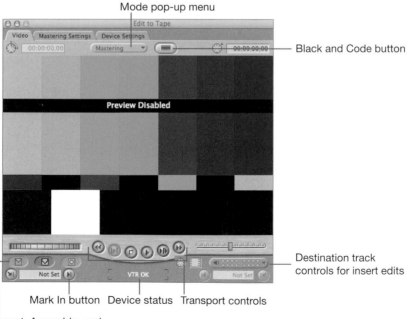

2   If you know the exact location where you want to begin recording, enter it in the Mark In field. If not, play the tape, and click the Mark In button (or press I) to mark where you want to begin recording.

3   Click the Mastering Settings tab, and select your settings just as you did in the Print to Video exercise.

4   Click the Device Settings tab and make sure they are set to control your recording device.

5   Click the Video tab. From the Browser, drag the *Believe Output* sequence to the Preview area of the Edit to Tape window and into the Assemble section, then release the mouse.

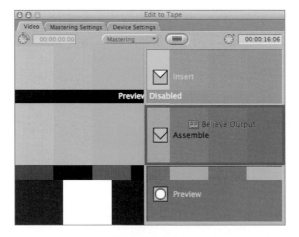

6   When the Ready for Playback dialog appears, click OK to start the recording process.

        The tape is cued up automatically, and the first elements of the output are recorded, starting at the In point you have set. As with the Print to Video option, you don't need to render anything in your sequence. Final Cut Pro automatically renders the video at full quality before outputting it.

7   Close the Edit to Tape window.

Making a Timecode Window Burn

Often during the editing and output process, someone will request a screening tape of the current version of the sequence with a visible timecode superimposed on the image. This timecode display is sometimes called a *timecode burn-in* or *window burn.* A window burn of your sequence is helpful when others need to screen your sequence and provide feedback referencing precise locations, or when you're working with a deck that cannot read timecode from the tape. In Final Cut Pro, the window burn is created by applying the Timecode Reader filter.

1   In the *Believe Output* sequence, select the first clip, **uw_rotations**, and choose Effects > Video Filters > Video > Timecode Reader. Then compare the Timeline Current Timecode field with the timecode window burn in the Canvas.

When you apply this filter to one of the sequence clips, the timecode that appears is that of the source clip, not of the Timeline. Since the objective is to have a display of the Timeline timecode, you have to nest the sequence clips, then apply the filter to the clips as a nested group.

2   Press Command-Z to undo the last step. Choose Edit > Select All, or press Command-A, to select all the clips in this sequence.

3   Choose Sequence > Nest Items. In the Name field, add the word *NEST* to the end of the name, and click OK.

All the clips in the Timeline are nested into a single track of video and two tracks of audio. In the Browser, a new sequence appears, *Believe Output NEST*. Since the window burn will be applied only to video clips, you could also select just the video clips and nest those.

NOTE ▶ To return to the individual clips in the sequence, you can double-click the icon in the Browser, or double-click the V1 nest in the Timeline.

4   In the Timeline, move the playhead forward to any full image frame in the sequence, that is, not in a transition. Choose Effects > Video Filters > Video > Timecode Reader.

Now, the Timecode Reader filter is applied to the entire sequence, and you see the sequence timecode in the Canvas.

5 Click a few different places in the Timeline ruler area and make sure the timecode display in the Canvas matches the timecode number in the Current Timecode field in the Timeline.

Depending on your media, you may want to change the timecode display, to make it smaller or more opaque, or to reposition it in a different part of the screen. To open the nest in the Viewer, you have to use a different approach from the one used to open a normal sequence clip.

6 Option–double-click the nested sequence in the Timeline to load it into the Viewer, and click the Filters tab. You can also select the nest in the Timeline and press Return.

7 Adjust the size, color, opacity, and position of the timecode display, so it is easily seen over the video in the sequence, yet not too distracting. If necessary, toggle on the Title Safe overlay from the View pop-up menu.

8 Output the sequence to tape using any one of the output methods described earlier in this lesson.

Backing Up Projects

After you have fine-tuned and output your sequence, it's time to back up your project. Each project may require a different backup strategy, not only when you are finished with a project, but throughout the editing process as well. If Autosave Vault is active, Final Cut Pro will automatically save a backup of your project at set time intervals as you work. In addition to this automatic backup system, here are a few other general strategies to keep in mind:

▶ Store your project files on a drive separate from your Autosave Vault drive. That way, if either drive goes down, you will always have your project on the other drive.

▶ Save a few versions of your project throughout the life of the project. This reduces the chance of file corruption by ensuring that you don't work on the same physical file for an extended period of time.

▶ Every few days, back up your project to removable media, such as flash drives, CDs, an iPod, or other FireWire devices. You can even back up your project to a server. The idea is to protect the project and yourself in case your computer or drive goes down.

> **TIP** ▶ An easy way to remember how to save your project is to think locally, globally, and remotely. Locally is on your own computer; globally is on a server or backup drive; and remotely is on a flash drive or drive you can take with you.

Some editors like to print or retain a list of all the clips in their projects, including the information they entered in the Browser columns. You can do this by using the Batch List function. However, you will need the help of a spreadsheet program such as Microsoft Excel, or a program that can interpret the tab delineations created in the batch list. Follow these steps to create a list of clips contained in your project:

1 In the Browser, select the Master Clips for Believe Output bin.

2 Choose File > Export > Batch List. Name the list *Believe Output*, and choose Exports as the target destination. Make sure that Tabbed Text is chosen as the Format option, and click Save.

3 In Final Cut Pro, choose File > Open. Navigate to the Exports folder, select Believe Output, and click Choose.

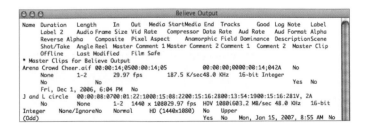

A window appears with your clip information. At the moment, it doesn't look helpful. But it will shortly.

4   Press Command-A to select all the information in this window, and press Command-C to copy it.

5   Open your spreadsheet program, and press Command-V to paste this information into the first cell. Adjust the column widths to allow the information to be read easily.

Name	Duration	Length	In
* Master Clips for Believe Output			
Arena Crowd Cheer.aif	00:00:14;05	00:00:14;05	
J and L circle	00:00:08;07	00:01:22:10	00:15:08:22
J hugs whale	00:00:14;27	00:00:54:14	00:00:10;19
J rotations	00:00:07:24	00:00:18:04	00:12:16:14
narration_2	00:00:18;18	00:00:18;18	
performance_S spray jump	00:00:09:14	00:00:10:29	06:19:47:15

Because the batch list is in a tab-delineated format, the information is placed into separate cells in the spreadsheet. You can now print the batch list as part of your backup process.

MORE INFO ▶ When you need to organize, copy, convert, or remove media files from your hard drive, you can access the Media Manager tool in the File menu. This is covered in the APTS book *Final Cut Pro: Beyond the Basics,* and also in the Final Cut Pro User Manual.

Lesson Review

1.   What is the most efficient way to find the audio peaks in a sequence?

2.   How are audio peaks indicated in the Timeline?

3.   What can you do to determine whether an image falls within the broadcast safe range?

4.   How can you correct an out-of-range clip so its range is acceptable for broadcast?

5. What two tools can you use to help prepare the audio and video of your sequence for output?

6. What is a self-contained QuickTime movie?

7. When might you use the QuickTime Conversion option to export a sequence?

8. What are the three ways you can output a sequence to tape?

9. What Export command do you choose to create a list of clip information?

Answers

1. Using the Audio Peaks function, located in the Mark menu.

2. By markers in the Timeline ruler area where each audio peak occurs.

3. Choose View > Range Check > Luma, and move through the sequence to see where the out-of-range clips are.

4. Apply the Broadcast Safe filter to the clip.

5. The Audio Mixer and Video Scopes.

6. A movie that uses Final Cut Pro sequence presets and that can be played on any computer without having the original media files present.

7. When you want to export a sequence at settings other than the current ones (for example, for the web or a DVD).

8. By recording manually, or by using the Print to Video or Edit to Tape options.

9. Batch List.

Keyboard Shortcuts

Command-Option-L	Opens audio Gain Adjust
Control-Z	Toggles Excess Luma Range Check on and off

Index

Making memories for today and tomorrow!

SeaWorld
ADVENTURE PARK
San Antonio

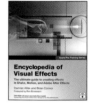